Coming of Age in the Hip Hop Generation: Warrior of the Void is **a brilliant narrative** that illustrates how what many consider challenging behavior of young black males can also be the biggest asset to exploring the frontier of their personal identity on the journey of re-examining who they are.

On the quest for independence, Akhenaton confronts, resists, and rebels against the path his father struggles to mold for him. During the struggle, he enters a "void" where "demons" fight to steal his power and narrate his life. The battles that ensue push him into deep reflection about his father that reveals the power of his own personal truth: the mutual love between them is in fact the potent identity that will overpower the "demons" and liberate his strengths. This book is for young males in search of their personal power and for the parents, teachers, mentors, and friends who seek to help them find it.

—Yvette Jackson, Ed.D.
　　CEO, National Urban Alliance for Effective Education
　　Author, *Pedagogy of Confidence*

Coming of Age in the Hip Hop Generation: Warrior of the Void is **a cross-generational vision of faith and unconditional love.** It is our collective story. This amazing narrative is poetry for our souls. It is the book that I wish would have been available for the countless students who came of age in the last decade in the schools my colleagues and I led in New York City. Nevertheless, it should be an asset to students and educators in schools and universities across America and beyond.

We can all relate to Akhenaton's struggles to define "the man in the mirror" as he comes of age. For those of us who have raised or are raising Latino and African American males, we can also identify with the struggles of his father, Askia, as he seeks to assist his son in navigating through the American maze of life.

—Carmen A. Jimenez
　　Former principal and deputy superintendent,
　　New York City Public Schools
　　Former presenter and facilitator, The Harvard Principals' Center

Somewhere between old school soul and new school swag, from the revolutionary politics of the Black Panther Party (of the 1960s) to the rebellious poetry of Tupac's "Gangsta Party," a bridge was built in Brooklyn. Linking the stories of a father and son who share **untold insight into the challenges and triumphs facing Black youth and their parents,** *Coming of Age in the Hip Hop Generation: Warrior of the Void* is a journey some just ain't ready for, but all who travel through these pages will be far more prepared for life in America today.

—Bryonn Bain

Prison Activist and Nuyorican Grand Slam Poetry Champion

Author, *The Prophet Returns* and *Lyrics from Lockdown*

Brother Fitzgerald

Storytelling is a divine art
Painted by the tongue to enable
us to fully visualize and express
our humanity!   AD

Coming of Age in the
Hip Hop Generation

Warrior of the Void

askia.davis@gmail.com

Coming of Age in the Hip Hop Generation

Warrior of the Void

Askia Akhenaton Suleiman Ali Davis
and Askia Davis, Sr., Ed.D.

Askia Book Publishing
Brooklyn, New York

Coming of Age in the Hip Hop Generation
Warrior of the Void
Published by:
Askia Book Publishing
Phone: 347-885-4625
Email: askia.davis@gmail.com
Websites: askiadavis.com
hiphopgeneration.net
warriorofthevoid.com
www.facebook.com/Warrior-of-the-Void

Askia Davis, Ed.D., Publisher
Edited by Deborah Jackson
Quality Press, Production Coordinator
The Printed Page, Interior and Cover Design

Copyright © 2012 by Askia Akhenaton Suleiman Ali Davis and
Askia Davis, Ed.D.
Trade Paperback ISBN #: 978-0-9855024-0-9
eBook ISBN #: 978-0-9855024-1-6.
Library of Congress Control #: 2012907190

Dedication

To the students of the New York City Public Schools and students in public schools across this great nation, may you rise to fully express your dreams and may those dreams transform our world.

—Askia Akhenaton and Askia, Sr.

Acknowledgements

"Who (what man) can understand his (own) errors?
O' Lord, cleanse me of secret faults."
—Psalm 19:12

Love to Nydia, mother and wife, who is an inspiration and guide. For their spiritual guidance, adoration to Mattie, grandmother and mother; and to Clemencia, grandmother and mother-in-law.

—Askia Akhenaton and Askia, Sr.

Honor to Miss Tracey Cook-Person, Miss Tai Ford, and Mr. Askia Egashira, English teachers of Benjamin Banneker Academy in Brooklyn, who elevated my love of the written and spoken word.

Admiration to Coach William Saunders and Coach Perry Williams of the Warriors at Benjamin Banneker Academy, Coach Will Curry of the New York City Boys Club, and Coach Terrence Felder of the New York Knights, all of whom taught me the value of teamwork, leadership, and personal responsibility.

—Askia Akhenaton

Honor to Mr. Scott, my eighth grade English teacher in Swainsboro, Georgia, who introduced me to "The Creation" and set me on a path to the love of poetry and prose:

—Askia, Sr.

And there the great God Almighty
Who lit the sun and fixed it in the sky....
This Great God,
Like a mammy bending over her baby,
Kneeled down in the dust
Toiling over a lump of clay
Till He shaped it in His own image;
Then into it He blew the breath of life,
And man became a living soul.
Amen. Amen.

—James Weldon Johnson

Contents

Introduction

From Askia Akhenaton, the son:

I emerged from my mother's womb on November 30, 1992, in a delivery room at New York Hospital, York Avenue and East 70th Street. Mom endured a C-section, so dad was there to be the first to greet me. As I rested in my basinet breathing rhythmically, in a manner that older humans struggle to remember, the nurse prepared to weigh and measure me.

She placed me on the scale, looked at dad, and announced, "Nine pounds and one ounce." Then she took out a 24-inch tape measure. She stretched it along the length of my body. "Oh, this baby is longer than 24 inches. I need to go and get another tape," she whispered.

She began to walk toward the door, but stopped short before exiting. She turned and looked at dad. "Well, I am the only one here and I shouldn't leave the room," she confided with stress lines on her forehead. "Uh, let me measure this baby again." She then stretched the tape as if it could extend beyond 24 inches to cover the full length of my body.

"Twenty-four inches exactly," she smiled, turned to the chart, and entered the measurement.

Dad let it go, although it seemed clear to him that I was more like 25 inches. He was just so happy to pick me up and cradle me in his arms. As I rested in dad's arms, we waited for mom to emerge from the anesthesia. Dad told me, "You are the magical child, my heartbeat, the Warrior of the Void." Those are words he would repeat to me often until the age of 8, and he still whispers them from time to time.

The "Void" is the space that exists between who we are and who we are called to become. It is the space where we encounter so many flamboyant demons while our few guardian angels often remain hidden from sight. Demons often choose not to appear horrific; they usually choose to appear enchanting.

When dad and I began writing this memoir, I was 17, soon-to-be 18. I was about to become a freshman at Hampton University. Go Pirates!

The odyssey from basinet to college has been an interesting and challenging one, and the challenges continue. One of my toughest obstacles has been defining my own identity through a continuing war with my father. Am I my father's son or my own man? Can I peacefully shape the life I want on my own schedule? Does my youth require me to follow my father's schedule for my life? It would be great to know the answers as soon as possible.

I am African American and Puerto Rican. I am a black man. I am this generation and the future of America. That last statement alone is enough to place fear in the hearts of some who do not want the future of America's changing face. But, as my father says, "Nothing can stop the ripening of time."

It would be erroneous to say my existence began on November 30, 1992, or even at the point of conception. Dad and mom often speak about me coming to dad in two separate visions, three months apart and prior to my actual conception. Due to those visions, dad finally relented and accepted the idea of having another child. One year and two days after his first vision, I physically appeared on earth outside of mom's womb. They recorded their memory of those visions in my yearbook when I graduated from kindergarten from Lefferts Gardens Montessori in Brooklyn.

Dad says I have a story to tell. In fact, as an educator, he believes that every student has a story to tell. He says a person doesn't have to be famous to have a compelling story. He believes some of the most revealing stories come from less than famous people and are often more interesting. Our hope is that the stories in this book will bring to mind your own stories and the stories of your parents and families. Retell them around your dinner tables and at your family gatherings. There is power in the word.

We send a special shout-out to the black and Latino males between ages 13 and 22 to encourage them to keep the faith in their strength and wisdom. Remember always:

> "The measure of a man is not taken when he is knocked down;
> it is taken when he quickly gets up."

When we appear on earth, we come with a history. The most pressing history is that of our mothers and fathers. We carry their genetic, cultural, and spiritual histories. As we develop, we also carry their life or social histories. We carry the images, words, and emotions of the stories they tell, the music they play, the songs they sing, the whack dances they step, the activities and experiences they involve us in. Our mothers, our fathers, and our history attempt to shape our character and our points of view.

Thus, in order to tell my history, I must tell some of my parents' history. I am a teen of the first decade of the 21st century and, inescapably, a teen of the 1960s (as my parents were teens of the 1960s). Listen to me sing in the shower and hear the range of music and emotions spanning through my time and, inevitably, reflecting my father, my mother, and earlier treasured tunes of their lives.

In 2010 at age 17, dad heard me singing in the shower and I was not just singing some catchy Bill Wither's tune. I was not just singing a song I heard my father play many times from the time I was 2 years old sitting in my car seat in the back of a Camry that my father still rolls in. I was singing "Lovely Day" because I was feeling it and knew it was the best expression of the light I wanted to bring to the world at that moment thinking about my lady: "Then I look at you, and the world's all right with me. Just one look at you, then I know it's gonna be a lovely day...."

Minutes later from that same shower, dad heard me shout: "Waka Flocka Flame! Waka Flocka Flame! Oh Let's Do It, Oledoit, Oledoit...." Yeah, I was singing drug-dealing music. I was singing as if I had f***ed my money up and was not able to re-up.

As I dried myself in front of the mirror, he heard me switch my iPod to Celia Cruz's "*Rie y Llora*" and sing: "*Rie y llora. Este negrito no pasa de moda.*"

Minutes later, dad called from outside the bathroom door demanding, "Okay, man, you need to get a move on!" I ignored him because I was looking into the mirror, putting on moisturizer, adjusting my iPod to hip hop poetry with B.o.B's "I'll Be in the Sky" and singing: "Remember when I leave, that the one in the mirror ain't me.... It's kinda me but it's not. It's just a mask that I got...."

With dad's blood pressure rising as he banged on the bathroom door again, I accepted the call to swiftly move toward the door of the apartment and thus closer to the door of the bus with my final destination of Benjamin Banneker Academy. On the way toward the first door, dad heard me singing Stevie Wonder's "As:" "Just as hate knows love's the cure, you could rest your mind assured that I'll be loving you always...."

During the bus ride, dad was not there to hear me sing the words of "A Song for You" by Donny Hathaway: "I love you in a place where there is no space or time. I love you for my life you are a friend of mine...."

Later that evening at Banneker, warming up on the basketball court with my boyz as dad looks on, Kanye and Jeezy are spitting "Amazin" on my iPod as I sky for several dunks: "I'm a monster. I'm a maven. I know this world is changing…."

At home later that evening after the game, I was cooling down with John Coltrane's "A Love Supreme" ("I will do all I can to be worthy of thee, O' Lord…") and meditating with Miles and Cannonball on "Autumn Leaves" as I prepared to sleep toward a new day with Facebook, Twitter, and AIM on my laptop next to my pillow.

The next morning dad found me checking my cell phone for texts and my laptop for Facebook messages and tweets before I climbed down from the bed. While checking, I was singing along with the songbirds that were in the nest on the awning outside my window. Minutes earlier they had taken the place of roosters while calling for me to open my eyes. As dad attempted to get my attention, I deliberately could not hear him through my headphones as I sang along with Corrine Bailey Rae: "Three little birds sat on my window and they told me I don't need to worry." I didn't have to worry because summer was coming "like cinnamon, so sweet," and I would walk by with a smile as "little girls double-dutch on the concrete." I was going to school to sing to my lady, "Put Your Records On."

Minutes later, while I was in the bathroom, dad heard me singing Richard Smallwood's "Total Praise," Yolanda Adams' "Victory," and Earth Wind & Fire's "Keep Your Head to the Sky:" "He gave me the will to be free, purpose to live His reality…." There I was singing for me to hear that I had to keep my head in "faith's atmosphere."

By the time dad began his usual knocking on the door, I had moved on to Kirk Franklin's "He Reigns/My God is an Awesome God." I was feeling the music and back in church as dad shifted from knocking to banging on the door while demanding that I get out of the shower and out the door. Gospel has to wait for school.

As I packed for school, dad heard me singing Otis Redding's "Try A Little Tenderness:" "Young girls they don't forget it. Love is their whole happiness, yeah, yeah, yeah…."

On the way out the door, I am hooked to my iPod. I am singing DMX's "Where da Hood At," and dad is shaking his head signaling that he does not want to hear DMX and the N-word.

Of course, you can't be an American teenager raised by parents who became teens in the 1960s without giving homage to the Temptation's "My

Girl," Marvin Gaye's "Distant Lover," and Bob Marley's "Is This Love." So I was singing all three as I ran to the Vanderbilt Avenue bus stop hoping to catch a glimpse of my lady just before the start of class.

I guess I really played with dad's blood pressure most of my junior year and all of my senior year while in high school. The shower and shouting routine with dad would be repeated almost every school day during my senior year. But, you know, everything is cool when you have your music and you think you know where you are headed. You can say, "I got this dad! It's not that serious. I can handle my business."

I have since learned that I am still trying to really learn how to handle my business.

This is the story of the first 18 years of my life growing up black and Puerto Rican in Brooklyn under my dad's guidance and dealing with our ongoing father-son struggles. My story is about finding my voice and seeking to find me, while struggling with the genetic, cultural, spiritual, and life histories I inherited that present the challenges to me being my own man.

It's about how my desire to be my own man had negative and positive affects on my progress as I came of age in the Hip Hop Generation. My story shares the clash between a father's view of the world, largely shaped while coming of age in the Black Power and Black is Beautiful Generation, and a son's world view that is being shaped while coming of age in the Hip Hop Generation. The clash of those two views of reality often has me "caught up and twisted."

It's also about Elmo, Cookie Monster, Miss Piggy, and rides in the car seat in the back of a 1992 Camry absorbing Motown, Earth Wind & Fire, James Brown, Otis Redding, Luther Vandross, Michael Jackson, Willie Colon, and Hector Lavoe.

It's about Psalm 91 and prayer at my father's side; "Next Friday," Mike Epps, Ice Cube, and three booty calls; the "missionary position" that ate the homework; and Pokémon, World of WarCraft, NBA 2K10, Madden, and Facebook.

It's about faith.

Come inside and take another look at Kobe, LeBron, Jay-Z, Lupe Fiasco, Beyonce, Trey Songz, Lil Wayne, Eminem, Drake, and R. Kelly. Come into my world of basketball with the Warriors of Benjamin Banneker Academy, the New York City Boys Club, and the AAU Knights of New York; my world of combat with Sensei Soke Majid and Scorpion Martial Arts; and my world of music, love, and heartbreak.

Come also and view New York and American history, music, media, sports, culture, education, and law enforcement during those 18 years.

My experiences during my first 18 years often encouraged dad to speak to me about similar or related experiences he had during his first 18 years. Many of those discussions are included because they reveal his efforts to shape my thinking, my values, and my future experiences. Thus, this book is somewhat of a dual memoir—mine and dad's. It is written in my voice, which speaks to my generation and to the parents, relatives, mentors, coaches, and educators who have attempted to shape us.

My father and I have collaborated on this memoir, which we expect will be the first book in a trilogy about our coming-of-age experiences. It captures both of our recollections of the first 18 years of my life. In many instances, we used family photographs, videos, written documents and records, and the Internet to aid our memories. In other instances, we wrote it as we each remembered it. We sought to be brutally honest about our shortcomings at the potential cost of substantial personal embarrassment. Mom was often there to ensure accuracy in our retelling of the stories.

BTW/By the way, if you see us on the streets, don't laugh in our faces about our revealed weaknesses. To live, we must all endure embarrassment. When will you reveal yours?

It is my expectation that one day I will sit with my own sons and daughters to co-author their histories and that the Davis clan will pass this tradition from generation to generation. We are Warriors of the Void.

Enjoy the stories, and spit your own.

—Askia Akhenaton Suleiman Ali Davis,
the "Warrior of the Void"

From Askia, the dad:

I have been blessed to be the father of my beloved son, Akhenaton, even though we have been locked in a struggle, really in a war. As a black man, I know from experience the special challenges America presents, especially for African American men. I also know the special possibilities America presents. My purpose has been to prepare my son to overcome the challenges and take hold of the possibilities through the fullest expression of his God-given potential.

At the founding of our nation when the "founding fathers" shaped America, they created a contradiction—a "land of the free" built on the brains and backs of the enslaved. They created a flawed "democracy" where people of African descent were identified as property and, in the Constitution, as three-fifths human and beasts of burden.

As a parent, I have worked hard to prepare my son to overcome America's challenges. My wife says I have worked too hard. When our son is stubborn and unwilling to accept sound advice, she says, "Let him make the big mistakes and suffer the consequences."

However, she doesn't really mean what she says. She recognizes that there are special consequences that black and Latino males commonly face that are never faced by any other group of kids in America, except Native Americans. For example, when black and Latino males fail in school, the path of consequences most often leads to lockdown as B.o.B writes in "I'll Be in the Sky." Nevertheless, she remains concerned about my blood pressure, which often rises as I struggle with him in an attempt to keep him moving toward God's promise.

My son says, "Let me live my own life." That is exactly what I think I am trying to do. However, I must admit that there are times I do get it wrong and am overbearing. My son would say, "Swag!"

What has been great about writing this memoir with my son is that I have gained some insight regarding my shortcomings, and I have come up with answers to some of the puzzling questions he presented. I could have used some of those answers a few years earlier. However, we can often only be as good as we are at the present moment. Enlightenment and personal growth involve a process that takes time to ripen. As Eminem suggests in "Not Afraid," it takes time and maturing wisdom for us to be able to command our demons to do jumping jacks.

Does any American parent have the perfect formula for balancing protection, guidance, and freedom in raising his or her sons? Our intellect suggests one course of action. Our emotions suggest a different course. Our faith suggests a third. Our love is the substance that breathes life into our intellect, our emotions, and our faith. Our love, our emotions, our intellect, and our faith are challenged by the reality of the moments that present storm clouds that obscure and attempt to destroy the possibilities that lie before us.

Has any black man invented that perfect formula for raising his sons in 21st century America? Has any popular media outlet bottled his formula for national distribution? A perfect formula for parenting our sons would truly transform America because no single group on the planet has more hidden and "locked up potential" than black and Latino boys in the USA.

In 2009 a friend, David Powell, told me that it is important that our teenage sons not listen to their dads. David, à la Kahlil Gibran in *The Prophet*, said their odyssey and their world are not ours. He said that if our sons were to listen, it would make it impossible for them to create a new and better world. He suggested that our own youth has passed and their time is now. Of course, he told me these words after successfully raising his own beloved son, Daoud, who was 30-plus at the time of our conversation.

It's amazing how wisdom comes after the fact. But, like many of you, I want my wisdom before I have life's experiences and before the facts are revealed! I hope God is listening.

Nevertheless, I think David is correct. There is no higher life goal than self-direction and self-management in the expression of our God-given potential. Self-direction and self-management involve a process that develops in different stages and time frames in our lives.

My father was not around, so I rejected my mom's plans for me. At age 15, surrounded by poverty, I left small-town Swainsboro, Georgia, and moved to New York City, the Big Apple. I had mama's last $10 and a slightly greased brown paper bag containing mama's fried chicken and teacakes when I jumped in Mr. Harper's Bonneville for that fateful trip to 145th Street and Eighth Avenue, Harlem, USA.

At age 16, I lived on my own in an apartment in the Bronx. At age 17, I joined Lumumba Shakur, Afeni Shakur, Sekou Odinga, and Dhoruba bin Wahid in the Black Panther Party in Harlem, not to be confused with the so-called "New Black Panther Party" and its positions on race and violence. At age 18, I rebelled against racism at Brooklyn College, was arrested with 18 other students, sent to Rikers Island, "the Rock," and faced 228 years in prison. Yes, I faced possible sentencing of 228 years in prison before I had one hair of Georgia peach fuzz on my face.

Mom was opposed to each of my decisions. She had given me her last $10, the fried chicken, and the teacakes because, at age 15, I had threatened to allow misery to overwhelm me if she continued to hold me in Georgia with my seven other brothers and sisters still remaining at home. I wanted to see the world, and New York City represented its gateway. My stubbornness was legendary, so she knew she had to let me go.

So, beginning at age 15, despite my intense love for her, I was no longer prepared to be guided by my beloved mother. But, thanks be to God, I carried the genetic, cultural, spiritual, and life histories of mom and dad that served as a foundation that made it possible for me to graduate valedictorian from a Brooklyn high school and, at age 32, from Columbia University with an A average and a doctoral degree.

Faith has shown me that my son will create a new and better world. I want him to do that with a generation of mentally and spiritually liberated black and Latino males in America. That is precisely what America needs to be as productive as possible in the 21st century global economy and creative space. My son and I hope this memoir, the projected work that will follow, and the lives we live will carry a message and contribute to that liberation.

As Akhenaton and I wrote this memoir, the experiences we re-lived gave each of us new opportunities to reflect and better understand what we have been attempting to teach each other, especially during the ongoing wars of his teen years. We had the opportunity to reflect on what we have learned that prepares us to be better men.

No matter how much I have learned and accomplished throughout my life's journey, "living" is always there, presenting new challenges, new doubts, and new possibilities. Even after so many years on this planet, it is astounding to find myself facing some of the same mental and spiritual challenges I had overcome previously in my teens and twenties. The same challenges often present themselves with another name, another face, another mask. When they appear, there are those moments when it seems as if I have had absolutely no experience and no history of past successes. My emotions and anxieties struggle against my faith, while my faith seeks to remind me that I have run through an army comprised of my own faithless fears, negative thoughts, negative emotions, negative actions, and foreboding circumstances and have leaped over a towering wall of heart-numbing doubts. Also, I am beloved and more than a conqueror.

Recently, one evening while in bed, I had a dream vision. I was on a long and desperate search for inner peace. I paused, confronted God, and asked, "Father, I have endured and continue to endure so many struggles in my life; so where is my Damascus Road and where is my Epiphany (enlightenment)?"

God answered, "Your Epiphany is: I Am still here."

—Askia Davis, Ed.D., "The Shadow Warrior"

Preface

What do you get when a father who came of age in the Black Power and Black is Beautiful Generation attempts to raise a son who is coming of age in the Hip Hop Generation? You get two views of reality, psychological warfare, harmony, disharmony, hope and ongoing transformation. *Coming of Age in the Hip Hop Generation: Warrior of the Void* is the joint father-son memoir written in the son's voice and covering his life growing up African American and Puerto Rican in Brooklyn.

With a creative use of oral history, spoken word, lyricism, humor and introspection, *Coming of Age in the Hip Hop Generation: Warrior of the Void* offers profound insight into the lives of an American family and American history, culture, education, media, law enforcement and sociology.

—Yvette Jackson, Ed.D.
CEO, National Urban Alliance for Effective Education
Author, *Pedagogy of Confidence*

Chapter 1

Meet Dad:
A Pilgrimage to a Cotton Field

The Temptations sang "Papa Was A Rolling Stone."

My father is no rolling stone, but his father was. My grandfather left my grandmother when she was six months pregnant with my father's baby sister, the thirteenth child of the Davis family. There were four neighborhoods for blacks in my dad's hometown, and my grandfather reportedly had a mistress in each one. When he wouldn't come home on a given evening, he could usually be found at the house of the mistress closest to the travelling poker game he had left.

However, a rumor later circulated that my grandfather had to leave town when he was caught running with a white woman from another neighborhood. She owned a prominent business that he managed for her in their small town in the heart of "Dixie," Swainsboro, Georgia. This happened in 1961 during a time when a black man could be lynched for even saying hello to a white woman, and when it was rare for a black man to have the kind of job that many white men in town envied. Dad was 10 years old when my grandfather left, and he has never laid an eye on him since.

My grandfather's treatment of my grandmother and his abandonment of his 13 kids motivated dad to be a better man, a better father. Dad's father wasn't there for him. Dad, at times, seems to be too much there for me. Sociologists and psychiatrists say that many African American boys experience extreme life challenges due to the absence of their fathers. Well, I can spit about the challenges of a black boy who, as a teenager, faces some interesting life challenges because his father is too present. You know what I mean?

My father's middle names are "intensity, determination, and focus." At 6 years old, he was assigned to Mrs. Graham's advanced class at Emanuel County Elementary and High School. However, dad had a little boy's crush on the much younger and beautiful Mrs. Miller and preferred to be in Mrs. Miller's first grade class. So, when my grandmother took him to school on the first day, he ran into Mrs. Miller's class and took a seat. No amount of cajoling, pleading, or demanding from my grandmother, Mrs. Miller, Mrs. Graham, my Aunt Gloria (dad's oldest sister) and the principal, Mr. D.D. Boston, could get dad to budge from that seat. He remained in Mrs. Miller's class the entire first grade and refused to be skipped early to the second grade, which was common practice for advanced kids. According to Aunt Gloria, that episode marked a high point at the beginning of dad's "legendary stubbornness."

The following year in second grade, dad was often given the responsibility of sitting in the teacher's chair and taking the class through the reading and math lessons whenever Mrs. Lawrence had to leave the classroom. One day little 7-year-old dad was told to take charge of the class. As Mrs. Lawrence departed, dad asked if he could first go and "pee." Mrs. Lawrence told him no and to wait until she returned. He told her that he didn't want to wait. A few minutes later, dad decided to deliberately "pee" on himself knowing that she would have to leave her assignment and return to the class immediately so that he could go home alone and change.

After that episode, dad was able to go and "pee" anytime he wanted to because Mrs. Lawrence wanted to keep him happy. Mrs. Lawrence relied upon him and did not try to skip him to the third grade. He was glad to stay because, despite his disappointment with being told "no," he had a little boy's crush on the beautiful Mrs. Lawrence as well.

Dad comes from a generation of African Americans who, before entering elementary school, were taught by the media and society to ridicule Africa, Africans, and being black. In the 1950s, calling someone "black" was considered one of the highest insults possible. While in elementary school, dad and other African American kids preferred to swing on trees from ropes, imitating Tarzan, rather than play the roles of the "Africans" who were depicted on television and in the movies as "savages."

Yet, before leaving high school, dad and many other black kids of that same generation threw off the shackles of their "mental enslavement" and became the Black Power and Black is Beautiful Generation. In less than a decade, they brought about a revolution in the thinking and actions of African Americans. Outside of school, they studied African and African American history, while inside of school they fought school and university administrators to ensure the teaching of that history. He and his generation believed education was the key to future success. They were willing to fight and go to jail to ensure African Americans had quality public schools to attend and an equal opportunity for admission into universities, especially public universities.

Consistent with the spirit in Maya Angelou's poem, "Still I Rise," dad's generation believed African Americans have demonstrated that they are capable of the most extraordinary accomplishments when challenged by the darkest adversity in America, and dad wants to make sure I continue in that tradition.

Dad is not only intellectually and psychologically intense, he is also physically intense. He is a kung fu man and an exercise fanatic. About five to six days a week he is at Bikram Yoga Park Slope for 90-minute sessions in a room heated up to 115 degrees with humidity up to 65 percent. He is most likely the only man in the room wearing long sleeves and long sweat pants. While most men are bare-chested and wearing yoga briefs or shorts, he's wearing a black undershirt under a black long sleeve Under Armor football shirt to drive his heart rate up as he goes through 26 postures.

When not at yoga, he can be found standing on a Spinner for 90 minutes of consistent intensity, without sitting for even a brief moment. He believes once a person reaches 50 years of age, that person has to "taste his own warm salty sweat every day or plan for the early cold embrace of the Grim Reaper."

America has an obesity problem, but at 6 feet dad weighs the same 175 pounds he did at 18 years old and has the same 31-inch waist. During the season of Lent in 2010, he went cold turkey, eliminating sugar, juices, and desserts from his diet, and he now only allows himself small desserts on special occasions. In May 2010, after his weight fell by 12 pounds, placing him at 167 pounds, Dr. Saw, his internist, suggested he needed to put on a few pounds. Since then he has taken to eating walnuts every day for "healthy fats" and as a substitute for the "bad fats" in desserts. He claims walnuts suppress any cravings for sugar. Since eliminating juices and desserts, he claims even carrots are too sweet. For me, they are not sweet enough.

As a baby boomer, dad does not want to be told by me that he will soon be a senior citizen. He is a baby boomer who believes he will be young forever. He won't. I think dad is already an old man, but he does not believe it. He ain't trying to hear that. He says that I can only hope that I have the same energy he has now when I reach just half his present age.

My father was born in a little town of about 4,000 folks in southeast Georgia, USA. His family didn't have much money, so my father had to take on many jobs to help his family survive. Before and during my pre-teen years, dad would often preach to me about the challenges he experienced and how he grew strong from meeting the many challenges he faced as a poor black boy in the South.

He told me about how, starting at 5 years old, he had picked cotton in the blazing sun. Throughout the following years, he also climbed tall pine trees to shake down pine cones to sell for the pine nuts they contain; "fired" a wood-burning boiler to provide heat above 1,400 degrees to produce steam for a dry cleaners; cropped tobacco; organized bales of tobacco for auctions at a tobacco warehouse; scavenged for bricks at demolition sites; harvested peanuts, pecans, green beans, watermelons, and peaches; dug a grave for a funeral; washed dishes at Keys Café; served customers at A&W Root Beer; cleaned the office at the local USA Army Recruitment Center; and served as a premier caddy at the Swainsboro Country Club and Golf Course. Those were just some of the jobs he had between the ages of 5 and 13, before there were laws against child labor.

By age 13, I had, of course, not worked a single day for a salary, and sometimes I was not trying to hear all the "rah-rah" or all of that "blah, blah, blah, uh huh, uh huh." I would stare into space as he spoke, and he would get my attention by pulling up the legs of his pants and showing me again the dark calluses that remained on his brown knees. He said he got them from the many years he had picked cotton, crawling on ground that was heated beyond 100 degrees by the hot Georgia sun. You see, when you pick cotton, you can stand and bend over. But dad said several hours of standing and bending over would "kill your back," even when you are young. To avoid the back pain, you would "walk on your knees" down the rows picking cotton as you go. Whether walking on your feet or walking on your knees, dad said you had to watch out for rattle snakes. Huh?

I think dad is weird sometimes. He actually has some fond memories of experiences he had leaving the fields at the end of a day of picking cotton. He told me that when he was 10 years old he used to love to stand on the back bumpers of pickup trucks, singing with his friends as they departed for home after a long day in the fields. He would stand at one end holding on to the side of a wooden frame that was placed in the bed of the truck. The frame was there to provide a structure for the canvas that would cover the bed to protect passengers from the sun and rain. Another friend, LeVonne Williams, would stand at the other end. They would often pass other trucks, which also had other black kids singing while standing on the bumpers.

Dad said he could still clearly see those days as they stood on the bumpers singing Sam Cooke's "Bring It On Home to Me," the King of Rock and Roll, Chuck Berry's "Johnny B. Goode" and Smokey Robinson and the Miracles' "Shop Around." When they sang Chubby Checker's "The Twist," he said they would dance twisting on the bumpers as the wind caressed their faces while they sped down the country highways at speeds greater than 40 miles per hour.

At times when they would pass other trucks carrying their friends, and even strangers from nearby towns, they would breakout with the call and response rhythms of Ray Charles' "What'd I Say."

Dad would shout "Hey" to the kid on the other truck and the kid would respond "Hey." Then dad would shout "Ho" and the response would be "Ho." Dad would shout "Hey" a second time and get the response "Hey." Dad would shout "Ho" a second time and get the response "Ho." Then the pattern would be repeated a third time, followed by dad shouting, "Ah! Make me feel so good" and getting the response "Make me feel so good."

Then, as the trucks separated, dad and his friends on his truck would continue singing: "See the girl with the diamond rang, she knows how to shake that thang...."

In Brooklyn, up until age 13, the only cotton I had seen was the cotton sticking out of a discarded mattress on the sidewalk waiting for the sanitation men, the cotton inside my torn teddy bear, and the cotton that got stuck to my Afro from wearing an American Eagle hoodie.

So, four months before I turned 13, when we went to visit dad's boyhood home in Swainsboro, he was eager to take me to a cotton field. Yes, we were going on a pilgrimage to a cotton field in Georgia. You might ask, "Why a pilgrimage to a cotton field?" Well, much of dad's focused and determined character was shaped in the cotton fields where he worked five days a week during the summers from ages 5 through 11, sometimes alongside his mother and often alongside his sisters, brothers, cousins, and friends.

During the cotton season in the summers of those years, dad spent more time in the fields Monday through Friday than in any other place, including home. At the beginning of those summers, he would spend time on work crews "hoeing" cotton or, in other words, clearing weeds and grasses among the cotton stalks with a hoe to ensure healthy growth. Later in those same summer months, when the cotton bolls had opened, he would return to pick the cotton from the bolls.

As dad, his brothers, sisters, and their neighbors did the work, they often moved up and down the rows of cotton singing. He said singing seemed to ease their minds a bit from focusing on the burden of the work, but not from the injustice of low wages and exploitation by men whose sons and daughters were seen only rarely in the cotton fields on the evenings when they would accompany their fathers as they drove the black workers home.

To somewhat lessen the financial and psychological impact of the exploitation, dad's older brother, Marcus, and first cousin, Waitus Jones, taught dad and the young field hands tricks that would get them credit for more cotton than they had actually picked. This involved strategically adding, to hundreds of pounds of cotton, water and another unmentionable liquid, stones, and a type of melon usually used to feed farm animals. In addition, they were taught to strategically insert pounds of "pulled" cotton into the middle of many more pounds of cotton picked from the bolls. "Pulled" cotton is still attached to the bolls. Usually, one could "pull" cotton at three to four times the rate one could "pick" cotton. The ratio was generally one bag pulled for every three bags picked. At times, Marcus would have to borrow some of dad's cleanly picked cotton when Marcus had gone on a "cotton-pulling escapade" while ignoring the ratio.

The farmers did not want pulled cotton because it reduced the value at the market. During a typical day, Marcus and Waitus would register three times the weight of the typical field hand who did not use the tricks and twice more than those who did. Field hands were paid by the number of pounds picked, and Marcus and Waitus always took home much more money at the end of each day than anyone else.

For dad and his young friends, Marcus and Waitus were walking and living cotton-picking legends. They not only taught them the tricks, but Marcus and Waitus would also move fast up and down the rows so that they would have a little extra time to disappear among some trees with some pretty girls. Dad and the others would remain in the hot field struggling to reach their target for the day, while Marcus and Waitus were in the shade. Before disappearing, they would say that they were going to pick some "bullets" (wild Concord grapes). However, they would return with smiles on their faces and not one grape in their hands.

Dad and his neighbors sang the blues and gospel moving up and down the rows. They chanted the opening to Sam Cooke's "(That's the Sound of the Men Working on the) Chain Gang," which was a call and response work song about black inmates in the South doing forced labor digging ditches and building roads while being guarded by white sheriffs armed with rifles. They lamented with Lou Rawls as they sang his version of "St. James Infirmary," a blues story where a young singer mourns the untimely death of his beautiful sweetheart while identifying her cold body on top of a long, white table in the morgue.

They also rocked to Lloyd Price's "Stagger Lee," a popular rock song about a legendary black gambler from St. Louis. The lyrics indicated that while gambling one evening in 1895, his friend Billy cheated and won all of Stagger Lee's money and his brand new Stetson hat. So Stagger Lee "…shot that poor boy so bad. Till the bullet came through Billy and it broke the bartender's glass."

Legends concerning Stagger Lee, who died in prison in 1896, began circulating in the African American community and were passed down through the years. "Stagger Lee" (the song) was recorded in 1925 by Ma Rainey, the "Mother of the Blues." It has since been recorded by more than 100 artists including James Brown, Ike and Tina Turner, Wilson Pickett, the Isley Brothers, Bob Dylan, the Grateful Dead, Jerry Lee Lewis, Pete Seeger, and Amy Winehouse. In 1959 Lloyd Price's version hit No. 1 on the rhythm and blues and the pop charts in the USA and in England, while dad moved up and down the cotton rows in Georgia shouting, "Go, go, go, go Stagger Lee!"

Sam Cooke's "Wonderful," the Five Blind Boys of Alabama's "I'm Going Home on the Morning Train," and the Impressions' "Amen" were among the gospel songs that brought church right into the cotton fields. Once in a while, someone would pause from the back-breaking work to do a little "shout" (ecstatic dance) while singing. On Sunday mornings, dad would sing those same songs at St. James Baptist Church with some of the same neighbors he had sung next to in the cotton fields Monday through Friday. He might also "shout" a little to the rhythms of the drums and tambourines when he would attend the Pentecostal church.

You didn't "shout" in a black Baptist church. The pastors would put you out. They weren't interested in having anything brought into their pews that reminded the congregation of Africa and the past of our enslaved ancestors. They wanted the members to be "proper" Christians. Yet, no matter the preferences of the preachers, the soulful spirit of Africa could not be fully suppressed in the music of the soloists and choirs.

As dad and I stood in that hot "dog days" August sun in 2006 with no shade in sight, dad asked me to look down the rows of cotton and "see the monkey that all the workers wanted to keep off their backs when picking cotton." He said, "That monkey is hot and heavy and known for causing workers to have heat strokes and fainting spells."

It was midday, 107 degrees, and we stood there with no hats or shades or bottled water. I thought dad was buggin' and talking nonsense about finding a monkey in a cotton field. It felt like 130 degrees, which it probably was standing unprotected in the sun. You would have thought he would have been better prepared, but, then again, maybe he was as prepared as he wanted to be. We were in the field under the brutal sun while all the other nine million sensible people in Georgia were somewhere else under an air conditioner, their own or someone else's.

Not even the farmers dared to be out in the field. At that time, it was just dad and me under a hot Georgia sun, which dared any cloud to appear in the sky. I stood wondering if it were possible for Georgia to have its own special sun. Even the distant trees at the edges of the field were too afraid of that sun to produce any shade.

As we stood there, the sun felt hot enough to fry my hair, to fry my head, and to fry my mind. I reached up to scratch my head through my Afro. I could smell the aroma of the coconut oil I had used on my Afro that morning grow in intensity as the sun sat directly overhead and on my head. I was waiting to hear sounds like uncured beef bacon sizzling in the frying pan because I was sure the sun was using the coconut oil to cook my hair and cook my head. Of course, inside my Afro, my fingers were even warmer than they had been seconds before.

With my hair "ablaze," the intense glare of the sunlight forced me to practically close my eyes. The absence of any breeze and the absence of clouds had me wondering if it could be any hotter in the room at Bikram Yoga Park Slope. Dad had once convinced me a few months earlier, with an incentive of $20, to try the class. I attended three times, and each time the teachers had the room approaching 110 degrees with 60 percent humidity. With the doors and windows shut, there was no air in the room as we went through 90 minutes of yoga postures. But with $60, I was able to buy a video game I wanted. And that was enough Bikram Yoga for me for a while, if not for a lifetime. After all, at age 13 I preferred sports with constant and fast competitive movements. Of course, dad has continued to appeal to me to return for instruction from his favorite teachers including Roody, Robbin, Havi, Saya, Christine, Nandra, and Amanda. Although I have agreed, I have always found something else to do when the scheduled times would arrive.

As we continued standing in that cotton field, little rivulets of sweat streamed down my face, my arms, and legs. My throat was dry. I swallowed hard several times, hoping against hope that I could generate enough moisture to ease my dry throat.

After a minute, I started to notice the aroma of fresh cotton rising from the cotton stalks to flow into my nostrils. It was the first time I recognized that cotton has a very different aroma from that which I had experienced with manufactured items. Manufactured cotton seemed odorless by comparison to the rich aroma of natural cotton on cotton stalks in the field under the hot Georgia sun.

While attempting to escape from the smell of cotton, I started seeking a quick end to our visit. I threw my hands into the air and whispered, "Dad, I see the cotton but I don't see no monkey!"

"I don't see any monkey," he corrected me, as usual. He then took my shaking head between his hands and asked, "What do you see now?"

The presence of his hands on my ears made the heat even more unbearable, if that were possible. I struggled to breathe. I struggled to remain respectful.

Soon, at a distance of about the length of a football field, I could see some very intense heat waves that appeared to move across the cotton field. I declared, "I am too hot, and all I see are some intense looking heat waves, but no monkey, dad!"

Not a second passed before he uttered in response, with a bit of a Southern twang, "Boy, those heat waves are the monkey. As a matter of fact, when they are that intense we say it is the go-rilla. And when that go-rilla moves across the field like that, you want to go in search of water and shade trees rather than risk being taken out on a stretcher with a sun stroke!"

It's funny how that Southern twang has remained in his voice even though he has been in New York most of his life. I do not have that twang, and that is a good thing. That twang might work for Andre 3000, Outkast, Waka Flocka Flame and B.o.B in hip hop, but I want to be a sports broadcaster. It would be difficult to spit my lines on ESPN with that twang. Folks in certain parts of the country would definitely need a translation.

I think dad is happy I do not have that twang. He often says I will be a great sports broadcaster because I have a passion for sports and sports statistics. He also says I have a better voice and am taller and more handsome than Dennis Haysbert, the star of *The Unit* and all those All State commercials.

Mom says Dennis Haysbert is considered "handsome enough" by most women, but that she must admit I am "cuter by more than a smidgen and was born with a microphone for a voice." Recently, dad asked mom if she still thought Haysbert was handsome after they saw an episode of *The Unit* where he took his shirt off to reveal a very hairy chest. She answered, "Yeah, but he needs to get rid of the hair on his chest."

I must agree with dad that a very hairy chest is not a good look on a man. I do not want to be like my first cousins on mom's side, Eric and Pito, who live not too far from "Little Puerto Rico" in Orlando, Florida, and shave their chests. Pito even has his sister Allyson shave the hair on his back that he can't reach (*eww!*). Pito and Eric are not metrosexuals; instead, they are into body building and Eric is an ex-marine who recently completed service carrying a gun bigger than himself in Iraq. I am glad I come from dad's genes that do not produce a hairy chest that needs shaving. But they do produce some feet that require a lot of lotion and Vaseline to keep them from being ashy. Thankfully, they are big feet and good for hooping!

Anyway, after 10 minutes out in that hot August sun, I was glad to leave the pilgrimage to the cotton field and that "go-rilla" and to quickly walk toward the comfort of the air-conditioned Camry. Dad had made his point, and I felt happy that I was not dad or anyone else who had to endure such intense heat for 10 hours a day for peanuts. I was also happy that he had not brought along a burlap sack with the intention of asking me to pick a few pounds. Thank God farmers now have machines to pick cotton and African Americans have other opportunities. Ain't that right, Mr. President?

Of course, I told dad none of my thoughts. As a 13-year-old teenager, I had already learned that it's not cool telling your parents you agree when they are trying to make a point. Even when you do agree, it's best to keep it to yourself or you might get more preachy lessons when you are not in the mood to hear all that. Parents, especially dads, seem to know precisely when you are not in the mood, and that's when they choose to lay it on you: "Blah, blah, blah, uh huh, uh huh." And I ain't trying to hear all that. Know what I mean?

With the most challenging part of the pilgrimage completed, we returned to the cool comfort of the car. As we neared the town limits, my thoughts were on grub and the noises coming from my stomach. The kind of noises only a hungry stomach can make.

"Hey, dad, can we stop at McDonald's?" I asked.

Dad must have thought he had made his point in the cotton field because he said yes to McDonald's even though he was a health nut who "wouldn't be caught dead eating the 18 grams of fat in a Big Mac or drinking the sugary, diabetes-hyping chocolate shake."

That day he didn't even mention that he thought McDonald's had a "special perfume it puts in the oil for its fries." He believed their fries had a very recognizable smell that is nothing like the smell of real potatoes from a farm.

He once told me when I was 8, "Morticians have to work for two whole days using special chemicals to remove that smell from some dead bodies. Man, if they don't get rid of that smell and people come to view a body that ate a lot of fast food, the smell would make them think they were back at McDonald's instead of in church at a viewing. While the preacher is trying to pray for the deceased, the wife, children, and relatives would be dreaming of french fries."

The Big Mac, shake, and fries were my reward for cooperating by watching, listening, and not complaining about preferring to hang out in the motel with Pokémon, Yu-Gi-Oh!, and my PlayStation. (Dad decided he would fast until he could get a decent meal.) Dad would later spend the next five of my teen years attempting to teach me that teenagers are more likely to get the things they want through cooperation rather than through lying, complaining, and defiance. He really thought he could teach me, an American teenager, that lesson. When teaching me about lying, he would sometimes quote Judge Judy who remarked, "How do you know when a teenager is lying? When his mouth is moving!"

Well, my mouth would move and Judge Judy would make her point. Lying is in our DNA. Stand inside any school or on any school yard full of teenagers and see if you have enough numbers to count all the types of lies you hear. Teenagers don't lie to sin; we lie to seek advantage and status.

I lie to get my own way and avoid dad's way. Even when I agree with what he wants for me, I want to go about getting there my way, not his way. For example, I want to graduate from college in four years, but sometimes I want to go to classes when I feel like it or stay sleeping when I don't feel like it. I want to go on Facebook and Twitter on my MacBook while also checking for texts on my cell and being hooked to my iPod when I feel like it, even sometimes while I am rushing at the last hour to complete a college essay. I want to play basketball and sometimes come home to play on my XBox 360 and Play Station 3 until way past midnight even as I work on the assignments that are due the next day.

I can do it all. Thus, I often ask myself, "Why is that so hard for him to understand?" If someone knows the answer, I would appreciate a posting on Facebook because I could use it to show how often he is totally unreasonable.

Thankfully, on the way from McDonald's to the motel, I had the pleasure of playing with my Game Boy Advance and busting out of dad's distant world for about a half hour. With my fingers, eyes and mind working in harmony, freedom was a sweet thing.

No more "rah-rah" and "blah, blah, blah, uh huh, uh huh."

Chapter 2

Meet Mom: A Banana Boat Ride from Puerto Rico

Eminem sang about his mom and, in comparison, my mom is very different. I believe my mom is a great mom, especially when she is not trying to be dad and when she is not taking sides with dad. I know she often places demands on me only to please dad. Sometimes I miss those days when I was her precious *"bambino"* and able to go to her for something while not including him. She has a sweetness that he doesn't even pretend that he wants to possess.

Mom was born in Aguadilla, Puerto Rico, which was at that time a little sleepy fishing village of about 15,000 inhabitants. Aguadilla is located on the northwestern tip of Puerto Rico and is bordered by the Atlantic Ocean. Today, it is a city with a population of more than 65,000 and it has an international airport.

Mom's parents left Puerto Rico for New York in 1956 when my mother was 2 years old. *Mi abuela/*my grandmother was pregnant with my *Titi/* Auntie Miriam when the family boarded the Pan American plane out of San Juan for New York with mom, three of her older brothers, one younger sister, and my great grandfather. *Mi abuelo/*my grandfather was waiting in *Nueva York* after having arrived a few months earlier to work and prepare a place to receive his family.

BTW, *mi abuela es blanca y mi abuelo es moreno/*my grandmother is "white" and my grandfather is black. When my grandfather approached my grandmother, her "white" sisters kindly warned her that if she were to marry him she could expect to have a difficult time combing her children's hair. *Mi* *abuela* was in love and the color of *mi abuelo's* skin and the future texture of her children's hair were not concerns. Later, when my *trigueña* mother was in fifth grade, my grandmother discovered a solution for dealing with her thick, long, and beautiful kinky hair.

One day while *abuela* was combing mom's hair, the comb got stuck inside a long mound of hair. Grandma, with her little arms, struggled to pull the comb through, but the comb wouldn't budge. So grandma got up, got the scissors, and cut mom's hair just above the point where the comb got stuck. Mom was not happy to lose her beautiful hair, but grandma had solved her problem. So, if you look at mom's school picture in *mi abuela's* photo album, she has two long thick ponytails one year and short hair cropped slightly below the beginning of her neck the next.

In search of a better life, in 1956 my grandparents settled on the Lower Eastside of Manhattan in a tiny railroad apartment in a rundown tenement. It was a railroad apartment without trains; an apartment with little boys without the story book train characters named Thomas the Tank Engine, James, Gordon, and Diesel. The bathrooms were in the hallway and shared by dozens of families from the various apartments. Now, that's got to be gross! Son, if you have been in a public bathroom in New York City, then you know what I mean.

Thank goodness *mi abuela* was known for keeping a very clean and organized apartment for mom and her then four brothers and three sisters. She kept a small bucket in the apartment for her kids to do their "business." After they would finish she would go and empty the bucket in the common bathroom in the hallway. (I heard that in old-time London and New York, before indoor plumbing was common, parents would go to the windows and empty the chamber pots onto the streets below. Folks below had to keep an eye above to avoid having their hair color and complexion changed in an instant.)

If one of *abuela's* little ones was sitting on the "bucket" when another had to go, she would inspect and clean the common bathroom each time before she would allow one of her children to enter, especially the girls. Though she was a tiny woman, she would often hold her very young daughters as they "sat" on her arms above the toilet. Her left arm would hold mom at the bottom of her legs at the fold under her knee caps. Her right arm would be positioned across the middle of mom's back. Thus, mom would be in a sitting position without resting on the toilet as mom took care of her "business." *Abuela* had four little girls, so I guess there was a lot of "business." ROTFL/Rolling on the floor laughing!

This happened in the late 1950s and early 1960s when waves of Puerto Ricans were coming to the shores of *Nueva York*. The New York newspapers wrote stories about the new arrivals. In 1960, shortly after my family's arrival, *El Diario*, a Spanish-language newspaper, wrote an article about mom's family complete with a picture of the family. The picture featured *mi abuela*, mom, and seven of her brothers and sisters sitting on a couch.

When I was 10, my mother took out a copy of the article with the picture and showed it to me to make a point about teasing other kids. If they had not been my family, I would have laughed out loud at how ridiculous mom and her little brothers and sisters looked in that picture.

Laughing would have gotten me into deeper trouble than I was already in for teasing this girl at school by calling her a name that I would rather forget even today. WWIT/What was I thinking! Miss Foote, the principal, had found out about the name calling, and she had called me to her office. It was my first time being called to the principal's office. I sat in the outer office with all eyes on me while waiting for her to call me into the inner office. When we spoke she expressed her disappointment, and I felt so alone and helpless. From her office she called dad to report my misbehavior, and her call set me up for a major confrontation with mom and dad.

Initially, dad told Miss Foote that he was shocked that I knew such a word to call the girl. He knew it was not spoken in our home. Miss Foote explained that I had learned the word in my sex education class in the school. Dad was instantly not happy with sex education in school and not happy with me.

In middle school in America teasing is a big thing. Psychologists say it is a form of bullying that is meant to humiliate another person. Everyone is afraid of being teased, and everyone wants to be popular. One way of making sure you are not teased is to call attention to someone else by teasing that person. You could become very popular in middle school as a master teaser, and no one would dare tease you because they would be afraid of your wrath and your popularity. I was not a master teaser, but I had decided on that day to repeat a tease that I had heard directed at this not-so-popular girl after we learned the word in sex education class.

Mom was almost 6 years old when the article in *El Diario* was written. In the old black and white news photo, mom and her sisters and brothers looked like brown-skinned versions of the Little Rascals. Mom and her siblings all had that *jibaro*/country hick look. *Mi abuela*, who had been a nurse in Puerto Rico, sat erect and proud *como una reina*/like a queen. *Mi abuelo*, who would die two decades before I was born, was at work at the sweat shop where he spent 12 hours a day manufacturing suitcases. There were two well-dressed male strangers. One was an apartment building owner and the other was a local politician.

As I looked, I could only imagine how poor mom's family must have been if they could make the papers as the example of the families arriving from Puerto Rico who desperately needed support to make it in mainland America.

My mother told me that in those days, on the Lower Eastside, kids born in Puerto Rico were often teased by African American kids, white kids, Jewish kids, and other Puerto Ricans who were born in New York. A famous tease was to claim that Puerto Ricans who were not born in New York came over to mainland America on a "banana boat." As one kid would make the claim, other kids would surround the victim and join in for the big laugh: "You came over on a banana boat, ha, ha, ha!!! How many did you eat? She ate the whole boat!! Ha, ha, ha!"

Mom said that she had been teased so often after arriving in New York that in the first grade, as the teasing continued, she became confused and started to actually think that maybe she had come over on a banana boat. She even started to have images in her mind and in her dreams of actually being on a boat full of bananas sailing past the Statue of Liberty!

Of course, in first grade mom had never seen a banana boat or even the Statue of Liberty. She had arrived on a Pan American jet and had landed at LaGuardia Airport. As American citizens, Puerto Ricans could easily travel anywhere within the USA. Although they were poor, with determination my grandparents found the money to pay for the passage of two adults (including my great grandfather) and five kids and my *Titi* Miriam "in the oven." Though they were already American, they were very much like today's Dominicans, Mexicans, Salvadorans, Costa Ricans, Guatemalans, Hondurans, Nicaraguans, Panamanians, and Haitians who are often very poor yet struggle against seemingly impossible odds and find the money to come to mainland USA in search of a better life for their kids.

It is ironic that mom was being teased by kids who had never even been on an airplane, because in those days a plane ride was a luxury that mainland-born families on the Lower Eastside just could not afford. The only planes that the haters had seen were planes overhead and the paper ones they threw around the classrooms when misbehaving. Another irony is that the parents of the kids born on the Lower Eastside probably had arrived in New York on ships from Puerto Rico and Europe before airplane travel became available and affordable to the general public. Maybe some of those earlier ships from Puerto Rico sailed with the teasing kids' parents and actual cargoes of bananas.

After mom told her banana boat story, to show me that I shouldn't insult any of my classmates, my father was overcome with anger and, for the first and last time, he picked up my ruler to suggest that he was disappointed enough to spank me. My father preached that boys must grow up respecting girls and, thus, become men who respect women.

"Would you want someone to say that to your sisters? To your mother? Your aunts? To Allyson or Nicole (*mis primas*/my cousins)? You are not to repeat the trashy words you hear other guys say in school or in the street! You are better than that!" he told me.

As dad spoke that day, mom stood by nodding her head in full agreement.

"Akhenaton, you must understand what your dad is saying. *Bambino*, that was not a nice thing to say to anyone," she admonished with the tenderness that was often missing in dad's voice when he would admonish me. Her tenderness was reassuring.

"Okay, mom, I'm sorry. It won't happen again."

Gucci Mane would later sing he was not "stoopid," but I must confess after hearing mom's story I could not say the same for me. I understood my mother's and father's words and said, "I agree." I spoke the words because in my heart I knew I had acted "stoopid" calling the girl a name whose meaning I did not even really know. The disappointment that I felt and the disappointment in my parents' faces were worse than the major punishment of taking away privileges, including video games and television, for more than a month.

However, I was really proud a year later when the same principal remarked to mom that I was "the one kid who seemed to be comfortable mingling with all the subgroups in the cafeteria" within my very diverse middle school in Manhattan. She said that I was comfortable with the nerds (she called them "smart kids"), the Goths, the athletes, the Asians, the Caucasians, the upper-middle-class, the Latinos, the African Americans, the hip hop crew, and the new immigrants (the Guatemalans, Mexicans, Senegalese, Dominicans, Salvadorans, Iraqis, Tibetans, and other new arrivals who could be the subjects of teasing and bullying in New York schools today).

Dad said that I was privileged in being comfortable because I will be well prepared to find success in a world that requires a person to work and be comfortable with people from all races and religious backgrounds. He said that in his hometown everyone was Protestant Christian and either black or white, and he had attended a segregated all-black elementary and middle school. Thus, he had to learn later in high school to interact with white kids of his age.

Dad said that he was 6 years old the first time he saw Puerto Ricans or even knew that such a people existed. A group of Puerto Rican migrant farm laborers had stopped in his small town and was being hosted by Mr. Hamp

Andrews, a neighbor and entrepreneur. Word quickly spread throughout the black section of town that an interesting group of people was nearby. The word that circulated suggested, "Come over to Hamp's place and see a group of people who look white but are treated like blacks." Thus, many curious African Americans left their homes to come to my father's neighbor's home to see the group for themselves.

Dad was one of the curious. He arrived just as the Puerto Rican migrant workers were reentering the four covered trucks that would take them "up north" to Newburgh, New York, for apple and pumpkin picking season. The summer harvest season in the South had ended, and the laborers were preparing to head north for the fall harvest.

Dad stood for a few minutes staring at the young men, young women, and teenage boys and girls wearing overalls and inexpensive straw hats sitting on the floor of a truck with barely enough room to fully stretch out their legs if they were to get a cramp during the long ride north. There were no expressions of joy on their faces or from their voices as they prepared to set forth. Images of himself with his brothers and sisters and other African Americans sitting in the back of pickup trucks on the way to cotton and tobacco fields came to dad's mind.

When dad walked around to the front cab of a dark blue truck, he discovered the truck driver was a Caucasian man. The Caucasian drivers had just returned from eating at Key's Cafe in the Caucasian part of town. They had returned to retrieve the Puerto Ricans who had to eat their meals with Hamp in the black part of town. For dad it was the same story. The Caucasian men looked very much like the Caucasian men who would come to the black part of Swainsboro to retrieve blacks at 5:00 a.m. for work in the fields.

Dad was fascinated but he would not see another Puerto Rican until he arrived in the Bronx nine years later. Later, as a baseball fan and teen in the Bronx, dad would read about the Negro Leagues and discover that Emilio "Millito" Navarro was the first Puerto Rican to play professional baseball in the Negro Leagues with the Cuban Stars, a team of African Americans and Latino players. In 2009, Navarro, at 105 years old, was the oldest living member of the former Negro Leagues. Navarro played in the Negro Leagues when Puerto Ricans, Dominicans, Mexicans, Cubans, and other Latinos were not allowed to play in the Major Leagues due to racism. Any potential Mariano Rivera, Albert Pujols, Jose Bautista, Big Papi, Robinson Cano, Alex Rodriguez, and any other Latinos with even a hint of black blood were not welcomed before

Jackie Robinson changed history. BTW, Robinson Cano, a Dominican, was given that name at birth to honor Jackie Robinson's achievement.

Dad's first Latino sports hero was Juan Marichal, the Dominican pitcher with the high leg kick, who was a star with Willie Mays, Willie McCovey, and the San Francisco Giants. In the 1960s, Marichal and the Giants battled Sandy Koufax, Don Drysdale, and the LA Dodgers for supremacy in the National League. The rivalry between the teams was like that of the Yankees and Red Sox today. Mays, Marichal, McCovey, Koufax, and Drysdale were later inducted into the MLB Hall of Fame.

While in college, dad's first Puerto Rican heroes were Don Pedro Albizu Compos and Ramon Emeterio Betances. Each had African ancestry and both were considered fathers of the Puerto Rican independence movement. Dad would also learn that a black Puerto Rican, Arturo Alfonso Schomburgo, or Arthur Schomburg, was a scholar and historian who is considered "the father of black history." Schomburgo, while attending school in his native San Juan, was said to have been told by his fifth grade teacher, "Blacks have no history, no heroes, no great moments."

Motivated to disprove that lie, in 1891 Schomburgo moved to New York and became a tireless researcher and collector of African and African American history and artifacts. He ultimately sold more than 10,000 items including books, manuscripts, letters, prints, playbills, and paintings to the New York Public Library which houses the materials at the Arthur Schomburg Center for Research in Black Culture on 135th Street and Lenox Avenue in Harlem.

Unlike dad's childhood in a black and white world, I was fortunate to have attended P.S. 59 where 19 of the 24 students in my fourth grade class had been born outside the USA, representing more than 10 other countries (including Afghanistan, Iraq, Iran, China, Tibet, Nigeria, the Philippines, and Russia) and several religions. My best friend, Cassie, was born in Germany. I liked her a lot because we could sit and talk like the best of brothers and sisters. Our parents also became friends. I was disappointed when her family moved on to California. They moved in 2001, before Facebook was invented which would have been an easy way to keep in touch.

Today, I have thousands of Facebook friends including friends who live outside the USA, mostly in Asia and Europe. Many I met during various summer programs in my teens.

At times I struggle with spending too much time keeping in touch on Facebook and Twitter when I should be studying. Word! (Did dad just say that?)

Anyway, Cassie, if you are reading this, hit me up on Facebook.

Chapter 3

Dad Meets Mom: Different Romance Rules

When I turned 12, dad told me the story of how he met mom. My father met my mother the old-fashioned way. This was before eHarmony, African American Singles dot com, and all the other sites for finding the love of your life. This was also before Lil Wayne sang about meeting and teaching a brokenhearted woman how to love in a strip club.

My father and my mother worked in two different departments of the same company. He saw her walking down the hall one day in April 1981. He said her appearance "caused the sun to enter the 41st floor of the suite of offices at Astor Plaza in Times Square on what was outside a very cloudy and rainy day." She walked very erect; *como una reina*.

Mom said when she met dad, "He walked at times as if he had the world on his shoulders." My father said she later taught him to walk more erect, thereby improving his posture and flexibility and adding to his ability to maintain a "youthful appearance" as he aged.

I believe my mom knows that sometimes there is a harmless, yet competitive spirit between her son and her husband. At times, I have a good feeling whenever I get the opportunity to burst dad's ego balloon. I love to challenge his knowledge about athletes, sports, issues in movies, music, and musicians. I also like to tease him about his physical appearance by putting up signs that read "old man" on the mirror in the bathroom that he and I share. I place the signs so that they frame his face when he raises his head from the sink to look into the mirror the first thing in the morning.

In contrast, for my benefit, his thing is to put up on the same mirror famous quotes of great men and psalms and proverbs from the Holy Bible. One that he tends to keep up for long periods of time and return to often is taken from the book of Isaiah:

"For you shall go out with joy and be led forth in peace:
The mountains and hills shall break forth before you into singing
And all the trees of the field shall clap their hands."

In my opinion, my mom has issues with owning her bathroom. Dad and I share a bathroom because mom insists. We must share the larger bathroom in the master bedroom of our apartment and stay out of the smaller bathroom, which "belongs" to her. She says it has to do with us not putting the seat down and me missing the target in the dark late at night. She said she does not want to be like millions of women who suddenly fall into the bowl thinking the seat is down, only to find the men have left it up. I think she still has bad memories of the common bathroom in the hallway on the Lower Eastside, which makes her exaggerate the problem with us using "her" bathroom.

Anyway, on that spring day in 1981, dad noticed that mom had the most beautiful nutmeg brown eyes. Dad said the eyes are where you start. He said the eyes are the mirror to the soul. Her eyes embraced his eyes in search of his essence, his spirit.

Dad said that mom's teeth were pearly white. Her smile was radiant. She had on jeans that represented her beautiful shape. He said she had the shape of a goddess that no sculptor could capture. She was the picture of health, and he was charmed. He said there was something about the change in the sound of his voice that let her know he was charmed. No, he didn't stutter. Instead, his voice became "melodious" (something hard for me to imagine). He explained he wanted to sing the words he was speaking to match the melody pulling on his heart strings. He said he was intent on finding the appropriate time to gently touch her hand with his fingertips as they conversed. That would be the signal to her that he was a man with proper character and intentions. He believed if she allowed the touch that would be a signal he would stand a chance of dating her.

"Hello. My name is Askia," he said as they were about to pass in the hallway.

Mom paused, turned with a subtle smile and whispered, "My name is Nydia," using the Spanish pronunciation. She had learned from Rosie, a co-worker, that he was interested in meeting her but she had not been sure she wanted to meet him. (That, I can understand). They both would say later that it was love at first sight when their eyes met.

Mom had never been married, and dad was in the sixth month of a separation from his first wife. Dad's heart was shouting "hello" while his mind was also saying "take it slow," long before John Legend came up with that line. So, despite the intensity he felt at the initial hello, for the next four months they dated regularly without dad ever attempting to kiss her lips.

He said that he did not kiss mom because he did not want lust to cloud his mind. He declared, "I wanted to first know what kind of person she truly was. I wanted to know her thoughts about God, herself, her family, and the world. I was a single father raising two daughters, and I wanted to make sure she was a woman I would be comfortable introducing into our lives. I wanted to know her values and if they would be in harmony with the values in my heart, including a devotion to improving the lives of blacks and Latinos in America."

Yeah, son, dad is weird. I believe you could see why I don't want his advice or opinion regarding any girl I might date.

So, at age 12, dad told me that there is more to a relationship than taking off your clothes. He explained that after a few times of that, a couple better have something else to keep them together, to sustain a relationship, and to build a family.

"Don't be fooled by the rappers' videos into looking at women the way they do," he advised as he spoke of their encounter. He further suggested, "Some rappers are not looking for real women. They are only looking for warm bodies. Word!"

He said that many years ago, before he went on YouTube and saw the "cold" dead women's bodies in bed with Kanye in his 2010 "Monster" video.

The late comedian Bernie Mac might have encouraged me to ask: "America, is dad right that many rappers are not looking for real women?"

Now, at age 18, I might ask, "Should I listen to Lil Wayne's 'How to Love' to get a real sense of how to build a healthy relationship with a good woman? Does Lil Wayne do a good job restoring a woman's confidence in love after her heart has been broken?"

In the video, Lil Wayne is rapping to a stripper, whose heart has been previously broken by a "whole lot of crooks," as she shakes her body and he looks on in the strip club. Even dad must admit that strippers need love, too. Did dad and mom meet the right way or is Lil Wayne's way with the stripper in the strip club best? Huh? Visit my Facebook page and let me know your thoughts; take the poll.

From the time I was 10 through the age of 13, while riding in that old 1992 Camry up the Westside Highway to the Fieldston Enrichment Program, dad would ask me on several occasions: "What are the four things you should look for in a wife?"

After many discussions of situations he had seen (and some I had witnessed), I understood and accepted the answer, and I even told him so:

"First, she must believe in God."

"Second, she must come from a loving and good family." (My father was raised in a poor household by a single mom, my grandma Mattie, who remains his principal role model for her love, devotion, and strength raising 13 children.)

"Third, she must have a lot of self-respect, be very intelligent, and have plenty of common sense to raise the children."

"Fourth, she should be beautiful to me, with no need for my friends to think she is beautiful."

I spat the lines as if they were mine. I even felt comfortable repeating them to mom when she asked.

When dad met mom, she had an Angela Davis big beautiful "Natural" or what most folks call an Afro. Like mom, in the 1970s and 1980s, many Puerto Ricans in New York wore Afros in celebration of their African ancestry, I was told. Mom said there were even whites who wore real Afros, not Afro wigs. Dad said even the young Billy Joel in the 1970s wore an Afro when he did "New York State of Mind." Imagine that.[1]

The Afro was the popular style for folks from Michael Jackson to Bill Cosby to Pablo Yoruba Guzman (today a reporter on WCBS 2 in New York), and Felipe Luciano, a member of the Last Poets who, according to dad, were spitting in the late 1960s and early 1970s along with Abiodun Oyewole, Umar bin Hassan, David Nelson, and Gylan Kain.

Dad suggests that the Last Poets and other spoken word artists of that era (such as Gil Scott-Heron) were inspired by musicians, including John Coltrane ("A Love Supreme" and "Naima"), Miles Davis ("So What" and "All Blues"), and Nina Simone ("Four Women" and "Wild is the Wind"); poets, including Langston Hughes ("Black Like Me" and "A Dream Deferred") and Claude McKay ("If We Must Die" and "Outcast"); and the speeches and leadership of Malcolm X, Martin Luther King, Jr., H. "Rap" Brown, Stokely Carmichael, Muhammad Ali, Huey Newton, and Eldridge Cleaver, who were incomparable spoken word masters. Those musicians, poets, and political leaders carried revolutionary messages to people of African descent throughout the world during the Harlem Renaissance and in the 1960s and 1970s.

The Last Poets and Gil Scott-Heron are given credit for planting the seeds for the birth of rap and hip hop in their original revolutionary form with revolutionary themes. Gil Scott-Heron's "The Revolution Won't Be Televised" and the Last Poet's "This is Madness" continue to inspire spoken word artists today in the Hip Hop Generation.

Grand Master Flash and the Furious Five with Grand Master Melle Mel's "Beat Street" and "The Message" are two of the best examples of early hip hop in its revolutionary form with revolutionary themes. Dad reported that, as he moved around the streets of New York City in the 1980s, he watched many spontaneous break dance "street battles" where the teams used "Beat Street."

I have watched the "Beat Street" video on YouTube countless times.[2] Everything in that song speaks about conditions that we can still see all around the streets of America and the world today. Dad declares that in that song Melle Mel warned us more than three decades ago—before the introduction of iPhones, "Crackberries," Play Station, XBox, MacBooks, Facebook, Twitter, etc.—not to become slaves to the computer, but many failed to listen.

Pablo Yoruba Guzman and Felipe Luciano with their Afros were also two founding leaders of the revolutionary Puerto Rican Young Lords of *El Barrio* in the 1970s. Even Carlos Santana ("Maria, Maria. She reminds me of a west side story…..") of Mexican ancestry, and many of the Latino members of his band, wore Afros in the 1970s when they sang, "She's a black magic woman and she's trying to make a devil out of me…."

I wore an Afro until age 14 when I went with the Toronto Raptors' Chris Bosh look—hundreds of small braids. The current Miami Heat Bosh is sort of plain looking with a hairstyle that has no character. I have my hair in dreadlocks now.

Mom told me that when she was a student in the early 1970s she was stopped and questioned by the police because they thought she resembled Angela Davis, the fugitive black revolutionary. Angela Davis was a university professor wanted by the FBI for alleged involvement in the murder of a judge. Her picture with the big Afro was constantly on television, in the newspapers, and on the walls of post offices. Her image was almost as well known in America as that of Muhammad Ali. However, Ali's face was considered the most recognizable and beloved face by people throughout the world.

Angela Davis was No. 1 on the FBI's Most Wanted List. President Nixon was putting a great deal of pressure on the FBI to capture her, and FBI agents were stopping and questioning hundreds of light-skinned African American and Latino women with Afros in cities throughout America.

In comparison to mom, Angela Davis was 10 years older and had that Michael Strahan gap between her two front teeth, while mom's teeth did not have any gaps. I guess the police who stopped and were hoping to arrest mom were practically blind.

Dad said that in the 1960s and 1970s when African Americans were fighting for their civil and human rights, they were also fighting to change their names from the European names given to their ancestors back during slavery. They stopped referring to themselves as N-words, Negro and colored, labels given by whites. They became blacks and African Americans. Cassius Clay became Muhammad Ali. Malcolm Little became Malcolm X and then later became El Hajj Malik Shabazz. Alice Faye Williams became Afeni Shakur, who would become the mother of Tupac Amaru Shakur. (Tupac Amaru II was a revolutionary Indian leader who led an Incan uprising against forced labor and oppression by the people of Spanish descent in Peru in 1780.)

At 17, dad was a revolutionary colleague of Afeni Shakur in the New York City Black Panther Party on Seventh Avenue and 122nd Street in Harlem. Dad's role model was Lumumba Shakur, Afeni's first husband and the leader of the New York City Black Panthers. He said, "Lumumba had the purest heart and deepest commitment to the freedom, education, and well-being of African Americans and people of African descent throughout the world. Lumumba was a fearless, strong, brilliant, charismatic, and visionary black man. His humility added a powerful dimension to the attractiveness of his character."

Dad said although he learned the theory about the importance of community service and commitment to the success and self-determination of black people throughout the world from reading Malcolm X's autobiography, his first example of the expression of that service and commitment was Lumumba. Dad suggested he has yet to approach the vision, commitment, and humility Lumumba possessed.

At 17, dad was also a student leader at Brooklyn College, fighting to open the doors of admission for African Americans and Puerto Ricans to City University's main campuses. At 17, he changed his name from Leroy (which means king in French and English) to Askia, the name of the 15th century king and warrior, Askia the Great, of the mighty Songhai Empire in West Africa.

Dad informed me, "In the 1960s and 1970s, African Americans also fought to bring forth their own definitions of beauty, rather than have the white-controlled society and media define beauty and impose the images the way they do today." He said he has read accounts where today even many young white women have trouble relating to the air brushed and tinted images with long flowing hair and bony bodies that the media imposes, seemingly nonstop. African Americans in the 1960s would have not accepted today's Victoria Secret or Clairol images.

"Black is beautiful!" was the word back then according to dad. The new symbols of beauty were Angela Davis, Afeni Shakur, Assata Shakur, Nikki Giovanni, the young actress Cicely Tyson, Kathleen Cleaver, and other black women active in the struggle. Those women stressed their African identity by wearing their hair as a "Natural," the name they preferred over the name Afro. The idea of "Natural" suggested natural and God-given beauty.

"What a woman had on her mind and expressed through a heartfelt commitment to improving the lives of African Americans was a very important aspect of her beauty. Those women set the standard," he explained.

Dad told me, "The beautiful Beyonce with her current look would have had a very difficult time getting noticed by revolutionary African American men as a beauty in the '70s." He said she would have had to do something about the L'Oréal weave and remove all that makeup. Gabrielle Union and Zoë Saldana, whom dad and I agree are dimes plus and as fly as fly could be, would nevertheless have had to change their hair in the early '70s, according to dad.

Of course, I would take them both just as they are, no matter what time or what year. I am even willing to move out! YGTR/You got that right. Gabrielle and Zoë, don't delay (and Gabrielle remember that Wade is boring you to death). Ladies, just ignore dad and ignore my age. I am 18 years old, 6 feet 4 inches, 200 pounds, handsome, and intelligent. Call, text, or email me. If you text, email, or Facebook, upload some pictures with your latest smiles, including at least one sending me a kiss. *Te quiero mucho! Si!* Swag!

When we worked on what we hoped would be the tenth and possibly final editing of this memoir, on August 21, 2011, the *New York Times Style Magazine* featured a beautiful Esperanza Spalding wearing a glorious "Natural" on its cover. Inside, in a photographic display titled, "Nightie Aphrodites," Solange Knowles, Corrine Bailey Rae, and Les Nubians (Helene and Celia Faussart) were also featured in their "Natural" beauty.

Dad made sure that I would take a long look at each photograph more than once. He told me each of the women represented real beauty that is rarely portrayed in popular media. Then he told me, "Get on British Airways and go to London and bring back Corrine Bailey Rae! She has the beauty that should be gracing the streets of Brooklyn. And, while you're at it, stop in Paris and bring home Les Nubians!"

That's my dad. Yes, I agree that they are beautiful women.

Mom told me the kinky hair of African Americans was not only admired in the 1970s. She suggested dreadlocks had been admired in ancient times and was a style worn by some ancient Egyptians, the Dravidians of India, and some blacks in ancient Mesopotamia (modern Iraq and Iran). She would later take me to the Brooklyn Museum of Art to show me the exhibit labeled, "Nubian Wig," which displayed the wig worn by Nefertiti more than 3,350 years ago. She explained Nefertiti was the Queen of Egypt and is still recognized today, nearly 4,000 years later, as a standard for female beauty. The "Nubian Wig," which remains on display in the Egyptian section of the museum, looks essentially like the dreadlock hairstyle worn by some African American and Latino women today.

When it came to handsome men, mom explained Muhammad Ali and the actor Calvin Lockhart set the standard admired by women all around the world in the 1970s. In 1975, Calvin Lockhart had starred as the original Biggie Smalls in the movie "Let's Do It Again," which also starred Sidney Poitier and Bill Cosby. (The Notorious B.I.G. later adopted Biggie Smalls as his name in honor of the character played by Lockhart. That is one funny movie where skinny Jimmy "J. J." Walker, after being hypnotized by Sidney Poitier, defeats a boxing champion. Dad and I have laughed together many times during repeat showings.)

Muhammad Ali was the most recognizable face on earth and the most admired. Ali was dad's hero. I cannot count the times we have ignored mom's presence while looking at ESPN's broadcasts of the Ali fights over and over and over again. I can see it in my head now. I can see Ali, after defeating Sonny Liston, running around the ring and jumping up into Bundini Brown's arms shouting: "I shook up the world! I shook up the world!! I shook up the world!!!" Yes, Ali shook up the world in more ways than one.

Dad remarked that he just loved it when Ali would deliberately pull out his comb and start combing his kinky hair after a fight in the 1960s and 1970s. Ali would make remarks about his handsome appearance as he combed through his kinky hair, which dad said our enemies in society and the media wanted us to define as "bad hair."

"Ain't I pretty?" Ali would ask. Dad said Ali was deliberately sending a message with that comb to African Americans and men and women of African descent throughout the world about our beauty and strength of character while tens of millions around the world watched. Dad said that act alone ensured that African American men would never go back to wearing a "process," that hairstyle the early Temptations wore that was created through the use of chemical lye.

After watching an Ali fight on different occasions in my pre-teens, dad and I would look at each other, jump off the couch, do the Ali Shuffle, play fight, flex our arm muscles, and, with intensity, shout one of dad's favorite quotes that Ali would use after devastating an opponent: "Ama baaad man!! Ama baaad man!!!" Then we would ask mom, "What's for dinner?" Of course, by then the dinners would need reheating for the baaad men.

Dad admired Ali so much that Ali became one of the four names I was given at birth. Dad wants me to know, Ama baaad man!!!

Mom and dad are not perfect, TBT/truth be told, especially dad. There have been times in my pre-teens and early teens when I would say, "I am so glad I have you for parents." I was happy that their destinies had crossed. Dad went from not knowing that Puerto Ricans existed to marrying one. I was so happy to accept them as my parents that I twice appeared to dad in a vision more than three months before my physical conception.

Earlier in my seventeenth year, I spent much of the time telling them they do not understand me. I have told them they do not know how to communicate with me and show me love for the person that I am. I have explained that they only show me love for the person they want me to be, not the person I am. That explanation has not been enough to get them off my back with their demands, at least not as often as I would have liked. Yet, I'm twisted because I know the love is right here.

Son, what is it with parents and the demands they place on teenagers? Why can't they understand that it is my life and that I don't need POTS/parents watching over the shoulders?

I am willing to make my own decisions and live with the consequences. I am smarter than they are because I live in the here and now, not in the ancient times of their teens. Shouldn't we have democracy in the lives of our families? "My way or the highway" is for the military, and you don't see me wearing a uniform.

One morning in spring 2010, in the midst of my "senioritis" while arguing with dad about getting out of the bathroom to get to school on time, I threw a verbal dagger meant to pierce his heart. "Dad, I'm going to be a better father to my sons than you are to me!" I shouted.

Dad replied, before my words had fully left my lips, "Every father who loves his son wants his son to be a better man, a better father. When you become better, I will be so proud and my grandsons will be blessed."

I heard him, but I gave no signal that I understood or agreed. I wanted him to know that he was talking smack, but how could I say that? I wanted to keep my anger boiling hot, and he was not making it easy. I wanted to punish his love. I wanted to punish his love because I did not know what else to do during many moments like that when I would feel frustrated because he would seem not to be moved by my anger. I was not getting any help from mom, and I could tell she was in agreement with him, even though she preferred that both of us would handle our disagreements in a different manner.

How do you keep your anger boiling hot against your dad? You adjust your posture. You squint your eyes. You sigh. You take deep breaths. You go silent. You shake your head, "No, no, no." You blow hot air through your nostrils. You speed up your heartbeat. You fade instead of charging.

You think, "That will show him," and on your way out you slam the door for all the neighbors to hear while shouting, "Mom, you were no help!"

Chapter 4
Fighting to Get to Earth

"Warrior of the Void. Warrior of the Void," dad often whispered to me from birth through age 7. "You are my blessing. I am like King David. Despite my deep sins, God gave me Suleiman (Solomon)."

You know, I've never once asked him the meaning. Somehow I instinctively knew what he meant. The Void is that empty, challenging, and treacherous space that must be conquered by a special awareness, a special existence, and a special warrior. The Void is the space that exists between who we are and who we are called to become. It is the space where we encounter so many flamboyant demons while our few guardian angels often choose to remain discreetly hidden from sight. Demons often choose not to appear horrific. Demons most often choose to appear enchanting.

Dad said that I am a magical child. You see, I first came to dad in a vision nearly four months before I was conceived. I had to reach him in order to reach earth. He had already determined that two children were enough, and, as my two sisters approached young adulthood, he was looking forward to the day when he would be "free to live his dreams."

Dad wanted to pursue a second career as a writer. Also, he was just beginning to adjust to the grave disappointment of believing his first novel, *A Love Supreme*, had been stolen by a film director and turned into a movie for which he had received no credit, after directing his lawyers during a second meeting with the film maker's lawyers to refuse to consider negotiating for a monetary settlement.

Six months before the night of my appearance in his vision, dad had married mom (his second wife) with an agreement that they would not have kids. It was a rather selfish, one-sided agreement since she had no kids and desperately wanted some. It must have taken a lot of love for her to agree, but agree she did. That agreement was a threat to my birth, and I could not let it stand.

Around 2:00 a.m. on Thanksgiving in 1991, as my father slept, I appeared. "Dad, it is time for me to come into the world!" I announced. "Dad, it is time for me to come into the world!"

I stood in the world as dad looked me up and down while attempting to get the clearest picture of "this strange yet familiar toddler" who stood before him speaking in the clearest of voices.

"Dad, it is time for me to come into the world!" I announced a third time.

Dad knew that although there was some physical part of him asleep, he was not dreaming. He had that ESP (extrasensory perception) and special knowledge that could "see" the difference between a dream and a vision. He had the knowledge to act willfully in the midst of a vision rather than remain just a passive observer. So he carefully studied my appearance and sensed that my presence was not to be casually ignored or placed in the category of a dream.

After a minute of studying my appearance, dad shook mom. "Nydia! Nydia!! Wake up! Wake up!"

"What is it?" mom mumbled with half-closed eyes and a racing heartbeat. "What is it?" Mom is not a person who likes to be awakened from a deep sleep. She usually wakes up cranky.

"This toddler just appeared before me. He looked me in the eyes and said, 'Dad, it is time for me to come into the world!' He was as clear as the brightest day. He was this little, light-skinned toddler about 18 months old, and he spoke with the clearest voice, a voice that could not be ignored. This was no dream; it was as real as this discussion between you and me."

"So why are you telling me this?" mom asked.

"I am just so struck by his appearance. It was my first time seeing him, but I see that I already know him. He exists, but is not on earth."

"So why are you telling me when you know we have already agreed that we would have no kids? Why would you stir these emotions in me?"

"You're right," dad agreed as he turned his back to her and closed his eyes.

Mom, however, was wide awake. She was silent and let the darkness embrace her emotions.

Two and a half months later, Valentine's Day occurred for lovers. So, as the first anniversary of their marriage approached, dad decided he would take mom to Washington, DC, to enjoy the museums. It was my time to make another appearance. As they slept at the Washington Hilton, there I was in dad's arms in another vision as he entered an elevator at his office. It was really cool because dad was carrying me as his son, as if I had already entered his world.

"Dad, I can read all the words in this elevator!" I exclaimed, as all the other riders looked on in amazement at the 18-month-old toddler in dad's arms. "No smoking. Capacity 3,000 pounds. *New York Times. Wall Street Journal. Washington Post.*"

"Nydia! Nydia!! Wake up! Wake up! That same little toddler just came to me again. This time he was in my arms, and I was at the Center for Educational Leadership on Hudson Street in Manhattan. We were in the elevator, and he started to read all the words in sight as the other people on the elevator looked on in amazement."

"The same toddler?" mom asked.

"Yes, the same one! It is his time to come into the world! He did not have to tell me this time. I just know that it is inevitable!" dad said with an air of anticipation and awe.

"So, what are we going to do?" mom asked.

"You need to go and see Dr. Edersheim and do all your checkups to make sure when you get pregnant there are no complications."

"Okay, I will see her as soon as we get back to New York," mom joyously responded while hugging dad intensely.

Two weeks later Dr. Edersheim examined mom. She said that mom was in good health, not pregnant, but that she should have no problem conceiving.

So they, and I, turned to preparing for my entry.

Chapter 5

The Name Game

Nine months is long period of time to wait for something you desperately desire. You know that when you wait in great anticipation for something to happen, at times minutes could seem like hours, days like months, and months like decades.

It's Friday, April 10, 1992.

"Askia, I have great news," mom said, as she closed the door leading to the parlor floor of my family's brownstone. Earlier she had visited Dr. Edersheim's office for a checkup. She entered the bedroom where dad sat next to the bed watching an NBA game. The walls of the bedroom were painted antique white and the furniture included antique mahogany dressers and bed frames. With the exception of the television, ceiling fan, and modern lights, the scene in the bedroom could have been mistaken for a scene from the 1800s. The brownstone was built in 1884 and became a landmark in 2009.

As mom took off her coat, dad rose from the antique chair, embraced her and said: "I know. We are having a son." They stood in that embrace for nearly a minute, not whispering another word. Their exhilaration smothered the words that were coming from the NBA announcer. Dad would later tell me that at that time it was if they existed as one being. There was no Nydia and no Askia. There was NydiaAskia united, one spirit recognized as one being. There were no longer two histories or two futures; there was just one.

"Well, although you have not had a sonogram, we know that it is a boy, the toddler who came to me in the two visions," dad continued. "Obviously, if this baby could come in a vision before he is even conceived, God has called him for a special purpose. I have his name. It's Askia Akhenaton Suleiman Ali Davis."

"Wow, Askia Akhenaton Suleiman Ali Davis? That is a mouthful! Don't you think we should keep two of those names for the next child?" mom asked while trying to maintain a respectful tone. "Will there be enough space on a birth certificate for all those names?"

"Askia, the mighty warrior king of the Songhai Empire," dad whispered.

"Akhenaton, the wisdom Pharaoh of Egypt, the husband of Nefertiti, and the first man in recorded history to say that there is only one God.

"Suleiman, Arabic for Solomon. I wanted to use the Hebrew name, but Stewart Lyons, a Jewish friend, said that Solomon is Shlomo in Hebrew, and I think Shlomo sounds too much like Slow Moe. And who would name a kid Slow Moe? Even Moe in the *Three Stooges* was fast.

"Ali, for Muhammad Ali." Dad breathed deeply and paused to let his words express their power.

"Wow, isn't that a lot to have a kid live up to?" mom asked.

"He does not have to be any one of those men," dad whispered. "His purpose, his calling, is beyond what we can determine. The names are there to remind him that he stands on a rich tradition, a rich legacy, and the shoulders of powerful ancestors, named and unnamed, known and unknown."

For little me, waiting inside mom's womb, there would be no names like Lil Wayne, no T.I., no Jay-Z, no B.o.B, no Fifty Cents, no Drake, no J. Cole, no Waka Flocka Flame, no Kanye, no Trey Songz, no Gucci Mane, no Ne-Yo, no Mario, no Omarion, no Juelz Santana, no Usher, no Andre 3000, no Lupe Fiasco, no Maxwell, no will.i.am, no Chris Brown, and no other European names. Dad wanted names with "power, spirit, and ancestral meaning." He gave me four: Askia Akhenaton Suleiman Ali. They are a mouthful and, at 18 years old, I think they fit (and they are all on my birth certificate).

So, dad had my names selected, but I was still almost 8 months from arrival.

It has been said that the history of the parents becomes the history of the child. It is that history that we struggle to break free of in our teens as we seek to define life and ourselves through our own eyes. Dad once told me that even Yeshua (Jesus) had to break free of the definition of the world Mary and Joseph had prepared for Him. He told me the story of how Mary chastised 12-year-old Yeshua for separating from the family to remain in the synagogue during a trip to Jerusalem. Yeshua, as a pre-teen, had to remind Mary that he must be about his Heavenly Father's business and not the business or world that Mary and Joseph wanted to place before Him.

Nevertheless, as Luke reported, at 12 years old Yeshua returned home and remained subject to his parents until the ripening of time. I am still waiting for my ripening of time.

Dad read that Biblical story to me but yet, in 2010, he continued planning to shape my view of the world from conception through old age. You see, dad is a master planner. He takes great pride in coming up with solutions to problems in an instant that, for long periods of time, would vex other professionals. Maybe he's a master planner because of his intellect and also his experience responding to difficult challenges in his childhood and teens like those in the story that follows.

On July 9, 2007, I was almost 15 years old. Dad and I sat to watch "The Bronx Is Burning" on ESPN. "The Bronx Is Burning" is a television drama that focuses on the Yankees playing and winning the World Series in 1977 while fires set by arsonists burned out of control in the neighborhoods surrounding Yankee stadium. Dad used that occasion to tell me another story of the challenges he had faced and overcome.

At the age of 16 in 1967, my father was living on his own in the Bronx near the Bronx Zoo when apartment buildings were constantly being torched by arsonists. The word on the street was that arsonists were often acting on behalf of white landlords who preferred to collect insurance rather than continuing to rent to Puerto Ricans and African Americans who were entering the Bronx in large numbers in the late 1960s and 1970s.

The Bronx was shifting from being mostly white as white renters and home owners fled to the suburbs and Co-op City. Due to the presence of African Americans and Puerto Ricans, the banks redlined the neighborhoods and made it impossible for the white landlords to get loans or sell their buildings. Many landlords often allegedly had their properties torched at night while the residents were asleep inside. So many buildings were torched, that the Bronx started to be compared to Berlin and other cities in Europe that had been destroyed in World War II during bombings. Some residents lost their lives, while many lost their possessions.

In 1967, my father was living at 2082 Bryant Avenue in the fourth floor apartment he had shared with Uncle Willie, dad's oldest brother. Uncle Willie had been drafted into the USA Army to support the war in Vietnam the previous year in 1966. Although my father had only been in New York less than two years, he was determined not to return to Georgia and the life his beloved mother had prepared for him. So when Uncle Willie threatened to put him on the Greyhound Bus back to Georgia, my father asked him: "You and what army?" Willie had been concerned about leaving his little brother alone to face the dangers of the big city. However, Willie didn't have an army ready to send my father back south.

My father remained in that building through several bouts of arson. He put himself through high school and the first year of college during that time. By then, most of the surrounding buildings had been completely destroyed and the tenants displaced. In dad's building by the end of 1969, more than a quarter of the 150 apartments had been closed due to almost weekly incidents of arson. The smell of burned furniture and other items filled the air constantly. Yet, dad walked up four flights of stairs each night and slept in his bed as though he were fireproof. He kept the key to the security gates on his windows handy just in case he had to make a quick exit down the fire escape to the yard 60 feet below.

In the fall of 1969 during his second year of college, the city paid him $3,000 to move so that the city could demolish his and all of the neighboring buildings. The city had plans to build the housing projects that are now on Bryant Avenue, a few blocks from the Bronx Zoo. Dad found out and quickly learned how to maneuver inside the bureaucracy of city government to obtain the right to the $3,000 for an agreement to move. Dad explained $3,000 was a lot of money in those days and, with good planning, almost enough to live on for an entire year. But he continued to keep his grind at Rapid Messengers delivering packages to corporations and wealthy individuals.

So, at 17, he lived in a really dangerous area before it was called the "Boogie Down Bronx." When I was 17 years old, I lived in a condo in Brooklyn and in a single dorm room in James Hall at Hampton University. Knowing that, you might think that I would never have any reason to complain about anything. But you are dead wrong. At that age, I didn't really care to think too deeply about his experiences and what they could teach me. I did not think his experiences could be as difficult as mine. Certainly life is much more complex today than it was in the late 1960s. Certainly I have more challenges.

Yes, I still think I have the worst of it. You see, he has lived through his challenges and fought the fight to shape his own life. I am still living through mine!

Chapter 6

Talk To Me, Baby!

It's Saturday, April 18, 1992.

"What do you think about what Reverend Jeffries had to say in today's sermon?" dad asked as he took off his jacket upon entering the living room that Saturday afternoon. Reverend Jeffries was the enlightened pastor of Philadelphia Church of Universal Brotherhood on Eastern Parkway and Nostrand Avenue in Brooklyn. He was known as a teaching preacher, the kind who wanted members to use their intellect and heart to get to know God and His Word.

"About what?" mom responded because Reverend Jeffries had spoken on a number of topics and mom was wondering where the conversation with dad would begin.

"About Napoleon Bonaparte's mother, Letizia Ramolino. You know how he said she spoke to Napoleon daily while he was in her womb. Dr. Jeffries said that she would tell Napoleon that he was destined for greatness, that he was destined to be a liberator of his people."

"Yeah, that was pretty interesting," mom replied casually.

"You know there are researchers who have determined that babies do respond to their mothers' voices while they are in the womb," dad declared in the confident tone of someone who had just gained some awesome knowledge.

"And there are those researchers who suggest that it is a good thing to play classical music while a baby is in the womb and in the months immediately after birth. They suggest playing classical music has a beneficial effect on brain development. They call it the 'Mozart effect.' If classical music has such an effect, jazz must be even more beneficial," he whispered as he placed "In a Sentimental Mood" on the turntable.

With the saxophone of John Coltrane and the piano of Duke Ellington embracing them, they danced slowly in front of the fireplace in the living room. He slowly began to rub mom's stomach with his right hand then knelt to place his ear.

"I think that we should take a few minutes each morning, afternoon, and evening to speak to Akhenaton," dad whispered as he looked up and she looked down.

"Okay," mom said as she moved to the sofa and began speaking to me as dad held her hand. With their hands on her stomach she whispered, "Akhenaton, you are destined for greatness. Greatness is living so that others will prosper."

Duke Ellington and Coltrane continued melodiously in the background while dad responded: "Akhenaton, greatness is living so that others will prosper."

For the next eight months the words became a mantra: "Akhenaton, greatness is living so that others will prosper." Mom would recite the mantra. Dad would recite the mantra. Coltrane was the music of choice most often during the monologues. At other times there were Miles, Keith Jarrett, Yusef Lateef, Ron Carter, Japanese Masters of the Shakuhachi Flute, Mozart, Bach, Beethoven, and Stravinsky, among others.

By 2010 in pre-college at Hampton University, I had experienced 18-plus years of listening to the jazz of John Coltrane. Though I was a big fan of hip hop, with Jay-Z, Drake, and Lupe being my favorites, I listened to Coltrane on my iPod while I studied. There is something about Coltrane's music that focuses me and reinforces my sense of purpose.

The mantras my parents whispered at times varied. "Akhenaton, you are coming into a world with a special place prepared for you," was one that surfaced frequently from their lips.

Even today when I mess up, dad always attempts to rise above the disappointments to remind me that despite the issues I "will rise to achieve the promise, the expression of my anointing."

It's ironic that mom started talking to me while I was in the womb with words that she assumed I could understand, yet today I often cannot understand the words that are coming out of her mouth. She's sounding more and more like dad. Maybe her words today are filled with too much of the wrong emotions.

TBBH/To be brutally honest, I don't hear "A Love Supreme" when she is talking to me about the clothes piled on the floor in my room. I don't hear Duke Ellington's piano when she is reminding me to wash my basket of dirty laundry before I depart to meet my basketball team for a scheduled game. I can't hear Miles' trumpet when she is asking me to bag and take out the recyclables.

I try to block her out with J. Cole on my iPod when she is asking when I am going to begin studying. "Hey mom, I am studying. I am studying J. Cole's 'Work Out.' I am preparing to go to my lady Niyya singing: 'Straight up, now tell me do you really wanna love me forever, oh, oh, oh, or is it just a hit and run?'" (BTW, J. Cole filmed the video on the Dean Street Playground's basketball courts across from my condo, which you can see in the video. I had my first dunk there at age 13.)

Thank God for J. Cole, iPods, and Dr. Dre's Beats!

Chapter 7

Baby Shower and My Peeps' Fashion

It's Sunday, August 23, 1992.

By the time of mom's baby shower, I was stretching out big time in mom's womb. Mom said I was a big kicker. She thought I was gearing up for a life of the professional soccer star, a little "Puerto Rican Pele."

Recently, I've had an opportunity to review the videotape and photographs of the baby shower. I saw a lot of faces that remain active in my life today. The year 1992 must not have been recognized as a year of high fashion, judging from the outfits that my peeps wore.

There was mom, big stomach and all. "What is that she is wearing?" I asked myself. In the video, mom is wearing a dark purple, loose-fitting blouse and black slacks. The blouse has stitching that falls at the bottom of mom's belly that accentuates the roundness that announces my presence.

I hoped she had retired that outfit, because she is famous for holding on to what she considers symbolic treasures. For example, she still has my christening outfit that I wore at two months old. I would not be surprised to go in the closet tomorrow and find the first cloth diaper she placed on her shoulder to burp me and the first cloth diaper I wore on my little hiney.

Standing next to mom is my first cousin Melissa who is mugging for the camera. Melissa is 5 at the time and appears to be the most fashionable person there. She just has on a plain white sweater, blue jeans, and sneakers. If she is the most fashionable, you could only imagine how the rest of my peeps looked. Today Melissa lives in Fort Lauderdale and dad teases her about dressing in the "Florida casual style" when she visits us in sophisticated New York. He says "Florida casual" outfits always look as if they were three steps below Sears. He says even when they are new, their "colors don't pop," and they make a pretty young woman like Melissa look middle-aged.

My first cousin Akil, who is 6 at the time, has on a blue sweater with some awkward designs. I believe the designer ran out of ideas and allowed his preschooler to select the designs. Akil's parents should have been arrested for putting that sweater on him. I am confident he was happy when he became old enough to insist to his parents, Aunt Irma and my godfather, Uncle Rufus, that he would choose his own clothes. By the way, Akil's sister Nyisha is my godmother so I'll be nice and skip my comments on her outfit. (I am fortunate to have two sets of godparents. My Uncle Robert and first cousin Sonia are also my godparents.)

Dad has on jeans and a black sweatshirt with a replica of a painting from Paul Gauguin, the 19th century French artist. The painting is titled, "The Siesta." It depicts a scene from the lives of four women in Tahiti. Dad had bought the sweatshirt in Paris at the Louvre during his and mom's honeymoon the previous year. On his head he wore a multicolored Kufi that he had picked up in Kano, Nigeria, from a merchant in the open-air market during the pilgrimage-to-Africa part of the honeymoon a few months after Paris. His jeans are form-fitting and boring.

As I continued to review the video and pictures, I remembered how happy I was when I was old enough to say, "No, dad, don't buy that 'cause I am not going to wear that." I said that often when he attempted to purchase jeans, slacks, and shirts for me at age 11 until he got the message.

By age 13, I had a different problem. At 6 feet, I was then as tall as dad, and he would keep and wear the shirts, jeans, and sneakers that I no longer wanted to wear.

No, he wasn't cheap. Instead, he thought it a sin to discard clothes that were in good shape when he would eventually have to buy similar items for himself. So he would pick a few of the items whose styles he liked, and donate the rest to the Salvation Army. Usually, those items were in good shape because, as an American teen, you know your mind could change from one minute to the next regarding what is fashionable, so you just stop wearing items your parents think are perfectly okay and "practically new."

So, can you imagine how I felt the first time dad showed up at my middle school wearing a shirt and a pair of jeans that I had worn just a few weeks earlier? "Embarrassed" was not the word to describe my emotions. Unlike most of my friends who were passing clothes down to younger siblings, I was passing clothes up to dad and he was crazy enough to wear them to my school.

Thus, I had to get him to agree to never embarrass me like that again. We quickly reached an understanding that he could wear my "old" Sean Jean, Rocawear, and Akademiks clothing as long as he did not wear them in my presence and in the presence of any of my friends.

By early age 14 in high school, I was thankful that he could no longer wear my sneakers because I was size 13 1/2, and his shoe size was a mere 12. I was also 6 feet 2 inches and growing. Thus, he could no longer wear my jeans. My arms were at least three inches longer than his and my chest much more mad brolic, so he could no longer wear my Rocawear, AE, and other shirts. Then I would often tease him about being a "midget" because I just couldn't resist popping that ego. He would give me that look that would let me know he did not appreciate being called a "midget," but other than that what could he do?

As a result of my growth, in my freshman year of high school I was happy when I became free from the possible horror of dad arriving for a ball game dressed in my clothes. Can you imagine how I would have felt had dad shown up at my high school, Benjamin Banneker Academy, wearing my clothes? I would have had to transfer. Thankfully, size does matter.

Beyond the clothing worn at the shower, the gathering was very much like other showers and parties that I would later attend with mom, dad, and other family members. There was plenty of food and there was plenty of eating. The decorations were those that my *Titi* Violeta is famous for handcrafting. Quite a few kids were present. They played together while the adults moved from conversation to conversation.

Mi abuela was there with her Rosary beads and the big crucifix she wore at all times around her neck. Dad told me, "Her cross was bigger than the ones carried aloft by the Spanish *Conquistadores* when they attempted to enslave the Native Americans, the Aztecs, the Mayans, and the Incas and impose Christianity on people they wrongly considered savages."

My crazy Uncle Nick was going around with his usual gadgets tricking people and stunning them with mild electrical currents. Uncle Nick is real cool and buys me a lot of cool and expensive things. He always dresses as a clown when my little cousins have their birthdays. He's good, and there is no need to go hire Bozo.

One thing that was missing was the music. That was unfortunate because I would have loved to have seen if they danced as badly then as they do today.

My *Titi* Miriam was the one taking the video. As she moved around the room, she recorded on camera comments from the participants. Most of the comments were aimed toward mom and dad, wishing them *bendiciones*/blessings. When she arrived next to mom, she asked her about me.

"Nydia, how is the baby taking in all this excitement?" *Titi* Miriam began.

"Oh, he is kicking up a storm. His little foot is right there," mom answered, pointing to a spot about three inches and 180 degrees to the right of her navel.

"Wow, kicking up a storm, huh? Now, we have all heard that you have all these names for the baby that none of us can pronounce," *Titi* Miriam continued in her Bronx/Puerto Rican accent.

"Tell us those names again," she said. BTW, *Titi* Miriam at times spoke very fast English, and I must admit that I could imagine some English-speaking folks asking for an interpreter.

"Askia Akhenaton Suleiman Ali Davis. I had to practice pronouncing Akhenaton and Suleiman myself. Ah-ke-na-ton. Soo-lee-man." Mom paused and let out a big smile.

"I told Askia that we should save two of the names for the next baby," she continued as *Titi* Miriam and others laughed in response.

As I prepared to turn off the video of the baby shower, I joined the chorus of laughter. Then I reflected on my names and the importance dad places upon the names. Before and since my birth, my family has referred to me by my second name, Akhenaton. That was dad's idea. He said that Askia should be treated like the family name for the boys, with each boy having it as a first name but being called by their second name. According to dad, each of my sons should have Askia as their first of several names, and so would each of their sons, and so forth.

Thus, for example, my first son might be named Askia Sundiata Yossef Malik Davis. He would then be referred to as Sundiata (Sun-dee-a-ta) within the family. Sundiata was the founder of the great Mali Empire.

My second son might be named Askia Taharka Musa Menes Davis. He would be referred to as Taharka (Ta-har-ka), the Nubian Pharaoh of Egypt and the Kingdom of Kush.

My third son might be named Askia Kwame Madiba Ali. He would be referred to as Kwame Madiba, representing Kwame Nkrumah, the first President of the Republic of Ghana and Nelson Mandela, the first true President of the Republic of South Africa. (Madiba is the Xhosa name South Africans use for the beloved Nelson Mandela.)

This pattern would continue even if I have 10 sons and would follow as they have sons, grandsons, great grandsons, and so forth. (It seems better than all of George Foreman's six sons being named and called "George," an English name with no meaning. How did Foreman get away with that? I guess their mother had no say in the matter.)

So that's dad, the master planner, having generations of Davis males already named from here to eternity. You go, dad!

However, maybe I will name my first son Jose Luis, and the second, Eduardo Ramon!

Naw, just kidding, dad.

Chapter 8

My Baby and His Foreskin

On Thursday, November 12, 1992, mom and dad visited Dr. Edersheim's office near New York Hospital. Dr. Edersheim had recently run some tests on mom, and she wanted to share the results with both mom and dad. Up until that point, there had not been any apparent reason or cause for concern. Thus, they arrived at the doctor's office in a rather calm state of mind.

Dr. Edersheim walked into the waiting room with papers in her hands and warmly greeted them. She explained she had analyzed the tests and the tests suggested there were decisions that have to be made rather quickly. She expressed concern that mom's platelet count at 160,000 was very low and has been steadily dropping for a period of months. She said she was concerned that if they were to drop any further, mom's blood would not sufficiently clot during delivery and that could lead to serious consequences for her health and well-being.

In addition, she explained I was draining mom of larger amounts of calcium than would normally be expected. She then proceeded to present two options and the potential consequences of each: natural child birth and a Cesarean or C-section.

Years later, in the winter of 2010 when my *madrina*/godmother Sonia was preparing to have a C-section, she asked mom about her experience. Mom wrote the following in an email to my *madrina* explaining the choices Dr. Edersheim had given her in 1992:

"I was all set to have natural childbirth and had gone to Lamaze class and everything, but my platelet count starting dropping dramatically in my eighth month. My doctor was concerned that I wouldn't be able to clot (this happens when platelets are low), so I had to see a hematologist. They did the 'cut' test, and it was fine. (In the cut test, they cut you on purpose to see how long it takes for your blood to clot and my clot time was normal.) They were totally confused as to why my platelets kept dropping. (I went weekly to get them checked). They didn't know if Akhenaton's platelets were low as well, so they gave me two options:

(1) Natural birth and wait until Akhenaton's head crowned (top of head appeared), take blood from his scalp and, if his platelets were low, put him back in and do a C-section; or

(2) Check my platelet count when I got to the hospital on the day of the scheduled C-section and, if it is above 100,000 (it should be between 160,000 and 450,000), then numb me from my waist down so I can stay awake and Askia can stay in the operating room while they performed the C-section.

No way was I going to have my baby pricked, blood drawn, and then pushed back in (he would have all of this pain and trauma inflicted upon him before he even entered the world) just to test his blood. So I chose the second option, the C-section, which was scheduled for the Monday after Thanksgiving. However, when I got to the hospital on Monday, my platelet count was 66,000 (dangerously low, so they tell me). They immediately put me under and had to rush me to the operating room. Askia couldn't stay, so the last thing I remember telling Askia was, 'Make sure they give me the right baby.' Then I was out."

So, on November 12, 1992, mom chose a C-section, which was scheduled for the morning of November 30, two weeks before her due date.

Mom and dad walked from the doctor's office, confident in their faith that all would be okay. They talked and laughed about the Lamaze classes that they had attended for months that taught breathing and pain control for natural vaginal childbirth. Dad said he had been looking forward to being in the delivery room, counting the seconds between contractions, and guiding mom through her deep breathing exercise. He said he wanted to be there to see the stressful grimaces of her facial muscles as she pushed my head through the small opening.

As they continued on the drive back to Brooklyn, dad told mom the story about the birth of my oldest sister Ife in 1972. Dad explained he had been in the delivery room and was hopeful for a son. A sonogram had not been taken since sonograms were not common in 1972.

When Ife emerged, the midwife looked and declared, "You have a boy!" Dad jumped with joy only to be pulled back to earth within seconds when the midwife corrected herself and said, "It's a girl. I made a mistake looking at the umbilical cord. Do you still want her or shall I put her back?" "No, no! Give her to me!" dad exclaimed. "Give her to me!"

Later, when dad told me the story, he said having a daughter first made him a better man, a better father, and forced him to mature quicker at the age of 22. It made him step outside of his male ego and his male plans to see the world differently.

Twenty years later, dad and mom are on their way back to Brooklyn from the doctor's office in Manhattan. They had a precise date and an approximate time for my birth. I would need to wait an additional two weeks. It was two more weeks filled with mom and dad speaking to me in the womb and me listening to Coltrane, Miles, Mozart, and the other musicians whose music was selected to enhance the growth and functioning of my brain.

On the morning of Monday, November 30, 1992, mom and dad arose at 5:00 a.m. to prepare to arrive at the hospital by 6:30 a.m. As they drove up the FDR Drive, there were many moments of silence. The day had arrived for them to be overjoyed, and mere words could not express the anticipation.

By 7:00 a.m., mom was settled at New York Hospital in the room she would be sharing with Ms. Oshima, a Japanese American woman who was there also for a Caesarian. Dad, mom, and Mr. and Mrs. Oshima struck up a friendly conversation while waiting for their doctors to arrive to have them wheeled to separate operating rooms.

Just before the arrival of Dr. Edersheim, mom turned to dad and suggested he should watch carefully to make sure she gets the "right baby." Mom was concerned that several babies would be born that morning, and she wanted to make sure none of the horror stories of mothers leaving with the wrong babies would happen in my case. She knew she might be knocked out under anesthesia and would not see me for several hours.

As soon as the doctor arrived, they rushed mom to the operating room. The original plans called for dad to be in the operating room. However, because of mom's worsening platelet condition, he was told he could not enter. Dad assured mom he would be outside of the operating room and would be the first to see me, other than the doctors. He would make sure they put on the little bracelet that says "Davis" and would make sure she received the right baby.

At 10:28 a.m. I arrived. It was "my time to enter the world," as I had first told dad a year and two days earlier. I was home, in my new world. I breathed deeply and rhythmically as mom rested unconsciously and dad waited outside.

When the nurse, an African American woman in her forties, brought me to dad, he looked in my face for "the Davis look." Only after seeing "the Davis look," did he look for the hospital bracelet with "Davis" inscribed. Dad wore the multicolored Kufi from Nigeria as headdress to honor my arrival. He would wear the Kufi in the house, at church, and when he took me to work and family visits during the next seven months.

Dad watched me as I rested in the basinet breathing rhythmically. My head was perfectly formed and smooth, not like the squashed heads that some babies get through vaginal births. I was 9 pounds 1 ounce and nearly 25 inches long.

Dad thought I looked like the picture of health and power with a warrior's physique to match. He took me in his arms and gave thanks to the Lord for His blessing. My eyes moved from being fully open to shut to fully open again. I took in the new world with my eyes.

At about noon, dad went to join mom in her hospital room. Mrs. Oshima and her husband were there as well. Soon after dad's arrival, the Oshima baby and I were brought in to our mothers.

Mom took me in her arms and lightly smiled while looking at the baby being passed to Mrs. Oshima. She lightly kissed my forehead. Dad eased as close as possible to us without sitting on the bed. He smiled that robust smile of happiness. With dad so close by, he soon sensed that mom was anxious and puzzled about something. His intuition was confirmed when mom began whispering, asking him to come closer. With dad as close as he could be without sitting on top of us, mom dropped the question.

"Askia, are you sure this is my baby?" she whispered. "Are you sure this is our baby?" she asked with extended eyes and a wrinkled forehead betraying deep concern.

"What do you mean?" dad responded, with puzzled wrinkles on his forehead.

"Are you sure this is our baby? This baby looks more Asian than Mrs. Oshima's baby! Are you sure they didn't switch our babies?"

Dad took a moment and looked into mom's eyes to determine if the medication was affecting her thinking. She appeared normal, but her questioning seemed illogical. He decided that he would hold her hand and speak in the most reassuring tone possible. With her looking at him and away from me, dad whispered, "No, Nydia, I was there. He looks like all the Davis babies at birth: slanted eyes and yellow skin."

"I just need to know that you are sure. Are you absolutely sure he is our baby?"

"Yeah, I'm sure. His features will change as he gets older and the melanin kicks in. You see, if you look at the edges of his ears you will see the skin is darker than the rest of his body. Eventually, when the melanin kicks in, he will be more like that brown color at the edges of his ears. But, until then, he has the look of the Davis babies at birth."

Mom took a moment to look at my left ear. She moved her right pinky along the edge of my left ear. Then she gently moved so that she was in position to look at my right ear. She ran her pinky along the edge of my right ear. Then, reassured, mom smiled more broadly. She was no longer prepared to reach out for Ms. Oshima's baby. Dad relaxed and smiled along with her. Then, reassured, she was prepared to breastfeed me. I was hungry and finally nourished.

Mom would stay in the hospital for five days, and she would never again mention to dad concerns about not having the right baby, not even when dad would later refer to me as "little Buddha." He made that reference when she took the picture of me at 5 months old in dad's arms in the Brooklyn Botanical Gardens.

Well, there I was: African American-Puerto Rican, and a mixture of Yoruba, Native American, Spanish, Taino, and Irish, and, as dad would say, all Davis in appearance, looking like "little Buddha," no disrespect intended.

I had to be circumcised before we left the hospital. Mom was not a big fan of circumcision. She thought it a bit barbaric to cut at the penis of a baby. Dad wanted circumcision although, as a Christian, he knew the Apostle Paul taught circumcision was not required to be in the family of God. Dad believed Paul's teachings, but chose circumcision in part because of early research that indicated it has beneficial results in preventing the spread of HIV and other venereal disease, and it helps to protect against cervical cancer in women. Dad says later research has confirmed those findings.

It's funny that 5 years later at age 5 I became a regular participant with mom and dad in the nightly rituals of watching *Seinfeld* on television. I know that I have since seen every episode. Now, there is one particular episode where Jerry Seinfeld's friends are going to have their son circumcised. They hire this very nervous and very funny mohel to perform the ritual. In the process, the mohel accidentally slices Jerry's finger as Jerry holds the baby. Jerry ends up complaining, more than the baby, to the mohel. That episode is hilarious.

When dad, mom, and I saw a rerun of that episode last year, mom told the story of my circumcision. Mom said residents, or doctors-in-training, would come by every day looking for male babies to circumcise. She made sure she was awake when they made their rounds so that she could explain that one of the experienced male doctors from Dr. Edersheim's practice would perform the circumcision. She doesn't know if he was funny and nervous. She doesn't know if he was a Jewish mohel on the side. All she knows is that he sliced a bit of me.

I was taken next door for the circumcision, and mom turned up the television volume as high as she could so that she would not hear me when I screamed and cried. She explained that she soon discovered that I had a microphone for a voice when she heard my screams of agony from the room nearby above the volume of the television as the doctor cut me. She felt a surge of guilt and wanted to get out of her bed and force the doctor to stop.

She said she was horrified when she first looked inside my diaper after the circumcision. "Your little wee wee looked like raw meat. I was so glad when it started to heal and look normal after several days," she told me.

I have since heard that some parents keep the skin. Now that's gross! Maybe I should go now and search in the closet of keepsakes for that, too, knowing that mom keeps anything with sentimental value if given the opportunity.

"Mom, do you have my foreskin?"

I can only hope the doctors did not give it to her. It would only show up at the worst of times, like as a gift to my bride on our wedding day. *Eww!*

Chapter 9

Brooklyn in da House

On Saturday, December 5, 1992, at 11:00 a.m. mom and dad gathered me into one of the beautifully hand-knitted blankets given as a gift at the baby shower. The blankets remain in the keepsakes closet until today. Dad drove us back home to Prospect Heights in our made-in-America 1992 Camry while mom sat in the rear holding me.

At home, my crib was prepared and waiting. It was placed a few feet from mom's and dad's bed in their bedroom on the parlor floor of the brownstone. It is where I would spend the next 18 months of my life.

In the days immediately following our return home from the hospital, family and friends began to arrive to see dad's magical child.

Mi abuela arrived. Within three months she would become my regular babysitter, living three days a week with us in Brooklyn to care for me. Mom said she felt blessed that she was able to return to work part time instead of full time due to a change in her job. She added that she felt doubly blessed that *abuela* would be caring for me. It is from *abuela* that I picked up the accent that you could hear when I speak Spanish, which is not that often. Mom says I can sound like a native speaker. Although dad knows more Spanish than I do, mom says he sounds like he is speaking Spanish with a Southern accent. For instance, he says the word *manzana*/apple like *man-zana* with the emphasis incorrectly placed on the first syllable and *ana* sounding like ann-na with a Southern twang.

Arthur Barnes, dad's mentor, arrived with his wife Sandra Feldman, who dad called the most dynamic and caring union leader in the USA. When

I grew older, dad showed me the picture of Arthur and Sandi holding me during their visit. Dad explained that Sandi pushed her teachers' union leaders to work with Chancellor Crew to reform failing schools to improve the education of kids. He suggested she had to fight many of her own leaders who seemed more concerned with protecting the privileges of teachers, including bad teachers. He further explained the innovative work he led with Dr. Crew, with Sandi's support, was the first of its kind in big cities that were trying to address failing schools.

My oldest sister Ife arrived. Ife means love in the Yoruba language of Nigeria. Her middle name is Monifa, which means blessed in Yoruba.

My youngest sister Kakuna arrived. Kakuna means love in the Herero language of Namibia. Pokémon picked up that name. Her middle name is Aziza, meaning precious in Kiswahili and Arabic. She was a freshman living on campus at Rutgers University in New Brunswick, New Jersey. Dad says she is better educated than he is. Within three months she would begin coming to Brooklyn from Rutgers to babysit me every Friday to relieve *abuela* while mom worked. She became like my second mom.

Though Kakuna and Ife have a different mom from mine, dad would often tease mom by saying I looked more like Kakuna and Ife than I looked like mom. And it was the brutally honest truth, although now there are people who say lately they can see a bit of mom in my face since my features have changed. Dad's response is always, "Naw, I don't see it." He says it is just mom's family members, her friends, and her co-workers projecting what they cannot possibly see to make her feel good.

When I was about 12, mom told me the story of a time we were leaving the playground in Prospect Park, long before my features changed. Mom said I was not quite 18 months old and was cranky because I was sleepy. As I complained, this woman walked over and asked mom if we were lost and if she was babysitting. Mom stepped out of character and remarked with annoyance, "Yes, I am babysitting, and I guess I'll be babysitting all my life. I'm his mother!"

The woman thought she was being helpful, but mom was in no mood for being questioned about our relationship. In a multicultural and multiethnic city like New York, she was tired of the unnecessary stares and the questions. I was her baby, and that was that!

From day one, at home and about, mom began chronicling my life in pictures, videos, in notes, and in written documents. There is an incredible picture of me taken on December 11, 1992, lying asleep on dad's chest as he sleeps in the bed. That's mom's favorite picture. We appeared as if we did not have a care in the world. We appeared as if we were on the same page in perfect harmony, one mind and one purpose. I can truly say time seems to have changed that, although he says the ripening of time will prove we are still united in spirit and purpose.

A few days after December 11, 1992, mom took a picture of me asleep in the living room with my little white skullcap on and my right arm and hand up in the air as if I am giving praise the way I would later do at Philadelphia Church of Universal Brotherhood, Bethany Baptist Church, Emmanuel Baptist Church, and at the church on the campus of Hampton University. Dad says they couldn't figure out how I managed to keep my hand raised on various occasions while asleep, unsupported by anything. So mom took the picture to document the improbable, if not the impossible.

From around the same time, there is a picture of dad measuring his forefinger against my feet to illustrate how long my feet were near birth. My right foot is stretched from the top of his right forefinger to no more than two inches from the beginning of his wrist. I had big feet then, and I have big feet now (size 14), but nothing like the size 23 on Shaq.

Starting when I was 4 months old, dad and mom would often take me to the Brooklyn Botanical Gardens. Our favorite spots were the field of cherry blossom trees, the Japanese Garden, the Rose Garden, and the little pond where the geese swam. One of dad's favorite pictures is the one of me at 5 months old in his arms. He is sitting next to the pond in the Gardens. He is wearing the multicolored Kufi. My skin is a pale yellow and my big round head is bald. I had been born with a head full of hair but it was gone by the age of 5 months. My eyes have a commanding look of awareness. It is this picture that dad labeled: "Dad with Little Buddha."

Then there is the picture of me being held by *abuela* at 5 months. She is standing and holding me in such a way that my body length is totally vertical. I look like I am more than half her height and I am a mere baby, not even a toddler. *Mi abuela* is vertically challenged. Thankfully, I got my height and my hops from dad's side of the family.

By the time I was 7 months old, dad had purchased a walker with wheels for me. By the time I was 8 months old, dad said that I was ready for the Daytona Speedway. After work he would come to the ground floor window of our living room and call out "Akhenaton, Warrior of the Void." I would hear his voice and race with my walker across the room to see his face. Upon seeing his face, I would turn the walker into a merry-go-round, spinning and shrieking with joy. He looked forward to seeing me racing and spinning while coming down from the work pressures of being the Senior Assistant to New York City Chancellor Joseph Fernandez and responsible for the Chancellor's primary education initiatives, School-Based Management and School-Wide Programs in 300 schools.

Within minutes of his arrival, I was usually strapped to his chest or back and on the way out for our daily stroll through Prospect Heights, Park Slope, and, at times, Prospect Park. I was always positioned so that I could see my surroundings as he talked and pointed things out to me. Those walks actually began before I got the walker and continued for months thereafter.

There is this great picture of me at 10 months old being held in my father's arms while he goes through his Northern Shaolin and Qigong forms in Prospect Park. Dad is moving to Deniece Williams' "Black Butterfly" which is being played on the boom box. Mom says she should have had a video camera instead because she could have caught me mocking dad's breathing and aspects of his movement as he went through the forms.

My father would begin to diligently teach me those forms when I was the tender age of 6 years. By age 8, under the guidance of Soke Majid, my Scorpion Martial Arts sensei, I would begin winning first prize in combat and kata competitions at karate tournaments in New York. My side kick and my axe kick would become beasts that my competitors would not have much success avoiding. I was chopping them down like trees. With my big feet, I was kicking them from the centers of the rings and they would land outside the perimeters.

Now, as I look at those and other baby pictures, I see nothing but the picture of pure innocence. I see a loving and protective father and mother. I see peace and harmony. I see parents who wouldn't question anything that I would do. When I puked on dad's shoulder, he smiled. When I peed in mom's eyes as she leaned forward to change my diaper, she laughed as she moved unsuccessfully to avoid the geyser. I know my number two, or what dad calls "the big number," must have stunk, but there is never a hint of a complaint.

I see confidence, boldness, and joy in my eyes. I see my eyes searching for knowledge. I see no distractions. There must have been times when I was cranky, tired, and pissed off for not getting an immediate or desirable response. There is no hint of that in the pictures.

Well, as a teen, the pure innocence and pure harmony are often absent. That search for knowledge competes with my search for fun and entertainment, talking to my girl on my iPhone, the video games, Facebook, Twitter, and basketball. My father and mother are still loving and protective, sometimes maybe too much.

I no longer pee in mom's eyes, and she now complains of me missing the target and peeing drops on the toilet seat that I forget to lift in the late night in "her" bathroom. And, yeah, now they think my number two does stink. So, as parents who do not smoke, mom leaves a book of matches in the bathroom so that I could light one following a dump. Mom was told that the sulphur dioxide released from a lit match immediately kills the smell, just in case she has to go in immediately following me.

When company is expected, mom cleans "her" bathroom before they arrive and places an "off limits" sign for me on the door since this is the bathroom that they will use. So, if you visit, you will always find a beautifully clean bathroom with fresh Eucalyptus plants or a beautiful arrangement of dried flowers.

Life is such that we must battle our parents in order to fully mature. Life is such that we must also battle ourselves. I am doing both.

No more "itchy kitchy koo!"

Chapter 10

C is for Cookie and Super Soakers

Is there an 18-year-old American born and raised here who did not grow up watching *Sesame Street*? If so, I want to meet him or her. He or she would be a rarity.

By the age of 15 months to about 7 years old, *Sesame Street* was a part of my daily routine. I learned to count, say the Alphabet, and laugh at televised humor. Often, mom and dad would be right alongside watching and laughing with me. When *Sesame Street Live* toured, I was sitting in the Theatre at Madison Square Garden laughing right along with Elmo, Kermit, and my parents.

The first televised love affair that caught my attention was the one between Miss Piggy and Kermit. Miss Piggy had that way of saying "Kermie, Kermie." Miss Piggy was a warrior. She knew what she wanted and no one could get in her way.

In 1999, I went with dad and mom to the movies to see "Muppets from Space." In the film, Miss Piggy rolls up on these two spies who do not want her present as they steal secrets. When she asks what they are doing, one tough guy tells the other to let him handle her. However, Miss Piggy is not intimidated. Of course, she ultimately uses her karate to "FedEx" the tough guys straight to hell.

Cookie was my favorite Muppet because he was out of control. I loved when he would try to control himself and not snatch and gobble up the cookies.

There's the episode where Cookie is the character Alistair Cookie on *Monsterpiece Theatre*. The episode is entitled, "Conservations with My Father."

In the opening scene, you cannot see Cookie but you can hear him gobbling up cookies and burping in the background louder than the *Masterpiece Theatre* background music which is playing. As the camera stops on an open book, streams of crumbs rain down on the pages as Cookie moans "uhm, uhm, ahh and ahh."

Cookie introduces the episode announcing that it is dear to his heart. It stars Cookie and his dad, Pop Cookie. Soon the scene shifts to Pop Cookie in the kitchen. He looks almost exactly like Cookie except he wears the kind of glasses that makes him look older. He calls for Cookie to come in. Pop Cookie tells Cookie that he had called him in to teach him something important.

Pop asks Cookie to describe what he hears. Cookie does not know until Pops takes him to the sink to see the dripping water from the faucet. Cookie asks Pop to explain the big deal or need to show him a dripping faucet. Pop explains it is important to not waste water that is needed for drinking, cooking, and bathing. He tells Cookie if it were to continue to drip down the drain, soon there would be no more. Cookie gets the point and turns off the faucet.

With the lesson learned, Cookie is ready to run back outside to play, but Pop points to the television. A cartoon episode is visible. Pop asks Cookie to explain what he sees. Cookie tells Pop he sees the television. Pops asks Cookie to explain what is the television doing on when there is nobody watching.

Cookie looks and scratches his head to indicate he is searching for an answer. Within five seconds he has the right answer: "Me know it ain't wasting water!" Pop responds by teaching Cookie it is wasting energy, and energy is needed for the radio and lights.

As they turn away from the television, Pop starts to sniff the air. Excited, Pop asks Cookie what is the smell they are detecting. Cookie's eyes spin excitedly at the top of his head. Together they exclaim "Cookies!" And they eat all the cookies that Chef John had been waiting to serve to the other Muppets.

What's really cool is *Sesame Street* is still around and should be for a long time. There are snippets of episodes posted on YouTube, including the two I cite above, and many have gotten hundreds of thousands of hits by viewers. Viewing them has provided a great opportunity to reconnect with the earlier years and to keep learning and smiling even today.

During a recent viewing, I realized Super Grover must have been the first super hero introduced to me. Super Grover flew around the planet in search of answers to questions that puzzle little children. He generally flew to a location and fell uncontrollably from the sky sending out shrieks as he crashed down next to the little boys and girls he would seek to educate. He was wise, yet vulnerable.

In my teens my super heroes have been Spiderman, Batman, Iron Man, Neo, Morpheus, Wolverine, Jet Li, Hwoarang, Kobe, Dwight, D Rose, Adrian Peterson, and Blake.

Dad recently told me that by age 2, I had learned to recite the alphabet, to recognize large case letters from A to Z, and to count objects up to 10, all with the assistance of Elmo, Ernie, Big Bird, Cookie, and the Count.

Mom said at 18 months W was my favorite letter and 7 my favorite number. Mom reported I would often stand in my crib while one of the Muppets slowly recited the Alphabet with each letter appearing on the screen. So, as the A appeared, I would say "A." Then I would say "B." I would continue in this pattern until right before W came up. In preparation for W, my favorite letter, I would stand on my tippy toes, expand my chest, and draw in a big gush of oxygen. Then as W appeared, I would shout "W!!!!" while expelling all the oxygen I had drawn in, along with the carbon dioxide.

Mom said that during this period I would "discover" letters and point them out excitedly wherever we went. She told me that during a visit to *mi abuela's* apartment, I stopped at the entrance to *abuela's* bedroom, pointed, and shouted "t!" I entered her bedroom, walked around, and continued to point at other objects on *abuela's* walls and shouted "t!" Then I picked up books and pamphlets from *abuela's* dresser while continuing to point and shout "t!"

Mom told me that after I pointed and shouted "t" a fourth time, she realized I was pointing at the many crosses on the wall, on the pictures of Jesus and Mary, on the Icon of the Madonna and baby Jesus, and on the Holy Bibles, pamphlets, and several sets of rosary beads. My excitement prompted mom for the first time to count all the crosses in *abuela's* bedroom. She reported counting 91.

You see, like so many Latina *abuelas*, *mi abuela's* bedroom was decorated like a Catholic shrine. She prayed more there than in church, even though she attended church every day. Everywhere I looked, I saw a "t."

Mom also reported that around age 2, during a visit to *Titi* Maria's apartment, I picked up a toy gun belonging to my cousin, Pito. I looked at the strange object trying to determine what it was. I maneuvered it in my left hand so that the tip of the barrel rested pointing down into the top of my closed fist. With the play gun in that position, I turned to *Titi* Maria, pointed to the semi circular metal around the trigger, and shouted triumphantly, "P!"

Mom said, "*Titi* Maria laughed hysterically and suggested that I was depriving you of experiences that all little boys should have playing with toy guns."

However, I would not get a chance to play with guns until I was 5 when, in the summer of 1998, dad bought a set of Super Soakers which we used to drench each other in war games running up and down the block in front of the house.

The Super Soaker had been invented in 1989 by a young African American engineer, Lonnie Johnson. Johnson was a graduate of Tuskegee Institute. In 1991 and 1992, it was reported to be the No. 1 best-selling toy in America. The design of the Super Soaker allowed you to produce a steady and forceful stream of water. "Wetter is better" was the slogan used to promote Super Soakers.

There were Super Soakers which had a nozzle that allowed you to point the gun in one direction and shoot a stream of water in another direction. The idea was to shoot a stream of water at an enemy hiding around a corner, or to point at one enemy yet shoot another. I had that one, and I am saving it in the basement of our brownstone for my sons and daughters.

The water compartment of our Super Soakers held as much as a quart and the power allowed a stream of water to reach more than 10 feet. So I had to be constantly moving to avoid the range. Of course, trees were helpful, but even then it was impossible to stay behind a tree the entire battle. The joy was not in defense, but in taking the battle to my enemy. So I would leave the safety of the trees on Park Place and charge at dad. Sometimes he would run away if I got off a good burst of water. At other times he would fall to his knees, and I would let him have it until I hit empty. Then off I would run as he would charge with a full tank.

When I reminisce, I want to still feel the intense cold water hitting my cheeks and chest as dad holds the trigger to produce a steady stream after having strategically waited until my water tank was empty to catch me defenseless. Of course, there were times when I would outsmart him and catch him when he no longer had water. We would laugh as I drenched him while he tried to keep the water from going up his nose and into his eyes and mouth. He would sneeze and cough to hold back the full effect of the penetrating water.

Life is a story. History is a story. Life is history. Stories nourish the spirit. Dad says we wouldn't be fully human if there were no stories to move us. There are stories in Super Soakers. There are stories in books. There are stories on television, in the movies, in music, in video games, in conversations around the dinner table and on the couches in living rooms, in the private moments with your girl, in the playground hooping with your boyz, and in the study giving my friend Samori a beat down on PlayStation with Madden.

Dad suggests as humans we have the capacity to return to a story we saw or heard ages ago and have it move us in the way it moved us then; or, we can have it move us even more powerfully now than it had moved us then.

Dad would say, "The ripening of time has added new insight and deeper meaning to the story."

As we reviewed the *Sesame Street* episodes, dad said his thoughts were on the episodes and beyond. His mind's eyes saw me again standing on my toes in my crib so that I could get a better look at Cookie on television. He saw again the excitement in my eyes on my third birthday as I opened my gift and pulled out my Tickle Me Elmo. Again he witnessed me rolling on the floor and laughing with Elmo as Tickle Me Elmo somersaulted, rolled, and laughed uncontrollably. He saw a time when our brownstone on Park Place was on our own *Sesame Street*.

In those days, our beloved warfare involved cool water shot from two Super Soakers on hot days to cool bodies and to build relationships. In my late teens, our psychological warfare would involve hot words and competing ideas shot from two divergent minds attempting to define the reality we both must accept.

Today, we need to find our way back to sunny days on *Sesame Street*.

Chapter 11

Special Ed Ain't Special

Even when you know you can fly, there are always haters trying to clip your wings. However, as T.I. and Rihanna teach in "Live Your Life," you should ignore what haters say and watch them as they fade away.

There are those haters who do not want you to fly because of who and what you are. Like Soulja Boy says, they have a place set aside for you, but you can always prove them wrong by putting your swag on and coming up with another hit.

BTW, "Turn My Swag On" is a song I should never have introduced to dad. He loved it too much. What teenager wants his old dad to be walking around the house singing "Hopped up out da bed, turned my swag on," as a way of waking the teenager up?

What teenager wants his dad to follow him around the house, to get in his face and sing, "I got a question why dey hatin' on me, I got a question why dey hatin' on me?" For weeks, which seemed like a lifetime in 2009, I had to listen to dad butcher Soulja Boy's lyrics. Dad told me he had "done nuthin' to 'em but count my money…."

Even my cousin Nicole had to hear dad when she visited. She had this image of dad as super serious and responsible at all times. When dad turned his swag on, Nicole couldn't stop laughing in disbelief.

Dad told me that one of his biggest responsibilities was to protect me until age 18 from folks who would seek to limit my dreams, my flying. I'm 18 years old now.

Dad reports that when I was about 2 years and 9 months old, I ran into the first two people who wanted to clip my wings and had a place set aside for me. It was a special education class in a highly exclusive private school in Brooklyn Heights. If I would only attend, they had the means to get the State of New York to pay the $25,000 yearly tuition until I would graduate from eighth grade.

The encounter with the two began rather innocently. I was approaching 2 years and 9 months old, and mom and dad thought that I should start preschool. Getting kids in the best preschools and kindergartens were huge concerns of middle-class and upper-middle-class parents in New York City. (Today those parents can pay as much as $40,000 in tuition for kindergarten.) Many middle- and upper-middle-class parents thought the quality of the preschool and kindergarten experiences would have a profound impact on the development and success of their children later in life. Dad said poor parents wanted the same for their kids but could not afford to even dream of paying tuition of $25,000, an amount that was often higher than their yearly income.

My father was a "big-shot" educator with a doctoral degree who wanted only the best for his son. So he did research and discovered several schools in downtown Brooklyn were highly regarded. We visited several, but he wasn't impressed.

Then on a bright sunny morning in late August 1995, we visited a Montessori school in downtown Brooklyn that mom and dad hoped would be ideal based on what they had been told about its curriculum. The school had small classes and great facilities. The tuition was about $10,000 a year.

Dad and mom were open to sacrificing many other items in their budget if the school could offer a high quality early education. In preparation, dad had begun to save for my pre-school and college education immediately after my birth. Dad and mom had been mindful to spend less on clothing, entertainment, travel, eating out, and gifts to each other. In addition, although dad had a demanding work schedule, he took full responsibility for basic home repairs, maintenance, painting, and gardening to save the expense of hiring someone to do these chores.

The Montessori school in downtown Brooklyn was minutes away from Prospect Park, the Botanical Gardens, and numerous cultural institutions. The school served mostly middle- and upper-middle-class families. The student population was more than 80 percent Caucasian, a percentage typical for most schools in Brooklyn that charged high tuition.

On the day we visited, I wasn't feeling it. As mom and dad spoke with the female principal, I clung to my father's leg and attempted to avoid the eyes of the principal. The principal noticed, and asked mom and dad if there was anything wrong with me. They explained that I was generally very talkative and outgoing and that this was the first time I had clung to dad's leg in the presence of anyone.

Up until then, I was seen as outgoing and forceful. Dad said as a baby and a toddler, I was accustomed to looking people in the eyes as if I were putting them under the deepest scrutiny. However, there I was clinging to dad's leg as if the principal were the Wicked Old Witch of the West from the "Wizard of Oz." I was not in the mood to speak in response to any of her questions.

After a few minutes of additional conversation with mom and dad, the witch, oh, I mean the principal, asked, "Have you had him evaluated or tested?"

Dad asked her why she would ask that question. She suggested maybe I "had a developmental delay with language." Dad said there had never been an indication of that, and I was doing just fine. He said I was outgoing, talkative, and energetic. I knew the alphabet, I could count objects correctly, and, when read to, I was able to follow along and make comments on the stories as well as ask questions. In addition, he said I could "read" my favorite books from memory.

The principal acted as if dad had not spoken at all, and she asked to have me tested for vision, hearing, and language development, although she had no basis for the request other than the sight of me clinging to my father's leg. My parents were stung and confused by the request. At home they talked about it and finally consented to the request with full confidence everything would show I was doing just fine. They assumed consent was required in order to have me enroll at the school.

I went to the testing sites recommended by the principal. My eyes and hearing were just fine. However, when we went to the so-called language specialist, the intrigue set in. The language specialist lived and worked in an expensive brownstone in the heart of Park Slope, an area of multimillion dollar homes. Her diagnosis suggested that although I was speaking clearly and interacting well in learning activities at that stage of my life, there was "something" in the diagnostic tests that indicated I would later have difficulty processing and understanding language and reading and speaking clearly. She then suggested enrollment in a different Montessori preschool in downtown Brooklyn at the state's expense of $25,000 to ensure my full development.

The area around downtown Brooklyn was the home of the Wall Street wealthy, and the price of real estate was as high as the price in prime areas in Manhattan. Today, that description remains accurate. For example, in 2006 a house in that area sold for $11 million. In 2009, an apartment near there was listed for sale at $25 million.

Dad and mom immediately rejected the so-called language specialist's diagnosis and recommendation. They told her that her diagnosis was totally unsound. They did not bother to ask to see the testing documents nor did they return to revisit the principal who had recommended the tests. Dad would later say he felt so stupid that he was then contractually obligated to pay a tester whom he thought was nothing more than a mere charlatan with a Ph.D. diploma from a top university hanging on her wall.

When they returned home, they placed the recommendation in the closet of keepsakes to show me later, when I would enter college, just how wrong so-called experts could be about the potential of kids, especially black and Latino boys.

When I was a teen, dad and mom told me they are thankful that "Divine Guidance" prompted me to cling to dad's leg as he stood before the principal. That response was the first signal to them that something was wrong with potentially placing me there. Dad said he and mom ultimately assumed the language specialist and principal were involved in a financial scheme to place perfectly able, middle-class kids without disabilities in schools at the state's expense. They assumed the tuition paid would keep the enrollment up and be gravy for the receiving institutions. The appeal to parents was attendance in a well-regarded institution at the state's expense, even though many of the targeted parents had the money to pay the tuition. The yearly tuition would start at $25,000 and rise to more than $35,000 by the time it would have taken me to graduate from middle school at the state's expense.

After rejecting the recommendation of the so-called language specialist, my parents were still faced with finding a preschool for me, preferably a Montessori preschool. So, in late August 1995, dad sat in our living room to pray and meditate.

"Lord you created the universe to take care of me," dad began. "Now I need you to reveal the school that my son should attend that is consistent with your will for Akhenaton's life. In Jesus' name I pray. Amen."

As dad completed the prayer, he sank into the rhythm of his breaths while meditating and returning to repeating the prayer. As he emerged from prayer, a thought touched his spirit: "Pick up the Brooklyn Yellow Pages and select the school."

Within seconds dad ran upstairs and asked mom for the yellow pages as he told her of the thought that had come upon him. He turned to the section on schools and his eyes immediately focused upon Lefferts Gardens Montessori, a school in what some would call the "ghetto" of Crown Heights. My parents had considered other Montessori schools, all in middle- and upper-middle-class communities, but until that moment they were unaware that this particular school existed.

"That is the school, Lefferts Garden Montessori on Rogers Avenue in Crown Heights. We are going there tomorrow," dad announced. Mom was all right with it. She knew dad had a way of gaining special insights, although they both recognized there was no logic in selecting a school from a phone book when a person had the depth of knowledge and contacts dad possessed. They were prepared to select faith over logic. So, from the prospect of attending school in one of the wealthiest neighborhoods in New York City, we were on our way to Crown Heights or, what my boyz would call, "da hood."

Dad, the "big-shot" wise educator, was thinking about sending me to school in wealthy Brooklyn "when the wisdom of The Most High suggested 'da hood,'" he explained.

When dad tells this story, he often says, "God's wisdom made my wisdom seem like mere folly, like mere stupidity."

Chapter 12

Montessori in da Hood

On a warm, early September morning in 1995, dad dressed me and we prepared to enter the Camry for the ride to Lefferts Gardens. Lefferts Garden Montessori was about two miles from our house, a drive of about 10 to 15 minutes depending upon traffic. Mom sat in the back seat speaking to me about our upcoming visit as dad listened in upfront.

Mom reported that when we arrived we were greeted by Miss Lenore Briggs, the principal, founder, and owner of the school. Miss Briggs' skin was cinnamon brown. She looked rather grandmotherly with her long black hair in dreadlocks. Although she was up there in age, she did not have any wrinkles. The classroom was bright and uncluttered. There were learning stations spread throughout the classroom for computing, blocks, math manipulatives, and other activities. Various students were at the learning stations, while a small number were gathered around the main teacher, Miss Alicia Martin.

My eyes were open with the look of excitement. Seeing the excitement in my eyes, Miss Briggs suggested that I go and join in wherever I wanted to while she would speak with mom and dad. I headed straight to join a kid named Omar at the computer.

Mom later said she was deeply impressed that Miss Briggs sat facing mom and dad with her back to the classroom as they conversed. Miss Briggs had seated mom and dad in a position where they could observe me and my interaction with the other kids. She behaved totally opposite from the way the other principals we had seen had behaved. The other principals immediately had placed me and my parents under a microscope while suggesting they had the ability to diagnose the lifelong potential of a 2-year-old.

Dad says even today there are thousands of parents all across New York fretting about upcoming evaluations of their children as they seek to gain a spot for them in the so-called best private and public preschools and prekindergarten classes. He also reports that since my encounter with the so-called language specialist, tens of thousands of little African American boys, little Latino boys, and even little white boys have been misdiagnosed and placed in special education classes in private and public schools in New York City and around the nation. As senior assistant to three chancellors and as superintendent, he said he fought vigorously to oppose the wrong placement of students in special education in public schools. He says there is much more that must be done.

Mom and dad loved what they saw that morning as I moved among the other kids as if we were family. Lefferts Gardens Montessori would become my learning family away from home.

Today, my parents and I cannot remember a single bad day ever in the classrooms on Rogers Avenue. My parents and I cannot remember a moment that I did not feel treasured by Miss Briggs and my teachers.

Each school day for three years (after the first few days of tearful partings from mom), I would get up from bed with a spirit of anticipation. Mom told me it had broken her heart the first day she had dropped me off. She said I bravely left her side and walked into the classroom, then I turned around to say goodbye with tears streaming down my face. She said I was such a trooper.

Anyway, mom said the only school days that she recalls me missing occurred during a time when she, dad, and I went to visit relatives in Puerto Rico from Christmas 1995 through *El Dia de los Reyes Magos*/Three Kings Day in January 1996. We stayed at the Caribe Hilton in San Juan and then, with scores of relatives, stayed at a *parador*/inn near Mayaguez after visiting Aguadilla, mom's place of birth.

According to dad, in the *parador* we got a real taste of Puerto Rican culture when scores of family members gathered and moved from guest room to guest room as if no walls existed while sharing the care of the kids, food, stories, entertainment, laughter, and rest. Mom reports all had fun listening to dad's Southern-accented Spanish, and they had a good laugh at his expense when he used *seno*/breast instead of *seso*/brain when trying to make a point about how alcohol damages brain cells. Even on vacation, dad can't help himself. He laughed along with them as he continued to enjoy *Titi* Andrea's *tostones* and her tasty excellent *mojito*/garlic dipping sauce.

As an educator, my father suggests the most successful teachers are those who build a strong bond with their students and know how to nurture a strong relationship among the students. He says brain research shows learning is accelerated by relationships. That's why conventional wisdom says parents and family are the first and the best teachers, he counsels. He suggests the same students who thrive in classes where strong bonds and productive relationships exist often shut down and falter mere minutes later when they are in a different class with negative relationships.

As I think about his words today, I am mindful of the extraordinary efforts many of my high school teachers at Benjamin Banneker Academy undertook to build productive relationships with and among their students, even students who were, like me, mule-headed at times. A shout out to Miss Ford, Miss Samuel, Miss Murray, Mr. Egashira, Mr. Bradhurst, Coach Saunders, Coach Williams, Miss Davidson, Mr. Tuggle, Mr. Fernandez, Miss Iverson, Mr. Miller, Miss Urena, Dr. Shabaka, Miss Cook-Person, Miss Abdul-Karim, Dr. Rock, Mr. Marshall, Mr. Higgins, Mr. Muhammad, and Mr. Walton from Banneker.

Miss Briggs was my preschool *abuela*, and Miss Martin and Miss Martino were my preschool moms. They took us out to explore the world. We travelled to the theatre to see *The Lion King,* and we enjoyed Prospect Park, the Botanical Gardens, the Brooklyn Children's' Museum, Sesame Place, Reis Beach, a Native American Pow Wow, Green Meadows Farm, and the movies.

In the classroom, the Montessori Method was about exploring based on a child's interests at a given time. So, when a student wanted to go to a particular learning station, he could do so without asking permission, as long as the station was not crowded with other students. The Montessori Method was about developing more responsibility for your learning than the responsibility you would develop in other schools where teachers had tight schedules and told you what you could and could not learn.

I was the little computer wiz in class. From the time I was 2 years old, mom and dad never restricted my access to the home computer. They said they wanted me to be computer literate. Mom reported that at 3 years old I knew how to turn it on, dial up to connect to children's websites, and save files. She said dial up was often particularly frustrating for adults as well as kids. It required patience because it would usually take a few minutes to get through on a conventional telephone line to AOL/America on Line. At Lefferts Gardens Montessori, I would help many of the other students and even the teachers if they would encounter difficulties using the computer.

Mom recently told the story of how she arrived at the school one day in October 1995 to find me easily clicking and scrolling using a mouse. She was surprised with how easily I used this new computer peripheral because she was just beginning to introduce and encourage the use of the mouse to her co-workers at the hospital where she works. At the time, mom was her department's data coordinator/LAN administrator. She had a Masters of Business Administration degree in Management Information Systems. She was amazed that I had taught myself since she had not yet purchased a mouse for our computer at home and many adults, including the teachers, were at that point not fully accustomed to its use. In the school's 1998 yearbook, there's a picture of me sitting at the computer using the mouse while several other students look on.

Adeze Wilford, Omar Samuel, Kayanne and Kendra Williams, Zoe Munlyn, Khalil Commissiong, Travis Patterson, Charles English, and Ekoya Atkins were among my classmates who ranged in age from 2 years to 5 years when I began. Outside of school we attended birthday parties and other events as our families grew close. Omar was my big brother since he was 2 years older. He graduated at the end of my first year. Khalil and Travis were my boyz who were with me the whole three years.

Lefferts Gardens Montessori published a yearbook at the end of each year of my attendance. In every picture I appeared in my trademark little Afro. Dad was committed to not cutting my hair for a spiritual reason revealed in a dream shortly after my birth. Mom and dad seemed to have dressed me fashionably in sweaters, collarless shirts, jeans, and corduroy pants. The colors and styles weren't all over the place. Khalil was often dressed in a suit and bowtie looking like a little man, or, as dad puts it, "like a little member of the Nation of Islam."

In the 1996 yearbook, there is a picture of Adeze hugging me during a graduation ceremony for the older students. She has on a white dress and has a white bow with ribbons holding her hair in place. I have my little Afro. I am wearing a white dress shirt and a bowtie and cummerbund made of Kente cloth. We both are smiling big smiles. Dad smiles every time he looks at that picture because he remembers when Adeze had told her mother that I was a "little wild child," full of too much energy to invite over to her house.

The picture dad and mom love most is one of Travis, Khalil, and me in the 1998 yearbook. Khalil has on a long tie this time and a navy blue blazer. I am stylish in beige slacks and a striped shirt. Travis has on a shirt two different shades of blue and made of soft velvet. We are smiling and posing together like a band of brothers, like the band of brothers I would later develop in high school with members of the Benjamin Banneker basketball team. (Go Warriors!) Dad says when one looks at that picture one is immediately impressed to witness a sense of spiritual unity leaping forth through the smiles and embraces of three

5-year-old boys. He says America should look at that picture when it wants to see three black boys who know that they are beloved at home and in school.

The International Montessori Society regularly sent educators from Italy and all over the world to visit the school to observe the methods that Miss Briggs and her staff modeled so well right there in "da hood." Fifteen years later, we are still giving thanks that the way to the school was revealed during prayer and mediation.

It was at Lefferts Gardens Montessori for three years that I would spread my wings to fly away with the love of a little Guyanese grandmother, Miss Briggs, and her staff. And dad and mom would fly away, too, knowing that I was being well loved and well educated.

Chapter 13

Mischief, Diesel, and Thomas

As long as I can remember, I was fascinated by trains. Living in New York as a child made it easy to fall in love with trains. At the age of 5 I often travelled with mom and dad by subway, and we frequently visited the Transit Museum in downtown Brooklyn. Whenever we rode the subway, I always wanted to be in the first car outside the train operator's cabin, watching the trains speed through the tunnels. I loved it when we would move fast past other trains or see other trains approaching from the opposite direction. I imagined I was the train operator on one of the engines on *Thomas the Tank Engine*.

A ride on a train was always about the trip, not the destination. When you are a little boy riding on trains, your mind takes you to places where the trains don't even go. You are caught up in the experience, and you would be content to have the experience last long past your scheduled arrival at the planned destination.

When we visited relatives in the Bronx, I was in for a special treat. After the 149th Street Station on the #4 line, the subway would emerge from the tunnel and travel on the elevated tracks. After being pleasantly surprised the first time this happened, I would wait with great anticipation on the trips that followed. Up on the elevated tracks I would see Yankee Stadium. At times, I would even be able to look into people's apartments and also watch the jets flying overhead.

In 1997, mom, dad, and I visited San Francisco. In San Francisco, I discovered the joys of riding on cable cars up and down some steep hills. Wow, it was a great feeling to have the wind caress my face as we sat on the outer edges of cable cars. We also visited the Cable Car Museum.

The episodes of *Thomas the Tank Engine* fed my love for trains. Today in our closet of keepsakes, I have the replica of almost every train that appeared in the episodes. I have Thomas, Annie and Clarabel, James, Duck, Gordon, Henry, Edward, Diesel, and many others. I have my first wooden tracks that they rode upon. I also have an electric set. There are more than 15 videos containing nearly 100 episodes, and I have the video of the movie "Thomas and the Magic Railroad." When my little cousin Jaden visits, he goes straight to the closet and asks to play with the trains. When he leaves, the trains go right back in the closet where I am saving them to pass along to my sons and daughters.

Thomas and Gordon were my favorites. Most of the engines tried to live by the lessons of Sir Toppan Hat who taught the importance of discipline, obedience, and teamwork. However, when Diesel appeared he brought a new attitude. I loved Diesel because he brought more mischief and excitement to the train yard. Diesel was strong physically and he wanted everything his own way, as most 5-year-olds (and teenagers) do. He thought he was smarter than all the other trains.

In the episode "Pop Goes the Diesel," Diesel attempted to prove to Sir Toppan Hat how strong and useful he could be. He attempted to control some unruly freight cars that end up getting the best of him. Then he got very angry when the freight cars ridiculed him singing, "Pop Goes the Diesel."

That was an episode that I must have viewed 20 or 30 times from the ages of 5 to 7. Dad and mom would often view it with me, and we would sing along with the freight cars: "When he pulled the wrong cars out, pop goes the Diesel."

Though Diesel was defeated once, he never lost his determination to have things his way and he never lost his will for creating mischief and excitement.

What would life be without mischief and excitement? There's a word for that. What would life be for teens who do not want to have things their way? There are a few words for that. Can you imagine being all of Thomas without a healthy dose of Diesel?

That's got to be somebody other than me.

Chapter 14

Good Teacher, Bad Teacher, and Leadership

As a former Superintendent, dad believes that good and highly effective teachers are our nation's most valuable resource. He also recognizes that in America teachers are not valued. He suggests that a good and highly effective teacher in every classroom would be the single most important factor for ensuring that all students receive a quality education and America maintains its economic and political leadership in the 21st century. He recognizes that political and business leaders speak as if they are committed to this idea but consistently fail to take the necessary steps to make the idea a reality.

On April 14, 1997, dad had been appointed as Community Superintendent for Community School District Five in Harlem. Harlem is a community known throughout the world. He would leave Brooklyn every morning no later than 6:00 a.m. to report to work. He would leave before I woke up, and he would return most nights after mom had put me to bed.

Dad had been sent to Harlem by Chancellor Crew to clean up the corruption in that district that had, for nearly 30 years, been taking away resources and stopping the kids from getting a good education. There were educators, school board leaders, politicians, and their supporters who had benefitted from the corruption. They were interested in keeping the corruption going, so dad had to work very hard to hold them in check.

As I prepared to enter first grade in September 1998 after graduating from Lefferts Gardens Montessori, dad convinced mom to allow me to enroll in Public School (PS) 36. The school was on 123rd Street and Amsterdam Avenue in Harlem, across the street from dad's new office. He would drop me in the morning, and mom would pick me up after school. It was a great arrangement for me because it meant that I would see dad every day, at least in the morning, and during our 30-minute drive to Harlem I could speak with dad and also enjoy the old-school music dad tuned into from the car's radio.

My first grade teacher was Miss Dalrymple. She was tall, young, and had natural reddish-blonde hair. She had a wonderful smile, and she knew how to make learning fun. I was excited every day to see her and my classmates. She taught us some wonderful songs that we would often sing during class and special presentations that dad would sometimes attend. A big hit with me and all the kids was "Celebration" by Kool and the Gang. My favorite part was screaming "Ya-hoo! It's a celebration." I think the other kids loved that part, too, because they would scream along with me.

Another big hit was "I Can See Clearly Now" by Jimmy Cliff. We were taught to imagine "bright, bright, bright, bright sun shiny days." We experienced many such days in Miss Dalrymple's class.

Dad said I thrived in that classroom and added that Miss Dalrymple has "excellent classroom management skills." Miss Dalrymple was patient as she helped me shift from a Montessori environment to a more traditional school setting. At my Montessori preschool, the classroom was arranged according to subject area, and kids were free to move around the room instead of staying at desks. Dad said he was disappointed to learn in May 1999 that Miss Dalrymple was planning to transfer to a school in midtown Manhattan to be closer to home after her upcoming wedding. But he was pleased to know that she would remain a teacher since she had so much to offer.

In July 1999, with the election of a new school board, dad learned that he would not be returning to Harlem. The majority of the new school board members and their corrupt supporters said they wanted a Community Superintendent whom the Chancellor had not imposed. Dad said some of the school board members and politicians wanted to return to the corrupt practices of the past. They were allowed to do so until school boards throughout the city were eventually abolished a few years later because of the corruption and interference with the educational progress of school children.

So, in September 1999, dad returned to the Chancellor's Office in downtown Brooklyn, and my parents enrolled me in PS 282 in Park Slope since it was just a few blocks from home. I was placed in the second grade gifted class. PS 282 had a good reputation and better facilities than PS 36, including an auditorium that PS 36 lacked. Soon my parents would discover that my class at PS 282 lacked something that my class at PS 36 possessed—a competent and caring teacher. Overall, PS 282 was a good school, but for the individual student, the school is only as good as his or her individual teacher.

I started school with my usual enthusiasm. I quickly made plenty of friends. But most of the joy of learning was missing in class. However, I continued to enjoy books and learning experiences at home and out and about in the city.

Soon after school began, dad and mom discovered that as second graders we were using fifth grade textbooks in social studies and science. I was not yet 7, but my classmates and I were reading stories about the American Civil War and other things that we did not have the experiences or maturity to really understand. For example, we were assigned the *Red Badge* of *Courage*.

As a consequence, my parents complained that being able to read the stories was not equivalent to really understanding them. However, the principal wanted to keep teaching that way. She was proud of the performance of students on city tests and, somehow, thought it was due to their ability to read books whose content they couldn't fully understand.

One day about four months into the school year I told dad that I had to bring a quarter to school the next day. Dad wanted to know the reason. I told him a girl in my class said someone had stolen her quarter, and the teacher said she was "punishing the whole class by making everyone bring in a quarter" to give to the girl. Dad said the teacher was "acting silly," and he was not going to give me a quarter.

In the following weeks, dad started to hear from me about the teacher's treatment of boys in the class. She was really mean to the boys. We were all black or Latino (mostly Puerto Rican and she was Puerto Rican as well). This happened during a time before most Puerto Ricans were pushed off Fifth Avenue and out of Park Slope due to gentrification. It was at a time before the *bodegas* were replaced by fancy restaurants and crowded bars.

Soon after that, mom visited the class with about 10 other parents for a "read-to-the-kids" celebration. The teacher was uptight with the parents' presence and would not arrange the kids into small groups, as is the custom during this celebration, so that each parent would have an opportunity to read to a group. The teacher wanted one parent at a time to read to the entire class so she could monitor the whole class at once. Thus, the period ended with only two parents getting a chance to read and the other parents regretting taking time off from work. Mom and the other parents were able to observe the teacher's bad treatment of the boys during the period. When mom and dad complained to the principal, the principal acknowledged there had been other complaints.

Toward the end of the school year, mom and dad again went to the principal when they found out that the teacher removed me and about 8 other boys from the class and put us in another classroom while the rest of my classmates had a pizza party. The teacher claimed we did not deserve the party because we had not behaved properly the day before. The principal said she had no idea this had taken place and would not have allowed it.

Yet, to all of these complaints, the principal's only action was to suggest that I would have a different teacher the following year.

That was not good enough, so my parents told the principal of their plan to remove me from the school so that I could attend a school where no teacher would view boys as problems and where classrooms were managed for the educational benefit of all the kids, not for the benefit of the teachers. PS 59, a school a few blocks from mom's job in Manhattan, would be my new school.

My parents would later learn from a parent of one of my female classmates that my second grade teacher at PS 282 was reportedly recommending that almost all the remaining boys not be promoted into the third grade gifted class. My father was outraged. He told the parent if that were true, the parents of those boys should get together and demand the removal of the teacher. Dad said all of the boys had already proven their eligibility by excelling on the required tests before entering her class.

Dad felt my second grade teacher was representative of a small but significant percentage of teachers who do not know how to work with and relate to boys and are not interested in learning how to do so. Those teachers see boys as problems when the problems are really their biases and their poor teaching methods. He said teachers who cannot relate to boys should be in another profession.

Dad does not know if the boys were ultimately allowed to attend the gifted class, but he did learn the teacher remained in her post.

In less than a year after my departure, Miss Alexis, the assistant principal, would become principal of PS 282. Dad considered her much more dynamic and more deeply devoted to all children than the principal who had been there the year I attended. Although I was already in another school, dad started to help Miss Alexis build up PS 282's library and technology using contacts he had in the city.

A few years later, in the early fall of 2002, the Department of Education completed its move from downtown Brooklyn to the Tweed Court House in

Manhattan. This would be dad's new location. The new headquarters were equipped with the latest technology and new office furniture.

Meanwhile, in the vacated offices in downtown Brooklyn, computers and other office equipment and office furniture, all in relatively new condition, were left to sit unused. In October, dad took the risk of contacting five principals to have them come to the offices his unit had vacated. Miss Alexis and other principals took possession of the computers and other office equipment and office furniture that were sitting unused. They hired movers and signed receipts to indicate they were in possession of the unused equipment and furniture.

More than a year after the move, hundreds of perfectly usable and nearly new computers and other office equipment remained in the other vacated units in downtown Brooklyn while schools continued to be in need of such items. Although dad had been forewarned that he could be subject to disciplinary action if he were to proceed in distributing the unused items from his unit, no charges were brought against him, and the equipment and furniture have been put to good use.

I was happy to leave PS 282. I looked forward to PS 59. I never questioned my parents' decision. Dad said I was fortunate I had parents who had the knowledge, contacts, and means to move me on to another school. He stated that most classmates' parents at PS 282, unfortunately, did not have the same opportunity to move their boys.

I remember when I completed third grade at PS 59 I asked mom what my new school would be for fourth grade. She assured me I was staying put. I guess I thought a kid had to change schools with each grade. Mom recently shared with me how sad she felt that my short school experience at the time made me come to that conclusion. But, she always says that we must look for something positive in all situations. She now points out that one good thing that came out of that situation are my abilities to adapt to new environments and to make new friends wherever I go. Leave it up to her to find a silver lining in a dark cloud.

Today I wonder about my second grade classmates. Did they survive the scars inflicted by that horrible teacher? Did they graduate high school? Are they now in college? Are they happy and strong?

I distinctly remember my second grade teacher deliberately mispronouncing the name of one of the boys. His name was Guy (pronounced gee). However, she called him "Gay." Of course, at that time I did not understand the meaning, but I always wondered why she would not call him by his name.

Today, Guy and I remain friends. He is a dynamite point guard whom I have often competed against at Basketball City.

I hope the teacher has retired and is no longer scarring the lives of children. In second grade, we had a teacher who treated the boys like the orphans in "Annie." As Jay-Z sings, we experienced the "hard knock life." Even today, dad still faults himself that he ever placed me in that teacher's class in PS 282.

However, we have come to understand that there is a bigger and more important picture. If dad, with all of his knowledge and contacts, could find himself temporarily helpless, it is even more challenging for most of the parents of black and Latino boys across the nation. Most do not have the resources or contacts to drastically alter the educational circumstances of their sons. They don't have a PS 59 waiting with open arms.

Dad says it's our nation's challenge to help empower those boys and parents. It is crucial not just for their prosperity, but also for America's long-term prosperity. He wonders when the politicians and the corporate and educational leaders of America will wake up and act truly and consistently in the interest of Latino and black children who will soon be the majority of school children in all of America. He says America must wake up and realize it cannot afford to continue to miseducate black and Latino kids. He says America is talking the talk but unwilling to walk the walk by investing in what will truly transform schools and kids' lives.

"It ain't happening now even under Secretary of Education Arne Duncan. Ain't that right, Mr. President?" he asks.

Chapter 15

Ridin' Dirty, Walkin' Dirty, and Runnin' Dirty

Like most American boys, when I was a little boy, my parents always told me to go to the bathroom before leaving the house or any other place to make sure I would not be overcome with the urge to urinate in the street. Of course, as a 3- or 4-year-old, there were times when I didn't listen. Thus, there were times when dad had me stand between two parked cars to let out my streams when I could no longer hold them.

A couple of times at that age, I peed on myself just as we reached our block, and I had to go into the tub as soon as I arrived home. For example, one night at the age of 3, after leaving the Greatest Show on Earth Circus at Madison Square Garden, I had run with dad down our block hoping to make it. We left mom behind as we started our mad dash toward home. Unfortunately, I needed one more minute which time wouldn't let me have.

Now, I know many teenagers would never admit it happened to them. Well, I suggest that they should ask their parents. It happens. Mom says it's a "boy thing." What do you say?

Well, it is one thing to run down the streets when you are 3 to urinate and quite another thing when you are 13. However, at age 13 when you've got to go, you have got to go, and a tall black boy running can quickly catch the attention of the "po-po" in Brooklyn. They are always eyeballing black and Latino males even when they are totally innocent and walking as well as running.

Chamillionaire sings about how cops can see us rolling while they are "hatin', patrolin' and trying to catch us ridin' dirty." In New York, where African Americans and Latinos walk to the subway stations and bus stops, the cops have a big Stop-and-Frisk Program designed to catch us walking dirty. DWB is driving while black. DWL is driving while Latino. WWBL is not a radio station in New York; it's walking while black or Latino. In my case, I was stopped for RWBL, running while black and Latino.

In 2006, according to statistics from the New York Police Department (NYPD), I was about to become one of more than 400,000 New York City residents stopped and frisked that year by police officers who were not investigating any crimes during the stops.

In September 2006, at the age of 13, I left Benjamin Banneker Academy planning to take the Vanderbilt Avenue bus which would, after a little more than a mile, leave me within one block of our condo. When I arrived at the bus stop, the bus was full of students and had already started to depart. I decided to walk home. It was a bright and beautiful day and a cool breeze caressed my face. As I walked on Vanderbilt Avenue and came to Lafayette Avenue, I realized the urge to urinate was coming upon me. In response, I increased the speed and length of my strides thinking I could reach home in 12 minutes. I thought I could hold it at least 20 minutes, but I sped up just in case.

Three minutes later as I crossed Fulton Street, I suddenly felt as if I had only nine minutes before the flood would pour down. At the pace I was moving, I figured it would take seven to eight minutes more to reach home. I didn't want to go on myself or in the streets, so I started to trot. One minute later, as I approached Atlantic Avenue, the trot turned into a run as I sped to cross the wide intersection before the traffic light changed against me. Two additional minutes had passed since crossing Fulton Street.

The only thing on my mind was getting to the bathroom. I was four minutes from home, but my bladder felt as if it were giving me only three minutes to get there. So, after crossing Atlantic, I picked up Usain Bolt's speed and accelerated toward Pacific Street. I really didn't see anything around me. All I saw was the image of me standing in my bathroom sighing in relief as a waterfall descended.

However, someone was eyeballing me. He and his partner apparently pulled their car close to the curb as I crossed Pacific heading toward Dean Street.

"Hey, you! Why are you running?" His tone was more that of a summons than a question. Hearing the tone, I stopped running but continued to walk as the patrol car crawled along at my pace. My thoughts shifted to the instructions I had been given by mom and dad.

"Hey, buddy, stop right there!" he commanded.

I stopped with a sigh as I attempted to recall the instructions dad and mom had given about dealing with cops. The white cop who had asked the question came out of the car on the front passenger side. I watched him approach. He did not look friendly. His black male partner was looking in my direction yet remained in the driver's seat. I slowed my breathing.

"Why are you running and what are you running from?" He asked, again using the tone of a summons.

"I am not running from anything. I live around the corner on Dean Street. I was walking from school, and I started running because I have to get home to pee."

"Huh, that's one I haven't heard yet," he responded sarcastically as he held his night stick. "What do you have in that bag?"

"My books."

"Open it!" He pointed the night stick at my bag to emphasize his command. I opened the part of the bag containing my books. He came closer and looked in.

"Now show me what is in the other part you didn't open," he demanded.

"It's my basketball," I explained as I opened the zipper.

"These bags are made so that you could carry a basketball," I continued. I was fortunate that he had not decided to humiliate me further by personally frisking me. I would later learn from reading statistics that during each of the next several years hundreds of thousands of innocent black and Latino New Yorkers were frisked in public as if they were criminals.

"What school do you attend?"

"Benjamin Banneker Academy."

"Let me see your school I.D.!"

This cop was really into giving commands, I thought. Yet, I was still mindful of mom's and dad's instructions. Thus, I took out my I.D. He looked at it and then at me. I guess he wanted to see if I matched the picture on my I.D.

"Where did you say you live?"

I was feeling a bit frustrated, plus I still had to pee, but I attempted to maintain a calm demeanor, as mom had instructed I should do if the cops ever stopped me.

"Around the corner and one block down in the condominiums. If you come to the corner, you can see my building," I answered calmly.

"I know the building. Well, here's your I.D. You can go, but you need to be careful when running in the streets. You can look like you are a criminal running from a crime."

He said the words as if giving me fatherly advice. I had an impulse to ask if they were investigating a crime, but I chose not to since I knew the answer already. Plus dad and mom had counseled me not to say things or ask questions that might provoke a reaction from cops.

That was good advice because I would later learn from statistics from the Center for Constitutional Rights that 26 percent of the nearly 400,000 blacks and Latinos stopped in 2005 had physical force used against them although very few were stopped as part of an investigation, and even fewer were later arrested for criminal conduct. I would also later learn that I was fortunate that I had my identification. It was becoming common practice for cops to take people and hold them at a police precinct until someone arrived with that person's identification before the cops would release them.

Given the freedom to leave, I put my bag on my shoulders and took a glance at the black cop in the driver's seat. He turned his head away to avoid eye contact. I walked and turned the corner toward home.

That afternoon, I experienced RWBL, running while black and Latino. I was so relieved to be free of the confrontation I almost forgot about the real urge to relieve myself. However, the urge returned when I entered the elevator of my building. With growing anxiety, I counted each floor as the elevator passed while praying that no one would press a button to interrupt the trip to the seventh floor.

There is something about the movement of an elevator which intensifies the urge to urinate. I think you could compare it to the intensity generated by the sound of running water when you have to go. Thus, by the time I reached my floor, the intensity had grown to an unbearable level so I practically separated the elevator doors by force and ran down the hallway.

When I reached the door of our apartment, I dropped the keys. After retrieving them from the carpet, I opened the door. I threw everything down and made a mad dash for the bathroom. I decided to run into mom's bathroom since it was closer than the bathroom dad and I shared in the master bedroom. Thankfully, mom wasn't home because she would have denied me that privilege. I had already started to unzip while nearing the front door to our apartment. So as I ran toward the bathroom door I reached in my pants and squeezed like I would squeeze a water hose to hold back the flow.

When I arrived at my destination, I didn't have time to lift the toilet seat, but I aimed carefully and loosened my grip on the hose. Thankfully, the yellow gush miraculously merged completely with the colorless pond in the bowl. I was relieved, in more ways than one, as I went to the sink and washed my hands.

Suddenly, I realized I was tired. I was exhausted. I went to the refrigerator and poured a glass of Tropicana OJ, Low Acid. I drank it standing near the fridge.

Our kitchen, dining, and living "rooms" are part of a large open loft. I crossed from the kitchen area into the living room. I thought of going out to the terrace to see who was at the basketball courts across the street. Instead, I stopped at one of the couches and plopped down without removing my sneakers.

I must have fallen asleep within 30 seconds with the sun shining on my face because the next thing I heard was the front door opening. I looked up from the couch and was glad to see mom. She came over to where I was sitting. I asked her the time and realized that I had been sleeping for nearly two hours.

"How was your day, *bambino?*"

"Mom, you wouldn't believe it if I told you."

"Try me. What happened?"

I took several minutes to describe my encounter with the cops. She expressed her outrage and she expressed satisfaction that I had demonstrated the ability to handle myself in a situation that could have become more negative.

Starting at about age 10, mom and dad began to warn me against running when out in the streets, no matter what the reason. They cautioned that many of the officers in the New York City Police Department have a tendency to suspect any black or Latino boy over 5 feet 5 inches of being a criminal or potential criminal. I guess 10 is the age when most parents warn their kids about this because many of my black and Latino male friends received the same warning from their parents around the same time I did.

Dad says he bets even the black and Latino cops who live in the city have had to warn their own sons to beware of some of their fellow officers. He said he heard that many black and Latino officers give their sons a decal or something similar to identify themselves as sons of police officers in case they are stopped, like I was stopped.

At age 10, I was already 5 feet 6 inches and growing. Mom was concerned that although I had a "baby face," I may be mistaken for a teenager, which could make me a target because of my height and my size 11 feet. Mom told me to be careful when running for the bus or train because police officers might stop me to ask me why I am running and whether I had committed a crime.

She counseled, "It is better that you miss the bus or train. There will always be another bus or train. If they see you running, they could use that as an excuse to search you, saying that they are looking for weapons. If you argue that they made you miss your bus or train for nothing, they could use that as an excuse to harass you or take you to the precinct. So it's best to just avoid them. If they do stop you, tell them that you are only 10 years old and on your way to or from school."

The year was 2002. We had just moved into our condo, and dad would soon be the president of the condo board representing 171 apartment owners. (My two sisters had moved back into our brownstone.) The building complex had a fully equipped gym and a roof-top playground and track. From our terrace, I could see all the way to New Jersey, more than 10 miles away. The garage had room for about 200 cars, and a renowned artist had rented space for more than 30 vintage Corvettes. The rapper and actor Common was an apartment owner, and I had the good fortune of running into him at the elevator. I am told the editor of *Vibe* also lived here, but I am not sure.

In addition to our apartment, there were eight other apartments on my floor. Two of the owners who lived down the hall with their daughter were actors. The wife had starred in many shows on television, including *Law and Order*, and had also co-starred in several movies including a movie with Bruce Willis. Her husband had also acted on television, including PBS, and had co-starred in movies including one with Russell Crowe. They are cool people.

Two other owners on my floor were medical doctors. One is married to a school teacher, and they would later have two cool kids. Another owner on my floor was a media pioneer and a futurist, and his wife was a visual artist and interior designer. The owner across the hall from us was a school administrator who would later become a principal. The complex included other owners who were black, white, Latino, and Asian with professions in the media, education, the arts, law, and on Wall Street.

So you would think such counseling from mom and dad was ironic and unnecessary given my family's educational and economic background. But think again because, after all, this is America and racial profiling has been proven to be real. They see a black or brown face, and assume the worst.

Research has shown that state troopers in New Jersey stop folks for DWBL, driving while black or Latino. The Center for Constitutional Rights has shown, after reviewing NYPD's own statistics, that the "po-po" in New York City are racially profiling black and Latino males walking to and from work, home, and school. In New York City, cops are looking to catch folks "walkin' dirty" plus "running dirty," as well as "ridin' dirty."

In 2002 dad was particularly sensitive because, as a school superintendent, he had access to data about all the young black and Latino males and females who were being arrested daily while in school and also when leaving school.

Mayor Rudolph Giuliani had placed officers on patrol in many schools and had directed the police department to pursue criminal charges against students who walked onto the subways without school-issued transit passes. Jumping the turnstile to avoid paying a fare that was less than $2 led to thousands of black and Latino school kids being led away in handcuffs instead of being released and given a written citation demanding payment of a fine. Minor fist fights in schools led to arrests for criminal assault instead of suspensions. Dad was concerned that many of the students would end up with criminal records for minor offenses and find that they would not be able to secure employment later in life.

Principals, superintendents, teachers, and parents began to complain more visibly about heavy-handed police tactics with school kids. In some cases, overzealous school safety officers under the direction of the police department were seen instigating conflicts with students and, in several high-profile incidents, had arrested principals who complained about some school safety officers' treatment of students. The school safety officers claimed the principals had interfered with the performance of their "policing" duties. In New York City's 1,200 schools, there were 4,200 school safety officers (and 100-plus police officers), yet only 3,000 guidance counselors. That math said a lot about what was important to Giuliani.

In 1995 dad's hero, Chancellor Ramon Cortines, had fought against Giuliani's attempt to give the NYPD control of school safety because Cortines feared there would be widespread abuse of police authority used to arrest kids. Cortines suspected Giuliani's motives were not really about improving school safety, and he was concerned that behavioral issues which would normally get a kid sent to the principal's office would instead get a kid sent to jail.

Cortines was viewed by dad, many educators, parents, and city residents as the best educator and promoter of the interests of kids to have sat in the Chancellor's office. He used his devotion to muster the courage to stand up to Giuliani, whom dad, many educators, parents, and community leaders viewed as a dictator willing to crush any opposition to his will.

Dad said Giuliani, in response, resorted to the tactics of a bully, including attempting to humiliate Cortines by issuing public comments in the media about Cortines' resistance while using stereotypical words regarding the Chancellor's sexual orientation. Giuliani received significant criticism in the *New York Times* for his comments, but a few months later, by late 1995, Giuliani succeeded in forcing Cortines to resign for not accepting his demand to turn control of school safety over to the NYPD.

In early 1996 Rudy Crew replaced Cortines as Chancellor and Giuliani immediately began to pressure him to gain NYPD control of school safety.

In 1997 Giuliani insisted that all public school yearbooks be given to the NYPD for inclusion in their database so that the police would have the names and photographs of kids throughout the city when investigating crimes. Giuliani's position seemed to suggest that most if not every senior of the public schools was a potential criminal. Chancellor Rudy Crew initially resisted and Giuliani was not pleased. Crew said that only specific yearbooks would be made available on a case-by-case basis if school officials found sufficient reason to share them with the police.

In 1998 after initially resisting NYPD control of school safety, Crew gave in to Giuliani and the police department took control of school safety. Many superintendents, principals, teachers, and parents were gravely disappointed with Crew and Crew's decision. Giuliani and Crew made a public display of being the best of buddies, including making a point of attending Yankee games and the circus together. Giuliani suggested that many criminals and potential criminals were students in the public schools, and he welcomed Crew's concession to the demand for NYPD control of school safety.[3]

However, within a year the friendship was in tatters as a result of policy disagreements about the conduct of police in schools and policy disagreements in other educational areas. Giuliani then used his influence with members of the Board of Education to kick Crew to the curb. To add insult to Crew's injury, he had the Board put Judy Rizzo, Crew's deputy and long-term friend, in charge of the schools on an interim basis. Rizzo was viewed by dad and some other leading educators, including superintendents, as selfish, deceptive, and incompetent. She lasted a few months in the role.

Giuliani's theory suggested that any minor offender was highly likely to later commit major crimes, and he wanted the police to have all of the minor offenders' mug shots and fingerprints on file for detectives to use when investigating any major crime. Thus, if a minor offender later happened to be near or live in the vicinity of a major crime he did not commit, his picture could, nevertheless, be examined by victims, and he could be brought in to participate in a lineup. Of course, there was always the possibility that the minor offender could then be erroneously selected from a lineup and spend time in jail for a major crime he did not commit.

By 2001, the last full year of what dad called "the dictatorial presence of Giuliani as mayor," police officers had been regularly going into schools pulling out black and Latino kids to participate in lineups without asking the permission of their parents, teachers, or principals. Most of the kids had never been arrested. Also, the police officers knew that the kids being pulled out for lineups were innocent because they knew the kids were in school when the crimes had been committed and the prime suspects had already been apprehended. Dad said they needed warm bodies to fill the lineups to then say they had a fair process through which the victims identified the suspects.

As this continued, superintendents, principals, teachers, parents, and a few courageous black, white and Latino political and community leaders began complaining of the practice. They began to publically ask, in the media and city council hearings, if NYPD and Giuliani believed the education of the innocent kids was less important than their participation in a lineup.

They were angry with having kids miss school and the possibility that victims could erroneously select innocent kids when viewing lineups. They suggested the NYPD would never try such tactics in wealthier neighborhoods with white students. Eventually, the practice of pulling kids from schools declined, although it was reported in the media that cops continued to pick up and put into lineups innocent kids riding their bicycles and skate boards on the streets.

So, in 2002, when mom and dad sat me down to talk, they had seen enough to caution me about conduct in the street, in school, and on public transportation. I was directed to refuse to participate in any lineup if requested and to call dad who would call a lawyer, if necessary.

In September 2003 when I was about to enter Middle School (MS) 89, I was almost 11 and nearly 6 feet tall. Attending MS 89 would require that I travel alone daily into lower Manhattan. Thus, their counseling sessions happened more frequently, and they adopted certain practices to protect me from false prosecutions. One practice involved giving me an additional $20 which I was to keep in my wallet at all times. It would be my proof that I did not need to shoplift if wrongly questioned by some store workers who might be in the habit of following every black and Latino boy who entered their stores to buy snacks. Even though I had a school transit card, I was instructed to use the $20 to pay for a single train fare if I were to lose my card. So every day I had more than enough money for lunch plus an additional $20 which I could not spend unless I needed it for train fare.

For the most part, the store owners near my new school were cool. I would enter alone or with a group of my black, Latino, Asian, and white friends, and I was never hassled. However, I watched the police officers assemble daily at school dismissal in the subway station at Chambers Street and West Broadway in preparation for arresting any student they might catch evading the subway fare. Though the subway fare was about $2, that was often $2 more than many poor students possessed. In some schools, as many as 90 percent of the students were eligible for free breakfast and lunch due to their family's financial situation. So, if they couldn't afford to pay to eat, how could they afford to pay to ride to and from school if they lost their free passes?

The white, black, Latino, and Asian police officers often stood where they wouldn't be immediately visible to the kids but yet would be in a position to see the turnstiles. There were many times when I watched them place handcuffs on different students, almost always black or Latino, who had lost or misplaced their school-issued subway passes. Thankfully, I avoided any reason to draw their attention. During the times I misplaced my transit pass, I was always able to pay the fare.

I would later learn that in New York City when thousands of residents, even high school students, are arrested for non-felony offenses such as jumping the turnstiles they are often asked to post bail of $1,000. Of course if they didn't have the $2 to ride home they certainly didn't have $1,000 for bail. Thus, most would spend as much as three weeks in jail awaiting trial and miss school if they were students. In 2010 Jamie Fellner of Human Rights Watch authored a report on the criminal justice system's unfair treatment of the poor. She wrote, "Bail punishes the poor because they cannot afford to buy their pre-trial freedom. Almost one quarter—23 percent—of jail admissions last year were pretrial detainees charged with misdemeanors who had not made bail."[4]

The notorious Bernie Madoff who stole billions and destroyed many lives was allowed to return to his New York City home to await trial after posting bail. Even some organized crime figures accused of murder have been able to post bail and await their trial at home. Yet some high school students have had to languish in jail for as much as three weeks awaiting trial for jumping a turnstile after losing their school-issued transit passes. Is that justice?

As we sat down for dinner that evening in September 2006, mom told dad about my encounter with the cops. Dad expressed great outrage. At that time, dad was Deputy Regional Superintendent responsible for 99,000 students and 140 schools in the Bronx. As a superintendent, he was more familiar than mom with the practices of the NYPD and the impact of those practices on black and Latino teens.

"What's the difference between New York City and South Africa during the Apartheid era?" dad began. "In South Africa, every black man had to carry an identifying pass. If he was stopped by white policemen, he had to produce the pass. He could be stopped simply because he was African in his own country that the Europeans had stolen."

Mom and I continued eating even as dad's words caused us to now think more deeply about my encounter and the encounters of countless other black and Latino men in New York.

"Is New York part of a democratic nation? Is it a coincidence that the stop-and-frisk policy was developed under Giuliani, who would not give a second thought to putting into practice a policy that does not protect the democratic right to privacy of people of color? Did he even respect his wife's right to privacy when he brought his mistress to official functions at Gracie Mansion where his wife and children lived? That's a man who had to be told by a judge that his mistress could not visit Gracie Mansion where he, his wife, and children were living. What manner of man would humiliate his wife and children with such behavior? What perverted and self-righteous sense of authority did he possess?"

"Yes, *bambino,* if you ever fall out of love with your future wife, you must always remember to respect her even as you prepare to move on," mom interjected. "It's impossible to disrespect the mother while at the same time respecting and acting in the best interest of any kids you might have together."

I replied, "Don't worry mom. I would never be that evil!"

Dad smiled at me and suggested, "Giuliani was looking at school kids as potential criminals while his police commissioner was the real criminal. He later tried to pass Commissioner Kerik off to President Bush and the nation as the Secretary of Homeland Security. The very man who brought his mistress down to sleep with him near Ground Zero while managing recovery efforts after the terrorist attacks was promoted by Giuliani to President Bush to lead Homeland Security. Kerik reportedly used an apartment reserved for exhausted fire fighters to please his lust with his mistress, Judith Regan. One report indicated he had 'nooners' with various women in the same apartment, while fire fighters, police officers, and volunteers were risking their lives removing toxic substances from the World Trade Center site."

"Dad, what's a 'nooner?'" I asked.

"*Bambino,* that means that he was having sex with various women in the middle of the day before going home to his wife at night," mom answered.

"*Eww!*" I responded. "That's mad stupid and nasty!"

"Yeah, that is mad stupid and nasty, but that's Kerik. Thankfully, just in time, the nation discovered that Bernard Kerik was corrupt and a crook. Bush cut him loose. Kerik should have been placed behind the jail bars Giuliani had reserved for others. The criminal Kerik and the morally corrupt Giuliani arrested teenagers for not paying $2 to get on the subway after leaving school. Meanwhile, Kerik was cheating the government out of taxes and getting $165,000 worth of free home renovations from a company that the government suspects was tied to the mafia. He was Giuliani's police commissioner though he never earned any scholarly diploma beyond a GED," dad declared.

In 2010 reports indicated Kerik was convicted of tax fraud and other crimes during the period he served as Giuliani's commissioner of police. Before his trial, Kerik was able to post bail and remain at home. After conviction he was sentenced to four years in prison. Dad suggested that he is probably doing time in a minimum security prison that allows him catered food and conjugal private visits with women while residing in a specially refurbished cell.

As a black boy in New York City, I had to learn to protect myself from criminals and to protect myself from having encounters with some racist and overzealous police officers. I had learned the lessons mom and dad taught me regarding how to conduct myself when confronted by some members of the police force who adopt and follow racist practices when dealing with blacks and Latinos. Nevertheless, as I sat at the dining table, I decided I would make an even more determined effort to avoid the police.

In 2011 as we worked on editing this book, dad researched the continuing impact of the stop-and-frisk policy in New York City. He discovered the following using the NYPD database, analysis of the data by the Center for Constitutional Rights, and an analysis of news reports:

- The Center for Constitutional Rights reported 1,600,000 New Yorkers were stopped in a period of 3 1/2 years beginning in 2005 (see http://www.ccrjustice.org/stopandfrisk).

- Of those stopped 80 percent were African Americans and Latinos, even though African Americans and Latinos were only 53 percent of New York City's population. Whites were 44 percent of the population but 10 percent of the stops. BTW, if you add in the tourists and the hundreds of thousands of commuters, the white population on any given day would easily surpass the total population of African Americans and Latinos.

- Only 8 percent of all the whites stopped were frisked; however, 85 percent of the African Americans and Latinos stopped were frisked.

- Arrest rates during the period of 2005 through the first half of 2008 were low for all racial groups—between 4 and 6 percent of all NYPD-initiated stops during that period. These figures suggest innocent citizens had nearly 1.5 million encounters with the NYPD on the streets, with police officers using force in tens of thousands of those encounters. It is also possible many of those arrested may have had their cases thrown out due to overzealous policing.

- Only 2.6 percent of stops resulted in the discovery of a weapon or contraband (marijuana, ecstasy, etc.).

Before 2005, the relationship between the police and African Americans and Latinos was already sour due to high-profile police shootings of victims and the manner in which the NYPD interacted with the communities. Thus, there was concern expressed in the law enforcement community that black and Latino jurors were less likely to convict suspects when district attorneys had to heavily rely primarily upon the testimony of police officers.

Although most of the citizens stopped and frisked were allowed to proceed after questioning, up until 2010 the NYPD nevertheless entered their identification into the NYPD database as if they were criminals. The database contained the names, addresses, and social security numbers of hundreds of thousands of citizens who had never committed a crime, mostly young black and Latino men. It was believed to be the only database of its kind in the whole nation and probably the whole world.

According to the *New York Times* and other media, when black and Latino men are stopped, they are often told to empty their pockets. If they comply and are found to have at least one marijuana joint, they are arrested and criminally charged with a misdemeanor for public display of drugs. In 2010, 50,000 people were arrested in New York City on public possession of marijuana, mostly during stop-and-frisk actions.

If the marijuana had remained in their pockets and the cops had searched them, they could only be given a citation or the equivalent of a ticket and not taken to jail. Thus, to get a higher charge, police officers would trick unsuspecting people into showing them the contraband.[5] (I am glad that my close friends and I don't smoke and aren't caught up in that madness.)

In case you live in New York or are visiting, see http://www.nyclu.org/bustcard for information including a palm card produced by the New York Civil Liberties Union regarding ID that should be carried, so that you are not taken to the precinct, and actions that should be taken when stopped by the NYPD. You will be able to download it as an App on your iPhone.

In 2010, State Assemblyman Hakeem Jeffries (an African American) and State Senator Eric Adams (an African American and former NYPD officer) introduced legislation in the New York State Assembly and Senate to destroy the NYPD database. They were joined by white, Latino, and Asian assemblymen, assemblywomen, and senators in successfully getting the legislation passed.

Although Mayor Michael Bloomberg and Police Commissioner Raymond Kelly (who wants to run for mayor to continue the stop-and-frisk policies) vehemently protested, Governor Patterson (an African American) signed the legislation.[6]

When the bill was signed July 16, 2010, Senator Eric Adams commented that the bill protected innocent people from being targeted by the NYPD, especially people of color. He said people should be protected from both aggressive criminal behavior and aggressive police behavior.

It is the police officer's job to protect the community from criminal behavior. Dad says we should appreciate police officers when they perform their roles with respect and professionalism. He also says they should be held accountable when they cross the line. He believes the culture and policies of the NYPD ensure that every day some officers are crossing the line by not being professional or respectful to law-abiding citizens.

You might ask, "How does he know?"

His answer is, "Stop and ask the thousands of innocent New Yorkers who were stopped and frisked yesterday or even at the end of the day of your reading this chapter. It's 2011, and the stop-and-frisk policy remains as active as ever because the legislation allowed the stop-and-frisk policy to continue."

Unfortunately, all the legislation did was to deny the NYPD the opportunity to collect and keep personal data on innocent people who were stopped. It was just reported that the NYPD recorded the largest number of street stops in 2010—a total of 600,601 individuals.

In the 1800s, free African American men and women had to carry papers called a "Certificate of Freedom" to prove they were not enslaved. Bounty hunters, lawmen, and even white civilians were permitted by US federal law to stop a black person on the streets of New York and other northern and southern cities to ask for proof of freedom. If the papers weren't available, a black person could be sent to serve a slave master.

Today, although African American men are no longer enslaved, in New York City it is best that they are not stopped without their papers.

"Sure, we are free," dad says. "But we ain't that free," he adds.

Today, when black and Latino men are stopped and are found not carrying I.D., cops could take the authority to detain them and transport them to a precinct until they could be identified using standards set by the NYPD.

Under Apartheid in South Africa, from the 1950s to almost the release of Nelson Mandela from prison in 1990, black South Africans over age 16 had to carry a passbook to verify their identity, to prove where they lived, and to verify their right to work. If they could not produce the passbook, they were subject to arrest and imprisonment by policemen who were protecting the authority and privilege of Europeans who had invaded and conquered the African country to take control of its diamonds, gold, and other natural resources, which they still own in large part even after the overthrow of Apartheid and the inspirational presidency of Nelson Mandela.

Dad wonders if African Americans in New York City are stopped today at a higher percentage rate than Africans were stopped in South Africa under Apartheid. He says he might never know because he suspects the whites living in South Africa did not make their statistics available. If the law did not require the NYPD to make its statistics available, it would hide them. Nevertheless, dad says he is confident that today Africans are freer to walk the streets in Johannesburg, South Africa, without fear of harassment from the police than the African Americans and Latinos who walk the streets of Brooklyn, the Bronx, Queens, Staten Island, and Manhattan.

In early May 2011 while working on editing the book, dad read a *New York Times* article regarding the new Chancellor of the New York City Public Schools, Dennis Walcott, who is African American and was stopped by the NYPD.

The article stated that Chancellor Walcott was just a few blocks from his home in Cambria Heights, Queens, near midnight when he was stopped. He was being driven home from an earlier meeting in Prospect Heights, Brooklyn, by one of the education department's drivers. When pulled over by two white detectives in plainclothes driving in an unmarked car, he was asked if he was "lost." This was code for, "Why are you in this neighborhood at this time of night with a chauffeur?" Walcott identified himself as the new Chancellor. He had just left his previous position as deputy mayor in the last month.

Walcott had been deputy mayor of New York City for the previous nine years and had often been in the newspapers and on television representing Mayor Bloomberg. But that night he was just a well-dressed black man in the wrong neighborhood in New York City, just a few blocks from his home, with a driver who was part of an official security squad the NYPD provides for chancellors.

When Walcott sought to determine the purpose of the stop, the officers accused the driver of not signaling for a left turn. Walcott told them they were wrong because he had watched the driver signal. The cops ignored the Chancellor and recent deputy mayor. They demanded to see the driver's license and the registration papers for the car. They ran the driver's information through the computers and checked the status of the NYC Official License Plates that identified the car as belonging to the New York City Government.

When everything checked out to their satisfaction, they returned the license and registration papers and told the Chancellor he was "free to go." (He could go, but was he truly "free" in their eyes?) No ticket was given and no apology was offered, not even to a recent deputy mayor. The detectives refused to identify themselves and give their badge numbers to Walcott, even though it is NYPD policy that they do so when asked.

So, if those detectives violated policy when questioned by a black man who weeks earlier had been deputy mayor, what chance would any other black man have of getting them to follow policy? Dad wonders if the two detectives had approached the car with their hands near their holstered guns as had the two cops who had stopped us in our car while driving from a Jay-Z concert in 2010.

It is ironic that Walcott, before becoming deputy mayor, had worked with a former police commissioner on developing training to have officers become more respectful of New York City citizens. Walcott is given credit for helping devise the NYPD slogan that is on every patrol car: "Courtesy, Professionalism and Respect." I guess he got no respect that night for committing the crime of BCWB, being chauffeured while black.

Of course, after Walcott complained to Police Commissioner Kelly, the detectives were put under investigation for failing to identify themselves. Dad suspects the public will never learn the outcome of the investigation since the incident is an inescapable black eye for the department. He suspects there will be a mild reprimand and a continuation of the same policy.[7]

Walcott wasn't the first high-ranking black man to be stopped by New York's "Finest" in executing their stop-and-frisk policy. In 2008, two white police officers confronted another black man in Queens. Douglas Ziegler was sitting in his parked SUV wearing civilian clothes when confronted by the officers. After Ziegler identified himself as an NYPD commander, one of the officers aggressively attempted to enter the SUV but was restrained by his partner.

USA Today reported the officer was disciplined by having his gun and badge taken away and given desk duty for 45 days. Of course, they didn't take away his racist attitude although he was disciplined for being "discourteous."

What makes the case of Ziegler interesting is he was one of the top NYPD commanders at the time of the confrontation, and the parked SUV he was sitting in was issued and owned by the NYPD. Zeigler was chief of the Community Affairs Bureau, the unit responsible for building "respectful and cooperative relationships" with African Americans, Latinos, and other citizens of New York. During that same time, his wife Neldra was the NYPD's deputy commissioner for equal employment opportunity.[8]

Starting at age 10, mom and dad had to tell me to be careful. Dad wonders what the Zieglers, the Walcotts, and other high-ranking black and Latino officials, as well as black and Latino police officers, have had to tell their sons, grandsons, and nephews. He has been told, as I mentioned earlier, that black and Latino officers give their sons and relatives a special decal to display when stopped by police officers so that their sons and relatives would not experience the humiliation that others have had to endure.

Dad asks, "Is the stop-and-frisk policy so-called American justice? Or is it simply Giuliani's, Bloomberg's, and Kelly's New York justice? That so-called New York justice exists while Barack Obama sits in the White House, Eric Holder sits as Attorney General heading the 'Department of Justice,' Sonia Sotomayor sits on the 'Supreme' Court, and the 'French Lady' or 'Statue of Liberty' stands in the harbor holding up her torch calling for *liberté, égalité et fraternité*/liberty, equality and fraternity."

Taking back a line that Cee Lo Green borrowed from the 1960s, dad suggests the question to America is: "Now ain't that some sh**?"

Chapter 16

King David, Ice Cube, and Three Booty Calls

Mom and dad did not believe in teaching me the "prayer" that was taught to them and has been taught for decades to little children in America: "Now I lay me down to sleep. I pray the Lord my soul to keep. If I should die before I wake, I pray the Lord my soul to take."

They said they never understood that prayer as children, and it was never a source of comfort. They said it revealed nothing about God and God's presence with us.

By age 3, dad had begun teaching me the Lord's Prayer and the Psalms 23 and 91. Every night for years he would kneel next to me at bedtime and together we would talk to the Lord. Dad taught me by example not to recite words but to express the prayers and to amend them according to the message we wanted to send forth any particular night.

Dad taught me to pray in a manner of speaking to God and to place my name and the names of family members before God if I had a concern or desire for blessings. For example, this is Psalm 91, as taught to me by dad:

He who dwells in the shelter of the Most High
Who abides under God's wings
Oh Lord I say to You that You are my rock and my fortress
My God in whom I trust

No evil shall ever befall me
Nor shall pestilence come near my tent

For You have given Your angels command about Akhenaton
That upon their wings I shall be lifted up
So that I do not dash my foot against a stone.

I was taught to pray not just for myself, but also for others including family members. So my two sisters and my first cousin Nicole were often in my prayers. Mom says when I was 7 I added my *Titi* Baby to my prayers, without any prompting from her, after visiting *Titi* Baby in the hospital. We also began our ongoing tradition of starting any long road trips with prayer. The prayers were led by me once we locked in our seat belts and pulled out for the long drive to Cape Cod, Florida, Washington, DC, and other places.

At age 3, dad also began to read and explain to me stories from the Bible including the story of David and Goliath. At that point he didn't tell me that King David had also been a Peeping Tom, a lover of booty calls, and the murderer of an innocent man whose wife he had impregnated. I would learn those facts later at the age of 13 during a sermon. As you will see later, those facts helped me to connect the life of King David to Day Day, a character played by Mike Epps in "Next Friday," a hilarious comedy produced by Ice Cube.

When it comes to the Bible and church, dad has never suggested that it's all about being perfect and going to heaven. He says the teachings of Christ are more the gospel about how God calls us to live with one another on earth than it is about a view of heaven. Therefore, our discussions are about how we must live righteously now with all people and how our current living prepares us for future life on this earth that is "consistent with God's will for our lives."

Dad likes to quote Jesus who said there is more rejoicing in heaven when one sinner on earth returns to God than there is rejoicing about 99 people who never went astray. Dad says, "Like David, and later Solomon and Peter, we must all go astray." He suggests we can choose to leave God, but even then God is always right there with us. All we have to do is accept the Presence. We must be the prodigal son who humbly returns home, he suggests.

There are times when I feel like I just can't help myself, just can't keep focused on the things that represent the good and best in me. Why did I tell that lie? Why did I send that text? Why didn't I take care of my responsibility? Why did I detest dad and mom when they questioned me about not taking care of my responsibility? All are questions that have confronted me. I know the difference between right and wrong, but I am not always able to do what is right.

Dad says, "That was true even for the Apostle Paul who brought the Gospel to the people of the world. The Apostle Paul said it was sin working in his body which caused the errors."

Lies have brought me guilt and lack of progress, just the opposite of what I have sought. When I lied in the summer of 2009, leaving every morning pretending to go to Banneker for a math class I needed for graduation, I paid the price that comes with failure. I had to take two additional semesters of math beginning the fall of my senior year. But that was not the biggest consequence. The biggest consequence was getting caught up in the momentum of lying.

In basketball, your team can be more talented than the opposing team. But if your team is overconfident and takes the opposing team lightly, the opposing team might play harder. As the opposing team plays harder, it could gain confidence and momentum. All of its members could begin to overachieve. As they overachieve, their momentum builds and builds and begins to overwhelm the abilities of the better team to respond. That momentum hands the better team an unexpected defeat. You cannot reach out and touch momentum, but you cannot deny its presence as a force that alters real life events.

Life has taught me that lying is a demon with its own momentum. Each day during the summer of 2009 I got caught up in lying's momentum, and each day one lie led to another. Even when I wasn't speaking lies, my actions were a lie. Every day, my actions were a lie. I began to wonder how I could break away from lying's momentum. I wanted to but did not know how. And though my intentions were to defeat what dad expected of me, the momentum of lying seemed to defeat me. Although I got through the whole summer successfully without being discovered by dad, my confidence as a person did not rise, at least not for the person I really wanted to be.

Who wants to stand and be well known for being a good and effective liar? Can I see your hands? Yeah, I thought so. Huh, even professional liars prefer to be considered "truth tellers."

I would love to report that I have thoroughly learned my lesson. I am still learning my lesson. However, I have yet to thoroughly defeat the momentum of lying from that summer and some of the patterns that it has set in motion or reinforced in my life.

Dad says when we focus too much on our mistakes and weaknesses, we hinder our ability to become better men, "the men we were created and called to be." Dad explains it is our sense of guilt that often keeps us focused on our mistakes until that focus overwhelms out thinking. Thus, unbridled guilt becomes a demon that influences wrong thinking that feeds more wrong actions. Unlike Eminem, our demons have us doing jumping jacks. "The demons of guilt and wrong thinking become our jailers, and we become partners in our own imprisonment" according to dad.

Dad suggests that we must, instead, sincerely turn our thinking to rising above our errors and pursuing the best in us. He teaches, "God's grace calls us to swim in truth, not to drown in our errors." Dad says, "As the Psalm 19 teaches, it is impossible for us to even know all of our errors, but God can acquit us of our sins that are even a secret to us and everyone else."

Thankfully, dad and faith are teaching me I must not be a prisoner to my past, current, and future mistakes, which will occur with the rising of the sun. Even when I lie, dad says I must know the Truth is still within me. He suggests, "Christ said you shall know the Truth and the Truth shall set you free."

Dad professes, "The Truth in our spirit is bigger than the demons in our lies, which are nurtured by the desires of our flesh. Money, popularity, notoriety, and a career as a successful rapper or a successful athlete could all be desires of the flesh that could lead to imprisonment by the demons of greed and vanity." He says we have to choose to focus on moving forward with the Truth in our sprit, rather than the demon in our lies.

I'm trying to say, "Amen. True dat."

At 6 months I was christened at Philadelphia Church of Universal Brotherhood by Dr. F. E. Roy Jeffries, the reverend who married mom and dad. Philadelphia is located on Eastern Parkway and Nostrand Avenue in Crown Heights. Worship services at Philadelphia occurred on Saturdays, and we usually attended every Saturday until I was 4, or shortly after the death of Dr. Jeffries. Even after we started worshipping at another church, dad would often play Dr. Jeffries' taped sermons in the car for the next six or seven years, especially when we were taking trips of one or more hours. Dad considered Dr. Jeffries a teaching preacher who brought insight of the Gospel that was often out of reach of the average preacher.

In 1996, we moved on to Bethany Baptist Church in Bedford Stuyvesant. Reverend Dr. William A. Jones was the pastor. We moved to Bethany because Reverend Jones was another great teaching preacher. At the age of 5, I began to enjoy sitting with mom and dad in the services rather than attending Sunday school in another part of the church. Almost every Sunday, for the next five years, we sat in the pews listening to Reverend Jones and the Bethany Choir. Bethany had a great choir, and at Bethany I fell in love with gospel music. Dad would often purchase the tapes of the choir and play them along with Dr. Jones' sermons while driving in the car.

Dr. Jones had been active in the Civil Rights movement and had been a close partner of Dr. Martin Luther King, Jr., especially in Dr. King's efforts to get Baptist churches more deeply involved in the movement. In 1969 when dad was arrested with other members of the Brooklyn College 19, it was Dr. Jones who stepped forward and placed Bethany as collateral to free dad and his friends from Rikers Island. The church building was only two years old in 1969 and was an architectural gem in a community of architecturally distinctive brownstones.

Dad has speculated that Reverend Jones must have used his most charismatic skills to convince the church board to use the church to free 19 kids who neither he nor the members of the church board had ever met.

"They didn't even know if we were Christians when they put up that church to get us out. Two of the Brooklyn College 19 were Muslims and I believe the rest were Christians, but, like me, not regular church-goers at that time," he explained.

Recently, dad read a 1997 article in the *New York Times* which described Dr. Jones' preaching as "a divine symphony played upon the instrument of a human tongue." Dad said Dr. Jones' "divine symphony" moved so many hearts and spirits.

Around my tenth birthday in 2002, Dr. Jones became ill and was often unable to attend service. Dad reluctantly decided to seek a church where there would be many more kids my age actively attending. He wanted me to share the Christian church-going experience with my age group and, at that time, Bethany's membership didn't seem to have many kids in my age group.

We visited Christian Cultural Center in Flatlands, Brooklyn, several times. Dad loved Reverend A. R. Bernard's teaching but came to consider the sanctuary too large. The church seated 6,000-plus members. Today, dad maintains a love affair with Reverend Bernard's preaching by listening to his *Faith in Practice* daily sermons on the Internet. He places the depth of content of Reverend Bernard's teaching at the highest level, equal to that of Drs. Jones and Jeffries. Yet, he still considers Drs. Jones and Jeffries as unmatched masters of Spirit-filled oratory.

After a few months of wandering from church to church, dad heard about Emmanuel Baptist Church in Clinton Hill, Brooklyn. Emmanuel had been built in 1887. In 1997, it had entered the National Register of Historic Places as one of America's best examples of Gothic Revival architecture.

When we started attending regularly in the spring of 2002, the church was entering a period of renovation of the main sanctuary. The sanctuary seats about 500, and the church offers three Sunday worship services. We were attracted to the 10:00 a.m. Sunday service, which drew many young people in their twenties and thirties and lots of pre-teens and teens.

I chose to be baptized soon after I turned 11, and we became members of Emmanuel. Following an inspirational sermon by Reverend Anthony Trufant, the senior pastor, I walked to the front of the church in response to his call to audience members to select Emmanuel as their church home. Mom and dad joined me as I stepped forward. Little did I know that, Sunday after Sunday, they had been waiting for me to make a decision about staying or leaving Emmanuel.

Mom and I were baptized by Reverend Trufant a few weeks later. Although mom had been a practicing Catholic from childhood until a few years after meeting dad, she had never been baptized by being dunked in water as Jesus experienced with John the Baptist. Dad had also been baptized at 11 in a swimming pool by a travelling evangelist during a revival in Swainsboro, Georgia. He, along with several family members, sat in the pews and watched as mom and I were baptized.

Starting in 2002 we established a Sunday morning routine. We would attend church at 10:00 a.m. At noon we would head to downtown Brooklyn and go to either Junior's Restaurant or to the Court Street Cinema. If we went to the cinema first, we would usually go to a restaurant other than Junior's. We loved Lemongrass Grill where I would usually order steak, and mom and dad would order red snapper. During the summers, we would stop at the bakeries along Court Street for semolina and whole wheat loafs, homemade Italian ices, and cookies before returning home. From time to time, the routine would be broken if I had a basketball camp to attend following church service. After basketball camp, Dad would often treat me to the best fried chicken and lemonade in Brooklyn from Mitchell's Soul Food Restaurant on Vanderbilt Avenue in Prospect Heights.

Of course, at age 11, the sermons could be very interesting one Sunday and not as interesting the next Sunday. I always carried my note book and something to read. I had developed the habit of always travelling with books since I was 2. Dad had encouraged this so that I would read while travelling on the subway or bus and at times in the car. When parts of the sermons were not as interesting, I would open my book and read or do homework.

"*Bambino,* close that book," mom would often suggest.

Disagreeing dad would whisper, "Let him be. He is still listening and will absorb the sermon better if he is not forced to listen. The sermon is still penetrating his conscious and subconscious mind. That's better than having him sit there in rebellion."

Thankfully, dad won that argument, but mom would win others. When mom insisted that we not put our coats on in preparation to leave while the pastor prepared to enter the benediction, she got her way. During the Sundays when church seemed to be going on forever and ever, she also got her way. We had to remain respectfully seated, even if the hour for the next service had arrived with members waiting outside in the pouring rain.

Dad had a habit of bringing his *Harper Collins Study Bible* to the service and reading it during parts of certain services, especially when the adult praise dancers would perform. Dad had grown up taking his Bible to church because the Baptist churches he had attended as a child had emphasized reading the Bible. Mom had grown up Catholic and had attended churches where there were no Bibles in the pews, and members were expected to read from missalettes developed by the Catholic Church. At first she was uncomfortable with dad reading during the service. She thought it was disrespectful. Dad said, "All the other men sitting at home reading the "Week in Review" in the *New York Times* or sports in the *Daily News* or still sleeping after spending the night chasing women at the clubs are being disrespectful."

There were also a few times that dad would close his eyes in meditation. He had learned Transcendental Meditation in 1975 and continues to mediate even now. Concerned that others would think he was asleep and being disrespectful when his head would start to nod at times, mom would elbow him while whispering, "Askia, wake up!"

Dad would growl clearing his throat and whisper, I am awake. I was listening and my meditation was just releasing pent up stress from work this week." Sometimes that "pent up stress" had his head bopping up and down as if he were asleep. After a few Sundays, she finally learned to leave him alone. He's a stubborn man.

My father was also in the habit of not following a certain direction from the pulpit. He was not into following directions when anyone from the pulpit would say, "Turn to your neighbor on you right and tell them...." He thought it was a useless gimmick. He couldn't imagine Christ using that gimmick. He felt it would be more productive to have a few minutes of the sermon devoted to small group discussions about some aspect of the sermon. When Emmanuel adopted the latter practice for certain sermons, he was happy to participate.

Many of those Sunday sermons and services were great for each of us. At every service, we started with a period of greeting members. Mom, dad, and I always began by "greeting" each other with a big hug and a kiss. Those were special loving moments for each of us. Then we were off around the church greeting others and expressing love. Dad always looked for Miss Linda Patterson and her mother. Miss Patterson was a principal and colleague. She and her mom always wore large rimmed fancy hats and beautiful dresses as if every Sunday were Easter Sunday. You could easily spot them from clear across the sanctuary. They always wore smiles as well.

Emmanuel had a super choir, Total Praise. The choir had more than 100 voices accompanied by musicians on the piano, organs, saxophones, guitars, cellos, and violins. The choir director was Pastor Frank Edmundo Haye, a black Latino of Panamanian ancestry. He was a former assistant conductor of the world-renowned Boys Choir of Harlem. Under his leadership, Total Praise sang contemporary and traditional gospel. The choir also sang many songs that were written by choir members. The choir incorporated hip hop and jazz into the music in a manner to reach young audiences with the message of the gospel. Several of the singers and musicians had worked alongside popular artists including Patti LaBelle, Yolanda Adams, Stephanie Mills, Bilal, Common, and Lalah Hathaway.

In December 2002, Total Praise released their first CD, *Total Praise Live*. My parents and I attended the Christmas concert where the music on the CD was performed. We instantly fell in love with the hip hop gospel of the song "Magnify Him" and the testimony of the sister who was the featured soloist on "Another Chance." "Another Chance" would later become the song that would always get my father out of his seat in all the services where it would be performed. He said it touched him deeply by reminding him of the many chances God had given him. He often struggled to hold back the tears as he would join in the singing.

Total Praise Live was nominated for a Grammy which represented a remarkable achievement for a choir that was still in the early stages of its formation. In an April 2003 issue of *Vibe,* Tom Terrell reviewed the CD and wrote: "There are few things on earth as soul satisfying as a gospel choir caught up in the rapture—especially if that choir is the Emmanuel Baptist Church of Brooklyn's Total Praise. Imagine 123 choralists, six soloists, one rapper, a classical string ensemble, and a jazzy 13-piece band that can make any secular R&B, Latin, soul, funk, or hip hop riff feel like God's own glorious groove."

Dad and mom suggest that Pastor Haye is a master of connecting our spirit to the praise of the living God. I agree.

For 18 years, my spirit has been enriched with music that I can call to the surface when I need it. Sometimes it's Total Praise, Kurt Franklin, and Yolanda Adams. Sometimes it's Coltrane and Earth, Wind & Fire. Sometimes it's Stevie Wonder, Michael Jackson, and Usher. Sometimes it's Bob Marley and Kassav. Sometimes it's J. Cole, Lupe, Jay-Z, R. Kelly, and Eminem. Whatever it is, it is a resource deep within which helps me to regain focus and confidence.

I can send a message of confidence and success to myself as I am singing Yolanda Adams' "Victory" and Eminem's "Not Afraid," one gospel and one hip hop.

By the time I was almost 14 in 2006, Emmanuel had selected a new youth minister, Reverend Shareka Newton. Reverend Newton looked as if she were in her mid-20s. I immediately fell in love with her sermons because she has a way of connecting the Bible to what is going on now in the lives of young people. She doesn't front about being perfect. She lets you know that she has been to clubs with friends and gives the impression that she might still be going to parties once in a while. She gives the impression that she has made mistakes selecting male and female friends. She lets you know that she has not always put forth her best academically. She lets you know that it is in the midst of living with mistakes and bad choices that we are able to hear God's voice, sometimes even when we don't know that we are listening. She says, "God has a way of getting our attention."

Reverend Newton has a great speaking voice, and she's funny. She is a wonderful storyteller. Dad and mom say it's obvious she puts a lot of study into the preparation of her sermons. Her stories are often about life situations that occurred with her friends in high school and in college. As a teenager, I can easily understand her stories because I have had similar experiences or know someone who has had similar experiences. I believe she tells the stories because they show that the messages of the Bible are important to us as we live our lives today.

Once in a while, Reverend Newton will use the language of hip hop or tell the story of the mistakes made by popular musicians, movie stars, and athletes to make a point for the young people. She might also cite a scene from a television series like Judge Mathis to make a point about men getting caught in baby mama drama. She lets you know that lustful and simple thinking can land you into damaging and complex situations.

During one sermon, she told the story of King David of Israel and Bathsheba and how the two tried to "play" Uriah, Bathsheba's husband. She explained that David was taking a stroll on the rooftop of the palace one night. While casually strolling, he peeped through a nearby window and spotted Bathsheba taking a bath. Bathsheba was a dime with a face and body that turned David on. Being king, David had her brought to the palace for what my boyz would say is a booty call. That night, he forgot about all the many other personal wives and concubines he had in the palace.

In David's arms, Bathsheba became pregnant. David quickly sent for Uriah at the battlefield. He wanted to have Uriah come home to be with his wife before her pregnancy was obvious so that Uriah would think that he was the father. He told Uriah he had been fighting too long against Israel's enemies and needed a break to go home and be with his wife. He brought Uriah home, but Uriah could not bring himself to be with his wife while other Israelites were dying on the battlefield. As a man of valor, he could not enjoy making love to his wife while his band of brothers was out defending Israel.

So David decided to get Uriah drunk hoping that would inflame Uriah's passions to sleep with his wife. Even drunk, Uriah kept his principles and slept in the servants' quarters away from Bathsheba.

With Uriah refusing to be with his wife, David needed to come up with another plan. His new plan was to send Uriah back to battle with a sealed note to the commander. The note ordered Joab, the commander, to allow Uriah to lead the charge against the enemy troops and to have all the men fall back when Uriah was near the enemy line so that Uriah would be slain. Being a loyal subject, Uriah didn't even look to see what was written. Uriah died. As soon as a respectable period of mourning had passed, David married Bathsheba with the two looking forward to the birth of the baby.

However, the Prophet Nathan told David that he would not be blessed with the baby as a consequence of his sin. The baby died. David and Bathsheba mourned the death. David wrote Psalm 51 asking God to cleanse him of his sin:

Be gracious to me O God, according to your loving kindness;
According to the greatness of your compassion blot out my
transgressions.
Wash me thoroughly of my iniquity
And cleanse me of my sin....

Despite his sins and weaknesses, David sought to repent in his heart and asked God not to take his Spirit away. God ultimately blessed David and Bathsheba with Suleiman (Solomon, "the wise").

Dad pointed out that the king of Israel was involved in a "booty call" and "baby mama drama." He said Israel's greatest king had committed murder. He declared David could not escape paying for his sins, but managed to pray for and receive Grace.

When Reverend Newton told that story, she also spoke about how some women today trick some men into believing they are the fathers of the babies of other men. After she completed the story of Bathsheba "playing" Uriah, my thoughts went to D'Wana "playing" Day Day in "Next Friday," a movie written and produced by Ice Cube. When we arrived home that Sunday, we popped the video tape into the VCR.

In the 2000 movie Day Day (Mike Epps) is being "played" by D'Wana (Tamala Jones). She is short, with a big pregnant belly that causes her to walk real funny like a duck. D'Wana appears at Day Day's home and begins to "key" his new car because Day Day is denying that he is the father of her unborn baby. From the living room Craig (Ice Cube) calls upstairs to Day Day to let him know the girl is keying his ride.

Day Day runs outside with the court's order of protection to confront the girl, and she sprays what seems like a full pint of pepper spray all into his eyes. She tells him that he had better live up to his responsibility to her and "his baby." Then, with her stomach stretched so far out that it forces her to walk like a duck, she leaves warning that she will be back with reinforcement.

As Day Day rolls in pain on the ground, his father uses a water hose to spray water into his eyes causing him to practically drown. When Day Day gets up, in a voice expressing deep frustration, he tells his cousin Craig the girl's accusations are ridiculous. With his eyes still stinging and his frustration boiling over, his crying statement to Craig went something like this:

> Man, that broad is crazy! I met her less than three months ago. I was back in the old hood looking for some fancy twenties (rims) for my car, the kind you can only find in the hood. I saw her walking holding that famous L.A. hamburger and I wanted a bite. So I pulled over and stopped to talk with her. She had a little "pudge" in her stomach. I thought she was cute so I overlooked the "pudge," thinking it was probably baby fat, plus I wanted a bite of that hamburger that I had missed since moving to the suburbs after hitting the lottery. So I said a little something something and I tapped that. That was just three months ago. Next thing I know, she is telling me that she is more than six months pregnant with my baby. Her stomach is so way out there that baby can't be mine! Now why did y'all just stand by and let her key my real baby (the car)?

Of course, the scene is hilarious. Every time I think of it I bust out laughing. For a bite of hamburger, he gets involved in a booty call. LOL! He saw a "pudge" and thought it was "baby fat."

The real star of "Next Friday" for me, mom, and dad was Jacob Vargas. He played the role of Joker, the leader of a band of three drug-dealing Chicano brothers. When confronting Craig and Day Day, Joker constantly used "*ese*" in the way my Uncle Eddie, a Bronx Puerto Rican, would use "yo, bro." When we first saw the movie in 2000, we were not familiar with the use of "*ese*" by some Chicanos on the West Coast to refer to guys. Vargas' use of "*ese*" fascinated us. His use of "*ese*" seemed so fresh and mad cool. So "*ese*" quickly became a word that we would use often in conversation around the house in the weeks immediately after our first viewing of the movie.

For example, dad while talking to me after dinner would say, "*Ese*, take out the garbage." When he could hear my music, although I had on my earphones, he would say, "*Ese*, turn that music down!" When it was time to get out of the shower, he would say, "*Ese,* get out of that shower now!" When it was time to put away the video games, he would say, "*Ese*, put that crap away and do your homework!"

In "Next Friday" Vargas kept us laughing hysterically with his crazy antics including the time he jumped into bed with a girl as if he were diving into a swimming pool. As he dove in, he screamed, "I am an Aztec warrior!" In reality, he was really a little dude (about 5 feet 5 inches and 130 pounds) with a big ego. He should have been embarrassed appearing on the screen standing in a girly type Brazilian bikini thong underwear which did not cover his butt cheeks fully.

His lack of embarrassment is what made that booty call scene gross and really funny.

Aztec warrior? I don't think so. Was he an embarrassment to Aztec warriors? Yeah, and all of their descendants *en todas partes de Mejico, en todas partes de los Estados Unidos, y en todas partes del universo/*in all parts of Mexico, in all parts of the United States, and in all parts of the universe.

Imagine a king, chosen by God to rule Israel, becoming a Peeping Tom which led to a booty call and then murder. Imagine Mike Epps wanting a bite of hamburger and finding himself in a booty call. Not too difficult. Imagine Jacob Vargas showing his ridiculous butt cheeks while diving into bed for a booty call. *Eww!* Close your eyes. Believe me, you don't want to see that!

Dad says men and women do the most stupid things just to have booty calls, often with complete strangers. He says after the glow of the booty call has left, dull and ugly drama usually arrives.

Moral of the story: no booty calls, and please keep your pants on!

Chapter 17

Soke and Self-Defeating Demons

Do you remember that song about Kung Fu fighting? Well, my father thinks his feet are as fast as lightning. When your father thinks he has it going on as a Kung Fu man, then you must expect to be drawn into the ring.

My father's father was a prize fighter on the side. My father was too young to attend the fights, but his older brother Willie told him of that history. Dad told me he must have inherited that fighting spirit from his father because from his elementary school years dad had a reputation for being a tough and fearless puncher as well as a brilliant scholar. Dad wanted the same for me and practically from birth he was preparing me to be a Kung Fu warrior.

Starting when I was about 6 months old, dad would put me in the baby carrier and walk to Prospect Park. At Prospect Park, with me still in the baby carrier on his back, dad would slowly practice Northern Shaolin, Tai Chi, and Qi Gong forms. As I grew older, he would put me in the jogging stroller, run the four miles around the park, and then stop to practice the forms as I sat and watched. As I neared my second birthday, we began our annual summer road trips to Cape Cod. On the bicycle trail, he would push me for miles in the jogging stroller and stop as we reached Coast Guard Beach to take time to practice the forms as I again watched from the stroller. Once I began to walk, I would at times rise and attempt to follow his movements. Mom was often there to photograph or video my attempts.

When I turned 7, dad started to search for a martial arts school. He wanted a school for me that would teach me discipline and self-defense so that I could walk the streets of New York with confidence and the appropriate caution to avoid places or situations where conflict was likely to arise. During 1999, there had been an increase in rumored gang activity in certain neighborhoods around schools in New York. Dad was keenly aware because, as the community superintendent of schools in Harlem, he had to respond to various rumors of potential gang encounters at school dismissals.

Generally, the rumors were about potential rumbles involving the gangs that carried the names of West Coast gangs but had no affiliation with the gangs on the West Coast, according to dad. He said the members were mostly wannabes or posers who could be "stupidly dangerous" but not nearly on the scale of the LA gangs with the drive-by shootings. Often the rumors were nothing more than kids spreading threats that were overheard by members of the Division of School Safety who then sent out an alarm to principals and administrators.

Dad had survived the means streets of New York, and when I turned 7 he began earnestly preparing me to do the same. In selecting a martial arts teacher, mom and dad wanted someone who would be firm with me and teach me how to control and direct the "unbridled intense energy" I possessed. They also wanted a black man who would also serve as a role model.

On Vanderbilt Avenue near Prospect Place they discovered Scorpion Martial Arts. Scorpion Martial Arts was located in a brightly lit storefront that had many trophies in the windows. Today that storefront is occupied by Namaskar Health (products and education), owned by the long-revered Bob Law and his wife, Muntu. Scorpion Martial Arts has moved on to another location outside of Prospect Heights.

At 7 years old, I was placed under the guidance of Sensei Soke Majid. Sensei Soke was a Fifth Dan Black Belt. He was in his late twenties, 6 feet, and 170 pounds of pure muscle. He had a wicked axe kick, and his powerful punches were delivered with blinding speed. He would enter boxing and kick boxing competitions and knock out his opponents long before Mixed Martial Arts became a craze.

Soke was intense and disciplined. Like dad, he was a storyteller. During every class for the next three years he had a story about life which he wanted us to understand as much as he wanted us to learn to block, kick, and punch. He would take about 10 minutes of each one-hour class to tell a story after we sat following an intense workout. Initially, I was antsy and found it difficult to focus completely on his lectures. However, I tried my best to remain seated and appear focused. I did not want to be called out to do additional pushups while the other students looked on.

With his lectures, Soke attempted to help me understand that my main enemy would be myself, and that I had to learn to defeat my own weaknesses and the self-defeating demons of my desires and of my own ego. At 7, I was a bit clueless about what it would mean to see myself as my own principal enemy, and I am still unable to fully understand.

Soke taught that we were learning to fight so that we would never or rarely have to fight. He said we would be able to walk away from conflicts without throwing a punch. He declared the highest example of the warrior was being able to walk away when you know you could beat a persistent enemy. He taught that we would know we were the better men and women without having to prove it with our skills. He said our opponents would be happy to let us walk away because they would have sensed we were more powerful, mentally as well as physically.

Soke taught that there are three types of a people in the world: those who watch things happen, those who let things happen, and those who make things happen. He taught there were three enemies I must fear most: "I," plus "I," and "I." He said that "I" was my most elusive enemy, and the only one capable of defeating me. He said most men go to their graves having been defeated by their "I." He said the first trick "I" play is to have what is worthless appear as treasure for my heart, mind, and body. He said that "I" tempt me through the five senses beginning with what "I" see, hear, taste, smell, and touch.

Soke counseled: "A true martial artist in the Scorpion system is not concerned with titles; he is only concerned with consistent improvement on every level of existence in life every day. This is the highest art to learn in the Scorpion system. This is the art of Self-Discipline."

Understanding the mental aspects of martial arts was initially beyond my reach, but I listened and absorbed for a later day because next to dad, Soke was my hero. That later day is still on its way. Dad wanted that day to arrive at least two years ago when he had to endure an intense period of my "junioritis" during my junior year in high school.

At age 7 with Soke, my most immediate concern was to learn to throw punches and kicks. I quickly demonstrated I was pretty good with throwing punches and kicks, and blocking and side-stepping those coming at me.

By age 10, I wore a size 11 shoe. I was nearly 5 feet 6 inches and 120 pounds. In early December 2002, Scorpion Martial Arts participated in the 18th Ryu Reinshi-Dan Tournament in Westchester County. This was a prestigious tournament that drew martial arts schools from all of metropolitan New York.

The referees were not from New York City, and Soke cautioned us they had a reputation for not giving earned points to New York City kids. We were counseled, "Therefore, when you kick or punch, leave nothing to the imagination. Make sure the other kids feel it so they cannot deny that it happened."

Of course, we were also counseled to always follow the rules and to fight fairly. Concerning katas, we were advised to deliver our moves with intensity and precision, because it was even easier for the referees to deny points for maneuvers in the katas. (A kata is a choreographed series of fighting movements, with stepping and turning, while trying to maintain perfect form.)

I would compete in the 10- to 11-year-old age group since I had just turned 10 a week earlier. Panther, our fiercest warrior, who had already developed a winning reputation, would compete in the 14- to 15-year-old age group.

In preparation for the tournament, beginning in October 2002 dad would take me at least twice a week downstairs to the gym in our complex. His goal was to build my endurance and to have me practice the techniques Soke was teaching during the three classes I attended each week. Dad was also interested in having me perfect the stepping and turning moves he had taught as a Northern Shaolin teacher.

In 2002, dad would carry a case of CDs to play while we went through our routine. The iPod had started to be sold a year earlier in October 2001, but dad would not purchase one until 2003 to use for our continuing routines in the gym. Dad was always at least a year behind in purchasing new technologies.

Dad would usually begin by playing a collection of Motown hits to get our routine started. The first hit up was usually "Please Mr. Postman" by the Marvelettes. As the music played, dad would have me work out in a space that was about 10 feet by 10 feet. I would begin dancing and circling à la Muhammad Ali as I threw kicks and punches at an imaginary opponent. My heart rate would quickly rise. I would have to maintain a consistent pace during the entire two and a half minutes of the song. If I showed laziness, I could expect dad to enter the space and challenge me with kicks and punches. Therefore, with a healthy fear of dad's ability to challenge me, I kept my intensity up.

The next song up was usually "Heatwave" by Martha and the Vandellas. "Heatwave" would set a blistering pace, and dad would join me in the ring as my competitor. My heart rate would kick up to another level to match my rising anxiety. I would wonder if dad would be compassionate or unreasonably demanding. He would often moderately punch and kick and block me as I would him, while trying to suppress my anxiety. Dad would generally pull his punches and kicks, but there were times when I would stumble into a few.

When I did, dad was unapologetic. He seemed altogether detached emotionally from our activity. His attitude about me running into a punch or kick was, "A fall in the pit, a gain in the wit." Therefore, I tried my best to use my wit not to fall into the pit too often.

Throughout the nearly three minutes of "Heatwave," we would move with the music. We would step, spin, and dance, adding foot moves and fighting techniques from Alan Lee's Northern Shaolin Kung Fu Wu Su, a system dad had taught in his mid-20s.

For nearly 30 minutes following "Heatwave," we would continue moving with various songs including Bob Marley's "Exodus," Kassav's "Rete," Youssou N'Dour's "Set," the Jacksons' "Torture," Con Funk Shun's "Got to Be Enough," the Eagles' "Hotel California," and Willie Colon's "*Calle Luna Calle Sol.*" After each song, or after about three minutes if the songs were longer, he was usually kind enough to give me a 30- to 45-second break before moving on to the next. He would use those 30 to 45 seconds to talk to me about techniques and discipline as he demonstrated techniques. I would listen and attempt to regulate my breathing.

I fell in love with Kassav during our routine and would sing the words in the shower some mornings even though I couldn't translate the French Creole. A few years later when I was at Video Game Creation Camp, I was pleased when mom and dad called me from the Sounds of Brazil Club in Manhattan. They were at an evening performance of Kassav and used the cell phone so that I could hear Kassav as they danced to the music. Also, a few years later when we visited Old San Juan, mom was quick to remind me of Willie Colon's song when we walked on *Calle Luna* and *Calle Sol* in Old San Juan.

In addition to those songs, there were a few songs with moderately slower rhythms. When the slower ones would come up, I would have an opportunity to catch my breath a bit before the ones with faster rhythms, like Jimi Hendrix's "Along the Watchtower," would have me breathing deeply again. By the end of the 30 minutes, I would usually be near exhaustion, but I couldn't show it because I feared that Dad would unreasonably keep going much longer.

During one session, I showed I was a bit tired and unfocused. Dad was quick to notice. "What's on your mind?" he asked with that determined look in his eyes that told me I had better carefully choose my response. He had a way of positioning his eyelids so that they were practically shut but open just enough to let you know that his eyes were focused on nothing else but you and your potential response.

"Dad, I'm okay," I remarked as I tried to step up my pace.

"Well you can't be okay if you are moving as if your mind is elsewhere!"

With his retort I attempted to adjust my facial expressions and add more force to my kicks, blocks, and punches and I attempted to step and spin more briskly. I was hoping that he would be satisfied.

However, I knew that I had failed to convince him when he gave me that look again as he started to play the Gap Band's "Oops, Upside Your Head" which is nearly nine minutes long. Within seconds he was in the "ring" with me as he threw more intense punches and kicks that I had to block and counter. I thought that he would make me fight him the entire song, but when my attitude, punches, and kicks took a step up, he let me go after three minutes into the song. That experience was enough to convince me to stay focused every time we entered the gym.

If dad was ever tired, he never showed it. For an old man he seemed tireless and young. I was a bit impressed and a bit concerned.

Usually after the fighting dance routine, dad would give me a break to drink water and to sit for five minutes in meditation. Those were minutes of relief. Afterwards, it was time to practice my katas, especially Kata #4 which I would use in the upcoming tournament. I would get up, look at dad, and have to quickly forget he was there to totally focus on the kata. An abbreviated version of Scorpion Kata #4 went something like the following:

- Bow and say "ush."
- Move into a left cat stance with knife hands.
- Strike with left knife hand to throat, punch straight fist to face, left fist to stomach.
- Jump into a flying right front kick to the face.
- Throw right and left punches to the stomach.
- Launch a spinning backwards right wheel kick to the face.
- Turn right 90 degrees, step into a bow and arrow stance, block and three straight punches to the midsection.
- Jump, delivering two hammer fists to the face.
- Launch a right leg, 360 degree sweep and rise.
- Step in horse stance, low block with right arm, upper block, right side kick, left roundhouse kick.
- Turn left, 180 degrees into cat stance, jumping right front kick, left roundhouse kick.

- Step back into horse stance, side kick with left leg, right roundhouse kick to face.

- Launch spinning wheel kick with right foot to opponent's face, three straight punches.

- Block opponent's counter with sweeping right circle leg sweep, step up into a left back kick to chest.

- Spin and throw right roundhouse kick to face.

- Face opponent and throw three more punches to face, gut and groin.

- Deliver spinning left wheel kick to opponent's face, shout "keyah!"

- Kneel on right knee, ceremonial low block with left hand, punch three times.

- Stand, bow and say "ush!"

After the katas, I was usually on the treadmill to complete a mile at a slight incline. Dad would start me at a slow pace and increase the pace gradually. Toward the end, he would have me running at a blistering pace for 60 seconds, followed by a three-minute cool down. As I cooled down, I often looked forward to going upstairs to Yu-Gi-Oh! and my GameCube. After the cool down, dad would send me upstairs, and he would stay downstairs for 90 minutes of his own practice. I was usually pleased to be leaving and satisfied with the practice.

Mom was not a big fan of how I smelled after arriving soaked from the gym. "Take a shower, and put your clothes in the washing machine," was her usual demand.

With Soke's teaching and dad's support, I was ready for my first real competition at the tournament. I had learned to look both tigers in their eyes and find my inner strength and confidence. I felt as though we were a team. I had learned to act with strength and courage when anxiety threatened to engulf me like the powerful waves that get the best of surfers. My heart beat with the rhythm of rising pride. I eagerly looked forward to representing my dojo and my family. I put my swag on before I fully knew what swag was.

When we arrived at the tournament site that Sunday, there were hundreds of kids getting ready to compete. The tournament was held in the gym of a local college that provided enough space for as many as 10 competitions to be played at the same time. As the competitions got underway, my parents and my friends' parents circulated within the gym to support the kids from Scorpion Martial Arts as they competed. Every competitor wore protective gear, including martial arts boxing gloves and a helmet so that no one would have a serious injury.

At the beginning, there were many complaints about unfair scoring. Nevertheless, the Scorpion Martial Arts kids were winning almost all of their competitions. The gym was noisy with parents screaming, "Punch him, kick him, block him!" and other commands to their children. Some of the parents seemed more excited than the kids who were competing. When kids failed to execute as the parents commanded, the parents would further deflate the spirit of the kids with criticism at the end of the matches.

As instructed, my parents and the parents of my dojo avoided giving commands. They left all the coaching to Soke and his assistants. I think that approach enabled us to relax and focus better. I would learn later when I got involved in competitive basketball that the presence and directions of some parents would often cause some of my teammates to perform significantly below their abilities.

Before my competition, we had the opportunity to watch Panther in his 14- to 15-year-old age group competition. As usual, Panther was dominant. He had this crouching technique from which he would spring delivering back fists to the face of the stunned opponent. Seeing him fight strengthened my motivation. With each devastating move he made, my heart rate would rise as if I were in the match. As I watched him circle his opponent, I felt as if I were circling as well. When he finished, I rose and went to an area where I could mentally reconstruct in my mind a few moves he had made that I thought could be helpful in my competition.

Soke's nickname for me was "Oak" as in oak tree. He said I was "strong and unmovable." Although I had just turned 10 a week earlier, Soke brought my birth certificate so that there would be no questions about my eligibility to fight in the 10- to 11-year-old age group. I was tall with big feet.

Early in my first match, I delivered a devastating side kick with my size 11 foot that sent my opponent out of the ring and out of the competition. During my second match, I delivered devastating punches and an axe kick that even a decade later my opponent is probably still trying to determine where it came from.

The competition would supposedly get stiffer as I went up in the matches because I would face opponents who had won their previous matches. So, before the third match, I took a moment to relax and refocus.

When I fought the third competitor, I stuck out my long arm and placed my right hand on his forehead. My 11-year-old competitor swung furiously at me, but I was always out of reach as his short arms continued to hit nothing but air. The scene was funny, but I was not laughing. After about three seconds of having my right hand on his forehead, I would remove it. With my hand removed, he would attempt to get closer but I would step back and put my left hand on his forehead. Again, with my hand on his head controlling his forward momentum, he would swing wildly. After about three seconds, I would remove my left hand. With my left hand removed, he would attempt to get closer only to be stunned by side, round, and axe kicks.

For the championship round, I faced an 11-year-old who was close to being 12 years old. He was as tall as me and at least 20 pounds heavier. Against him I shifted toward speed. I sprang forward, grabbed his collar, and pulled him into a devastating back fist. As I landed, I quickly sent front kicks to his stomach which were followed by jumping roundhouse kicks to his head gear. I kept him from gaining any kind of fighting rhythm with my quick fighting moves and use of the circling step techniques Soke and dad had taught me. My opponent was accustomed to fighting in straight lines, moving back and forward at 180 degrees. With me circling, he had no clue where to deliver a blow or where my next blow would come from.

I won the fighting championship and received a trophy two and a half feet tall. My heartbeat was still elevated when the trophy was presented. Soke stood next to me, and mom snapped a photograph. I felt as tall as Soke in spirit.

When it was time for the kata competition, I observed katas that were incredibly simple being performed in my age group. None of the kids incorporated flying kicks or spin moves the way I would. None of their katas had as many varied moves as my kata. They were playing it safe, while I had selected a kata with a very high degree of difficulty to execute.

As my competitors went through their katas, they performed well. They delivered their katas with intensity and accuracy. Anyway, I thought their katas were boring because they moved like robots in straight lines stepping, kicking, blocking, and punching. When they turned stiffly to move in another direction, they would proceed in a straight line often repeating the same moves they had performed in the previous direction. The referees gave them high scores.

When I got up for my kata, all eyes were on me because of the way I had won the fighting competition. Amazingly, I was able to look past everyone and "enter" my kata. I circled, jumped, and spun in the air, delivering imaginary punches and kicks with precision. As I finished, I could hear Soke and dad screaming with excitement. When it was announced I had won first place for the kata competition, my parents and teammates gathered around in celebration.

Dad was more excited about the kata trophy than the fighting trophy. He said it showed that I had internalized the techniques and the spirit of the martial arts. "You entered yourself and threw out the demons of fear and doubt," he proudly announced to anyone in earshot of us.

In all, Scorpion Martial Arts captured over 16 trophies that day, more than any other participating school. Panther had won two first-place trophies, while adding to a widespread reputation as an untouchable martial artist. Nikosa Majid, Soke's daughter, had won two and was on her way to becoming well known for her form in katas and fighting. I was the "Oak" that ironically had chopped down quite a few trees while winning two trophies.

At the next class at Scorpion Martial Arts, we brought in all the trophies for display. Soke had us sit as he talked about his pride in the discipline and courage we had displayed. He presented a brief story about each of us as our parents sat listening. When he got to me he told the following (mom's paraphrase):

> You know when Akkie, when Oak, first came here he was just
> one ball of fiery undisciplined energy. He couldn't sit still in class
> for one minute. It was as if he had just had three cups of coffee.
> That energy was always ready to get him going. I had to be hard
> on him just to get him to sit still. Now look at him two years
> later. You wouldn't know that he is the same kid. Look at him sit.
> He's focused. He's disciplined. He listens. You know, I tell you
> guys a lot of stories, and you say I talk too much. You may not
> understand many of the things I say now, but you will understand
> later. When you are caught in certain situations, you will deal with
> them successfully and look back and say, that's what Soke was
> trying to teach me.

As I listened to Soke, I was filled with pride. To me, Soke was super special. To have him compliment me was very satisfying. I had worked hard and had earned the compliments of a man who, at first, caused me a lot of anxiety. I had to learn to act with focus in the midst of the anxiety. I had to learn not to focus on my mistakes but, rather, to focus on improving. I had begun to understand that the enemy I had to defeat was me.

For the longest time dad has told me to never say that I am unable or cannot do something in particular. Instead, he counsels that it is always more important to say with meaning, "I must learn" to do something in particular. He says when you say you cannot, your subconscious mind hears that, and you are setting yourself up for failure. However, when a person says "I must learn," the subconscious mind hears that and helps the individual move toward success. I had begun to learn that lesson on a practical level with Soke in Scorpion Martial Arts.

Dad further explained that there are five kinds of people in the world when it comes to succeeding in accomplishing something of lasting value. "First, there are the many who never try. Second, there are the many who try, fail, and give up. Third, there are the few who try and often fail, yet they keep on trying. Fourth, there are the few who try and often fail until they succeed and are satisfied. Fifth, there are fewer who try, often fail and finally succeed, but then are not satisfied as they move on to higher challenges. Ali is a great example of the fifth type, and his failures, successes, and continuing passion are not just reflected in boxing."

Since my experiences with Soke, I have had plenty of mental challenges where I have had to use what he taught. For example, Soke taught that most folks know where trouble could be found and that it is best to avoid such locations, if possible. So in September, 2010, in my first month on campus at Hampton, I was invited to a party in an apartment opposite the campus. When I arrived, I noticed what appeared to be 500 people attempting to crowd into a two-bedroom apartment. Although I really wanted to dance and get to know people, I understood the party contained a recipe for potential trouble. So I did what Soke would have instructed. I didn't bother to go in. Instead, I left and went with a friend to a nearby Burger King.

I have also had a few physical challenges which required his teachings. One of the first came during my freshman year at Benjamin Banneker Academy. It occurred when my friend David and I were walking home from school in September, 2006. As we crossed Atlantic Avenue heading south on Vanderbilt Avenue, we could see a posse of 10 teenaged African American and Latino boys and girls crossing unto our side of the street and walking toward us. Sensing they were looking for trouble, we thought of crossing to the other side but we quickly figured that would only provoke them to chase us. So we walked straight ahead hoping to avoid eye contact.

Before we could reach them, they charged us. I wondered if it were possible for them to hear our thumping heartbeats and smell our fear the way they say dogs are able to smell fear. A small group knocked my friend to the ground and started to punch and kick him. Meanwhile, the rest surrounded me. Although it had been two years since my last class with Soke, I had the choice between allowing my fears to beat me and finding a way to beat my fears. Thankfully, Soke's teachings rose up within me even as the fears refused to relinquish total control of my mind.

As instructed by Soke, I would show no fear and, most of all, not allow them to get me pinned on the ground. As I rediscovered the side kicks and punches that I had once delivered in competitions, I was able to keep them at bay. A few had a taste of my size 13 sneakers. As I gathered further strength and courage, I reached down and pulled David up to his feet. Then we began running after I threw a few more kicks and punches at the strangers who had attacked us just so that they could have some fun. They pursued us about a half block and stopped. I guess they figured some other innocent victims would soon come along for their sort of entertainment.

All of this had happened as scores of cars and even public buses passed us on one of the busiest intersections of Brooklyn. No one honked a horn or attempted to intervene. No one came out of any of the businesses nearby. No one called the cops. It is ironic that this incident happened on almost the exact spot on Vanderbilt where the cops would stop and search me a few weeks later for running home to urinate.

At home I told mom and dad about the fight. They took me that afternoon to the 58th Precinct to place a police report. The precinct is a block from our apartment, yet the officers casually said they could not look into the attack or seek to prevent others since Vanderbilt Avenue was two blocks east of their precinct's boundary line. They suggested we go two miles east to another precinct to file a report asking cops to look out for gangs of kids attacking other kids on Vanderbilt Avenue at school dismissal.

Dad and mom knew it was highly unlikely that officers from a precinct physically that far away would bother to come to Vanderbilt Avenue to ensure kids receive safe passage home. So the next day they reported it to Banneker's principal to encourage the principal to warn the kids to be careful going home.

Following my encounter on Vanderbilt Avenue, dad told me how proud he was I had handled my business and had helped my friend. He said he hoped that one day I would return to Martial Arts classes, and he was sorry we had lost contact with Soke who had closed the dojo and moved. Dad said it was important to walk the streets with confidence, and that is why he had placed me in Scorpion Martial Arts. Then he told me of a confrontation he had with a gang in Harlem at the age of 15 that had taught him the importance of skills for self-defense.

When dad arrived in New York in June 1965, street gangs could be found in most neighborhoods. The gang life as depicted in "West Side Story" was mild compared to real gang activity in all five boroughs of New York City and among most racial and ethnic groups. Dad knew to be cautious in avoiding contact with the gangs but did not know quite how to be cautious. He did not have a Soke to teach him the ropes.

On Friday, August 13, 1965, around 7:30 p.m., dad left his brother Rufus' apartment on 148th Street near Seventh Avenue. The sun was about to set on a beautiful day. Dad was headed for Duckee Donuts, a diner that his brother Willie managed on the corner of 145th Street and Eighth Avenue. Dad walked with an air of lightness, fueled by the pleasant thoughts of later seeing Chris, a girl he had communicated with prior to arriving in New York in late May. Chris lived at 308 West 145th Street, and he had attended a party at her apartment the previous Friday. Dad considered himself a great dancer so he had spent most of the party dancing with girls he was meeting for the first time. Dad thought he had been "the life of the party, dancing up a storm with the pretty girls of 145th Street."

As dad crossed 147th Street and Eighth Avenue that evening, a boy about dad's age stuck out his elbow and bumped dad in his chest. In 1965, it was apparently customary for Southern African Americans to say "excuse me" even if the other party was responsible for accidentally causing the bumping incident. Being a naive Southerner, dad politely said "excuse me," assuming that no stranger would deliberately bump into a person. Less than a second of the words escaping dad's mouth, the boy turned and angrily announced, "You didn't say excuse me!"

"Oh, yes, I did," dad retorted as he picked up on the aggressive tone of the stranger. Anticipating a confrontation, dad started to quickly size up his opponent. He narrowed his eyelids, and he felt the muscles in his upper arms become a bit tauter as his chest expanded.

"I say you didn't!" The stranger nearly shouted while putting up his dukes. With his dukes up, the stranger started to bounce and bob and weave. His action was a display of confident manhood on the streets.

Dad had grown up on one simple principle: "If a man raises his hands, don't wait for him to throw 'em." Dad had previously observed a few fist fights on the streets of New York and had noticed that New Yorkers tended to throw up their hands and dance a bit before throwing a punch. He said it was sort of like watching Bruce Lee circling his opponent for about 10 seconds and thumbing his nose before putting his foot through the opponent's chest. Dad called the New Yorkers' moves "styling and profiling" to demonstrate confidence and instill fear. So while this guy "styled and profiled," dad quickly clocked him with a right to his jaw knocking him to the pavement.

Within seconds, one of the guy's friends stood up from where he was hiding behind a nearby parked car, and another came from the stoop of the building five feet away. As they attempted to surround dad, dad threw four or five punches that held the three at bay. Dad had learned to be a "head hunter" in any "throw down," so his fists only landed on noses, jaws, and cheek bones. He wasn't wasting time with body blows. Dad had several advantages. He was accustomed to hard manual labor which had built his strength. He was athletic and had experience boxing in competitions in school. He had a surge of adrenaline fueled by his anger that someone would just start a fight with him for no apparent reason.

After delivering the first few punches, dad started to run toward 145th Street. The three guys chased him. Dad would run a few yards, stop, and throw some punches, hitting the closest guy, and then resume running. This sequence of events repeated itself until he arrived at Duckee Donuts. Dad quickly entered the restaurant which he thought would be a sanctuary of safety.

Once inside, dad sat on a stool attempting to control his heavy breathing. While he sat, he assumed the fight was over since his adversaries had disappeared. He sighed deeply to release the stress, even as he noticed his brother Willie was not out front. Unalarmed, dad assumed Willie would soon emerge from the kitchen in the back and he would order a shake, a burger, and fries.

However, within five minutes of sitting, dad looked at the restaurant's window to discover about 70 kids standing with their faces pressed against the restaurant's glass. The windows together were at least 50 feet long, wrapping the corner of 145th Street and Eighth Avenue. The kids seemed to range in height from 4 to 6 feet and in ages from 10 to 18. Each brandished a glass bottle that had once contained soda, wine, beer, or liquor. A grimace of contempt shaped each face, including the faces of the youngest who should have been home preparing for bedtime. With dad in view, they sent an emissary in to ask dad to come outside.

In those days even gang members generally waited until they were outside a business or an apartment to fight an adversary. If a confrontation started indoors, one or both of the adversaries would usually suggest, "Let's take this outside!" Back then, there was an unwritten code about fighting indoors and destroying an innocent person's property or fighting where innocent people were likely to get hurt.

As the emissary entered, all of the 20-plus customers sat observing in complete silence while continuing to eat hamburgers and donuts and to drink coffee. Cell phones had not yet been invented, but dad said even if they were, no one was looking to get involved. He said the time was just like today, unfortunately, a time when too many black folks would rather see a fight than to stop one.

"Hey, man, those cats outside want to talk to you," the emissary announced at a distance of about five feet from dad.

Dad carefully looked at the emissary up and down. Like dad, he too was about 15 years old, about 6 feet, and about 160 pounds. When dad realized the emissary was the same dude who had bumped him, dad proceeded to do something I can say was truly mad stupid. As a surge of adrenaline took control of his body and mind, he lunged for the guy. "You're the one who started all this!" dad announced. "I should get you while your boys are outside!" The gang banger, apparently remembering the blows dad had thrown earlier, turned and ran for the door.

With the gang banger back outside, dad now faced another problem. The owner of the restaurant had stood nearby watching the exchange between dad and the gang bangers' emissary.

"Hey, man, are those guys out there looking to talk to you?" asked JT, the owner.

Dad turned on the stool to look at the owner and address his rhetorical question. Dad paused as if he could find a different answer. Dad could feel more than 20 sets of eyes focused on him and the owner simultaneously. Dad's heart sank.

"Yeah, that guy who came in here started up with me outside for no reason," he reluctantly told the owner.

"Well, he said they just want to talk to you. So why don't you go talk with them? I don't want them to break my windows," the owner suggested.

The African American owner was originally from Swainsboro, Georgia, and he was a close friend of Willie, dad's brother. He was 10 years older than dad and had left Swainsboro for New York the year before dad would enter fourth grade. Since he had not seen dad since his departure seven years earlier, he did not recognize dad and dad did not recognize him.

Dad was keenly aware the owner was prepared to quickly move from a polite plea to an enraged demand. He also knew what was waiting for him outside, and he preferred to "pass" on that conversation. With JT preparing to throw dad to the dogs, dad managed to clear his throat, to slow his racing heartbeat, and to clear the fog in his mind long enough to form a question.

"Uh, uh, is my brother Willie here?"

"Are you Willie's brother who just got up here? I am JT the owner."

"Yes, I am Willie's brother."

"So why didn't you say that before? Well, no problem. Sit right there." JT spoke with the empathy that was missing when he had suggested dad go outside and speak with the fire-breathing gang bangers. One minute he had appeared to be a gigantic ogre prepared to send defenseless dad to a sure death, and the next minute he was prepared to offer a sanctuary from the dragons waiting outside.

Seeing the sparkle of empathy in JT's eyes, dad sighed with relief that was beyond relief. He felt the heaviness in his chest lifted. He felt he then had a chance to live to see another day. Nevertheless, the guys remained outside armed with Coke, Pepsi, RC Cola, Thunderbird wine, Bacardi, and other bottles for just about every soft drink and alcoholic beverage sold in New York in 1965. So dad was in no mood to order a burger, fries, a shake, and definitely no kind of soda.

In 1965 on 145th Street there were two black police officers who had established a reputation for not taking any "static" from anybody. Their tags were Batman and Robin. As dad sat wondering how he would get home, the two officers strolled casually into the restaurant. "In the midst of all the high drama they strolled in as if they were taking a walk in the park eating ice cream," dad reported. It was dad's first sight of them, and it was a welcomed sight.

Batman calmly asked, "Hey, why are all of those kids outside?"

"One of 'em came up to me and threw an elbow as I was walking over here. I was just walking, and I never saw the guy before. Then he started a fight while two of his friends jumped in. One came off the stoop and another came from behind a car. I ran here to see my brother Willie, and within minutes all of those guys showed up with all of them bottles!"

Dad had spoken the words so quickly with his Southern twang that he wondered if they had fully understood him. However, after hearing that Southern twang, the officers must have figured dad was the new kid on the block being picked on.

"Okay, we'll handle this," Robin announced as they calmly turned to go outside to confront the gang bangers. As the two walked toward the door, dad noticed they had a "little bop in their steps and a bit of Florida A&M style in the way they twirled their night sticks." He said they had more "bop" (swagger) than the average gang banger on 145th Street. Once outside, the two officers spoke a few words, twirled their batons, and "the bangers split the way rats would run from a sinking ship."

With the corner eerily cleared, Batman bopped back into the restaurant and asked dad to follow him. The officers took dad to the other side of the street about 40 yards from Chris' apartment building and placed him on the bus that goes across 145th Street to 149th Street and Grand Concourse in the Bronx where dad would take the subway.

Once on the bus, dad exhaled. He was no longer seeing past episodes of his life quickly flash through his mind as death seemingly approached. Dad was glad to be heading home and no longer planning to party that evening with Chris and her fly girlfriends. He had put two plus two together and come up with four, meaning the guy who had started this must have been at the recent party at Chris' place and was looking to teach that little "jump off Georgia" boy a big lesson for being too friendly with the fly city girls on 145th Street. Dad figured he had made the mistake of slow dragging with the wrong girls, and their guys had been out to break his legs and his head.

Chris reportedly hosted some great parties and had pretty friends who hosted others. Dad said no one could find a greater collection of pretty girls anywhere else at any other party in the city. Dad said he could never remember seeing Chris' parents when he attended the parties. However, he never saw any of the teens drinking alcohol or smoking reefer. He said the lights were always down low, but not so low that you couldn't pick the girl you wanted to ask to dance when a slow record came on. He said the first thing that he and other guys did when arriving at a party was to "scope out" the girl that would be the most desirable partner when a slow record would come up.

"Slow dragging" and "grinding" to The Miracles' "Oh Baby Baby" and The Temptations' "My Girl" were the highlights of dad's and many other guys' nights on 145th Street and many other streets in 1965. Dad said a guy had to be alert to hear the opening of the songs so that he could get to that special fly girl to ask her hand for the dance before another guy could. Once dad had her, he had to utilize the special embrace, the special timing of certain movements, and the special pace. He also had to have his right knee in the right place. He had to coordinate movements with her.

Dad said he never wanted to be like some other guys who would step on their partners' feet and stumble through Billy Stewart's "I Do Love You." He said the offended girls would not give the guys a second chance, and the other girls who noticed would not give them a first chance. So dad "always had a smooth groove" (according to him).

When the Bronx was asleep, Harlem was awake. Way past midnight you could find more people activity on 145th Street than you could find on the most active Bronx streets at five in the afternoon. Dad had left sleepy Georgia to be awake, to be fascinated "with the great white lights of New York, New York, the Big Apple; the city so nice, they named it twice." There were more girls on a few blocks of 145th Street than there were in his whole hometown. There were more parties on any Friday night than there were in any combination of 30 Fridays in Swainsboro.

Nevertheless, on the bus ride back to the Bronx, he concluded he would attend no more parties at Chris' apartment at 308 West 145th Street because he did not have anyone to cover his back if the gang bangers were to arrive to "invite" him outside "to talk" about his desire to embrace the fly girls on 145th. After being in New York only two months, he did not yet have any male friends who would leave the Bronx with him to party in Harlem. They had the intelligence he had been missing. Also, dad couldn't count on the presence of his older brothers, Willie and Marcus, who had already earned the gang members respect by showing they were willing to stand up to threats from the gang's leader.

So, for dad, there would be no more "slow dragging" and "grinding" to Billy Stewart's "I Do Love You" or the Righteous Brothers' "Unchained Melody," and no more "swanging" to the Four Tops' "I Can't Help Myself" or Junior Walker's "Shotgun" at Chris' crib.

There would be no more boo-ga-loo-ing on 145th Street!

Chapter 18

Video Games, Cowboys, and Indians

The Hip Hop Age is also the age of video games. American youth's love of hip hop and video games is often the cause of concern for their parents. When I was just 6 years old and in love with Pokémon, the war with my parents over video games began and that war continues even today even though I am now an 18 year old adult!

My dad hated Pokémon and didn't attempt to disguise his hatred! He saw Pokémon as a threat to the development of my brain and reasoning ability. During my early teens, he believed that much of the hip hop he viewed on cable was dragging black and Latino youth into sexual, sociological, and psychological illusions and delusions that would thwart their readiness for successfully assuming the responsibilities that come with "real" manhood and womanhood.

You see, parents of my parents' generation grew up in the age of rhythm and blues, jazz, Motown, and rock and roll. They also grew up in the age before video games were invented. Can you imagine the curse of being born and becoming an adult before the invention of video games? Can you imagine being cursed to grow up without hearing Jay-Z, Lupe Fiasco, Kanye, and J. Cole as a teenager? I can only imagine their childhoods must have been mad boring. My parents, especially dad, want me to live the same clueless and mad boring life he led. Son, I ain't trying to hear that.

In 1975, Atari released Pong, the first video game for home computers. Dad and mom had passed their prime when Pong was invented; they had recently graduated from college. Pong was old school and could only display two colors (black and white) at one time. It was a two-dimensional game modeled like a ping pong or table tennis game. On the screen, the players saw what was supposed to be the top of the playing surface. The little ball bounced slowly toward the opposite side of the table when it was "hit" by an unimaginative little line. The little lines supposedly represented paddles. The table had a flat line across the middle which I suppose represented the net.[9]

Only three words should describe Pong: "Boring! Boring! Mad boring!" Yet, dad admits playing it a few times on what he thinks was an Atari game console at an arcade near Times Square in the early 1980s. He suggests that he also played Space Invaders during that same visit. He must have dropped in out of curiosity. If dad's slow and clumsy fingers were the last line of defense, I am sure the invaders were successful in their mission.

At age 2 in 1995, I was on my way to becoming very comfortable with the computer. It was dad's idea to let me have access to the home computer at an early age because he knew that kids of my generation would have to be very comfortable with computers and other technologies to have the broadest possible educational and career opportunities. By the time I was 3 years old I was attending a Montessori preschool and kindergarten and was often called upon by teachers to assist other kids in using the school's computers.

In 1995, the educational games on computers were limited and did not make use of complex graphics and animation. I cannot remember the games I played. Dad and mom recall basic math and word recognition games. They also recall not having any anxiety about the computer games using up too much of my time or distracting me from doing my academic work later in kindergarten. However, today they maintain a high level of anxiety that started to appear before I would even complete first grade with my intense interest in Pokémon and other video games.

Even though most American parents, like my parents, are clueless about video games, their lack of knowledge does not stop them from having opinions which they attempt to impose on their kids. I am sure that my experience is like the experiences of many other kids of my generation. At age 6, it was easy for dad and mom to put the games away and only let me have them when they were ready for me to have them. When they thought enough was enough, they would simply take the games and put them away until they were ready to allow me to use them again.

In my pre-teens and early teens, I was old enough to demand more access to my video games. Yet, there were hundreds of times in my pre-teens and early teens when dad's favorite command when he wanted me to stop playing my video games was: "Okay, man, now it's time for you to do something productive! Put that crap away!"

In response, I would usually ask for a few more minutes to complete the level I was in, and he would usually say, "You've had enough time. Put it away!"

"But dad, give me a few more minutes. I'm in the middle of the game and I am trying to set a record score," was a common response.

"I don't care. What is that doing for your education? You need to go pick up your books."

"But, dad, you are being unreasonable! I don't have any homework tonight and I read on my way home on the subway," I would respond as I continued to work my fingers.

"I will take that game and throw it in the trash if you don't turn it off this instant!"

Dad was unreasonable, but I had to obey.

Initially at age 6, when dad would permit use of video games, he expressed a special distaste for Pokémon. Pokémon made absolutely no sense to him. Thankfully, he did not completely stop me from having experiences with Pokémon. BTW, one of the Pokémon was named after my sister Kakuna. In Pokémon Platinum, the official name of No. 14, the Cocoon Pokémon is Kakuna. How mad cool is that? My sister, who was like my second mom, was a Pokémon.

Like many clueless American parents, my parents saw video games as potentially dangerous for the educational development of kids. For the most part, dad stepped forward to set the rules, but mom was also an enforcer of the rules starting when I was age 6. They were concerned about my love of Pokémon.

Mom suggested, "*Bambino*, kids today have too many Game Boys and other gadgets that do not require them to use their imagination. When your dad was growing up at age 6, he didn't have the gadgets so he had to be imaginative and creative when he went out to play. I want you to do the same as your dad. I want you to use your mind and your imagination. You will have more fun than just sitting playing with your video games."

Even at 6 years old I must have known that mom was speaking mad gibberish. I had no clue about how dad used his creativity and imagination at age 6, so her suggestion made no sense to me. However, I would later learn in my teens that in Georgia at ages 6 and 7, dad tied a string to the top of a broomstick, straddled it, and that was his horse. He wore a cheap straw hat, and that was his cowboy hat. He had a cap pistol, and that was his cowboy gun. When he couldn't find his cap pistol, he picked up a stick, and that became his rifle. He rode around on that broom screaming "Pow! Pow!" as he "shot" at his best friend, Charles Young, or at his imaginary enemies when Charles was unavailable.

When dad and Charles weren't riding their broomsticks, they could often be found playing with miniature toy soldiers, Indians, and horses. They would grudgingly take turns being the Indian chief and leading the Indians because in all the television shows the Indians were defeated by the white cowboys and soldiers. Oh, they did see Sitting Bull and the Sioux warriors defeat the soldiers at the battle of the Little Bighorn, "but that didn't count when I was 6 and 7," according to dad. Since the toys belonged to Charles, dad more often had to be the Indian chief.

In preparation for the beginning of the battles, Charles and dad would organize their forces on opposite sides of the floor at a distance of three to five feet. Once that task was completed, dad, as the Indian chief, would stand and mimic the pow-wow dance he had seen the Indians perform on television. After about 15 seconds of "pure" pow-wow dancing, he would dance for another 10 seconds adding the swinging of his hands in the "tomahawk motion" and make the same so-called Indian war cry that Florida State University football fans and the Atlanta Braves baseball fans make today. That war cry went something like, "Hoo, hoo, hoo, hoo, hoo, hoo, hoo, hoo, hoo, hoo."[10]

Finally, after completing the dance, it was time for the Indian chief to stand before his adversary and make a brief speech speaking "funny English" the way dad had often heard the Indians speak on television. Standing before the cavalry lieutenant with his home-made bow and arrow in hand, dad would say with a deep voice, "White man come-um and take-um our land. White man make-um peace after take-um our land, but white man no keep-um peace. White man speak-um with fork tongue!"

After the Indian chief spoke, it was time for the head of the cavalry to speak. Charles would stand erect with a puffed up chest. He held a toy Winchester rifle he had received as a Christmas present. Tucked in his belt, he would have a long stick which represented his sword. "We are stronger and smarter and braver than you," he would announce. "God gave us this land. You are red savages! We are going to pay you back for killing General Custer, scalping our men, and stealing our pure women to make half breeds!"

Following the verbal confrontations, the battle would begin. Dad and Charles would make sounds they thought were similar to rifle fire ("pow!")

and arrows flying through the skies ("zzzzzzz"). Then, with their little brown index fingers, they would knock over members of their forces that the bullets and arrows supposedly hit. As horses fell, they would let go the sounds that they had heard falling horses make on television. The sound went something like, "Ehn, ehn, ehn, ehn, ehn!" At the end of the battle, Charles would stand over all of dad's fallen Indians and make a brief victory speech about having saved America from the "red savages."

Does anyone see anything wrong with those images of dad and Charles killing off Native Americans? Would any sensible American want to see his son play that game today? Is there anyone who wants to go back to those "good old days" before the invention of video games when kids supposedly had to use their imagination and creativity in order to play and have fun? Imagine games which imitated genocide of Native Americans, as shown on television, from kids like my father (who has Native American ancestry).

Imagine games that reflected what dad and Charles had heard in numerous cowboy movies and television programs: "The only good Indian is a dead Indian." Those words were reportedly spoken by US General Phillip Sheridan in 1869 at a conference with 50 Indian chiefs at Fort Cobb in Oklahoma after one chief introduced himself to Sheridan as a "good Indian." The conference had been called to ensure Native Americans would be located and remain on desolate reservations and not threaten the progress of white settlers who were occupying the best land.

A PBS program, "The West," pointed out that after the Civil War, Sheridan unleashed a campaign of "total war" without concern for killing Native American women and children. Sheridan had been the Union general who blocked confederate General Robert E. Lee's retreat from Richmond that helped to bring an end to the Civil War. In 1884 he became Commanding General of the US Army, a post he held until his death.

Believe it or not, dad and Charles used their "creativity and imagination" to not only kill off Native Americans, but also to kill off Africans. When they weren't killing Native Americans, there were times they could be found playing Tarzan killing off Africans. They would take equal turns playing Tarzan, the white hero surrounded by "black African savages." They would even go in the little wooded area near their homes and tie ropes to low-hanging tree branches. Then they would grab the rope, swing through the air, and send forth the Tarzan yell, "O o o o o o! O o o o o o!"

One day dad's brother Thomas, who was two years older, joined their Tarzan reenactment. Thomas swung on the rope, and, as he neared the ground, his knee hit a tree stomp. Almost all of the skin around his right knee disappeared, and they were able to see the white bone of his kneecap. A few days later, dad and Charles were back swinging through the trees of Africa.

Tarzan was the smartest, strongest, and bravest man in the "jungles" of Africa and, on television, all of Africa was a jungle. As a baby, Tarzan was found and raised by apes who acted as his parents. The Africans were never intelligent. Cheetah, the chimpanzee and companion of Tarzan, was smarter. The Africans were the bad guys who ran around with big animal bones in their noses and loin cloths around their waists. They did not speak a language; they just uttered sounds that couldn't be understood.

When dad played the part of the Africans, he would repeat the uttered sounds as he remembered them from television. He would scream, "Hu gah mu gah! Hu gah mu gah! Bu da bu da! Bu da bu da! Ungawah! Ungawah!"

Dad was imitating the "Africans," who were probably African American actors. The actors would utter the sounds quickly while jumping up and down like excited chimpanzees with ostrich feathers in their head bands. Since no ostrich feathers were available, dad usually secured a chicken feather from an animal his mom had slaughtered in his backyard. Instead of a head band, he would use a big red rubber band around his head.

So that's how Africans from the "jungles" of Africa were portrayed on television in dad's childhood. Meanwhile, television portrayed African Americans (in those days they were called colored people, Negroes, Negras, darkies and nig***s) as buffoons, servants, and con artists. When dad was ages 6 through 9, he and Charles could often be found watching *Amos 'n' Andy* on television when they were not shouting, "Hu gah mu gah! Ungawah!"

Before the arrival of television, *Amos 'n' Andy* could be heard on the radio from 1928 through 1955. White men, in "black face," wrote the scripts and played the characters of Amos, Andy, Kingfish, Sapphire, Lightnin', and Mama. White men starred in the radio version, *Amos 'n' Andy*, which had a huge white and black audience. The radio show set the standard that popular radio programs followed during that period, the so-called "Golden Age of Radio."

When television arrived in the 1950s, white men in Hollywood decided to "try out some darkies" in the roles. Initially, the two white men who had acted on radio were programmed to be the voices of Kingfish, Amos, and Andy, with the African American actors on screen lip synching the lines. When that idea was dropped, the African American actors were required to sound as much as possible like the white actors who had played the roles on radio because the white producers thought the two white men had the better sense of the language and speech patterns of African Americans. In other words the two white men could speak more like black men and women than any black male or female actor. Yeah, that point of view was mad stupid and yet highly acceptable in Hollywood.

Andy Hogg Brown (yes, "Hogg" was his middle name) was a big, dark-skinned, heavy-set, and kind-hearted "buffoon" who was always being "played" by brown-skinned Kingfish, whose full name was George Kingfish Stevens. Amos Jones was thin, tan in color, and the smartest man in Harlem, the setting for the series. He was a taxi driver and high up on the food and intellectual chain.

Lightnin' was dark-skinned, worked as a janitor, wore a gray janitor's cap, and would scratch his head if you asked the simplest question, such as: "What day of the week is it?" He also had those "bug eyes" that Hollywood loved to have its black male characters display to make them look scared and stupid. To display "bug eyes," he would open his eyelids as wide as possible while his eyes would roll upward and his mouth would stretch wide to signal fear as if he had seen a ghost.

Other principal characters included Sapphire, Kingfish's wife. She was sort of like Alice on the *Honeymooners*. Mama, Sapphire's mom, was a lot like Martin Lawrence's "Big Mama," when she was loud, "throwing her weight around," and acting just plain dumb (a long-standing and very popular Hollywood portrayal of black women).

Amos was the light-skinned mediator between brown-skinned Kingfish and dark-skinned Andy. Kingfish would steal a nickel off a dead man's eye. Andy was dumb enough to replace it with two quarters, only to have Kingfish steal the two quarters. Andy worked and Kingfish's only work was acting as a con man "playing" Andy.

Amos struggled to keep the peace in Harlem. At one point Amos laid down the law and threatened to have Kingfish arrested by the police if he didn't change his ways. Kingfish was always quick to misuse big words in order to show how "intelligent" he was, so he responded, "Holy mackerel! Oh, so you givin' me an ultimato, huh?"

Of course, when Kingfish responded, he stuck his "Angelina Jolie lips" out as far as they could reach as the live audience in the television studio exploded in laughter. That line would keep dad and Charles laughing for weeks and coming back to the television for more. (BTW, I've gotten a lot of "ultimatoes" from dad regarding putting away my video games.)

Today, dad still laughs every time he repeats that ultimato line to his friend, Yvette Jackson, whom he met on the graduation line at Columbia University when they were receiving their doctoral degrees. He likes to use that line when she requests his assistance on an educational project.

However, instead of laughing at Kingfish, he now laughs at how "gullible, ignorant, and stupid" he was to look at those shows and laugh at the images of Africans and African Americans portrayed in Hollywood and the media. Today, he would not pay a penny to see Martin Lawrence play the "buffoon" as "Big Mama." He will not pay a penny to see any movie whose major purpose is to degrade black women or any other group of women or ethnic group. Even horror movies which depict violence against women are not shown in our home, and we have never together seen one in the theater during my 18 years on earth. Dad has never entertained himself with *The Sopranos* and he will not look at a minute of *Jersey Shore* after having read about what he considers its stereotypical depiction of Italian American women and men.

If you had told dad he was an African American or black at the ages of 6 through 15, you would have had a fight on your hands. Dad was colored and Negro. If you had told dad that he and all humans could, through DNA, trace their ancestry back to an African man who lived in the region of South Africa about 60,000 years ago, he would have said you were "talking crazy." If you had told dad that human language and the earliest form of human art were first developed in South Africa, he would have told you that you were speaking gibberish.[11]

Furthermore, if you had told him Africa had produced the civilizations of Egypt, Zimbabwe, Kush/Nubia, Timbuktu, and the Songhai Empire, he would have asked, with a look of stupidity and disbelief framing his face, "Huh?"

You might ask, "What was the turning point in dad's view of the world?" Dad picked up and read *The Autobiography of Malcolm X* when he was a sophomore at John Jay High School in Brooklyn. That book transformed his life. After he read the book in March 1966, he became an eager reader of African history and the speeches of Malcolm X. He later read *Bury My Heart at Wounded Knee* and other books of Native American history, poetry, and literature and learned to celebrate Sitting Bull and the Lakota Sioux warriors who defeated Custer at the Little Big Horn. He dismissed Johnny Weissmuller, the Olympic swimming champion who portrayed Tarzan, as "the real tree-swinging fool."

That spring in 1966, dad entered his new-found knowledge into discussions in honors history classes in John Jay High School, mostly populated by whites with a few Asians and African Americans. One day in class, after dad had spoken at length, Betty Begleiter, a cute blond and one of the most popular girls in school, interrupted his speech in class and asked him so that everyone could hear: "If you are so proud of Africans, why don't you go back to the jungle and swing like a monkey from a tree?"

Her taunt immediately threatened their developing friendship, and he responded: "During the time Africa was home to great civilizations, Europeans were living in caves and painting themselves blue." Miss Fitzgerald, a white teacher he still cherishes, encouraged dad to continue to study African history and express himself, which he did even though those discussions made others uncomfortable.

Dad and Betty remained friendly through their senior year because he somehow recognized she had only responded based on what she had been taught about Africans through television and movies. She was intelligent, not a racist, and she possessed a good spirit. She, like most other black, white, Latino, and Asian students at the school, had absolutely zero knowledge of African history and no one to teach them. Most, including the blacks, probably had the same view of Africans as savages who swing on tree limbs. Betty learned to listen with a more open mind.

Yeah, I should have agreed with mom that I should have put down video games and used my "creativity and imagination at play," as dad did when he was a little child. As Bernie Mack might ask, "America, ain't that right?"

Around 1982, dad purchased two Atari computers for my sisters, Ife and Kakuna. (Today, those computers are in the basement of our brownstone.) Back in 1982, Pac Man, Donkey Kong, and Space Invaders were the popular video games. Although the action in those games was incredibly slow and the graphics were dull compared to today's games, dad played but never mastered those games. Although the Atari joy stick did not intensely challenge a person's eye-hand coordination, dad's stiff fingers and slow eyes never mastered the joy stick. So, it is fair to say, he never found any joy playing with the joy stick.

Can you imagine most of the parents of dad's generation never played or mastered Atari and the ancient Pac Man, Space Invaders, and Donkey Kong? My generation would not even waste our time playing with that ancient stuff. What is the point of Pac Man? What is the point of Donkey Kong and Space Invaders? Who in my generation would waste time with the slow Atari joy stick? Atari may belong in a museum, but certainly not in anyone's living room.

Thus, if they never mastered the Atari joy stick, they are not prepared to handle the controllers for the PlayStation and the Xbox. Even with the Wii, they are too stiff and clumsy to perform well.

When I was 14, dad purchased the Wii and I was on it right away playing and mastering baseball and other sports. After about a month of watching me dad decided that he could play baseball.

"Akhenaton, I can play that game. Move aside," he suggested as he took the control.

I gave up the game thinking that it would be nice to see him play. I even gave him instructions to help him have a successful experience. However, after he struck out for the twentieth consecutive time, there was no more we in front of the Wii. Dad was not Pujols.

If most parents never mastered Pac Man and Space Invaders, and are incredibly clumsy even on the Wii, then they are unprepared to understand and master Tekken 6, God of War III, Halo 3, Grand Theft Auto III, Madden, Pokémon Red Blue, Call of Duty, Star Wars Battlefront, NBA 2K10 and 2K11, Street Fighter II, Super Mario Galaxy, and Resident Evil 4.

Of course, I saw the video games as productive, full of fun and imagination, and also educational. Dad saw them as potentially a threat to my education and the development of my brain. He thought they had no useful purpose other than providing a reward of a little fun after focusing on my "real responsibilities," especially studying.

Thankfully, early on I discovered the love of books and was an eager reader in elementary and middle school. Thus, when I didn't have homework, I would spend time in books that I chose. I read the classics like *A Wrinkle in Time*, the Harry Potter books collection, *The Chronicles of Narnia* series, *A Series of Unfortunate Events* collection, *The Autobiography of Malcolm X, Down These Mean Streets*, and the books by Walter Dean Myers, the master author, including *Monster, Hoops*, and *The Dream Bearer*.

Before age 6 I was introduced to Pokémon and, by 2001 at the age of 8, I was becoming a Pokémon master. I started trading Pokémon cards at age 6 using *Prima's Official Strategy Guide*. I am sure mom and dad did not have a clue about what I was doing with the cards, but apparently that did not stop them from purchasing cards and the strategy guide. Looking back, dad said he went along because I showed interest and the guide required reading. As an educator, he said he knew kids would read and study more the things that appeal to their interests.

Also at age 6 I was using my Game Boy to play Pokémon Ruby and Sapphire, and I was watching the *Pokémon* series on television. My parents purchased the *totalgames.net,* a magazine that contained the "complete mapped solution" for Pokémon Ruby and Sapphire.

By age 8, I had graduated from Pokémon Red Blue to Pokémon Emerald. I used the official guide book to direct my strategies on my Game Boy Advance. I spent a few minutes in that guide book each day and dad started to notice my intense interest, so he didn't complain about my reading the guide book. Within months, the pages were mad wrinkled and the cover was coming apart because of constantly opening it and turning the pages. Dad said the only other book in the house that seemed as wrinkled from constant use was his *Harper Collins Study Bible.*

So reading Pokémon was acceptable. However, dad figured watching Pokémon on television did not require reading and studying. He did not see the link between the books, the cards, the video game, and the television series. He thought the *Pokémon* series was nothing more than a cartoon series, and one that was far inferior to Bugs Bunny, Daffy Duck, Foghorn Leghorn, Pepe Le Pew, Tom and Jerry, Top Cat, Yogi Bear and Boo Boo, and the stars of other cartoon series that he and Charles had grown up watching.

At age 7, he even tried to get me interested in Bugs Bunny and those cartoon series. I wasn't feeling it. I was feeling *Pokémon, The Simpsons* and *SpongeBob SquarePants*. Later I would graduate to *Family Guy, The Cleveland Show,* and *Static Shock*, and I would sneak to see *South Park* when dad and mom were asleep since they thought it was too grown up for me.

In 2000 when *Pokémon, The Simpsons* and *SpongeBob SquarePants* came on, dad at times had negative comments. With *Pokémon,* he complained that the Japanese directors used main characters who appeared robotic in speech and action. Regarding *The Simpsons* and *SpongeBob SquarePants*, he thought the humor was silly and uninteresting.

Dad preferred Elmer Fudd's humor. So he showed me an episode where Elmer had a rifle and hunter's outfit and cap while going hunting for Bugs. Elmer Fudd was seen softly moving on his tippy toes when he stopped and turned toward the camera and whispered to the audience, "Shh, I'm wooking for wabbits!" Of course, dad exploded with laughter.

Later in the episode, Elmer encounters Bugs who, as usual, asks, "What's up, doc?" Elmer tells Bugs it's "wabbit" season. Bugs says it's duck season and sends him after Daffy, the little black duck. Within seconds, Elmer confronts Bugs and Daffy. Bugs screams, "Duck season!" Daffy screams, "Rabbit season!" Elmer doesn't know who to believe and who to shoot. So Bugs screams, "Duck season!" Daffy screams, "Rabbit season!" Then Bugs screams, "Rabbit season!" Daffy is tricked and yells, "I say it's duck season!" Bugs says, "Rabbit season!"

Daffy shouts, "Duck season!" Elmer blasts Daffy, spinning his beak around on his head.

Now that was humor for dad and his generation. Dad told me that as a child at the movies he would often see Bugs Bunny, Elmer Fudd, Foghorn Leghorn, and Looney Tunes which were featured before the main movie. Can my generation believe that? Can any generation believe "wabbit" season is funny? Can any generation believe that has imagination?

Of course, dad was clueless about Pokémon. However, he allowed me to continue to progress with new versions of Pokémon as they were issued. He would buy me the new guides, and he eventually stopped making negative comments and learned to barely tolerate my interest.

By the time I was 8, it was time for me to move on from Nintendo 64 to a GameCube. I hung with GameCube for a while. Need for Speed: Underground, Metroid Prime, Enter the Matrix, and NBA Courtside 2002, with Black Mamba on the cover, were among the first games I played on my GameCube. Then in 2004, I purchased Madden 2005. That game would ultimately change my relationship with dad regarding playing video games.

Like most American dads, my dad is a big fan of football. With football, basketball, and baseball, he is not living in the past. In football, he might fondly remember "the great Jim Brown" (whoever that is), but he does not allow memories to stop him from loving what Adrian Peterson is able to do today. When the Giants and Jets are winning, dad is an enthusiastic fan of those teams. When they are not, he can be seen pulling for the Steelers, the Colts, the Bears, or Philadelphia, if they are having great seasons.

Unlike me, he dislikes the Cowboys and "Romeo," a name he mockingly gives to Dallas' quarterback, Tony Romo. When Brandon Jacobs scored the one-yard touchdown run that put the Giants ahead for the win in the 2008 Divisional Title Game, dad began reciting his version of *Romeo and Juliet* to piss me off as he pointed to the television: "Romeo! Romeo! Wherefore art thou Romeo? I am here taking a beat down from the New York Giants. Ha, ha, ha, ha, ha!" That's football humor for dad.

Like me, he always dislikes the Patriots (and the Red Sox, too, although he loves Big Papi, yet was cheering for the Orioles). We loved and celebrated Plaxico Burress and the Giants when they destroyed Brady, Belichick, and the Patriots' perfect season in the 2008 Super Bowl. Together we talked smack to images of Tom Brady, Randy Moss, and Bill Belichick on our television after Manning's incredible 32-yard pass to the incredible one-armed David Tyree. We jumped from the couch, ran across the room, and reached one arm out to simulate Tyree's reception. When Tyree's catch was soon followed by Plaxico's touchdown, we leapt from the couch again to simulate the fake slant inside move that tricked Ellis Hobbs, the Patriots' defender, and allowed Plaxico to dish some serious misery to the Patriots.

After Plaxico's touchdown, we started talking smack to the announcers who were predicting Brady, Moss, and the Patriots could not be counted out after that touchdown even though precious little time remained in the game. When Osi Umenyiora, Michael Strahan, and the rest of the Giants' defense clamped down on the Patriots' offense, while not allowing them to move forward even a yard, we celebrated what we hoped would be the end of the Patriots' so-called dynasty. It was. Sorry, Boston (don't be hatin' on dad and me).

From 2004 through 2010 on Sunday afternoons if we were home watching a game, I'm sure our neighbors could count on hearing dad and me scream and talk to our favorite players. Adrian Peterson appeared on the cover of Madden 2005, and he was one of our favorite players. When Peterson would break out for a long gallop that would cause opponents to hit the turf, dad and I were screaming with each step. We would often awaken mom, who was not pleased. We would apologize and promise to keep our voices down. Of course, we would often break that promise as soon as Peterson made another astounding gallop. As America knows, Sundays are for football, not for mothers taking naps after a tough week at work.

On Sunday, February 5, 2006, dad and I were home watching the Super Bowl XL. The Pittsburgh Steelers played the Seattle Seahawks. We were both pulling for Pittsburgh. Big Ben Roethlisberger was having a bad passing game. However, with less than two minutes to go in the first half, Roethlisberger stepped back and threw a fantastic 37-yard completion to a leaping Hines Ward. From start to finish, the play may have taken six seconds.

As soon as the play was over dad shook his head, threw his hands up and asked out loud, "What happened?" The Pittsburgh offense had been mostly ineffective before that play. The play was called on third down with Pittsburgh needing 28 yards for a first down. Therefore, dad had not anticipated the play, and his question was just there to express his surprise and confusion, rather than to seek an answer.

However, I had an answer, and I quickly told him what had happened. I told him the type of play called, and I described the moves and blocks that were expected and performed by the offensive linemen and backs, and the routes of the tight end and the wide receivers, including Hines. I told him what defense the Seahawks had used. I described how Seattle had used its guards and tackles, defensive ends, corners, and safeties. I told him why the defensive play Seattle had selected was not the best for stopping the offensive play Pittsburgh had selected. I explained Seattle expected a more conservative play since they had the Steelers in a bad position back in Steelers' territory.

As I spoke, dad's mouth opened as if he were astonished that I had seen and understood that play. Also, before I finished speaking, John Madden started to describe what had occurred and his description was in harmony with mine. It really impressed dad that I had seen as much as, if not more than, Madden.

"Did you see all of that?" Dad asked with the element of surprise ringing in his voice.

"Yes, dad, I saw all of that," I responded casually as if it were no big deal. I knew dad had limited knowledge of what video games could teach and was not sure that he was prepared to learn.

"I played a little football in high school, and I missed that play. Akhenaton, you have played nothing but touch football. How did you see it?"

"Madden, dad," I responded casually as if he should have known.

"Madden? What do you mean?" Dad shook his head as if he were clueless. He was.

"Dad, I learned how to watch football using Madden 2005 and Madden 2006. I know the plays on offense and defense, and I know the plays each team prefers to use in certain situations. So I looked at the situation and anticipated the play Pittsburgh would use based on the way Pittsburgh lined up. When you know what to expect, you are able to better see what exactly happens."

"Wow, you saw all that from playing a video game?"

"Yeah, dad, I've tried to tell you that you can learn a lot from video games." I spoke in a polite tone, but one which suggested I was wise and he was confused and needing my wisdom.

The 37-yard pass was soon followed by a touchdown. Ward scored another touchdown and went on to be named MVP of Super Bowl XL. Dad and I were especially happy for Ward, Coach Cowher, and "The Bus," Jerome Bettis.

As we sat for dinner, dad opened the topic of video games again. "Akhenaton, you have said you want to be a sports broadcaster," he began.

"Yes, dad. I get so much information from Madden, NBA Live, and other video games. I get to know all the players and all the teams and what they could do best. I also get to know all the individual and team statistics."

"Now I know why you can quickly quote statistics of so many individuals and teams in so many sports, not just of your favorite players, favorite teams, and favorite sports. You get that knowledge from the various video games. So

I am thinking it is important to learn the mechanics of making video games. You do not want to be the average kid who just learns how to play the games; you should want to learn how to create the games."

"Yes, dad, I would be interested in learning how to create the games," I responded.

Later that same evening, dad decided to pick up and study my Pokémon guide books for the very first time. He started with Pokémon Emerald that he had purchased for me when I was 12 years old. He opened the book and discovered it had 248 pages. He told me he discovered it had complex vocabulary words. He discovered it had many complex rules and instructions that were too demanding for his adult mind to find interest in following. He discovered the whole book, all 248 pages, contained what seemed like an endless list of direct and indirect instructions that must be learned in order to play the game effectively. He also discovered the following:

- More than 200 Pokémon are represented and a player must be familiar with each one.

- Each Pokémon has a set of distinct abilities such as levitation, illumination, synchronization, immunity, cute charm, liquid ooze, magma armor, and intimidation.

- There are 25 different natures Pokémon could possess that affect the evolution of their abilities as the Pokémon gain experience in the game.

- In the midst of the game, a Pokémon's experience can grow and it could suddenly evolve acquiring new abilities that would make it more effective in an attack or defense.

- There are more than 400 battles and 400 contest moves, including zap cannon, thunder shock, volt tackle, swagger, transform, teeter dance, seismic toss, spore, memento, octazooka, hypnosis, guillotine, acid armor, and conversion. Each battle move has a set of different scores for basic attack power, accuracy, power points, two-on-two battle range, and direct attack. The contest version of each move has appeal points, jam points, and a target of disturbance.

- Battle moves and contest moves must be chosen wisely because they have certain effects upon the attacking and defending Pokémon. For example, blast burn is fire type. In battle moves its effect is it causes massive damage to the opposing Pokémon but forfeits the attacker's next move.

Now dad "discovered" all the above from reading the guide, not from playing the game. Dad had stopped after about an hour of examining the book. At that point, he was fighting off a headache from trying to understand so much information. He wasn't willing to put in the required time to read and analyze many of the complex charts and graphs.

Dad's brain is wired to play first and read instructions later. That is how he approaches assembling household products ordered online: he begins assembling and doesn't bother reading the instructions until he realizes he has made mistakes and cannot go further. That is why mom does most of the assembling of household products, including my current platform bed. She has the patience to read and follow instructions. If something needs five hours to assemble, she's prepared to give it five hours, while dad wants everything done in 45 minutes or less.

Any 12-year-old could have told dad that there is much more to Pokémon than what he had "discovered." The real discovery comes in playing the game, especially playing against skilled opponents.

Dad did not know that Pokémon expanded the imagination of kids. He didn't know that I had to read, analyze, and remember scores of pages of charts containing instructions and data about Pokémon that were vital for my success playing the game. He didn't know that I had to combine or synthesize information and data into strategies that would bring success to my Pokémon.

Also, dad did not know that as I played the Pokémon games there were always new and unpredictable experiences and worlds evolving in the Pokémon universes. A lot of the evolutionary changes in my Pokémon and my opponent's Pokémon occurred according to the knowledge, skills, and strategies my opponents and I displayed in the games.

While playing Pokémon, I had to learn to function effectively in various environments. I had to learn challenging vocabulary. I had to recall the characteristics of hundreds of species of Pokémon and their different evolutionary paths. I had to apply that knowledge in the development of my strategies and the changes I made to my strategies. I had to apply that knowledge to defeat and capture Pokémon of my enemies to use in winning. I had to use that knowledge to resist capture and defeat of my own Pokémon. When the Pokémon of my enemies quickly evolved, to present more challenging types of powers and environments, I had to enable my Pokémon to evolve and adjust my strategies to defeat my opponents with their Pokémon's new strengths and opposing strategies in new environments.

Of course, dad didn't know I had to apply all of what I knew within seconds and fractions of a second to remain competitive. Of course, this required incredible analysis connected with incredible hand-eye coordination.

Thankfully, my brain had not been stunted from using my fingers to knock over miniature toy Indians or from running around with an unimaginative broomstick between my legs screaming, "Pow, pow!" My brain had not been stunted from swinging on tree limbs and screaming, "Hu gah mu gah! Hu gah mu gah! Bu da bu da! Bu da bu da! Ungawah! Ungawah!" Thankfully, I had not spent my early years "wooking for wabbits!"

With new-found respect for Pokémon, Madden, and video games, dad spent the following several days online seeking opportunities for me to learn video game design. In his search, he discovered iD Tech Camps. iD Tech offered courses in video game design, animation, web design, robotics, and programming. The summer camps were hosted by major universities throughout America. The instructors were mostly college students and recent graduates who had a lot of experience working with media, technology, and film production. The camps were usually about 10 days in length.

My parents and I reviewed the information, and we decided I would attend the summer camp in July 2006 at Princeton University. As a 13-year-old, I wasn't sure what to expect. I did not know if the camp would be boring or exciting, but I felt it would be interesting to know how to create my own games. I also trusted dad's judgment.

On the first day of the camp, my parents dropped me off. Registration was held on McCosh Courtyard which was near the impressive McCosh Arch. The 600-acre campus seemed huge and beautiful. Best of all, it was not crowded since it seemed to be mostly reserved for iD Tech Camp participants and, I believe, entering freshmen. After registration we were shown to our rooms. We were housed in Princeton dorms. After I settled in my room with my roommate, dad and mom departed. Their departure marked the beginning of the first extended period that I would be away without at least one of them being by my side. I felt that I was prepared.

I do not remember a boring session. All of the sessions were interesting because the teachers knew how to motivate and demonstrate. There were no long, boring lectures. There were no short, boring lessons. The teachers asked us about our interests and worked with each of us alone and in small groups to develop our projects. Our overall assignment was to develop the knowledge and skills necessary to independently create a video game with multiple characters, multiple action scenes, and multiple competitive levels based on our original ideas.

In the evenings, we gathered to play video games and to walk to the market for ice cream cones. The kids were cool and so were the teachers, so I felt really good about being at Princeton. I called home every evening to talk to mom and dad.

During the day sessions, I worked hard on my project. I soon found that I had skills with video design software. I created a fighting game and completed two levels before the 10-day period was over. I brought the software home with the game I had created. I demonstrated the game for dad and mom. They were pleased, and we all agreed that I would return the following summer.

The following summer I attended the iD Tech Camp at Seton Hall University in New Jersey. The Seton Hall campus was also large and beautiful. At camp that summer, I was able to help students who were not as skilled as I was, which gave me a good feeling. The lessons were interesting, and we had a lot of after-hours fun playing video games and sports.

By the time I arrived at Seton Hall, I was long past dad monitoring my selection of video games and determining how much time I should devote to playing them. I was interested in the games marked "M" for age 17 and above. I had reached the point where I could go alone to GameStop on Court Street with my allowance and birthday money to buy what I pleased. It was time for Grand Theft Auto San Andreas, Halo 3, Street Fighter II, Need for Speed: Underground, Tekken VI, and Resident Evil IV. It was time for street crime in Southern California, fast cars, butt kicking street fighting, and warfare for blasting enemies and blowing things up.

For years I have been a master with Tekken VI. My favorite fighter is Hwoarang. He is a master of Tae Kwon Do. He reminds me of my fighting style with Sensei Soke and Scorpion Martial Arts. Like me, Hwoarang has devastating axe, side, and roundhouse kicks. In all of the battles with me at the control, he has never lost a match. When he knocks out an opponent, I make sure he keeps kicking the opponent even though the opponent is unconscious and on his way to the canvas.

Dad says the young Mike Tyson would also hit an unconscious opponent as the opponent fell toward the canvas. He says Ali was the opposite. He points out that when Ali fought George Foreman during the "Rumble in the Jungle," Ali pulled back his punches as soon as he saw Foreman stumble and begin to fall. Well, with Tekken VI, I am sticking to Tyson's style so that all of my opponents would know what they are facing.

Today, at age 18, I have created my own player with NBA 2K11 and 2K12 modeled after my playing style and abilities. The virtual me has played with Derrick Rose and Joakim Noah and has been the MVP as we defeated Miami and Kobe and the Lakers. Of course, my playing has kept me up way past midnight, and dad and mom have not been pleased. They suggest that I need more sleep. However, I find a way to get the sleep that I need.

Today my struggles with mom and dad are not just about video games. Today we argue about the iPhone, Skype, Facebook, Twitter, Beats (head-phones), and the MacBook. We argue about me using them on what seems like 24/7 to mom and dad. Of course, they are clueless and, like so many other teenagers, I have given up on trying to educate them. It's impossible to educate parents.

Teenagers can anticipate my parents' nagging, I mean questions, because they have heard the same things from their own parents. I'm sure they have similar conversations which go something like this:

"Why are you wasting so much time on nonsense instead of studying?"

"Well, dad, it's nonsense to you but interesting to me. You just wouldn't understand."

"Why are we paying all that money for data on your iPhone? And why are we paying for apps?"

"Dad, do you even know what an app is? Most only cost $1 and besides you have money."

"Didn't you register the warranty for your iPhone? Why didn't you make sure the warranty was active?"

"I did register it. I registered online. It's not my fault Steve Jobs lost the registration."

"Why are we paying for an iPhone when you do not immediately return our texts or calls?"

"How can I text or call if my power is dead?"

"Well, aren't you with your friends when we have told you to text at a certain time to let us know what time to expect you home? Why can't you borrow a phone?"

"Their batteries were dead also."

"Why did you place your iPhone where it could be stolen while playing basketball?"

"I was watching the whole time? I think it was the new kids who were there."

"Why did you put your Beats where they could be stepped on while playing basketball?"

"I put them in my bag out of the way. I didn't expect that someone would be pushed and fall into that area."

"Why do you need to borrow dad's MacBook? What happened to yours?"

"I don't know. It won't let me log on."

"Why do you need to borrow dad's iPod? What happened to your iPhone?"

"I need to listen while I warm up for my game and all my songs are not loaded on the iPhone."

"Why are you taking the other iPod? Did you now lose your dad's?"

"Oh, no. It's in my room somewhere and I'm in a rush."

"Why did you leave the Xbox in the middle of the living room floor again?"

"I will move it."

"Why was the PlayStation left on all night?"

"I fell asleep."

"How did you manage to drop dad's MacBook in your dorm room? You mean to tell me you had it in bed while sleeping and it fell when the fire alarm rang and startled you?"

"Well I was studying online. And I know you want me to study. Don't you?"

"Why do you think you deserve another iPhone with those grades?"

"I am doing okay in my courses."

"Are you staying off those websites with viruses?"

"Of course! Which ones?"

"Shouldn't you put away NBA 2K12 and go to bed? It is 2:00 a.m."

"I am not tired. My first class is at 1:00 p.m. Getting too much sleep will only make me mad tired later and I will fall asleep in class."

"Are you going to blame 'the ghost' again for stepping on the Ethernet cable? We already know "the ghost" left the crumbs where you were sitting using your Xbox."

"I wasn't even eating in that area last night."

"Why are you taking the MacBook to the beach? What happens if sand gets in it?"

"Sand will not get in it."

"Why shouldn't we set controls to keep you off Facebook after midnight on weekdays?"

"I am an 18-year-old man and should make my own schedule."

"Blah, blah, blah!"

"Uh huh, uh huh."

Recently, mom reported to dad that my godfather, Uncle Robert, revealed to her the message I have posted on my Facebook page to highlight my relationship with mom regarding use of Facebook: "Yeah, mom. I know, mom. Uh huh, mom."

Parents just don't get it. I have put a lot of time and mental energy in trying to figure out how to educate them. However, they are long past their prime and they suffer from mad brain freeze. They can't possibly understand the world in which we live. They see an iPhone and see a gadget. We see an iPhone and see new worlds. Does anyone have parents as clueless as mine?

What does dad know about iPhones? Two tin cans attached to a string were dad's first mobile phone as a kid. It couldn't send text messages, and it had no apps. He couldn't use it for research or to take pictures and videos. He couldn't watch football or basketball or movies on those tin cans. The word "download" did not even exist. The dead zone was everywhere in the universe beyond the length of the string and two cans.

Yet, as we worked on this book, dad asked mom to purchase an iPhone for use in his business. Can you picture dad with his thick clumsy fingers using the touch screen on the iPhone? Did Steve Jobs and Apple make a special one just for him? If so, the Apple CEO would have a lot of explaining to do at the next Apple Convention.

How possible is it for dad to go from stringing two tin cans together and using them to communicate with Charles to learning to master an iPhone?

Dad's brain just doesn't seem wired for that.

Chapter 19

War! What Is It Good For?

Edwin Star asked the question, "War! What is it good for?" In *Rush Hour*, Chris Tucker tried to teach Jackie Chan to sing the song and to understand the words that were coming out of his mouth.

As a child, you always want your parents to express confidence, to give you a sense that they are in control of things that could influence your life. When you see uncertainty in their eyes, no matter how hard they try to conceal it from you, you know that something really important is happening in their lives and yours. Fear in them brings fear to you.

In September 2001, I began fourth grade at PS 59 on East 57th Street in Manhattan. PS 59 was a school well known for the international mix of its student population. Many of the students were born outside the USA, and some were the sons and daughters of parents who worked at the United Nations, which was situated less than a mile from the school.

Dad and mom had chosen PS 59 because it was diverse, had great teachers, and was a five-minute walk from mom's job. Since my birth, mom had shifted to a part-time schedule which allowed her to drop me off and pick me up after school. So each school day, after a kiss from dad, at 7:30 a.m. mom and I would take the subway to 59th Street and Lexington Avenue. I loved trains, so a subway ride was always welcomed. Usually at 3:00 p.m. mom would be waiting outside for us to begin our walk to the subway to head back to Brooklyn.

I loved my teachers, my school, and my classmates. Only four of my classmates were born in the USA. My other 19 classmates were all born outside the USA in countries such as China, Iraq, Iran, Ghana, the Philippines, Mexico, and Senegal. Cassie, my best female friend, was born in Germany. With our mothers, we would go to the movies with other friends in school. I loved having conversations with her in the movies and during recess. At times, we would sit under the shade of the playground equipment and talk as other kids played. She was like the sister of the same age that I didn't have at home. Dad said we were "kindred spirits."

Alex, my best male friend, was born in New York. Alex's father was Cuban American and his mother was Jewish American. I spent a lot of time playing video games at his apartment in Manhattan, and dad and I had Passover Seder there. Our parents became close.

For an 8-year-old in the fourth grade, recess is a big thing to look forward to. Since our school was located in a congested part of Manhattan, our playground was on the lower roof of our school building. So each day we would go out with the September sun shining on our heads to run, play tag, and jump and swing on the equipment the way kids that age love to do.

Looking back, dad says that the weather in September 2001 in New York was just splendid. He remembers highs in the 70s and blue, peaceful skies during the first week of the month and the beginning of the second week.

On the morning of September 11, I travelled with mom to school. She dropped me off and continued on to work. Our morning routine at school started as usual. However, by 9:00 a.m. my classmates and I noticed a great deal of excitement among the adults. But no one would tell us what was happening. My school was located on East 57th Street near Third Avenue, nearly four miles from the World Trade Center (WTC). So we were not in a position to see the Twin Towers like kids in some schools in Lower Manhattan and some parts of Brooklyn and Queens. For the most part, we were left in the dark.

At around 10:00 a.m., many parents began arriving at school to pick up their kids. The parents must have been instructed not to say anything that the kids in the classes could overhear. At about 10:45 a.m., mom arrived. She looked concerned, but only told me that we were going to her office which was just six blocks away, about a quarter of a mile. I liked visiting mom's office so her suggestion was all right with me.

Mom told me years later that dad had called her at work that morning from his office in Brooklyn sounding very stressed and worried. She said she became increasingly concerned when he urged her to pick me up from school immediately. Her concern grew upon exiting her office building and walking to my school. She said the streets were eerily empty of people and cars when just that morning they had been bustling as usual with noise, traffic, and activity. The few people she did see were walking silently as if in a daze.

After mom picked me up and we walked to her job, she held my hand tightly although I would be 9 in two months and was almost her height. She would rarely release it for a few seconds before gripping it tightly again during the entire trip.

Earlier that morning the director of mom's department, Rosemarie, had gathered the staff to discuss how my mom and her co-workers would get home or where they would stay if they were not able to do so. So, when we reached mom's job, I could see her co-workers getting ready to leave. We noticed that all of the women were taking off their fancy shoes and putting on walking shoes. As mom got her things and we prepared to leave, that's when she told me about the planes that had crashed into the World Trade Center and that the buildings had fallen. I asked how that could happen. She said that she was not sure, but that dad had called and was all right.

She told me the trains were not working and we could not return to Brooklyn. Instead, we were going north to my Aunt Gwen's apartment in Harlem to spend the night with the hope that dad would come and get us the next day. Harlem was further north of mom's office, and more than 10 miles from the WTC. Our house in Brooklyn was about three miles southeast and across the river from the WTC.

As we entered the street, we joined a stream of people walking north. Unlike the eerie emptiness of a few hours earlier, each block was packed with hundreds of people all moving in one direction. Many were marching in silence, which seemed strange to me. Some seemed to be anxious. Some people had white dust on their clothes and in their hair.

Mom said we would have to walk about five miles because it was impossible to get a bus. The streets were congested with automobile traffic heading north. I didn't complain about having to walk that distance because I was accustomed to long and fast walks with dad. Also, I looked forward to spending the night since my cousin, Devin, who was three years older, had a lot of video games, though not as many as Alex.

As we walked several blocks, mom started to notice that all the stores that sold flats, sandals, and sneakers were packed with women who had come to work that morning in heals but did not have any spare comfortable shoes stored under their desks. As we passed the stores, we noticed many of the shelves were already empty. Good thing mom kept several comfortable shoes under her desk. She had even lent a pair to her co-worker, Juanita, before we left.

After about a mile, mom took me inside a Duane Reade pharmacy to buy toiletries. Mom said the shelves were almost bare because so many people had rushed in before us to buy the items. She explained many people would not be able to return home that evening, and we all needed tooth brushes, toothpaste, and other items.

We arrived at Aunt Gwen's after a two-hour walk. Mom picked up some KFC near my aunt's apartment since my cousin, Devin, loves popcorn chicken. Aunt Gwen suggested we watch a video, so she made popcorn and we settled in for the evening. Looking back now, I guess she suggested the video because she knew all of the television channels would be carrying news of that morning, and she did not want us to get scared. However, as an 8-year-old I wasn't thinking about it every minute. I would later learn that mom and dad were thinking about it every minute and wondering what news would follow once America would get a clear picture of the cause.

The next morning as soon as the subways were open dad arrived in Harlem. He had left the car in Brooklyn since there were restrictions on cars seeking to enter Manhattan. I was glad to see him and happy that he was safe. I was happy to be going home. I was told that school was canceled for the rest of the week and that I would remain home from school for three days with mom and dad. I do not remember being happy with the thought of being off from school.

On the subway to Brooklyn, everyone seemed to be in a somber mood. Even dad seemed strangely somber. A few weeks earlier he had suffered the death from illness of a younger brother, Uncle Junior, the father of my cousin Devin. I had watched him cry tears for the first time in front of me at the location we went to identify my uncle's body. Mom would later explain that dad was still grieving the loss of my uncle when 9/11 occurred which added more to his grief.

When we arrived in Brooklyn, we could smell the results of the flames at the WTC. For the first time in our lifetimes, we noticed F-16 fighter jets flying over the city. When we entered the house, mom and dad noticed that the floors and furniture were covered with a thin sheet of gray "dust." In 2010, as we reviewed our experiences, mom explained that the "dust" was carried by the wind from the WTC to our neighborhood and home. She explained the "dust" was on the surfaces of the television, the chairs, the bed, the counter tops, and everywhere imaginable. She wrote the following:

> So we head on home to Brooklyn on the train which made me
> very nervous since no one knew if the next terrorist attack would
> strike the subway. But I couldn't show Akhenaton I was nervous.

Nothing bad happened, and we got to the brownstone safely. As I walk in, I notice a very thin layer of gray dust over everything (our windows had been left opened on 9/11). It's on the furniture, on the TV, everywhere. I touch it and wonder what it is. And then it hits me. This dust is from the Twin Towers. This is from the people's bodies, their furniture, their office supplies, their files, from the buildings, from the Twin Towers. And that's when I finally lost it. I rushed up to my bedroom so Akhenaton would not see me, and I started crying uncontrollably. Their ashes had come across the river and were now in my house. I asked God to let them all rest in peace. Then I started to tenderly dust and clean up their ashes as I prayed for them.

My father has explained that his experience on 9/11 was somewhat different. He wrote the following:

Weather wise, 9/11 started out beautifully. I remember clear blue skies and a warm temperature in the low 70s. Shortly after arriving at work, a co-worker came in to my office and suggested that I come and look at TV. I went in the room next door where Fredda and a number of co-workers were gathered. We soon watched as the second plane hit the Twin Towers. I was stunned. I began to wonder how many innocent people would die. I was angry. There wasn't a lot of talking among my co-workers. Looking back, I guess everyone was dealing with his or her own private thoughts. We watched for nearly an hour, listening to the commentators speculating about the ability of the Towers to remain standing following the explosions. I was silently praying that the people would get out and that the Towers would remain standing.

When the first Tower fell, I remember distinctly thinking that there were 30,000 innocent deaths at the WTC that would be followed by the deaths of many more innocent people in the Middle East. I knew that terrorists had attacked the WTC before, and I figured similar terrorists were responsible. I was angry at the terrorists who had caused the deaths of innocent people at the WTC. I was also angry that their evil actions would lead to the death of innocent people elsewhere when our nation went forward to find them and hold them accountable.

Within minutes, my co-workers and I went to look out of the windows of our office. We were at the Board of Education building in downtown Brooklyn. We looked out of the windows on the eighth floor at 110 Livingston Street to witness the stream of individuals who had walked across the bridge from the area of the WTC into Brooklyn. Many were covered in a gray ash from head to toe. It looked like a scene from a horror movie. I am sure many were in a state of shock, but they had the presence of mind to move toward safety. I remember thinking that they were the mothers, sisters, brothers, fathers, sons, and daughters of my neighbors and of my fellow citizens. I must say that I had the deepest feeling possible of being a devoted New Yorker connected to all other New Yorkers as I looked out the window.

I soon left the window and I called your mom and told her to leave work and go pick you up at school. I instructed her to take you to Harlem, and I said I would join you all later or the next day, hoping travel would be possible.

Later at home I sat on the stoop and was stunned and amazed to smell gases and toxic compounds in the air. I also began to think about the dust that I had seen covering the furniture and floors when I had entered the house before coming to sit on the stoop.

As I continued to sit, my anger rose regarding the failure of our government to protect our people. I was angry that we had allowed some evil terrorists to kill so many people in our country. I was angry that our government seemed clueless about the extent of the threat we faced as fear seemed to rise in the country about the possibility of more immediate attacks. America had been told that our President was not immediately returning to Washington after the attack on the Pentagon. I was angry at President Bush and all the men around him who had to be taken to a secure location outside of Washington when all Americans should have been in a secure location: America itself.

Only one other time in history has an American president deliberately stayed from Washington while Washington was under attack or the threat of attack. That was President James Madison who did not return to Washington as 4,000 British soldiers in

August 1814 marched into the city and burned down the White House, the Senate, and most public buildings. While he was outside the city, he sent a messenger to his wife, Dolly Madison, asking her to quickly leave before the British arrived. That incident took place during the English-American War of 1812-1815.

I was also angry with Bill Clinton. I was angry that in previous years the Clinton administration had not been aggressive in handling the threats, attacks, and buildup of Al Qaeda.

While considering all those matters, my anger rose sufficiently to suppress the strength of my rising fears. I grew determined to move on with life in New York City.

On Monday, September 17, schools reopened in New York. As mom and I prepared to leave home, dad walked us to the door and kissed us both. He walked out unto the stoop to watch us as we walked down Park Place toward the subway. The sun was shining, and I looked forward to returning to school. Dad worked nearby and would leave in about 30 minutes.

For each school day during the next several weeks, dad would stand on the stoop until we disappeared in the distance on our way to the subway. It was a new habit he did not explain until recently in 2010. He said he was very concerned the subways were a target for terrorists, and he prayed each day that everyone would be safe riding them. He felt we had to move on with our lives, and he used that time on the stoop to see us off and to pray.

I imagine my father and mother were like so many other New York fathers and mothers, praying for the continued safety of family members who had to take the subways to schools and work.

During the first three months following 9/11, there were also concerns being expressed regarding the possible use of truck bombs to destroy bridges and tunnels in New York City. Whenever we took the Brooklyn Queens Expressway, we could see the still smoldering area where the WTC once stood. When we took the Holland Tunnel to New Jersey, we had to pass police check points. When we drove over the Brooklyn Bridge, we always passed police cars that were permanently stationed to avoid possible attempts to destroy the bridge. On the subways, we witnessed more police patrols and, at times, military patrols. Dad was taking Praying Mantis Kung Fu classes with Master Su Yu Chang in Chinatown where the smell of the smoldering ruins at the WTC remained in the air for months following 9/11, while members of the military patrolled Chinatown and downtown.

As recovery work continued at the WTC, some news reports began to suggest that New York would see a significant decline in its population as supposedly hundreds of thousands would leave to escape the terrorists' preference for targeting NYC. But we did not plan to leave, and in less than 10 years after 9/11 the population of NYC had grown by more than 200,000 residents.

During the immediate months following 9/11, there were several reports of harassment of some Arab adults and some Arab children in New York. As Superintendent in the Office of Corporate Partnerships, dad successfully reached out to Best Buy and other foundations to create a conference and training program for student leaders to ensure that all NYC students would act with respect toward their fellow students, especially Arabs and Muslims, during the aftermath of 9/11. The program was called "Diversity is Our Strength." Monies also flowed in from other companies who wanted to do something special for students who had been in schools that were situated near the WTC. Those resources were mostly directly by dad and used to build new playgrounds and library media centers in schools downtown and in Chinatown.

In late September 2001, when President Bush announced that America would go after Bin Laden and the Taliban, dad was in full support of the decision. Every night leading up to the war he followed the developments on the *News Hour* on television. He preferred the *News Hour* because he felt it provided more substance and analysis than the other nightly network newscasts. He also began to look at CNN more because it had many correspondents on the ground in the region of Pakistan and Afghanistan.

At some point in November 2001, as America prepared to go after Bin Laden and the Taliban, dad began to get frustrated with some of the news stories that suggested Bin Laden and the Taliban would be nearly impossible to beat. He questioned aloud the news stories that suggested Bin Laden had built many cave complexes that held all the supplies and war materials he would need to beat any attack from the USA.

In late November 2001, CNN, the *New York Times*, the *News Hour*, NBC's *Meet the Press* and other news outlets began reporting on and displaying what they called an artist's illustration of Bin Laden's supposedly "hidden mountain fortress." His fortress was said to contain offices and "hotel-like rooms" for Bin Laden and 2,000 Al Qaeda soldiers. There were supposedly rooms for tanks and heavy equipment, and an armory for ammunition and heavy weapons, including Stinger Missiles. The fortress supposedly had hydroelectric power through generators connected to a nearby river. A ventilation system reportedly carried fresh air some 12,000 feet into the complex, and the complex was said to be as tall as the WTC and built within a 13,000-foot mountain. The doors were said to be made of solid iron, and the whole complex was reportedly high tech with computers.[12]

Dad said, "The reporters made it sound as if a night in the Lincoln Bedroom and the President's Bedroom at the White House would be considered second class." Dad was also angry that some of the reporters spoke as if Bin Laden were some kind of a military genius who had defeated the Russians and had then used his knowledge in construction to build a fortress that would be impenetrable for American troops. Dad wasn't buying the reporters' hype about Bin Laden. He said it was American military training and weapons that provided the added power the Afghans needed to defeat the Soviet Union.

When the battle of Tora Bora began in December 2001, during every available moment it seemed as if dad was sitting before the television looking at CNN and channel surfing to get maximum news while avoiding the interruption of commercials. He said it is rather stupid that even in the midst of live reporting on an actual battle involving our nation, our news outlets must pause constantly for commercial interruption, even as bombs fall and soldiers and civilians die.

At the beginning of the battle, dad was again bad-mouthing reporters of CNN and the other American networks who bad-mouthed the soldiers of the Northern Alliance, representing Afghans who were opposed to Bin Laden and the Taliban. Dad said the reporters made the Northern Alliance soldiers seem like "the gang that couldn't shoot straight, while the Taliban was described as the masters of warfare." He was already tired about hearing how the Afghans had resisted conquest by Alexander the Great and the Russians and how they were prepared to turn Afghanistan into another Vietnam nightmare for America.

While the Northern Alliance fought on the ground, the American military bombed from the air. It took the Northern Alliance, with the assistance of the American military, less than two weeks to defeat Al Qaeda and the Taliban at Tora Bora. Dad said Bin Laden, who was reportedly directing his troops, was really trying to find a way to escape the fate of his troops. Eventually, Bin Laden escaped on a donkey to Pakistan.

With cameras rolling, news crews went into Tora Bora after the battle to film the caves after the Taliban had abandoned them. The big complex that Bin Laden reportedly developed was found to be a myth. Dad said that they had found only little caves "not much bigger than a rat's hole." He said it provided additional proof of why it is difficult to trust reporters, especially those who feel the need to paint the worse possible picture for America to keep the audience interested and tuned in to read and listen.

A few years later, dad was tuned in to hear Secretary of State, General Colin Powell, present "proof" about the existence of Saddam Hussein's "weapons of mass destruction." Dad was a Colin Powell fan. For dad, Powell was a symbol of the efforts African Americans had undertaken to defend this nation, starting with Crispus Attucks during the Revolutionary War, despite the racist treatment against the very soldiers who had defended America. For dad, Powell was also a symbol of the discipline and wisdom of African American men, which often go undeveloped due to institutional racism in our nation.

After the defeat of Saddam Hussein's army and the failure to find weapons of mass destruction, dad said he had allowed his admiration for Powell to misguide him into believing that Powell would never knowingly lie to the American people. Dad thought Powell would have turned down the assignment or resigned before knowingly lying about the presence of weapons of mass destruction. Nevertheless, he came to believe that if Powell didn't knowingly lie, he was duped by Vice President Cheney and the Bush administration to present the lie because Powell was widely respected among the American people.

Dad suggested Powell should have been in a position to know the truth and cannot be excused by giving the defense of being misinformed by the Central Intelligence Agency. Dad said, "No one would have believed Secretary of Defense Rumsfeld, so Powell was chosen to tell the big lie, which caused the needless deaths and injuries of tens of thousands of American soldiers and hundreds of thousands of innocent Iraqi civilians."

For dad, like most Americans, Afghanistan began as a "just war" against the terrorism and brutality of Al Qaeda and the Taliban targeted against America and the people of Afghanistan.

To him, Iraq is not a just war. Iraq had not attacked the USA nor, in his opinion, did it represent an imminent threat to the USA. He believes the war has taken a terrible toll on innocent Iraqi civilians with reported deaths of tens of thousands (mostly by the hands of Al Qaeda and Shiite and Sunni militias and zealots who deliberately target civilians.) He agrees with President Obama who said that it took our nation's attention from successfully completing the job started in Afghanistan.

Several of our relatives have fought in Iraq. My first cousin Eric volunteered and joined the Marines when he could have chosen to remain in college. Dad was impressed when "little skinny Eric wrote from Camp Lejeune that he was capable of doing more than 100 pull-ups and was graduating to become a Marine." Dad and mom are thankful that Eric and all our relatives have returned home safely.

Dad always pauses in silence when the *News Hour* or ABC's *This Week* list the names of American military personnel killed in action. After the silence, he sometimes makes comments about the families confronting the tragedy of lost loved ones, including soldiers as young as 18. He believes America must do more and all it can to support those families and to support wounded soldiers who return. He also believes Americans must do all that is possible to put more pressure on President Obama to bring our troops home from Afghanistan and to demand reforms that prevent zealots for warfare among our politicians from leading our nation into future unjust wars. He cites Cheney as a zealot who wanted President Bush to start a third war by bombing Syria. Dad says even Bush knew Cheney was crazy and refused to bomb Syria.

Dad also believes that General Powell and the politicians in Washington have never fully explained how the American people were "hoodwinked" into a war so that the people could determine what actions should be taken to avoid being "hoodwinked" in the future.

War has been with people since the beginning. We are counseled to love our neighbors, but we prepare for war. The wisdom of peace escapes us all, us and our enemies. So when Edwin Star sings, "There's got to be a better way," we know that mankind has not found it.

Until then, dad says "When necessary, fighting 'just wars' is the answer." Then, on reflection, he says, "The 'just war' is the just response, if indeed not the answer. Cause even in 'just wars' so many innocent people die and there is no justice in that!"

Chapter 20

The Kama Sutra Position That Ate the Homework

The SOS band is old school. The band had that song about taking the time to do "it" right. Well, "it" takes more than time to do "it" right; "it" also takes knowledge of how to do "it" right.

Did you ever as a teen tell your father something about your knowledge of sex that you would never tell your boyz? Did you ever think that you would have to tell him something that you would have preferred to keep to yourself? Well, when I was almost 14 something happened that caused me to reveal an embarrassing secret about my knowledge of sex to my dad. Read on and find out about my secret which I never thought I would reveal, and certainly never thought I would publish.

When a father sat a son down to teach him about sex in the old days, dad's days, they usually called it a conversation about "the bird and the bees." Imagine that! A straight conversation about sex was taboo. The birds and the bees? What do they have to do with sex?

Many of the fathers of my granddad's generation never had the conversation with their sons. Some were too embarrassed or thought it was best for their sons to learn as they had by experience or just doing "it," without really knowing what "it" was. You know "it" has a lot of different meanings to many different people. I learned that from listening to my classmate Juan discussing porn in middle school.

Dad's father was not around to have the conversation with dad. Granddad was a rolling stone. He was too busy doing "it" with his mistresses in different neighborhoods to take the time to tell dad how to do "it." The few fathers of my granddad's generation who had the conversations with their sons were described as using all kinds of confusing language and words to avoid speaking directly about the real deal of sex. So their sons learned nothing they could put to use.

However, by the time dad was 13, he had heard a lot of bits and pieces of information from being around men and older teenagers while working and hearing them talk about sex and relationships. He had also overheard adult women saying certain things when they must have thought he wasn't paying attention.

Since dad did not have that talk with his dad, and many of his friends did not have that talk with their dads, dad created a scenario of a likely conversation between an imaginary father and his pre-teen son that incorporates much of what dad and his friends heard from various sources at various times in their pre-teens and early teens. Thus, a conversation about sex in the late 1950s or early 1960s in rural Georgia could be expected to flow somewhat like the following (with dialect and a Southern accent):

"Well, son, ah, uh, well, uh, let me tell you 'bout the birds and the bees, and the flowers and the trees, and the moon up above, and a thing called love. You see, son, Mommy Sparrow and Daddy Sparrow have lil baby sparrows. To have dem lil baby sparrows, they rubs their bodies together. Then Mommy Sparrow and Daddy Sparrow build a nest, and a few months later lil baby sparrows hatch from eggs in the nest.

"Now when it comes to people, mommies and daddies loves just like the sparrows, and they rubs their bodies together just like the sparrows. Instead of a nest, we build houses. And nine months later, a stork 'livers the baby."

"A stork, dad? And how do you rubs mommy? And what do you call it other than rubbing?"

"Son, a stork don't 'liver no baby. That was a joke. Miss Sally Jane or a midwife 'livers that baby. You got in mommy's stomach when I laid on top of mommy's stomach and rubbedid her just like the sparrows. Muddy Waters, the King of the Blues, call it 'doing the hoochie koochie koo.' The 'portant thing is that we loves each other, and that made us want to have you. So we did the hoochie koochie koo so that we could have you.

159

"So when you gets married, you will do the same with the woman you love. Always make sure you on top, boy, there's no other place to be. You don't want no woman looking down on you. You be less than a man! And you can do it on the bed or on the flo'. But I wouldn't try no kitchen table. People have to eat dere, boy. Nobody wants to be smelling that when eating dem dere greens, corn bread, black-eyed peas, fat back, pig tails, and neck bones."

"Okay, dad, when I gets older I won't do it on the kitchen table."

"And, son, make sure you marry a good woman. Lord knows ain't nothing worse than been hooked up to a mean and ornery woman! If you want sumthang ornery, go get ya'self a mule. Dem ornery women from Bummingham, Alabama, one day dey kissing you, and the next day dey throwing hot grits or lye in your face! I hear dem gals from Jacksonville, Fla'da, pour hot grease down a man's ear while he 'sleep. If you marry one of dem, ya better sleep with one eye open. Those high yallow Creoles from Nawleans, Loo-see-anna, dey be working dem roots in that jamm-ba-laya and that hoo-doo (*brujeria*) on you.

"And dem Geechee gals from Charlston, Sous Calina, dey feed a man too much white rice. Dey don't care that you don't like rice. Dey feed it ta ya for breakfast, lunch, dinner, and supper. And don't let dem feed ya tomatoes and rice. You don't know what dey put in those tomatoes. All you'll know is that ya might no longer love her, but ya won't be able to leave her, no matter how hard ya try after eating the secret ingredients in tomatoes and rice."

"Wow, dad! Really?"

"That's right. So, son, I suggest you stick to good country girls from Jawja. Gals from good families. But make sure she ain't hi-falutin 'cause you'll never have nothing. She'll spend every dollar you got and then ask for $100 more. She'll work you ta da bone and send you to an early grave, and won't even give ya a decent burial with yur own money you left behind. For your burial you be lucky to get a clean used cardboard box that some cheap furniture came in. Boy, dem worms in dat ground be eating you before yur family and pastor even close the hole in the ground and go home for some of ya mama's fried chicken, biscuits, Kool-Aid, peach cobbler, macaroni and cheese, and collard greens cooked with a streak o' lean (that's a mound of fatback with one thin line of lean meat running through it).

"And don't expect no hi-falutin' woman to wear no black. She's gonna be wearing the prettiest flowery dress cause at yur funeral she's gon' have her eyes out looking for the next man with some cash. With her prancing around like a peacock, even the pastor might have to run home and take a cold shower and ask the Lord to forgive him."

"Dad, do you mean to say that Reverend Jackson could be tempted?"

"Son, Reverend Jackson is a man, and every man has a bit of dog in 'im! Most men can't tell the difference 'tween love and lust. Lust is often their first and last love. You better tell your daughters that!"

"Wow, dad! I will."

"And, son, make sure you 'void those fast gals down at dat dere juke joint when you get older. You don't wanna be making the same mistake your stupid no 'count cousin June Bug did. At age 21 he messed round with those fas' Jezebels down at that juke joint and ended up with three different babies by three different womens in the same year, and he ain't married to nann one."

"Dad, I didn't know that the three mas (Southern for moms) of James, Williams, and June Bug, Jr., is each named Jezebel. And, dad, does the hoochie koochie koo feels good? Is it fun?"

"Son, Jezebel is just a name given to all fas' womens. Those babies' mamas have other names. And the hoochie koochie koo can feel real good and be a lot of fun if it's done right with you on top, with the right woman, and at the right time. Don't let her look down on you, though. Anyway, boy, you have a long time before you should be doing any hoochie koochie koo. Don't be messing 'round boy. Don't be trying to bring no babies in here!"

"Thanks, pa! Now I knows errything I needs ta know. I's ready for life!"

Dad overheard that line about the tomatoes and rice at Beatrice Spann's "hair salon" (a neighbor's kitchen) when he went to get some money from his mother. A group of ladies at the "hair salon" were talking about a woman who had used that recipe on her husband. He overheard the line about the hot grease from his ex sister-in-law Barbara, who happens to be from Jacksonville.

In 1968, Mask Man and the Agents, led by Harmon Bethea, who wore a mask when he performed, produced the rhythm and blues dance hit, "One Eye Open." The song was a cautionary tale reminding men that the "sweet" heart they marry can quickly turn awfully sour as soon as the wedding bells are silenced. In the song, Bethea complains that he has to dodge boiling water, eat hot sauce she sneaks into blueberry pie, watch out for glue in the gravy because she is trying to keep his mouth shut, sneak the stew to the cat to avoid the "herbs" ("hoo-doo") she put in it to put a spell on him, and sleep with one eye open in order to awaken to another day.[13]

You can see from the conversation above between the imaginary father and son that, although the father said a whole lot, the son was left clueless about the actual experience of sex. You know, it is simply amazing that dad and his generation learned anything about sex. But, apparently, they did learn a little because my existence and the existence of my friends are living proof. I think they learned to do a bit more than rubbing.

Dad's generation did not have sex education in the schools and couldn't count on their fathers to explain sex. A lot of what dad and his friends learned, they learned from listening to older and experienced men and boys brag and from catching a quick glimpse at a pornographic magazine, when one was available (hardly ever).

In the television shows and movies of dad's generation, the married characters even slept in separate beds in the same room, so there was no rubbing or intercourse on the screen. The Internet wasn't invented, so they couldn't go online for information, and no newsstand back then would carry pornographic magazines the way newsstands do today. There was no sexting, so a teen had to use his imagination to guess what a girl might look like naked. Huh?

Dad says that he cannot remember ever hearing the word vagina or penis before he was 13. Until then, he thought vagina was the p-word and penis the d-word. Intercourse was the f-word. Those were the names that he and his boys knew and used.

Son, I would say they had a limited vocabulary, even though dad was considered highly intelligent.

However, my generation, before we reached our teens, learned to label the female and male "sexual organs." Consider those fancy words: "sexual organs." We learned the fetus is attached to an umbilical cord in the woman's uterus, not her stomach. We learned to actually use the words vagina, penis, and even intercourse, as the label for the sexual act between a man and a woman. We learned fancy words like clitoris, labia, and vulva. Our teachers even supplied pictures and we had access to certain books with the female anatomy so we knew where the vulva, labia, and clitoris were located.

Before age 18, dad had never heard the words vulva, labia, or clitoris. Dad didn't even know the p-word has different parts. All he knew was the p-word has a hole. LMAO/Laughing my a** off! He said later when he became active he "had to fumble in the dark" and half the time didn't know what he was searching for. I believe he had to get up and turn on the lights. ROTFL!

Now I want all the teenagers in America (and Canada, Mexico, Puerto Rico, the Caribbean, Nigeria, and England) who want to have that serious talk about sex with their parents, to go to their parents tonight and ask to sit and talk. Of course, we should look to our parents to educate us. Ah, we'll listen a little, but I believe no teenager wants to be hearing a lot about that from his dad and, especially, his mom. No, mom, don't even go there! *Eww!*

If boys in my generation didn't learn the correct words and locations at home, they learned them in sex education at school. Oh, yeah, everyone knows that we learned a great deal of other things about sex from our teachers, who must have qualified as "experts" on the subject before being allowed to teach the subject. Didn't our teachers qualify as "sexperts" in order to teach the subject? Isn't there a "sexpert" college degree? Huh? Can you imagine your typical teacher ever having sex? Huh?

Although dad is an educator, he is not supportive of the way sex education is taught in the schools. He does not think teachers are well trained in creating the lessons and getting kids to take seriously what is being taught. He suggests his experience is that many of the sex education lessons turn into joking sessions and opportunities for students to tease one another.

For whatever the teachers didn't teach, my generation had school mates in middle school like Juan who would gather boys around in conversation and give out the list of porno websites for illustrations of what the teachers would not present. Juan said our teachers were clueless and not giving us the real deal. Dad said the Juans of the world are full of bad information and bad advice.

So, if the teachers, teenagers like Juan, and moms and dads are not the best for sex education, at least my generation has hip hop and the rappers to teach us. Isn't that right? Huh? Shouldn't we learn about sex from Ludacris? Isn't his teaching the best way for teens to learn to protect themselves from heartache and disease? Doesn't he teach what true love is all about?

"Uh, uh, no, no," dad says. "Listening to Ludacris, Kanye, and the rappers' instructions about sex in some songs and videos is like inviting Satan into your bedroom." He declares, "Satan is the master of making the profane appear profound. He is the master of making what brings death appear as if it would bring life. Think about all the young black and Latino teenage girls and young women who have died of AIDS in the last decade the next time someone plays 'My Chick Bad' by Ludacris."

Dad adds, "Does an enlightened man spend time singing to other men about what he does sexually with 'his chick,' whom he doesn't have enough respect to see as a woman? Does an enlightened man want to imagine what some other man is doing with some other woman? Does an enlightened man take pride in having all the guys in his crew wanting to "bone" his chick?

My response is, "Dad, stop hatin' on Ludacris!"

What do you say? I know what many adults think, but I want to hear from the teenagers, boyz and girls.

Dad wants me to hold the Anthony Hamilton "Charlene" video in my mind to cancel his view of "garbage" shown in some of the videos from celebrities like Ludacris and Kanye. Dad believes that Anthony Hamilton sets the model with the most beautiful heartfelt sounds and images of a real man in love with a real woman in his video. He says "Charlene" is the "Try a Little Tenderness" of the Hip Hop Generation and Anthony Hamilton is this generation's Otis Redding when it comes to pouring pure soul into a love song.

He further believes "Charlene" is an instant classic that will be around centuries after the "gimmickry buzz" from "My Chic Bad" and "Monster" has been long buried, "despite the music critics having put Kanye on a throne with Jay-Z, and 'My Chick Bad' having reached the top of the chart but losing the Grammy."

I was 12 when I first saw Anthony Hamilton singing "Charlene," and dad and I both instantly fell in love with that song and its feeling. "Promise I'll be here to the very end. By your side, to protect you, and to love you, and be with you for life. Come on home to me, Charlene."

I must admit if I want to sing songs of my generation to my girl when we are alone, I am choosing "Charlene," Maxwell's "Pretty Wings" and John Legend's "Ordinary People." But that doesn't mean that I don't listen to Ludacris and Kanye when I am alone or with my boyz. Dad, I can handle it all, and listening doesn't mean that I am following. Dad, did you hear that? I ain't following although a lot of guys thought Ludacris and Kanye did have some good ideas in songs and videos when they suggested, _____, _____ and _____. (I ain't filling in those blanks.)

In September 2006, I started high school at Benjamin Banneker Academy. I was 13, and, like all teenagers, I wanted to be popular or at least to avoid being considered an outcast. I had been popular in my middle school, and a star on its basketball team. I had also been the star soloist on clarinet in the school's jazz band. I was determined to be a star on Banneker's basketball team, and I expected being a star would enhance my popularity at Banneker.

During my first year at Banneker, talk among boys would sometimes turn to talk about sex, when not about music, video games, and sports. Of course, everyone was a "sexpert" and no one was willing to admit knowing very little about sex, and no one was going to proclaim being a male virgin. (Only in the movies would a guy admit he is a 40-year-old virgin. Mad "stoopid.")

All the guys in my school had experience, not just a little bit but a whole lot of experience, if you could believe them. Of course, there were those guys you believed and the guys you did not believe. Then there were the guys who would talk about having 'tapped" some specific girls as they passed by. There were also guys who would leave school early to do some "tapping."

In our daily lives, sexual images were in some of our video games, on the Internet, in the movies, on television programs, and in the musical videos, especially the hip hop videos with what dad calls "the hoochie mamas."

Dad recently reminded me that I told him I wanted to wait until I was in college before having sex. (I don't think I told my boyz that.) I said that at age 13 during one of our conversations about sex when dad seemed to want to go into greater detail than before about having sex and protecting myself from venereal diseases. However, a deeper conversation would happen following an incident in September 2006 when I was almost 14.

One sunny afternoon in mid-September around 4:00 p.m., I was innocently upstairs with my friend Denise. Mom and dad had previously warned me not to bring anyone to the apartment when they were not at home. Denise, who hung out with me at the basketball court across the street from our condo, needed to use the bathroom. Though my parents weren't home, I let her come up. As she went to use the guest bathroom, I went into the bathroom in the master bedroom. However, before going our separate ways, I suggested it would be okay to sit in the study and talk when we came out of the bathrooms. I felt we had a lot to talk about since we were close friends, and we were both playing basketball on our school's teams.

About two minutes later as I emerged from the bathroom in the master bedroom into the living room, I heard the key turn in the door. I was momentarily startled. Mom walked in and gave me a warm smile.

"Mom, you're home!" I blurted out with stunned surprise framing my voice.

"Yes, *bambino*. I had a doctor's appointment and got out early. How was your day?" The sweetness in her voice, that was always there when she called me *"bambino,"* could not calm my racing heart.

With a racing heart, I responded, "Great, mom. Mom, my friend Denise came up to use the bathroom, and we were just getting ready to go back across the street to the basketball courts."

Mom turned and walked with me into the study where Denise was sitting. I could sense mom was not pleased to see Denise, but she held her temper and managed to politely greet Denise. Then I was directed to walk Denise across the street and to return immediately upstairs.

I talked with Denise as we walked, but my mind was really on constructing the story I was going to tell mom, and the story mom would tell dad.

When I returned upstairs, mom turned out to be totally unreasonable. No matter what I said, mom was not listening. No matter what I was selling, she wasn't buying. She promised a showdown between me and dad. At that time, she seemed a lot like what I had learned to expect from dad. You know dad, when he would get emotional he would practically spit out his words, and I do not mean "spit" as the rappers use that word. I mean he would shower me sometimes with the foam rising with the angry words coming from his mouth. All of that would be followed by a list of punishments, mostly regarding denying certain privileges, especially access to video games.

As mom continued speaking, the only thing missing from mom's monologue was dad's foam. "You and your father need to have a serious talk! I am not accepting your story. I do not want anyone up here when we are not home!"

"But, mom, she just came up to use the bathroom. You know there is no bathroom across the street. I don't know why you are acting unreasonable, just like dad."

Dad arrived home late that evening around 8:00 p.m. from a long day at work. He was regional deputy superintendent responsible for 140 schools and 99,000 kids in the Bronx, which kept him busy. As soon as he entered the apartment, mom pulled him aside. They spoke in the kitchen while I sat in the study. I had my Xbox on, but the images and the game could not hold my interest. I was thinking about another kind of "World of Warcraft" that had real consequences for me.

After about 15 minutes, dad came to the study. To my surprise, he seemed calmer than mom. There was no foam and no angry words, yet my heart was beating even faster than earlier.

"Akhenaton, your mother told me you had a girl up here today," dad began in a mild-mannered and exhausted tone. "You know I have told you not to bring anyone here when we are not home. We are going to have a serious talk, and I do not want you to lie to me. And, I do not want to deal with this emotionally. So go to your room, and we will have a serious conversation about this when I get off from work tomorrow."

There was no tenderness or anger in dad's voice. There was no emotion, just words almost as if he were reading from notes.

"OK, dad, but I told mom Denise just came up to use the bathroom." I had spoken with a bit of defensiveness because something in me told me that it would not be long before he changed his tone and his tune.

Again, the words rolled forth from dad with no emotion. "Say no more tonight. I want to hear the truth tomorrow. I will know if you are lying by the words you choose to say tomorrow. If you lie to me, your punishment will be beyond anything you could imagine."

As I passed dad on my way to my room, I wanted to feel relieved, but something wouldn't let me enjoy that feeling. Although dad had remained cool and had not mumbled a threatening word, my head told me war was on the horizon. Forgetting about my video games and my laptop, I picked up a book as I passed my bookcase. I reclined on the bed and read until I fell into the sweet sleep of relief.

After dinner the following evening, while mom worked at the computer in the study, dad found an opportunity to speak with me at the counter in the kitchen area. "So, as I said yesterday, I want to hear the truth. I do not want to hear a lie. Why did you bring that girl up here?"

Unbelievably, dad's voice was still without emotion. Yet, I knew he was serious, so I carefully considered my response. I shook my head, shrugged my shoulders, and sighed deeply to signal my frustration.

"Dad, I don't know what mom told you. She thinks I brought Denise up here to have sex!" I exclaimed through the voice of frustration. "We were playing ball across the street, and the playground has no bathroom. She needed to go, so I let her come up."

With piercing eyes that almost became narrow slits, dad asked, "Did you bring her up here for sex?"

"No, dad, I did not. Why would I? I did not bring her up here for that!"

A moment of silence followed as his piercing eyes continued to examine my eyes. I shrugged my shoulders with growing frustration, believing that I would never convince him. Then, with my frustration boiling over, I leaped into the silence.

"Dad, I am not lying. How could I bring her up here for sex when I don't even know how to have sex?" With that question before us, I continued to shake my hands, as if pleading, while shrugging my shoulders and shaking my head all at once. I felt trapped and embarrassed. I couldn't understand why he was giving me a hard time.

"Dad, I don't even know how to have sex," I announced again in a deflated voice that was also swollen with frustration. "I wouldn't even know where to begin."

I had told my father something that I would never have told my boyz or Denise. I felt exhausted and empty due to our conversation. Those few stressful minutes had taken a toll. I felt defeated. I felt as if I were less the man than I should have been.

With my words freshly minted, it was my father's turn to look puzzled. He asked, "What do you mean when you say you don't know how to have sex?"

In a barely audible voice I responded, "Dad, you have taught me about sex, but you have not taught me about the way to have sex. I wouldn't know how to have sex. I wouldn't know how to do it. I wouldn't know how to start. Do you ask her if she wants to? Or do you start with a kiss on the lips? I just don't know."

Dad placed his right hand under his chin as if he were in deep thought. There was another moment of silence. Then he clumsily walked into the silence and asked, "You mean the positions? What to do with a girl's body and what to do with yours, and what she will do with her body and with yours?"

After a couple of more deep sighs I responded, "I guess so, dad. You have never told me exactly what to do when having sex with a girl."

Then it was my turn to look dad in his eyes. I had spoken not to accuse but to express disappointment. I looked him in the eyes as he sat again in deep thought searching for a response.

In a tone that suggested he had missed explaining an important element of my education he responded. "Wow! I see what you mean. I've taught you about what to look for in a woman, how you must respect women, and what you must do to build a meaningful relationship. I've explained the importance of love happening before and after sex. I've told you about the purpose of sex and the parts of the body involved. I've given you books about your changing body and teen sexuality.

"I've also explained to you the importance of being mentally mature before having sex. I've told you about STDs and the importance of using condoms. I've explained what and who to avoid. I've told you to avoid the loud-mouthed girls and all girls who smoke and drink booze. I told you to be careful of those girls with a large portion of their buttocks publically displayed to reveal their so-called sexy tattoos and the waist bands of their thongs while seeking to get public attention. But I have never told you exactly how you do it, or the mechanics of doing it."

Dad grew silent again, and I accepted the silence as a time that we could both take a look inside of our minds.

"I see what you mean. I've told you what to do in general, but not in specifics. Well, now is the time to change that." Dad shook his head affirmatively, and paused in silence again. All the built-up tension in me released.

After a few more moments of silence, dad began to describe what he called the missionary position. (I vaguely remembered he had described that sexual position to me years earlier, but I had not been paying much attention.) He described how I would position myself above a woman, and how I would enter her. He described how I would kiss her lips, her neck, and her ears. He described how our bodies would move in coordinated rhythm. He said it was important to be in love and that love made it much more than just a fun exercise. He said it was also important to be old enough and mature enough to handle the emotional and other responsibilities that come with sex. We agreed that I wasn't old enough or mature enough.

Dad explained the first desire for sex comes from the eyes, and that is why we have the term "eye candy." We see someone attractive, and we think she is sexy. So our bodies are aroused, and often our thinking is suppressed, except the thinking that agrees with our arousal. With men, it is called lust and "letting the little head do the thinking for the bigger head." Dad suggested we must remember that every piece of "eye candy" ain't sweet and "eye candy" can be bad for your health, mentally as well as physically. The bigger head was there to control the eyes and to examine the "eye candy" in a manner that is beyond the ability of the eyes.

Minutes later after asking mom to vacate the study, dad took me to the study and we began to look for Kama Sutra websites that describe intercourse and have drawings of various sexual positions. He found and opened one. He showed me only depictions of what he called the missionary position: one with the man on top and one with the woman on top. We also looked for various institutes developed by doctors and psychologists who produce videotapes with young couples having sexual intercourse as teaching videos for couples.

After about five minutes, dad located the website of the Sinclair Intimacy Institute which produces the *Better Sex Video Series for Black Couples*. He ordered "Sexual Techniques for Lovers" that featured an African American couple in their early twenties. Dad also reemphasized that I should look at the books he had given me a few months earlier which address sexuality for early teen boys.

Dad said he wanted me to know what to do. Part of knowing what to do was picking the right partner and the right time, and protecting myself physically and emotionally. Thirteen was too young to do, but not too young to know. I wasn't completely comfortable with all the attention and teaching from dad, especially with mom not too far away. As a guy, I didn't want mom thinking that I was thinking about sex.

A not-so-funny thing happened the following week while waiting for the instructional video to arrive. As dad continued to teach me, he went online seeking to find an instructional video of the missionary position only. He was sure that such a video existed without all the "wild and crazy things that some people, including some rappers, say are part of sex" that he did not want me to see, such as a man having sex with two or more women.

One day he actually found such a site. After searching with the words "video of the missionary position only," several possibilities were presented. He chose a site whose description indicated it included a link to "an instructional video of the missionary position only." The McAfee anti-virus software signaled that the site did not pose a threat. However, when dad opened the site, the screen changed into a crimson red with a skull and crossbones image which must have contained a virus that killed the computer. That computer was two years old. Practically new to dad, but way past its time as far as I was concerned.

Dad was not happy to see it die. He had a lot of his office "homework" and many other files on that computer. He panicked and was not hopeful that he could retrieve the data and information he needed. He ran to ask mom for assistance. An exasperated dad explained to mom, "Help! The missionary position ate the computer and ate my homework!" Mom, who has an MBA in management information systems, tried her best, but all the computer did was to make a noise that sounded like a burp. Dad's homework and files were digested.

I was happy because that computer didn't even have a flat screen. We would eventually get a new computer with a flat screen, and I would get a new laptop. Mom wasn't thrilled about losing her files, and I would later learn she wasn't thrilled about dad's sex education efforts. She had the philosophy that I should learn from experience as I grew older. She said that is how dad and her brothers had learned. Dad told her that was a dangerous philosophy in the age of HIV and explicit sex in media, movies, the Internet, video games, music, and the arts.

At 13, I wasn't looking or ready for sex. I now hear mom thinks I tricked dad regarding my innocence in the incident with Denise. Did I? Huh?

Sex means a lot of different things to different people. You quickly learn that when you hear guys talking about sex. You also learn some of the things some guys talk about are not what you are seeking. So you learn to avoid the conversations, or you just listen in silence when the conversations are not avoidable.

My sex education did not stop at age 13. During the following years, dad and I would have other formal and informal conversations. He would often take the opportunity while we were viewing a program on television to make certain points about negative and positive relationships as depicted by the characters in movies or individuals in court television shows such as *Divorce Court* and *Judge Mathis*. For example, he would comment on what judges on television like Judge Mathis and Judge Toler describe as the lack of wisdom in the choices some people made that led to drama in identifying the actual fathers of children.

Another opportunity for these conversations would be the mornings when we would listen to the "Strawberry Letter" segment on the "Steve Harvey Morning Show." Steve Harvey, the comedian and author, would present his remedies for people who wrote to him about the dumb mistakes they had made in their sexual and love lives.

By the time I was 14, dad would allow the car radio to be tuned in to Hot 97, the local hip hop station, instead of his usual stations like KISS FM and WBLS FM. He wanted to know what I was I listening to so that he could continue to use my listening as a stepping stone to more conversations about choices before me. He remained concerned about the sexual content of some of the music, and would often take the opportunity to contradict or talk to me about the negative consequences of the actions some rappers promoted.

As dad listened to Hot 97, he said the golden age of hip hop had passed in the late 1970s and the 1980s. He reported he had been a fan of Grand

Master Melle Mel, Grand Master Flash and the Furious Five, Run DMC, Afrika Bambaataa, A Tribe Called Quest, the Sugar Hill Gang, Public Enemy, and other rappers who often carried meaningful messages in their recordings.

Dad suggested that he has not heard anything new that comes close to standing up to the insight in the "Beat Street" lyrics with Grand Master Melle Mel performing with Grand Master Flash and the Furious Five. He said, "That song spoke so much truth back then and even remains the truth today. It is the closest thing one could find in popular music to being visionary and prophetic."

Nevertheless, he also began to listen to and appreciate certain new hip hop artists and their songs. He later fell in love with songs such as:

- Chamillionaire's "Ridin' (dirty)"
- Eminem's "Mosh" and "Not Afraid"
- B.o.B's "I'll Be in the Sky"
- Kanye's and Jeezy's "Amazin'"
- Kanye's "Touch the Sky" and "Good Morning"
- Yung L.A.'s "Ain't I"
- T.I.'s "Dead and Gone," "Live Your Life," and "Whatever You Like"
- Flo Rida's "Right Round" (Dad didn't know he was singing to a stripper.)
- Woka's "Oh Let's Do It"
- Fort Minor's "Remember the Name"
- Gucci Mane's "Stoopid"
- Common's "Universal Mind Control" and "Testify"
- DJ Khaled's "Fed Up" and "Victory"
- Lupe's "Daydreaming," "Hi-Definition," "The Show Goes On," and "Super Star"
- Wale's "Mama Told Me"
- Roscoe Dash's "All the Way Turnt Up"
- Murs' "L.A.," "Better Than the Best," and "Lookin' Fly"

Before being introduced to those artists, dad already knew and listened to Jay-Z, P. Diddy, Fifty Cents, Black Eyed Peas, Mos Def, Tupac, Ice Cube, LL Cool J, Ice-T, Naughty by Nature, Method Man, Lil John, Soulja Boy, Sean Kingston, DMX, Nas, Notorious B.I.G., Dr. Dre, Geto Boys, Blackstreet, Andre 3000, Snoop Dogg, Common, and Outkast. Dad admired Jay-Z, P. Diddy, and Fifty Cents as entrepreneurs who had the vision to take their talents and create and influence commercial enterprises. He and I wore Jay-Z's Rocawear and P. Diddy's Sean John clothing (that I passed down to him), and we drank Fifty Cent's Vitamin Water (which earned Fifty Cent more than $500 million as an investor and promoter).

In 2003 when dad worked at the Department of Education, he coordinated and worked with P. Diddy on a partnership during P. Diddy's running of the NYC Marathon. Based on his courage to run and put in the time for training, P. Diddy received donations from Jay-Z, Bruce Willis, Jennifer Lopez, Chris Rock, Jamie Foxx, Ben Afleck, Ashton Kutcher, and other celebrities to support improvement in educational and social programs for youths. P. Diddy raised more than $2 million while completing the 26.2-mile run in 4 hours and 14 minutes. Of the money raised, $1 million was used to support the renovation of eight school libraries selected by dad in communities such as Spanish Harlem, Central Harlem, Bedford Stuyvesant, East Flatbush, and the South Bronx. P. Diddy used the other funds to support youth with the life-threatening challenges of HIV and AIDS.

Dad with P. Diddy in one of the libraries (Life Magazine, The Year's Most Memorable Photos of 2011)

Of course, I introduced dad to other hip hop artists such as Drake, Juelz Santana, and Lil Wayne. He liked the voice of the early Drake. He says the later Drake retains a great voice but needs something else to say with meaning. I agree. Since he got with Lil Wayne he ain't saying anything interesting. Juelz Santana expressed the rhythm, rap, and meaning dad wanted with "Second

Coming." "Mr. Carter" and "Let the Beat Build" convinced dad that Lil Wayne had some unique talents.

There's an upside and a downside to introducing a father to Lil Wayne and current hip hop music. Unfortunately, you may have to hear him attempt to sing or see him attempt to dance. For example, when dad fell in love with Murs' "Lookin' Fly," I had to see and hear him. It was not a pretty sight or a pleasant sound. I once walked in on him as he worked on this memoir. There he sat in the study, typing away while listening to and singing Chamillionaire's "Ridin'" as I attempted to close my ears. Who wants to hear their father singing, "The po-po be hatin' and trying to catch me ridin' dirty..."? Does any teenager want his father to wake him up singing "All the Way Turnt Up" when the teen is trying to snooze for 15 more minutes?

Throughout the period of working on this memoir, dad would continue to listen to various hip hop songs he categorized as "the good, the bad, and the ugly." He listened to them for inspiration and to stimulate his memory of the conversations and arguments we had back then when I was too busy listening to these songs myself to really do all the studying I needed to do.

BTW, dad purchased the MAGIX MP3 Maker 15 software that would enable him to edit out the N-word and the B-word in hip hop songs he wanted to roll with. He wanted to hear Murs sing, "Long time comin', but I been runnin', hands underground like Harriet Tubman" and "I'm getting play on both coasts like the LA Knicks" without hearing the N-word. He said he doesn't see any added value of using the N-word in "Looking Fly" and many other hip hot hits. I say it's hard to take the N-word out of Woka's "Oh Let's Do It."

Dad classified "My Chick" in the "ugly" group. He just didn't want to hear "My Chick" or allow it to penetrate his thoughts when he was not working on this memoir (although he'll listen to "Oh Let's Do It" even when not working on it). So, whenever Ludacris popped up on the car radio in 2010, dad popped off the station. Dad was not trying to hear that Ludacris' chick was doing "stuff" someone else's chick wishes she could.

However, most of the guys at Banneker and I were singing right along with Ludacris.

Dad suggests some of the things some people do and call sex have no place in the human experience. Dad says drugs plus alcohol plus sex with several bad chicks at once, noted as some rappers' formula, is a recipe for disaster. Dad counsels that "an hour-long, great time with Ludacris' bad chick could lead to a short lifetime full of continuing misery."

He said a man would be better off just having those "bad chicks" throw hot grits in his face. "The grits will cool, but that continuing misery can stay hot for a lifetime and early death."

Huh. I must secretly admit that is something to think about.

To that admission, dad says, "Swag!"

Chapter 21

Hakuna Matata: A Teenager's Philosophy

One of the great things about living in New York is you could be in a school in Brooklyn in the afternoon and find yourself transported to another world that evening via *The Lion King* or another Broadway play just a subway ride away. *The Lion King* was the first Broadway play I saw with my parents a few days before I turned 7 in 1999. However, I had seen *The Lion King* with my Lefferts Gardens Montessori class at the age of 5. Within a period of two years, I would have the opportunity to see the play four times. In November 2010, my parents and I were planning to see it again, and who knows how many more times we will see the play before it leaves Broadway.

Each and every time I saw *The Lion King* I would identify with Simba. Even today my girlfriend often affectionately refers to me as Simba. Mufasa reminded me somewhat of dad. I love dad and have learned a great deal from him, but I yearn to be free to move off the path where he is guiding. Dad and mom think that I have too much of the hakuna matata philosophy guiding my life.

Sir Elton John wrote the music and Tim Rice wrote the lyrics for the "Circle of Life." I can't count how many times I have been re-inspired hearing that song since my first attempt to sing it at the age of 3.

Tim Rice tells us that the circle of life moves us all. He says it moves us through despair and hope. He says it moves us through faith and love. He also suggests it moves us "Till we find our place on the path unwinding." Dad declares, "That place is a special place reserved for each of us. We are all on that path to that place. Unfortunately, for some the path seems to never unwind; it seems to maintain its twists and turns, denying peace."

Dad suggests, "The orbit of the earth around the sun is not circular, it is elliptical, or as some nonscientists would say, almost circular. The earth does not maintain a consistent distance from the sun as it moves through its orbit. Despite what you may have heard, in life everything that goes around does not come back around. Karma is pushed aside by Grace. Life does not move in a circle. The circle is a metaphor for the ellipse or spiral that life moves in. We use the word circle because who would dare sing 'The Ellipse of Life?'"

Dad further suggests, "In the orbit of life, as in the orbit of the earth, one finds consistency and change. It is the consistency that can make us appear like our fathers, but the change that makes us not our actual dads. The consistency brings stability, but the change brings progress. Life in a circle would lose its value. Karma without Grace murders all hope."

The Lion King opens with Tsidii Le Loka from the nation of Lesotho in southern Africa. She plays the role of Rafiki, a mandrill-baboon hybrid. Willie Wilson, an African American, is supervisor of puppets and the puppet workshop for *The Lion King*. Two hundred puppets are used and 17,000 hours were necessary to create all the puppets and masks.

The Lion King is the story of a young prince, Simba, and his father, King Mufasa. As a father, Mufasa attempts to prepare Simba for his destiny: kingship of the pride land. Mufasa is a wise and successful ruler who oversees great prosperity for the animals of the pride land.

Simba loves his father, but must disobey him in order to really reach his destiny, which cannot be truly defined by his father's view of the world. Mufasa gives Simba all of the privileges of being a prince. Mufasa gives him his time, his presence, and his guidance. He takes Simba exploring. He dreams with Simba about the future and Simba's role in shaping that future. He wants Simba to stand on his shoulders and the shoulders of past kings to create a better future than the current one created under Mufasa's leadership. He shows Simba the path he should walk and the paths that he should avoid. He attempts to keep all negative things from Simba's view and experience.

Simba has it good. However, like other boys who have it really good, good is not good enough nor is it satisfying enough to Simba. He is bright and curious, but his confidence does not allow him to see his naïveté. He is smart but not wise. He has knowledge but lacks wisdom.

Simba's overconfidence and lack of wisdom are used by his evil uncle Scar to bring about the death of Mufasa.

Feeling guilty and confused, Simba departs and lives the Hakuna Matata life as a teenager in exile. He lives a life with no responsibilities or cares. Then one night he looks into a star-filled sky, sees his father's image, and hears, "He lives in you." He returns to the pride land to dethrone Scar and restore prosperity to all. Soon he welcomes a son, a new prince, who must find his own way on the path unwinding.

Some people might think that *The Lion King* is a simple fairy tale that is too good to come true. However, it is a metaphor for human experience in real life. In some ways, it's similar to the story my father often retells to me and my sisters about the "Prodigal Son." In that story, told by Jesus, the prodigal son must also disobey his father and sink very low before gaining awareness that allows him to return home to a place his father has prepared for him to achieve his destiny. Soon after becoming a young adult (but probably still in his late teens), the prodigal son asks his father to give him his inheritance. With his inheritance, he goes to a land far away to live a wild and loose life among people who go about doing wild things. Soon his wealth is gone. He starts to work caring for pigs and becomes so hungry and desperate he considers squatting in the mud next to the pigs to eat what they are eating from the same trough.

Then, at his lowest point, he remembers his father and starts home. For years his father has been watching the road hoping for his return. His father sees him coming in the distance, and he runs to meet him. When he sees his father, he tells him that he has "sinned" and that he is willing to be treated as one of his many servants. His father kisses him, places a ring on his finger, and treats him like a prince.

His older brother, who had stayed home all those years, complains that he has not been treated like a prince. The father responds saying that all he has was always available to that brother who could have chosen to live like the prince he is at any given moment. Instead, the brother had chosen to work hard and be responsible as if he were a servant of the father even though all that the father has belonged to him. The father further explains that there is cause to celebrate because the younger brother had died and has returned home alive. The older brother ain't trying to hear that.

Yet, the father's response echoes Jesus' revelation that suggested, "There shall be more joy in heaven over one sinner who repents than over 99 persons who need no repentance." There is more joy expressed when one son returns home than the joy expressed with 99 sons who never go astray.

Dad also suggests that *The Lion King* brings to mind the story of Buddha as told by Herman Hess in the book *Siddhartha* and Deepak Chopra in the book *Buddha*. He explains Siddhartha was a prince whose father would not allow him to see sick, old, and dying people. Siddhartha's father kept him away from dangers and exposed him only to beauty and health. However, Siddhartha, as a teenager, stumbles upon sick and dying people when he disobeys his father and leaves the palace grounds. With that exposure, Siddhartha defies his father and sets forth into the world to discover a remedy for the suffering that he now knows every human must experience. He leaves behind a world of wealth and pleasure for one of extreme discipline and extreme self-denial.

In search for the remedy from suffering, Siddhartha tries many paths including extreme fasting that could have led to his death, extended periods of meditation and isolation, and finally the path of lust and riches with Kamala, a beautiful courtesan. Kamala assists him in becoming an incredibly wealthy merchant as the life of meditation and self-denial recedes. Then, at the top of the world, he realizes that there is a compelling emptiness. The songbird that resided in his heart is dead. The songbird is dead from his pursuit of passion, from the deadening whispers of the great wealth and power he had accumulated, and from the meaningless high respect that all around him shower upon him. He leaves that world and finds his way to a distant river.

On the bank of the river he sits under a coconut tree. He looks into the water and spits at his image. The river knows that he has lived a life full of folly and had lost sight of his original mission of finding a remedy for human suffering. He looks into the moving currents and sees the currents of his life passing. While he is absorbed in the images of the past, the river laughs at him. He realizes he is a wretch. He bends and falls headlong in search of death. On the riverbed, the mantra "Om" suddenly emerges from a very remote part of his soul. He is horrified by the folly of his actions. He falls asleep under the tree so that "Om" could set free his enlightenment.

Enlightened, he begins the simple task of working as an apprentice fer-ryman assisting an older man, Vesudeva. Soon he discovers he has a son when Kamala arrives after searching years for him. Kamala is ill and she soon dies. His son is a rebellious teen who is used to a life of luxury. Siddhartha attempts to hold him by the river, but his son steals the available money and makes his way back to the town and the rich estate that Siddhartha had developed with Kamala. Siddhartha is heartbroken because his only love has departed to live life as he chooses. Siddhartha discovers that enlightenment doesn't prevent a broken heart.

However, Vesudeva teaches Siddhartha to listen to the river. The river instructs Siddhartha to let the child find his own way. Vesudeva dies. Siddhartha is an old man and all alone, but he is not lonely because the river has revealed the remedy for suffering. He remains by that river as a teacher of freedom from suffering and as a simple ferryman, rowing monks in search of the remedy and rowing life's travelers along the rivers of their experience. He teaches a philosophy that attempts to free mankind from the suffering that comes from mankind's desires, thoughts, and illusions. He teaches that our desires, thoughts, and illusions, the ones we cherish most, are the real demons and dangers to our well-being.

Finally, dad believes *The Lion King* is the story of many young men and women in America who are going astray but will one day find their way back to the kingdom. He says it's the story of Malcolm X rising from dropout, prisoner, drug addict, and pimp to genius and liberator.

It's the story of Michael Vick, rising from dog abuser and prisoner to become a prominent speaker against animal abuse and a model of someone who overcomes self-inflicted adversities borne of his desires, thoughts, and illusions.

It is also the story of Mark Sanchez, who, despite all of the great early guidance from his father, was arrested when accused of rape. Although the charges were later dropped, he was disciplined by the Trojans football team for underage drinking and the use of fake identification on the night of his arrest. Nevertheless, Sanchez picked himself up and led USC to victory in the 2009 Rose Bowl, and dad believes he may be a few years of added experience from leading the Jets to a Super Bowl.

More importantly, before leaving USC Sanchez chose to learn to be fluent in Spanish to improve his interaction with Spanish-language media and to become active as a leading role model in high school sports leagues and after school programs in the Los Angeles area. Gustavo Arrelano wrote that Sanchez has inspired other Mexican American high school football players to seek to destroy the stereotypes which suggest that they are "too small, too inexperienced, and too Mexican" for college scouts to notice.

From experiences with my friends, I have discovered that I am not the only teenage son in America who has been locked in a battle with a father who wants to show the paths that must be walked and the ones that must be avoided. I am not the only son currently resisting to take full advantage of a legacy my father has established.

Am I Simba seeking excitement in the physical and mental wastelands that my father cautions me to avoid? Do I have too much of the Hakuna Matata philosophy guiding my teen years? Dad's response would be "yes," but I think he could be wrong. Don't you? The answer is as clear as black and white to me.

Hakuna Matata means don't worry, chill. "Do I need to get to class on time? Dad, why do I need to get to class minutes before time? Do I need to log off Facebook and Twitter? Must I make the bed? Why not eat in my room and leave the crumbs on the floor? Do I need to eagerly do boring homework? Why not wait until the last minute to write the essay that is due? Why not download my music now? Why not leave stale food in my backpack with my school books? Why must I print the completed assignment now instead of waiting until tomorrow when I am ready to walk out the door and might find the printer having technical difficulty?"

Do I really need to use my Beats just because my parents say they need silence while working on their professional projects from home? Shouldn't I order from Antonio's Pizzeria when dinner with vegetables is ready? Why not leave half-empty bottles of water in my room? Should I have to place my MetroCard consistently in one place where I could find it instead of risking being late to class if I am unable to locate it at the last moment? Why not put my sweaty basketball jersey in the bag with my school work? Why not leave clothes scattered on the floor? Why strive for an A when a B will do?

Hakuna Matata means don't worry, chill, I am handling my business. Hakuna Matata, it's the teenagers' philosophy, and I am an American teen. We're living in a Hakuna Matata world.

"Dad, I don't drink. I don't smoke. I don't gamble. I don't do drugs. I don't even take aspirin when I have pain from hooping. I am not asking for my inheritance to go away and spend on loose living. I don't go looking for trouble. I choose my friends carefully. I am comfortable dressing in a professional manner for interviews, class presentations, and when taking my girl out on special occasions." (Claudine's VIP French Cleaners, on Vanderbilt Avenue in Prospect Heights, does an excellent job keeping me looking good, and mom is a master on the iron, when necessary.)

"I also come home every night. I don't hang with friends who would encourage me to do stupid things. I like one girl at a time. I don't curse, unless you or mom pisses me off beyond reason. Even then, the most I would rarely say is 'WTF/What the f***!' You'll never find me seeking to hurt anyone mentally or physically. I don't use the N-word in conversation, although I must admit listening to and singing DMX's and Lil Wayne's songs that often use it. I don't have ignorant friends who would walk the streets of New York using the N-word for public entertainment. I ignore loud-mouthed females who ride the subways and buses no matter how physically cute they may be.

"Furthermore, I am not walking around as if I have no mind with pants down around my knees and stink underwear displayed. I'm willing to volunteer to help the homeless and senior citizens. I am intelligent. I love my family. I love God. Hakuna Matata, why isn't that enough?" EOR/End of rant!

Dad responded, "Akhenaton, when will you look skyward into a lonely starry night and hear: 'He lives in you?'"

Dad wants that to happen while he still walks the earth in full health. He wants the part of the brain that controls my reasoning to become fully mature before its time, which he knows neuroscientists say is age 21. I am only 18 years old. Can one enjoy fruit pulled from a tree before its season? Sometimes one has to go without experiencing what would taste tart today to enjoy a taste sweeter than honey in the proper season. Someone needs to tell him that.

Dad grew up in the Black Power and Black is Beautiful Generation. The themes of that generation emphasized racial respect and self-respect, brotherhood among African Americans, Latinos and people of color, the pursuit of justice and higher education, respect for black women, and the acquisition of political and economic power. According to dad, the themes of that generation were deliberately diluted beginning in the 1970s, for example, when America's media, entertainment industry, and Hollywood promoted among African Americans the selfish theme of "do your own thang" and the pimping theme of "Super Fly" and "Sweet Sweetback's Baadasssss Song."

By the late 1980s and the beginning of the 1990s, the media were promoting the theme of the "Mac Daddy," a super-sexed black man that every black man supposedly wanted to be, even black students and professors at HBCUs (Historically Black Colleges and Universities) and Harvard. "Mac Daddy" had been a name associated with pimps for nearly 100 years, but dad said the media was making it cool for nonpimps to claim the title as a testament to their supposed sexual prowess.

Being a "Mac Daddy" had nothing to do with being a daddy who would take care of his children and family. Chris "Mac Daddy" Kelly and Chris "Daddy Mac" Smith of Kris Kross helped to popularize the term with the hit "Jump" which was No. 1 for eight weeks on Billboard in 1992. Kelly and Smith also wore their clothes backwards, and many of their fans chose to do likewise. They were so popular that Michael Jackson gave them a spot on his world tour in 1992. Soon afterward, Kris Kross and the backward style became old, and sagging became a new style of fashion promoted by some rappers in the early 1990s. Sagging eventually spread to the larger American culture with whites adopting the style.

Sagging has also crossed the oceans into other cultures. Some people are sagging in London and even Tokyo. Kazuhiro Kokubo was ranked No. 2 in the World Cup in 2010 for the halfpipe in snowboarding at the beginning of the Winter Olympics in Vancouver. However, when the 21-year-old Japanese arrived in Canada, he was widely criticized for sagging. As a consequence of bad publicity and embarrassment for Japan, the Ski Association of Japan banned Kokubo and the team's manager and coaches from participating in the Olympic opening ceremony.

I was born in 1992, the year of "Jump" and Kris Kross' backward fashion. I was born into the Hip Hop Generation. Dad says by then the media and some ignorant yet popular black musicians, actors, and actresses had done a pretty good job of significantly diluting the revolutionary themes of the Black Power and Black is Beautiful Generation in the minds and culture of African Americans. He says the most negative aspects of the message of some in the Hip Hop Generation have continued to dilute the themes and the psychological accomplishments of the Black Power and Black is Beautiful Generation.

Dad suggests, "The power elite, which thinks incarceration before education, understands the importance of culture, language, symbols, images, and music in shaping the habits and desires of a people, especially the youth. Therefore, that elite will pay for someone to peddle the most negative and degrading language, images, music, and symbols to blacks and Latinos to perpetuate their mental enslavement and physical incarceration. Plus, while some rappers might make big dollars, Chris Tucker has taught us in *Rush Hour II* that there is always a representative of the power elite, the one percent, waiting for his cut, and that cut is always the biggest portion."

When dad was in his teens, the peace sign, the Black Power handshake, the raised clenched fist, a poster of Malcolm X, the Black Panther logo, and the black beret were among the powerful symbols and images of resistance. "Off the pig," plus "right on," plus "brother," and "sister," and "peace," plus "free your mind and your a** will follow," and "Power to the People," were words and phrases that conveyed meaning and brought folks together in the struggle for justice when spoken with the right rhythm and spirit. When one black man greeted another with "What's up?" the response was usually "Everything is everything." Those words suggested possession of discipline and the will to transform the world.

"Lift Every Voice and Sing" became our national anthem which was supported by James Brown's "Say It Loud, I'm Black and I'm Proud" and the Impressions' "Keep on Pushing," among other songs of resistance.

Dad says he can still remember around 1970 when President Nixon sought to diminish the power of the words, symbols, and images in a speech. "Law and order" Nixon flashed the peace sign and said "right on" in a televised speech as if he were in harmony with the very people and the struggles he was attempting to suppress.

Soon after Nixon's speech, dad reports, Hollywood started to release all the movies that offered blacks other images and symbols of a more compliant "Negro" such as "Shaft," "Super Fly," and "Foxy Brown," plus "The Mack" and "Sweet Sweetback." Hollywood presented "shucking and jiving Negroes" as pimps, pushers, street criminals, prostitutes, and cops unconcerned with the larger issues of economic exploitation, white supremacy, unjust wars against people of color, and the exploitation of Africa, the Caribbean, Asia, and Latin America.

Dad says Hollywood could have made a movie about John Carlos and Tommie Smith and their heroics at the 1968 Olympics in Mexico City. Instead, Carlos and Smith were left to suffer the sting of society upon their return home. When Carlos and Smith raised their fists in the Black Power salute on the podium, the USA Olympic Committee forced them to leave Mexico City immediately afterward. To blunt the sociological impact of their salute, the USA Olympic Committee a few days later had George Foreman enter the boxing ring in Mexico City waving two American flags. George Foreman's image with the American flags was used to counter the image of John Carlos and Tommie Smith with their raised fists. George Foreman's image was used to suggest everything was just fine in America, and America's white sports broadcasters praised Foreman and denigrated Carlos and Smith.

However, Foreman would suffer a lack of support among African Americans and Africans who preferred images of the righteous defiance Muhammad Ali was very adept at presenting. Foreman would later complain in the run up to the "Rumble in the Jungle" that he couldn't understand how Africans preferred Ali because he was "blacker" in appearance than Ali. He didn't understand that preference was given to perspective and not skin color.

Dad declares "Glory Road" would have been more pertinent in the early 1970s than during its release in 2006. That movie was about the 1966 NCAA Championship where Texas Western's all-black starting five defeated Pat Riley, Adolph Rupp, and all-white Kentucky. "The Great Debaters" would have been more pertinent in the 1970s than during its release in 2007. That movie is based on the story of how an all-black debate team from Wiley College beat an all-white debate team from Harvard in the 1930s. However, Hollywood was not interested in producing anything that would boost the determination of African Americans for seeking freedom, justice, and equality.

BTW, in reality, the Wiley team beat USC which had been the undefeated national debate champion. Although Wiley College won, Wiley could not be declared champion since the debate society did not allow black membership until after World War II.

I am coming of age in the Hip Hop Generation while living under the guidance of a father who came of age in the Black Power and Black is Beautiful Generation. I am pulled by two worlds, two visions of what the world should be. As Usher might remark, that reality is enough to have me "caught up and twisted" at times.

During one discussion of music dad said, "I know all of hip hop isn't negative. I like many of the artists with positive messages that you have introduced to me including B.o.B and Lupe Fiasco. Many other groups are very talented and carry positive messages, like the message in Lupe's, 'The Show Goes On.' Yet, they don't seem outrageous enough to get contracts or even cable or radio play. There is a consequence: a big difference between the messages and images chosen by the Black Power, Black is Beautiful Generation, and the negative messages that some artists constantly place before the Hip Hop Generation."

Dad further declared that when one considers the differences in the images and messages, "It is as if one is looking at two different worlds."

He continued, "One world emphasized natural beauty, while the other world emphasizes cosmetic beauty. One chose natural hair; the other often worships the weave. One was blessed with the presence and dedication of Ali; the other is often called to worship a self-centered and self-righteous LeBron. One quoted and sought to live by the words of MLK and Malcolm; the other often quotes and sometimes tries to live by the words of Lil Wayne. One followed Angela Davis; the other follows Rihanna ('rum bum bum bum, rum bum bum bum, rum bum bum bum').

"A black man and a Latino would be called brother, soul brother, brother-man, or blood by one; the other often calls him nig***, b*tch, jigga, or dawg. A black woman and a Latina would be called sister, soul sister, or my queen by one; the other sometimes calls her ho, b*tch, or b*atch. One often wore the Panthers' black beret and fatigues; the other often wears doo rags and sagging pants. One emphasized discipline and studying; the other often emphasizes rapping, drinking, gambling, life-risking sexual activities, fronting, and sports. One often issued songs of defiance demanding a revolution in the education and economic circumstances of our people; while the other too often issues songs that celebrate the mental enslavement of African Americans and the terrible living circumstances that send them to an early grave.

"Devotion to improving the lives of black people ruled one, while cash rules everything around the other, 'C.R.E.A.M. Get the money. Dollar, dollar bill, y'all.'

"To lift black people, one often sang songs to 'fight the power;' the other often fights and degrades/takes down his brothers and sisters and asks 'the power' to pay him millions to rap about it!"

When I introduced dad to Lil Wayne, he had already heard bits and pieces of his raps but had not sat down with an open mind to really listen. When he sat and really listened, he instantly understood why Lil Wayne is near the top, along with Lupe, Wale, Jay-Z, Kanye, and J. Cole.

Dad suggested that Lil Wayne's "Let the Beat Build" and "Mr. Carter" instantly let him know that he was listening to one of the few unique master lyricists plus a master of rhythm and spoken word, who, like Jay-Z, could take hip hop to another level.

Dad wanted to imagine what Lil Wayne, Jay-Z, Kanye, and a few others could do with their unique gifts if they were to fall under the influence of a modern-day Malcolm X, as Cassius Clay had fallen under the influence of Malcolm X in the early 1960s.[14]

Clay was initially controlled by 11 white men from Kentucky (the Louisville Sponsoring Group) who held control of his career starting at age 15 and signed him to a contract at age 18. Ali later reported that as the 18-year-old Cassius Clay, he was extremely talented and dreaming of being the best ever. However, he had no internal confidence about who he was as a man, a black man. In 1991, Ali told *Sports Illustrated*, "I was a Negro. I ate pork. I had no confidence. I thought white people were superior."

Dad remarked that Cassius Clay was transformed under the influence of Malcolm X and began using his unique gifts to "rap" words and poetic phrases and take courageous political actions to uplift black people and people of color who were oppressed, robbed, brutalized, and murdered by white supremacists throughout a turbulent and colonized world.[16] That is why his face is still considered the most recognizable face in world history, and he is still revered and beloved by people throughout the world today. Dad suggests that Jay-Z's

Water for Life Project is the kind of humanitarian action that would make Malcolm X very proud.[17]

Dad says it is important to remember that Malcolm Little was nothing more than a pimp, thief, hustler, and drug abuser before he met the Honorable Elijah Muhammad and was transformed as Malcolm X. Malcolm Little was entirely into "shucking and jiving" until he heard another voice from within that turned his life toward discipline and a sense of purpose.

I am black, beautiful, and proud. However, I didn't have to struggle like dad with the negative images of *Tarzan* and *Amos 'n' Andy* being fed into his mind every day. In my early years, he kept a lot of what he considered "garbage" television shows, like *In Living Color*, from my eyes and ears.

When dad made the transition from being brainwashed, he had to choose to be vigilant about preventing the re-pollution of his mind. His sensitivity meter remains high. He will not listen to certain songs or look at certain movies or television shows no matter how popular they might be. He does not want his subconscious mind influenced in a manner that his conscious mind might not quickly detect.

Meanwhile, dad says that I am as vigilant as I mistakenly think I need to be. Some of what I listen to and watch he would prefer to censor, but censoring days are over. Hakuna Matata, I control what I think! Don't I? Hakuna Matata, it is easy to control what we think. Isn't it? Hakuna Matata means don't worry. Should we?

Dad did not have a father around to disobey. Thus, his mom was there to disobey. Dad told me that a few days after turning 15 years old, he told his mother he had found someone to take him to the enchanting land of New York. His mother gave a look of disapproval.

Grandma must have been concerned that dad had only met the person that afternoon and had only spoken with him for less than five minutes. She saw New York as a wilderness possessing all the dangers and evils to which she did not want her Simba exposed. He said he told his mom that if she made him stay in Georgia he would not be happy. She had held him back from leaving since the age of 11, and he was no longer willing to be held back.

He said he told her, "Mama, you know I am a good son. If you make me stay, I will still be a good son, but I will not be happy."

When his mom looked into his eyes and saw that he was serious about deliberately making himself miserable, she let him go. She had learned what to expect from her past experiences of dealing with his legendary stubbornness when he did not get his way.

In my first month at Hampton University in September 2010, dad believed Hakuna Matata had its grip on me. My father was still struggling to let me go. As a 17-year-old, I was expected to call every Saturday afternoon and respond immediately to his text messages and emails. I didn't. When I had to change my schedule, he wrote an email and called my advisor when he thought I was not moving quickly enough to avoid missing the deadline for schedule changes. When he reached my advisor, my advisor told him that he had just completed the process with me a few hours earlier. I had two weeks to change my schedule, and I beat the deadline by 24 hours. That was good enough for me because it was very difficult to get to see the advisor due to long lines of students each day. But that was not good enough for dad because dad is the type who does anything important immediately. I do, too. It's just that I do not agree with some of the things dad thinks are very important or the response time he thinks is necessary.

Concerning my dorm room, he wrote me emails and called me several times suggesting actions I should take in speaking with the dorm leader about ensuring that I remain in a single room. Hakuna Matata, I didn't follow his suggestions but handled it in my own way and managed to stay in a single room, but only because student enrollment did not increase.

When dad and mom arrived for homecoming in October, he insisted upon visiting my dorm room against my strong arguments. I knew my room was messy, but figured I would eventually get around to cleaning and organizing it on my own, in my own time. However, when he discovered the room in "unimaginable disarray," he and mom insisted upon helping me clean it. After three hours of the three of us cleaning, I must admit I was thankful for that help. Hakuna Matata, in six weeks, when mom and dad returned to take me home for Christmas, the room was almost back to being in the same messy condition.

In October 2010, when I had not returned his calls or texts for over a period of 10 days, dad went to Bank of America and removed all of my cash from the debit card except for $13.52. I must admit that Hakuna Matata wilted because he got my attention. I called within a few minutes of finding I had little cash available.

"Hi, dad."

"Who is this?"

"Akhenaton, dad."

"Who?"

"Akhenaton."

"Oh, I see your phone is working now."

"Yes, I was waiting for a ride to take it off campus to the AT&T Store. I couldn't get a ride right away but there is a guy in the dorm with mad skills. I found out and paid him $5 and he was able to fix it."

"How are your classes?"

"Oh, everything is cool. Things are just fine."

"That's good to know. You need to make sure you keep us posted on your progress."

"No problem. By the way dad, could you place money on my debit card and put in $40 extra for laundry?"

"I've put nearly $100 weekly. That should be more than enough for food, laundry, the movies and entertainment."

"Dad, I don't eat the cafeteria food. It's nasty."

"But I have paid for 19 meals weekly."

"Dad, the vegetables are soggy and even the fried chicken is messed up."

"You are just saying that."

"Dad, no one here eats that food and the last time I ate it, the other day when I had no money, I threw up! I am not going to be making myself sick eating that food!"

"Well I am not going to be paying for Red Lobster, Chick-fil-A, Domino's, and Chinese food every night!"

"The food is horrible here! My friends at Delaware State say the food is much better there!"

"They are telling you that because they don't have anyone giving them nearly a $100 to eat out and to do laundry!"

"Dad, I am 6 feet 4 inches and 200 pounds. I need food. Ain't nothing here to do but play ball when they let you in the gym. It's boring and so you eat with your friends and that's like your entertainment. I don't drink and I don't do drugs. If I am not playing ball, I am in my room with a few friends playing video games and we order takeout."

"Well, you need to keep the schedule and call home once a week Saturday afternoon and respond to texts when you receive them."

"I did until my phone stopped working."

Previously, by way of email, I had given the excuse that my cell phone was not working. However, when I discovered I had no cash, I had quickly found a way to make it work and quickly called home. With cash back in the bank, dad said Hakuna Matata blossomed again.

Like most of the students at Hampton, I informed my parents that the food in the cafeteria was not edible. Trust me, it's not! Dad insisted that he was not going to give me "unlimited money" to eat. For some reason, the cafeteria food started tasting a little bit better. Weeks later, I even told him about enjoying the cafeteria's Sunday brunch. I started to find out what was on the menu and would go to Sunday brunch and lunch once or twice weekly when I thought the food might be bearable (hardly ever).

It's sort of funny, but as we started to work on *Warrior of the Void* in November 2010, he started to loosen his grip. The college advisors had warned parents to loosen their grip. The advisors wanted us to find our own way with the assistance they would provide, if you could reach them with their heavy workload. Many Hampton students will tell you, "That ain't happening."

Like Simba I am preparing myself to shape a greater kingdom than dad could imagine. And I want dad on earth and in full health to watch that new kingdom unfold. Although at times we have been and remain at war, love has really never been far away even when I accused him of being like a dictator and told him I could no longer respect him for trying to control my life.

When he picked me up at LaGuardia Airport when I came home for Thanksgiving in 2010, the first words out of my mouth were, "I miss you dad." Did I say that?

As Akhenaton, with the sun rolling high in a sapphire sky, I will find my way on the path unwinding.

Hakuna Matata, dad, don't worry.

Chapter 22

Hooping and Talking Smack

Before Lil Wayne's "Kobe Bryant," we all knew Kobe was the best. He has shown he doesn't need Shaq or Robert Horry. He doesn't need eight healthy fingers and two thumbs. He doesn't need LeBron, "the king" and "the chosen one" (only in name). LeBron is not a finisher. Jay-Z might be paying Dwayne Wade, but I ain't. Oh, I just remembered. Jay-Z ain't even paying him anymore.

Miami had their victory parade before even playing one game together. Bosh, Wade, and LeBron were a hit for Miami standing on top of that truck. Ego brings celebration; losses bring tears. In the future they might succeed in winning a championship, but there are too many good teams that will ensure Miami will not have a dynasty. Let's go Bulls and Thunder!

Mom has two early basketball memories involving me. The first occurred one Sunday when I was nearly 4 and dad was not at home. Mom walked into our living room to discover I was standing on the couch. Why was I standing on the couch? Ask mom. Here's her reply:

> Akhenaton, when I walked into the living room, you were
> standing on the couch screaming at the top of your lungs.
> You were talking to the television. The Lakers were on. I don't
> remember who they were playing, but I remember Kobe Bryant
> was going up for a dunk. As he went up, you screamed, "Posterize
> him, Kobe! Posterize him! Show him what you got!" After the
> dunk, you just continued standing, jumping, and talking as if
> Kobe could talk back to you through the television screen.

That is when I realized you were just like your dad when watching basketball. He would also stand, but in front of the couch, and talk to the players, as if he were on the floor moving up and down the court with them.

The second memory was also of an experience which occurred a few months later on another Sunday afternoon. Mom and dad had taken me to the Bedford YMCA on Monroe Street in Bedford Stuyvesant to register for swimming. After registering, we stopped by the gymnasium. From here, I will let mom tell the rest of the story:

> There was a basketball team practice in progress for kids 6 years old. When the instructor saw you, he rolled the ball toward you so that you could show him what you could do. At 4 years old, you were taller and beefier than most of the kids, so he thought you might be interested and would be a good addition to the team. Of course, none of them knew this was the first time you had ever held a basketball in an actual basketball court. From the door near the half-court line, you picked up the ball as all eyes turned to you. With the ball held in both hands over your head, you ran the length of the court, not dribbling once. When you got to the basket, you threw the ball up and it clanked off the front of the rim. You turned around to see the surprised looks of the players and of the instructor. That was when the instructor took a closer look to discover your baby face and asked your age.

So, at 4 years old, I wasn't a little Kobe, but who was or is? However, I was a Kobe fan then, and I am a Kobe fan now. There is no one in the game who has the focus, the will, and the skills of the Black Mamba. After 15 years in the NBA, he is still dominant. He is a coach on the floor guiding his team-mates to successful play.

When Boston defeated the Lakers in the Finals in 2008, Kobe showed respect for what Boston had accomplished. He congratulated Boston and became even more determined to defeat any team standing in the way of future championships. He led the Lakers to victory in 2010 against Boston after leading them to success in 2009 against Dwight "Superman" Howard and the Magic.

How great was Ron Artest's performance during the Western Conference Finals in 2010? Remember when Phil and the LA fans didn't want him to shoot, and the sports critics said he couldn't shoot? In Game 5 against the Suns, he shot and missed a three-pointer which pissed off Phil who felt he should have run time off the clock. Seconds later, with the score tied, Kobe went up for a contested three, had his hand hit, and shot an air ball. Artest came across the floor from a great distance while the ball sailed. He caught it, and put it in as time ran out. That shot changed the momentum of that series, and the Lakers won the next game to close out the series.

In the NBA Finals against Boston, Artest continued to play well and his defense and offense were major factors in the Lakers' championship. Dad and I were amazed when he decided to put his first, and possibly only, championship ring in a raffle which raised more than $500,000 for teenagers in need of therapy for mental health issues.

Dad remarked, "While some rappers and some athletes are so devoted to acquiring and showing off their bling (Artest's description of the ring), Artest demonstrated that it is much more important to be dedicated to improving the lives of young people."

In 2009, LeBron demonstrated he does not know how to handle defeat. Most fans remember how he walked off the court refusing to shake hands with Dwight Howard and the Magic after the Magic kicked his butt in the Eastern Conference Finals. When he was asked by reporters if he regretted not shaking hands, his response was the response of an overconfident man, "I don't regret anything that I do."

When dad read that quote, he suggested Nike had promoted LeBron as if he were some false "god" and apparently LeBron had started to believe the hype. Dad said the use of the title "King James" and the Nike poster with his arms outstretched declaring "We Are All Witnesses" seem to represent idol worship or idolatry.

Dad is not a witness to Nike's or LeBron's gospel. He asks, "What is his title 'King James' really about? Are LeBron and Nike bringing us a new gospel?" He answers, "We have the King James Edition of the *Holy Bible*, completed in 1611 during the reign of King James I of England. John the Baptist came bearing witness to Christ. It's only Nike and deluded fans bearing witness to LeBron. And bearing witness to LeBron is all about taking money from fans for overpriced sneakers, sportswear, and tickets."

Well, way back in 1996, before LeBron arrived on the scene, dad was a big basketball fan but not a fan of getting his son involved in worshipping the game and developing illusions about a future career in basketball. Thus, I would spend nearly four years in swimming classes at the Bedford Avenue Y without ever stepping into its gym to learn how to play basketball. He took me to my swimming lessons, but not up to the gym. Mom said just because I was tall and black did not mean I had to play ball. So they enrolled me in swimming, piano, clarinet, karate, and tennis lessons. I would not begin to play organized basketball until I was almost 9, even though I was taller and stronger than most kids my age from the ages 4 through 9.

As my ninth birthday approached in 2001, dad enrolled me in basketball camp on Sundays at the 92nd Street Y in Manhattan. Before enrolling in basketball camp, I had picked up some skills from playing against dad and in school at PS 59. When I enrolled, I joined the 9-to-10 age group. I played center. The camp was usually about 90 minutes long and programmed from noon to 1 p.m. Sundays after church. We went through drills. Toward the end of the period, we would play on various teams. My teams generally won because I would often be paired with a good point guard who could get me the ball down near the basket. I had a lot of energy and was developing good defensive skills.

At the Y, I began to discover my love for the game. Dad was my ride, so he attended all of the camps. He seemed satisfied that I was enjoying the camps, and he always made sure to stop for refreshments after each session. On the way home, we didn't generally talk about basketball. We would usually listen to old school music by tuning into "Hal Jackson's Sunday Classics" on WBLS, and I would often fall asleep. Dad encouraged me to sleep for the 30-minute ride so that I would be fresh to do my homework after we arrived home.

The following year, I continued to play well at the Y, and my knowledge of the game grew. My father was at my side when the competition became more intense. While some parents would shout instructions, demands, and encouragement to their kids, he would often remain silent. He would comment and encourage after the games. I remained the dominant performer in my group.

In the summer of 2003, dad enrolled me in Basketball City at Chelsea Piers in Manhattan. Basketball City had two leagues—the Big East and the Knicks. The Big East covered kids aged 10 to 12. Kids came from all over New York City. Many were players on their school teams. The competition was really stiff. The camp started at 8:30 a.m. and lasted until 4:00 p.m., Monday through Friday. Dad registered me in two camps that would not interfere with my academic prep schedule at the Fieldston Enrichment Program.

At Basketball City, my confidence in my abilities grew. In my first year, I had an impact and my team won the championship. I received individual trophies for hustle and rebounding. I loved my rebounding trophy the best. I was really proud when dad arrived to see me receive the trophies from Calvin Ramsey, a current official and former player with the NY Knicks. Calvin Ramsey had mentored dad at the start of his education career. Stephon Marbury,

Allen Houston, Walt Clyde Frazier, and other Knicks were present during various activities to also give us guidance and encouragement.

In September of 2003, a few months short of my eleventh birthday, I began sixth grade at a new school, IS 89. I was excited when I found out my new middle school had a basketball team. A few weeks later when Mom picked me up from school, she noticed my sad expression and asked what was wrong. I told her I had tried out for my school's basketball team and had not made it.

She said, "Don't worry about that. Remember, most of the players on the team are older and have been playing longer than you and have more experience. Next year there'll be open spots because the eighth grade players are graduating this year. In the meantime, just practice hard, and try out again next year."

In that instant, I went from feeling sad to jumping with happiness. I had a smile from ear to ear. Mom asked what I was so happy about.

I said, still smiling, "I thought this was it. I thought I would never be on the basketball team. I didn't know they would let me try out again next year. That's great!" That's when she knew that karate, clarinet, piano, and swimming had lost the battle. Basketball had beaten them.

So during that fall of 2003 and spring of 2004, I attended brief holiday camps at Basketball City and my skills continued to rise. Basketball City had great teaching coaches who had played on the college level. I had to learn to focus and to be in top conditioning to endure the drills and the games. I enjoyed the challenges they presented, and I became well prepared for the 2004 summer league.

During the summer league at the beginning of August 2004, I was ready at 11:00 a.m. to compete. After the morning drills, the 150-plus participants were organized into teams. Throughout the week, the teams would compete to participate in the Friday championship game that would feature the teams with the two highest winning records. The coaches had organized the teams with individuals of comparable talent so that no team would be dominant. They wanted the talent on all the teams to be evenly balanced. So to win, a team would have to demonstrate extra effort and team skill. To stand out, an individual player would have to demonstrate his skills and efforts in a team concept.

At the end of the Thursday session, the coaches announced the tally of the teams. At that point my teammates realized we would have an opportunity to compete for the championship if we performed well in the final elimination games on Friday morning. We performed well and went on to compete in the championship game. We won the championship, and I was named

"Most Valuable Player" of the league. My scoring, rebounding, and defense were all impressive.

To honor my accomplishments, I was presented a huge and unique "sculptured bronze" trophy from the NY Knicks, unlike those tall metallic trophies that are typically given out at tournaments. Dad was at the trophy presentation, and he was beaming about my accomplishments. When we arrived home, he placed the trophy on display in our living room and brought a few of the other trophies I had won from my bedroom to display them as well.

I was excited about playing at Basketball City, and I looked forward to watching America's Dream Team defeat the world and win the gold medal trophy at the Athens's Olympics. Nine of the 12 players on the dominant 2003 FIFA World Team, including Kobe, Kevin Garnett, Shaq, and Ray Allen, would not be there. But dad and I were sure we had enough to beat anyone, with the veterans Iverson, Marbury, Duncan, and the young Melo, LeBron, DWade, and Stoudemire.

So, on August 15, 2004, dad and I sat in front of our television anticipating a beat down of the Puerto Rico National Team with Carlos Arroyo and Jose Juan Berea. We were ready to trash talk into the television screen. Unfortunately, that evening Arroyo and his teammates did all the real trash talking. They beat the USA 92-73, and all dad and I had left to show for our initial enthusiasm was a bowl of cold popcorn and tired and deflated egos.

But, of course, we knew the USA would bounce back with vengeance since it was still possible to pursue the gold. However, when there were close wins over Greece and Australia in following games, we began to recognize that the USA was in real trouble. In the fourth game, Lithuania defeated the USA. After that defeat, we no longer prepared popcorn before the games. We also forgot that we ever knew how to trash talk at the opposing players through the television screen.

During the fifth game, the USA smacked Angola 89-53. We didn't celebrate because we knew Spain and the Gasol brothers were up next, and Spain was undefeated through four games. Ah, the USA defeated Spain 102-94. However, we didn't celebrate because Ginoboli, Scola, and Argentina were coming next, and the commentators were telling everyone the USA possessed the most talented players but was not the best team.

In the sixth game, Ginoboli had his finest hour with an 89-81 defeat of the USA. With that defeat, the USA was no longer eligible to participate in the championship game. We would have to play Lithuania for the bronze medal. Lithuania? Really?

Meanwhile, on the women's side, the USA remained undefeated under the leadership of Lisa Leslie. Dad and I had watched every game, and the USA smacked all of the competitors. We managed to cheer for the women's team but weren't prepared to talk smack to the screen the way we would have if our men had been winning. On August 28, by a score of 74-63, the women won the gold medal against Australia, the team some commentators had suggested capable of defeating the USA. Dad and I cheered, standing in front of the couch with raised fists.

Also on August 28, the USA men defeated Lithuania 104-96. Dad and I sat deflated on the couch. The Olympics were over, and the USA had lost even though that evening we had won. We watched with deflated emotion as the team took the stand and received the bronze medal. The team members also displayed deflated emotions through their body language. There was no sparkle in their eyes, and no smiles on their lips. They were not the Dream Team.

Recently, dad and I went on Google Images to examine photographs of the 2004 USA Basketball Team. Those images were not pretty. There was an image of the team wearing the bronze medal. Tim Duncan's head was cast down, Stoudemire was looking off in the distance, Richard Jefferson looked as if he were lost, and Odom appeared as if he were in a state of shock. Each was wearing a wreath which represented a crown, but everyone could clearly see that they did not feel like kings or princes.

Another image taken during the game shows Duncan near the bench on his knees as if he were pleading while knowing a miracle was not possible. In that same photo, LeBron and Jefferson are each standing with their hands on their hips in postures of defeat. Wade is crouching in defeat with his mouth open as if, like Chris Carter and Keyshawn Johnson, he were screaming in frustration, "Come on, man!" Melo and Okafur are standing behind Wade as if they really do not want to be caught in the picture. Stoudemire is just standing, holding his towel as if he could not wait to wash off the defeat, as if the stench of defeat could be removed by soap and water.

With the defeat, the American sports broadcasters had plenty to talk about. Some bad-mouthed Kobe, Dwight, KG, and other NBA players who had not participated. They said the absent players showed disloyalty to the nation. Some bad-mouthed Marbury and Iverson as selfish and unprepared for leadership in the international game, which has different rules than NBA basketball. Others said American players are very individualistic and unwilling to focus on the fundamentals of team basketball. Some said they were the "Nightmare Team."

All the critics seemed to say that other countries were catching up with the USA and implied that soon some country would prove it is better at basketball. They said the foreigners played better fundamental basketball while Americans focused on entertainment basketball. Some said Americans were undisciplined.

Dad and I listened, but we didn't believe the commentators. Everyone who has followed sports knows that the commentators are more often wrong in their analysis and predictions than they are right about the outcome of championships in all the major sports. When two teams are playing, they only have a 50-50 chance of picking the winner, the same odds that a couch potato possesses.

In June 2010, the "experts" said Miami Heat would lose no more than five games with James, DWade, and Bosh. Many picked LeBron and Cleveland to defeat the Magic in 2009. What about the 2010 Cowboys? In September 2010, they were on their way to winning the Super Bowl according to the broadcasters. At the beginning of the spring of 2010, not one broadcaster on the entire planet picked the Giants to win the 2010 World Series.

In 2008, USA basketball had an opportunity to prove the broadcasters wrong. We all know the outcome of the 2008 Olympics. Kobe focused on defense and making opportunities for his teammates while providing supreme leadership. Melo, DWade, and LeBron dominated scoring and playing defense. Dwight and Bosh rebounded and played defense. Both made more than 75 percent of their shots, and Wade and LeBron hit on more than 60 percent of theirs. CP3, Deron Williams, and LeBron dished the assists.

In 2008, the USA women and men stood tall and proud, and all the teams in the world tasted defeat. The USA men's team proved it was the most talented and most disciplined team. Dad and I saw every game together, and we talked so much smack to Gasol, Ginobili, Scola, Nowitski, Bogut, and Yao through the television while eating warm popcorn. I was 4 years old again, only this time I was standing in front of the couch talking smack, not on top of it.

What would sports be without us being able to talk smack? Smack talking is what makes sports even more entertaining. As fans, we love the players on the floor who talk smack with their lips and fantastic plays. There are many ways that they talk smack. One way is to posterize an opponent. Everyone tries to get out of the way of Blake.

A second way is to give the signal for choking when an opponent begins to fade, à la Reggie Miller in that playoff game against the Knicks.

A third way is to give your opponent a beat down, like Ewing did Miller and the Pacers in the 1994 Eastern Conference Finals. After the beat down, Ewing proceeded to stand on top of the scorer's table and beat his chest, which is talking smack without saying a word.

A fourth way is to go through the legs and place your elbow through the rim and give the "it's over signal" as Vince Carter did during the 2000 Slam Dunk Contest.

A fifth way is to be Gerald Green dunking with head above the rim while blowing out the candle on top of a cupcake!

Talking smack is Superman Dwight leaping over tall bodies in a single bound throwing down thunderous dunks as his puny opponents slap at the arms that even the best sculptors cannot create.

Talking smack is Kenny Smith introducing Blake's dunks at the 2011 Slam Dunk Contest before Blake leaps over the car. I am sure Barkley and all the judges wanted him to just shut up and let Blake just do it.

Dad says, "Talking smack is JaVale McGee beating the odds that favored the crowd's and judge's preferred player (Blake) while dunking two balls simultaneously through two rims. This was never done before, and probably never will be done again. Talking smack is JaVale going up with two balls, dunking them, and catching and dunking a third before returning to earth. The judges would not let him win the dunk contest, but he was entered into the *Guinness Book of World Records* for that dunk."

Dad also says, "JaVale wuz robbed! JaVale, go get your trophy out of Blake's trophy case! Blake knows it's yours, brother!"

I say, "Blake, keep your trophy. Dad is buggin'."

Chapter 23

History Manifests Destiny

In August 2010 at Madison Square Garden, Kobe and the USA Basketball team were playing the French national team lead by Boris Diaw. Dad and I were sitting close to an ardent group of about 10 French fans (males and females), who also appeared to be residents of the USA. When the French took a substantial early lead and held it for more than 10 minutes, the French fans unfurled and began waving a huge French flag and started to sing the French National Anthem, "*La Marseillaise.*"

To the amusement of four male fans of the China national team, dad immediately stood up and started to berate the French fans. "Don't bring that flag in here!" he began. "Not here in our house!"

However, the French fans attempted to ignore him as they continued to wave the Tricolors and sing "*La Marseillaise.*" Not to be outdone, dad began mocking the fans while singing "*Frère Jacques*" in a supposedly French accent. The Chinese fans roared with laughter, and two of them gave dad high fives and fist bumps.

That only encouraged dad more, so he began to imitate the voice of Pepé Le Pew trying to woo a female cat: "Come with me to ze Casbah, and we will make beautiful musique to-ga-ther." That was followed by a fake French accent imitation of Steve Martin's attempt to pronounce hamburger in "The Pink Panther."

Hearing those imitations of Pepé Le Pew and Steve Martin, the Chinese fans roared even louder and gave thumbs down to the French fans as the Chinese repeated, à la Steve Martin, "I would like to buy a 'amburger! 'amburger!"

Meanwhile, on the floor within minutes Kobe and Durant started to get hot and that only emboldened dad and dampened the zeal of the French fans. Seeing a new opening dad declared, "You all come here waving that French flag, and if it weren't for us Americans it would be '*Sprechen Sie Deutsch?*/ Do you speak German?' for you!"

After hearing those words and watching dad's effervescent performance in delivering them, the Chinese fans stood up in celebratory fashion laughing and throwing high fives as if the China national team had won the championship, yet the China team wasn't even playing! They were having fun while the French became quiet and settled down, probably because the momentum on the floor had changed significantly.

Shortly after the game on our way home, dad reflected on his behavior and said he was deeply embarrassed he had acted like an arrogant American who exhibits a false sense of patriotic superiority when confronting foreigners who do not share the same interests.

He said he really crossed the line with the "ugly remark" about rescuing the French from having to speak German. He remarked that the line dishonors the vital role that the French played in helping America liberate itself from England. He also suggested that the line is not true because the French, the British, the Poles, the Czechs, and others were the first to challenge Germany and continued to challenge Hitler even after the occupation of France and other parts of Western Europe. Meanwhile, America had remained on the sidelines hoping to avoid entering the war even as Hitler used genocide against Jews and other groups he considered inferior. America had even prevented the landing of ships arriving in New York from Europe with Jewish refugees. Refugees were sent back to Europe and many, unfortunately, died due to the terror released by the Germans and their allies in other European countries.

"Dad, if you feel that way now what made you say those things earlier?" I asked.

"That's a good question. I surprised myself. I really don't have a rational explanation for my behavior. I mindlessly repeated '*Sprechen Sie Deutsch?*' I had heard that comment many times during news programs in recent years about America's supposed role in rescuing the French from having to speak German. It generally arose when certain commentators and politicians would criticize the French government for being critical of America and competitive against what the commentators and politicians saw as American interests in Europe and the world."

Later in the fall of 2010 dad further remarked, after watching *World War II in Color* on the Military Channel, "The liberation of Europe was a collective effort on the part of the Americans, the French, the British, Canada, the Soviet Union, the Poles, and others, yet most Americans probably cannot name any of the Russian, British, or Canadian generals whose leadership contributed immensely to the defeat of Germany. I imagine most do know of the French de Gaulle and a few might have heard of the British Montgomery.

"However, only through the *World War II in Color* series on the Military Channel have I begun to learn about the tremendous contributions of commanders other than Patton, Eisenhower, Bradley, and McArthur and about nations other than America and England in defeating Hitler.

"Before watching the series, I had never heard of Marshall Georgy Zhukov of the Red Army who defeated the Germans at Stalingrad and marched on to Berlin while crushing the 'invincible' German Army on the eastern front. I had not heard of Major-General R.F.L. Keller who commanded the Canadian 3rd Infantry Division that broke through the German defense at Juno Beach on D-Day. I was unaware that contingents of Polish, Australian, Belgian, Greek, Czech, Dutch, Norwegian, and New Zealand soldiers and sailors landed on Normandy on D-Day to defeat the Germans."

"Dad, why are you so interested in history?" I asked.

"Marcus Mosiah Garvey said, 'A people without the knowledge of their past history, origin, and culture is like a tree without roots.' To a large extent our knowledge of and perspective about history have tremendous influence on shaping our values and beliefs and how we interact with others in the world. Sometimes that influence is obvious, and other times it is subconscious. Sometimes it is productive, and other times it could be counterproductive like when I insulted those fans."

"What do you mean?"

"When I was a kid in Georgia, the history I was taught suggested that God had blessed America like no other nation. In fact, I was never taught that God had blessed any other nation. It was as if America were God's only child, not just a favorite daughter. I was taught that America was special and destined to be the leader of the world. America was exceptional. Today, President Obama gets a lot of criticism from political opponents like Gingrich and Romney and certain other Republicans who say that he does not believe in the doctrine of 'American exceptionalism' or the idea that America is blessed above all other nations and called to be the leader of the world.

"I was proud to be an American because if God determined we were special, then indeed we were and there was no reason to question American history or present policy. I swelled with patriotic pride. Today I am still patriotic. I love my nation and would have not chosen to have been born anywhere else, even though I was born in racist Swainsboro, Georgia. But wisdom has taught me that my patriotism requires that I question past and present decisions and policies that are inconsistent with the best ideas of democracy, equal justice, equal opportunity and fellowship and peace with people and nations throughout the world."

When dad was in elementary school he was taught history full of facts, myths, legends, and values which do not ring true for him today. "His-story" is how dad's generation ultimately learned to label history as taught in American schools. "His-story" was the story consisting of facts, distortions, omissions, myths, doctrines, and values that the power elite, representing the one percent, wanted all Americans and the world to believe.

As a kid in elementary school dad was deeply interested in history and took great pride in fourth grade in being able to recite and explain the Emancipation Proclamation and the Declaration of Independence. He admired Abraham Lincoln and Thomas Jefferson, but had not been taught that Jefferson was a slaveholder and the father of six black children due to having sex with Sally Hemings, starting when she was only 14 and he was over 40. He was not informed that Jefferson died without freeing Hemings and several of his own children. He suspects that his teachers at that time did not know those facts. They too had been fed "his-story."

As a fan of history, dad paid apt attention to every lesson and accepted the story lines as truths and guides for his own thinking and values. So in fourth grade when dad learned about the war with Mexico for the independence of Texas, he learned the importance of the 1836 battle at the Alamo and the doctrine of "Manifest Destiny."

As a 10-year-old, with that history in mind, dad went to the movie theatre to see "The Alamo," directed by and starring a recognized hero of American cinema, the late John Wayne. As dad watched the movie, he felt as if he wanted to write a different ending if he couldn't enter the screen and fight alongside the defenders when the Mexican Army penetrated the walls of the Alamo and began killing the white "Texans" and Americans and their "loyal black slaves." Dad squirmed in his seat because Davy Crockett (played by Wayne) was a hero and legend to most American kids, including dad, for his leadership in expanding the geographical boundaries of America.

BTW, there was even a television show about Crockett's life, and dad still remembers the song he used to sing as a child with his friend Charles while playing cowboys and Indians:

Born on a mountain top in Tennessee,
Greenest state in the land of the free.
Raised in the woods so he knew every tree,
Killed him a bear when he was only three.
Davy, Davy Crockett, King of the Wild Frontier.

Son, while looking at that movie dad did not want to see Davy Crockett killed at that Alamo in San Antonio. Dad says even though he has only seen the movie once, he can still picture the scene at the end where John Wayne begins to swing his rifle at the rapidly advancing Mexican soldiers in a futile effort to stay alive and avoid defeat. Dad suggested that as he sat watching he was more concerned about saving Davy Crockett and Jim Bowie than about any of the enslaved blacks who fought alongside them. Huh?

While in school, dad was not taught that in 1829 slavery had been abolished throughout Mexico including *Tejas/*Texas (which was then part of Mexico) by Mexican President Vincente Guerrero. Guerrero was an Afro-Mexican or Mexican of African descent on his father's side and "Amerindian" on his mother's side. Guerrero was a leading general in the 1821 defeat of Spain in the war for Mexican independence. However, the whites in *Tejas* resisted the decree abolishing slavery and white American immigrants illegally continued to hold blacks in bondage and continued to illegally bring blacks into *Tejas* with them from American states.[15]

Later, while back in class at Emanuel County Elementary School, dad and his segregated black school mates were led by their black teachers in singing "This Land is Your Land" following a discussion of the Mexican American War of 1846 through 1848.

Dad and his classmates were taught the importance of the doctrine of "Manifest Destiny," a doctrine which suggested that it was God's will to have America spread to occupy all the land between the Atlantic and Pacific Oceans, "…from California to the New York island." Dad was taught President James Polk believed in the doctrine and that God had guardian angels watch over the settlers as they moved west taking more than half of Mexico and the western lands of Native Americans. Dad admired every president, including Polk, and took great pride in being the only student in his class able to name every president in order, from Washington to Eisenhower, and the years of each president's administration. He taught himself to memorize all the details without any requirement from his fourth grade teacher, Miss Murray.

Even today, dad still admits that despite the later transformation of his thinking and beliefs, there are times when he is reminded he has not fully purged the sense of American superiority that was drilled into his mind. Sometimes that sense of superiority emerges from his subconscious mind in ways that surprise him, such as in the midst of that basketball game.

Today, dad declares that most Americans calling for harsh and brutal actions against Mexicans seeking to enter America have no knowledge of the devious actions President James Polk undertook. President Polk exploited Americans' belief in "Manifest Destiny" and "American exceptionalism" to provoke a war with Mexico to seize its land. Despite the disapproval of many in Congress, Polk provoked Mexico by sending troops into an area of Mexico he wanted to claim was a part of Texas after Mexico refused to sell its Northern Territories to Polk for $30 million. Polk had promised in his 1844 campaign to see America spread from the Atlantic to the Pacific when America was essentially east of the Mississippi River at that time.

Dad declares that most Americans don't even know the US Army actually occupied Mexico City for months in 1847, after defeating a contingent of Mexican soldiers and civilians during the Battle of Chapultepec. Dad did not learn that fact until recently while watching a PBS special, narrated by Oscar De La Hoya, on the war with Mexico. He learned General Winfred Scott was appointed the military governor of Mexico while the USA Army continued to pursue General Santa Ana, whose troops were mostly hastily recruited from poorly trained and poorly equipped Mexican civilians.

In 1848 at the Treaty of Guadalupe Hidalgo, Mexico was forced to sell 55 percent of its land including (*Alta*) California, Arizona, New Mexico, Nevada, Utah, and Colorado, and parts of present day Texas (the Mexican area that troops entered following Polk's command), Kansas, Oklahoma, and Wyoming. Polk paid $15 million, half of Polk's original offer.

Dad asks, "Did we learn in the history taught in school that *Baja* (Lower) California is a part of Mexico directly below California and that California was named *Alta* (Upper) California before America seized it?"

During the Senate vote to ratify the treaty, Jefferson Davis, who would later become the president of the Confederacy and move to divide our nation to keep slavery alive, introduced an amendment calling for America to also annex northeastern Mexico. Northeastern Mexico was composed of the Mexican states of Coahuila, Nuevo Leon, and Tamaulipas. Those states were then and continue to be among the richest and most industrially developed states of Mexico. That amendment to seize and make northeastern Mexico a permanent part of the USA failed 44 to 11.

Like most elementary school children of dad's generation, dad was taught and believed that Manifest Destiny was God's will because God supposedly favored America above all other nations and that Americans were God's new "chosen people." It took a great deal of later study and contemplation while in college for him to "free his mind' and realize that Manifest Destiny was "a propagandistic tool which allowed certain Americans to rationalize genocide against Native Americans and imperialism and invasion against an economically and technologically poor Mexico."

When I was in school, I was also introduced to the doctrine of Manifest Destiny and the war with Mexico. However, it seems that my teachers did not attempt to indoctrinate us the way dad and his generation were indoctrinated. I wasn't taught to admire Jim Bowie and Davy Crockett in school nor in television and the movies.

While dad remains a devout black (Baptist) Christian American, as he was at 10, he suggests it doesn't prevent him from seeing how some Christian Americans then and now use religion (not the teachings of Christ) for political purposes to demean, render illegitimate, and sometimes demonize people who are "different" due to race, ethnicity, national origin, religion, and sexual orientation.

Therefore, when he is watching historical documentaries and the *PBS NewsHour*, he often asks me to observe certain segments with him. He does not want me to be ignorant and follow in the footsteps of Herman Cain who, as a black Christian American, apparently thought it was clever to draw laughter from a crowd of mostly white Christian Americans while declaring he was willing to build a fence that would electrocute Mexicans attempting to come across the border into American states which were once part of Mexico. Dad says he suspects that Cain's bias comes from an open and conscious sense of America's supposed superiority which was nurtured while he was in school.

Of course, I think Herman Cain's sense of humor about electrocuting Mexicans is mad stupid and offensive. My *madrina*/godmother Sonia, who is also my first cousin, is Mexican/Puerto Rican American and was born and raised in San Antonio, not too far from the Alamo. When I see her next I plan to ask her what was she taught as a Mexican American in elementary school in San Antonio in the late 1980s regarding the Alamo and the war with Mexico. Dad says he is willing to bet "she was taught pretty much the same his-story."

As Christians and Americans, dad wants to make sure we challenge the false religious myths about America and the religious bigotry of some Christian Americans against Muslims, Jews, Buddhists, and members of other faiths and nations. He remembers as a little boy when many Christian churches supported segregation and racial discrimination as "God's will." From studying history, he knows that churches throughout the world supported the enslavement of Africans, and in some cases Native Americans, as "God's will."

Dad suggests, "The Conquistadors came with guns, priests, and crosses. Pope Alexander VI decreed that what today is Brazil shall belong to Portugal, and most of the rest of South America shall belong to Spain as rewards for 'converting the heathens' in those lands. Portugal and Spain made the Pope and Vatican richer with the gold and natural resources taken from those lands using slave labor."

The Pilgrims came with guns and Bibles, and soon after enslaved Africans were brought to these shores with the blessings of the Church of England. In 1833, when the British Parliament voted compensation to former slaveholders rather than emancipated Africans in the West Indies, the Archbishop of Canterbury and the Bishop of Exeter received monetary compensation for the loss of slave labor on plantations they owned. Meanwhile, slaveholders in independent English America attended church every Sunday and placed their ill-gotten gains in the collection plates of churches throughout this great land. Thomas Jefferson and James Monroe, former presidents and slave owners, also used their ill-gotten gains to establish the University of Virginia. George Washington used his ill-gotten gains from slavery to build Washington College which later became Washington and Lee University, following Robert E. Lee's service as its president after his defeat in the Civil War.

Dad suggests that Americans must study and meditate on the teachings of Christ and not just follow the dictates of preachers, pastors, bishops, archbishops, popes, and political leaders. He says there are so-called religious leaders with political agendas that are higher than God's agenda of love, peace, and the "feeding" of all of God's children.

Dad finds it fascinating that religious leaders in South Carolina could stand before television cameras while clapping and making Rick Perry's wife feel very comfortable and self-righteous as she stood before them while saying God appeared to her in a "burning bush" to tell her to tell Perry to run for president.

Dad wonders if God also told Mrs. Perry that God will give Perry another Aaron to speak for him, since Perry has "never been eloquent and is slow of speech and tongue."

He remarks, "It should be clear to all Americans by now that Perry is not the sharpest tool in the shed, but now we need to know if someone found him as a baby in a basket floating down the Rio Grande!"

A Photo Gallery
Through the Years

Presenting the Authors

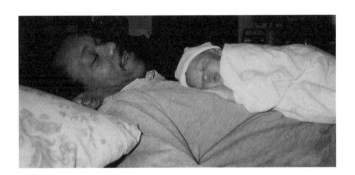

Harmony at 12 days

With mom at 5 months

With dad at age 4, Old San Juan, PR

With dad and my sisters at the zoo, Washington, DC, 16 months

With dad & mom, Lefferts Gardens Montessori, age 4

Piano lesson at age 4

PS 59 Spring Recital at age 9

With Travis & Khalil from Lefferts Gardens Montessori, age 5

Mom (far right) at age 3 with her siblings

Dad & me, White House Easter egg roll, age 7

With the Prez in North Philly, Sept 2008

Estos Niños Serán Los Centinelas De Nuestra Ciudad

Problema De La Vivienda En América

EL DIARIO DE NUEVA YORK — Viernes, 25 de Noviembre de 1960

Abuela with mom & siblings, El Diario article, Nov 25, 1960

Mom at 19 with "the Angela Davis Afro"

Dad, the 19-year-old revolutionary

QUIET PROTEST: Students carrying signs in support of black and Puerto Rican students' demands on the steps of Wagner Hall at the C.C.N.Y. campus yesterday afternoon.

20 Indicted in Brooklyn College Arson;

Students Arrested Here

By EMANUEL PERLMUTTER

Seventeen Negro and Puerto Rican students at Brooklyn College were arrested at their homes early yesterday on a 23-count indictment charging arson, conspiring to commit arson, and other criminal acts on the college's Flatbush campus.

Although the indictment, handed up Monday night by a Kings County grand jury, named 20 defendants, three have not been apprehended. One has not been identified.

The Brooklyn school has been plagued by student disorders, disruptions and vandalism in recent weeks. At the request of the college administration, helmeted policemen have been guarding the grounds and buildings since last Friday.

Other Developments

There were these other campus developments in the nation yesterday:

¶At Southern University in Baton Rouge, La., the police fired tear gas and shotguns at students who were throwing firebombs, rocks and bottles. Thirty persons were injured, including eight with gunshot wounds.

¶About 40 students took over the Interfaith Lounge on the campus of Northeastern University in Boston in a protest against the Reserve Officers Training Corps.

¶Tension rose at Cornell University with the impending arrest of several students involved in the armed occupation of the student center four weeks ago. The Tompkins County grand jury handed up 21 sealed indictments.

¶In San Francisco, the trustees of Stanford University decided to sever ties between the university and its affiliated Stanford Research Institute. The action followed demonstrations over war-related research.

Continued on Page 30, Column 1

17 Youths Seized as Arsonists In Brooklyn College Outbreak

Continued From Page 1, Col. 2

count, each defendant in the case could be sentenced to a maximum of 228 years in jail. Eighteen of the counts are felonies and five are misdemeanors.

In addition to arson, the defendants, who included three girls, were charged with criminal mischief, riots and recklessly endangering to the college and its students.

The accusations included a fire set in the college library on May 2; fires set in four classrooms on May 6, and damages to the faculty lounge on May 7.

The Brooklyn College indictments followed a growing trend of court actions to cope with student disorders. Other court actions have been resorted to by the police or college officials at the University of San Francisco State University, Columbia University, Dartmouth College and City College.

In a news conference in his office after he announced the arrests, District Attorney Eugene Gold said that batteries, gasoline and other materials for setting fires, and fire bombs had been found in the homes of some of the defendants.

In the home of one of the defendants, Nello Pile, 20 years old, of 1679 Prospect Place, Brooklyn, the police said they found "a blueprint for campus violence that gave a charted account for her bombing and burning of the college buildings and clubs," the police said.

Mrs. Blanche Pile, mother of young Pile, was arrested on a charge of interfering with a policeman after her son was seized yesterday morning. A mother of 11 children, she is a member of the Ocean Hill-Brownsville School Demonstration Project.

Weapons Are Seized

The Brooklyn prosecutor said that a revolver, a sharp-edged spear and clubs were among the weapons found in some of the homes.

The accused were picked up between 3 and 5 A.M. by 122 detectives who left in teams from Mr. Gold's office and fanned out over Brooklyn, Queens, Manhattan and the Bronx, Chief of Detectives Frederick M. Lusson was in charge of the operation.

The prisoners were taken in handcuffs to the District Attorney's office in the Brooklyn Municipal Building and then photographed and fingerprinted at Brooklyn Police Headquarters.

When arraigned, they were arraigned in the afternoon before Justice Dominic Rinaldi in Supreme Court in Brooklyn. At the request of Assistant District Attorney Elliott Golden, Justice Rinaldi held each of the 17 defendants in $15,000 bail pending trial.

When George Wade, a Negro lawyer representing most of the defendants, complained that the bail was excessive and "punitive," Justice Rinaldi replied: "We live in a civilized community. These people are accused of setting fires."

Near the end of the court proceedings, they are another Negro attorney, asserted: "There are S.D.S. students involved, and the students brought in because they are S.D.S."

This caused Justice Rinaldi to lean over the bench, point his finger at Mr. Wade and say: "This one court room is not a forum or a vehicle to be used by you or anyone else for a racist statement."

About 100 relatives, friends and supporters of the defendants paced outside the tiny ninth-floor courtroom while they were being arraigned. A detail of 50 policemen guarded the court corridor and the downstairs entrance to the courthouse to prevent disorders.

About 200 students held a rally on the campus of Brooklyn College in mid-afternoon to marshal support for the defendants. Collections were made to raise bail for the prisoners.

The demonstrators, many shouting obscenities, accused George A. Peck, the college president, of helping the police identify these arrested.

At a news conference in the Diplomat Hotel, 108 West 43d Street, Mark Rudd, who led the boycott by the Students for a Democratic Society that closed Columbia University last year, charged that the United States Justice Department was responsible for the Brooklyn College arrests.

Accusing the department of "coordinated repression" against the S.D.S., he asserted that "it was no coincidence that they busted our national office [on Monday] and then blacks and Puerto Ricans were busted today."

The following were arrested yesterday in addition to young Pile:

Leroy Davis, 19, of 2592 Bryant Avenue, the Bronx.
Elmurita Commiss, 19, of 29-30 Gilmore Street, Elmhurst, Queens.
John Leigh, 19, of 509 Newman Avenue, Brooklyn.
Frank Fernandez, 23, of 734 West 14th Street, Brooklyn.
Drew Johnson, 19, of 1571 Sterling Place, Brooklyn.
Harold Outlaw, 20, of 23 Nostrand Avenue, Brooklyn.
Larry Murphy, 20, of 919 Myrtle Avenue, Brooklyn.
Edward Brooker, 19, of 5707 Farragut Road, Brooklyn.
Sterman Fabo, 20, of 2070 Vyse Avenue, the Bronx.
David Powell, 21, of 1043 37th Road, Corona, Queens.
Curtis Dennis, 19, of 29 Halsey Street, Brooklyn.
Rodney Aviles, 17, of 477 St. Johns Place, Brooklyn.
Bennett Cecle, 19, of 147 North Eliot Street, Brooklyn.

The two other identified defendants who have not yet been apprehended were listed as Larry Sparks, 22, the only one who is not a Brooklyn College student, of 228 New Lots Avenue, and Antonio Nieves, 19, of 377 Bergen Street, both Brooklyn.

The New York Times
Published: May 14, 1969
Copyright © The New York Times

BC 19 arrest, New York Times article, May 14, 1969

With Sensei Soke at Scorpion Martial Arts, age 7

With dad after winning sparring trophy at age 10

MVP of League, Basketball City, July 2004, age 11

Cape Cod at age 15

Boys Club Manhattan Housing Authority Champions, 2009

NY Knights at AAU tourney, July 2010

Celebrating NYC PSAL Quarter Finals win, March 2010

Coach Saunders strategizes, NYC PSAL Quarter Finals, March 2010

Age 16 is sweet

HS Graduation with mom & dad

Chapter 24

Latino Screen Heroes

Around the age of 5, I fell in love with the "Sandlot," a movie about baseball and a team of working-class white, black, and Mexican American pre-teens battling it out with a team of rich and arrogant white kids for bragging rights as local champions of a community next to Los Angeles. Dad and I would watch this movie often well past my eleventh birthday, and it sits in the closet of keepsakes awaiting my sons and daughters. That movie sent me many early messages about how I should behave in a team sport, and today I am proud to say that I have one of the best team spirits you could find. I have kept that spirit when playing on losing as well as winning teams.

My hero in the movie is Benny Rodriguez, played by Mike Vitar. He was the first Latino hero I ever saw presented in an American movie. He was super cool, had super batting skills, and could burn rubber in his PF Flyers tennis shoes. He kept the team together and, if a kid wanted to enter the group, he was the one who gave permission.

Benny was the one who had the courage to face "the Beast," this huge dog who lived in the backyard where a very valuable autographed ball landed after being hit by the newest member. Babe Ruth had told him in a dream that he could face the legendary "Beast." So Benny climbed over the fence, retrieved the ball, and made it back over the fence to apparent safety. However, the "Beast" broke his chains, jumped the fence, and chased the boys through town. Ultimately, they tamed the "Beast" and were the champs of the town. Benny would go on to become Benny "The Jet" Rodriguez, playing for the Los Angeles Dodgers. So, in a sense, the movie was a memoir of Benny Rodriguez with his friends.

After "The Sandlot," Mike Vitar starred as Luis Mendoza in "The Mighty Ducks" film series. So on film he continued to be a model of the Latino cool hero kid for me.

As a teenager in 2005, I was introduced to another model of the righteous Latino kid. Rick Gonzalez, a Puerto Rican, played Timo Cruz in "Coach Carter." Timo was drawn to the streets of Richmond, California, when Coach Carter (played by Samuel L. Jackson) insisted that the team study. Timo did not consider studying to be related to basketball or the success he sought on the streets. After leaving the team, he assisted his cousin in his drug dealing until he watched his cousin being murdered on those very streets that seemed to have so much more appeal than studying.

Coach Carter was well known for asking his players: "What is our deepest fear?" He would ask the question to get the players to understand why he was pushing them so hard academically before he would allow them to play athletically. None could answer, and most could only moan about the pressure to succeed academically.

When Timo returned, Coach Carter continued to put pressure on the team to study. The team members remained defiant and complained to their parents who put pressure on Coach Carter, demanding he should not ask the members to reach for "excellence" in education.

Later, when Coach Carter decided to quit due to overwhelming pressure from the school board and the parents who thought he demanded too much of their sons academically, it was time for Timo to teach Coach Carter a lesson. Timo and his teammates were finally awakening to the value of Coach Carter when he was walking out of the school after packing his possessions. As he prepared to walk out, Timo and his teammates confronted him. Timo made a passionate appeal asking him not to quit. To reach Coach Carter, Timo decided to use the quote of Marianne Williamson in an attempt to get Coach Carter to face his own fear:

> Our deepest fear is not that we are inadequate. Our deepest fear is that we are powerful beyond measure. It is our light, not our darkness, that most frightens us. Your playing small doesn't serve the world. There is nothing enlightened about shrinking so that other people won't feel insecure around you. We are all meant to shine, as children do. It is not just in some of us, it is in everyone, and as we let our own light shine, we unconsciously give other people permission to do the same. As we are liberated from our own fear, our presence automatically liberates others.

Coach Carter's anger dissolved because he was impressed that Timo had discovered and used the quote. Enlightened by Timo, Coach Carter chose to face his own fear of success, and he led his ragtag team to the state championship in California. Eventually, they lost the championship game by two points but were not losers because they go on to lead productive lives. No, no one went to the NBA. However, six went on to college from a school where only five percent of the graduates usually attended college.

After watching Gonzalez' performance in Coach Carter, I was very excited when "Illegal Tender" was set to be released in 2007. In the movie, Gonzalez stars as Wilson De Leon, Jr., a 21-year-old college student who lives a lavish life style at home with his mom in Connecticut. Wilson is a straight-A student but pretty clueless about dealing with the complexities of life, especially the complexities his father had set in motion as a drug dealer before Wilson's birth.

John Singleton, of "Boyz and the Hood" fame, produced "Illegal Tender." The movie has some great Reggaeton songs performed by Tego Calderon and Que No including *"Dame Dame"* (da may, da may), a song that makes you desire to dance all night long.

It was great seeing those movies with my parents. They provided opportunities for us to laugh, to applaud, and to discuss the messages. I saw courage, teamwork, and love expressed. I heard the message about the value of education. I saw the importance of serving the community and strength in placing the needs of others before my own needs. I had a powerful view of the importance of family and the extended family. I witnessed the power generated from conquering mental as well as physical fears. I reflected upon my parents' love and their willingness to risk their lives for me, if necessary. I saw that even the most intense conflict between a parent and child cannot destroy a deep-rooted love. Those and other DVDs remain in the closet of keepsakes awaiting my sons and daughters.

It would be great if Hollywood produced more movies with Latino heroes instead of just movies with Latino villains, gang bangers, hustlers, pimps, and drug dealers. But Hollywood has to keep the stereotypes rolling on the screen during the very few opportunities given to Latinos.

Today I can quote Timo word for word about my deepest fear. Truth is, I am still moving to overcome my deepest fear and deal effectively with the complexities of life.

With the ripening of time, dad, I will. Keep the faith.

Chapter 25

Love, Heartbreak, and Basketball

Keyshia Cole in "Love" said she didn't know what she was missing until she and her man started kissing. That's when she found love.

Smokey Robinson in "Shop Around" said his mom told him that pretty women come a dime a dozen, and his job was to find one who would give him true loving.

I was in second grade when Valentine's Day first became meaningful. I guess someone might ask, "What does 'meaningful' mean to a second grader?"

In second grade, all you know is that you like being around a certain girl. You like the way she smiles. You like the way she talks. You even like the way she spells words and reads out loud.

In second grade, I was at PS 282 in a class with a rather mean teacher who did not like or respect boys. No matter how mean she was, I still looked forward to going to school every day. I managed, for the most part, not to become the specific target of her meanness. After all, there was always recess and there was also Imani. Imani had nice, pretty, milk chocolate, Gabrielle Union skin and beautiful, round, deep, dark brown eyes. She wore her hair in long pretty braids embraced by many colorful barrettes, red, blue, purple, pink, green, and yellow.

On Valentine's Day in 2000, I had wrapped a dozen red roses to take to school with me. I had retrieved the white wrapping paper covered with red hearts from the recycling bin where my mom had placed it the night before. My wrapping technique wasn't that neat, but that didn't stop me from wearing a big smile as I carried the package from my room.

Mom was taking me to school. With our coats on as we got ready to walk out the door, mom noticed what I was carrying. She paused and calmly asked me, "*Bambino*, what are you doing with the roses your dad gave me?"

"I need them for Valentine's Day," I responded with the innocence of a child who thought he was doing a good thing and what was expected. Dad had given flowers to mom. Therefore, shouldn't I give flowers to Imani?

"For whom?"

"For Imani, mommy."

"*Bambino*, you just cannot give my flowers to someone else."

"Why not, mommy? You had them already yesterday."

"I tell you what, *bambino*, you can have one rose, but not all of them."

So on Valentine's Day in 2000, I took one special and beautiful red rose to school for someone whom I considered special and beautiful, Imani, a little pretty Gabrielle Union.

On Valentine's Day in 2001, I was in a different school, PS 59 in Manhattan. I didn't take mom's roses this time. In fact, I took absolutely nothing at all to school for anyone. But I did bring home two cards from school. When dad and mom opened the envelopes to read the cards, they found $20 in each envelope.

"Akhenaton, what is this?" dad began. "Who gave you this money?"

"These two girls in my class."

"Why did they give you money?" he continued, in a tone of disapproval.

"I don't know. I didn't even know there was money in there. I didn't ask for it," I responded, as I shrugged my shoulders, sat on the rug, and turned on the television to watch the *Magic School Bus*.

"Well, we don't want you accepting money from any girls. That is something we believe boys shouldn't do. You have to return it tomorrow."

"Okay, dad, I will."

At that point in the conversation, I was already into whatever was on television and not thinking much about the money. For me, returning the money was no big deal since I had not expected the money and mom and dad gave me everything I needed. The two girls who had given me the cards were born in Asia. I had not asked for the cards, nor had I given them any cards. I had been mildly surprised when they gave me cards on Valentine's Day since we were only classmates.

As agreed, the following day I returned the money to each girl. I don't remember saying much except telling them that dad said I cannot accept money from girls.

In addition, three other girls in my class had given me cards and money for my birthday back in November. Dad had questioned me then and had not allowed me to keep the money when I couldn't explain whether other classmates had received money on their birthdays.

I would later learn more about dad's philosophy about not accepting gifts from girls and women. I would learn that in 1985 dad had refused to accept a loan from mom, who was his girlfriend at the time, when he needed to gather money for a down payment on the brownstone we would later live in. By 1985, she had been dating dad for almost four years. Dad explained to her that he was raised to never accept money from a woman. He explained he thought real men do not accept money from women, and real men should be financially self-sufficient. Mom responded that she was offering a loan not a gift. He suggested even a loan was unacceptable because the exchange of money has a tendency to complicate relationships.

Thus, dad spent several additional intense weeks attempting to put together the money for the down payment. He succeeded, in part, by accepting a loan from Aunt Irma, his sister-in-law. Acceptance from Aunt Irma was all right because she was a relative, and they shared a common goal: helping dad to secure a home where his daughters would feel safe and happy. Dad managed to repay the $4,000 loan within three months, before he had even moved into the house.

Today, Valentine's Day is still a special day for me, and I understand its meaning even more than I did back in second grade when I wanted to give mom's roses to Imani. Now I look to purchase a special gift (with dad's money, according to him) and spend some special time (my own) with my girl. I love to get home from that special time long past midnight after failing to respond to dad's texts asking, "Akhenaton, where r u?" I usually don't mind coming in knowing he has been anxiously waiting up to see me walk safely through the door after failing to get a response. He should have been asleep. I can handle things without having to text back, "OMW/On my way."

In second grade, you can only "like" someone. Love is not in your vocabulary, and it is beyond your understanding. It is said some people go a lifetime without understanding or experiencing love. No one wants to be included in that group.

By the time I was 15 and in eleventh grade, I was ready for love. I was ready for my first love.

It is said that a person could never forget his first love. They say you will always remember the first time you saw her, the nervousness you felt when you gathered the courage to speak to her for the first time, the first embrace, and the first kiss.

What does a 15-year-old boy look for in his first love? To tell the truth, at 15 you don't even know that you are looking. You may be looking at girls, but that is not necessarily the same as looking for love. However, all of a sudden, you find your heartbeat accelerating and your breathing quickening in response to the presence of that special someone, at that special place, and at that special time. You find yourself instantly more deeply self-conscious about your appearance, the smell of your breath, and the manner in which you are presenting yourself.

Maybe it's not the first time you saw her. Maybe during the first sighting you recognized nothing unusual about her. Maybe she didn't even strike you at first as the prettiest girl among the group of girls she was walking with when you first saw her.

Then one day she looks at you, and there is something special about that glance. Then she speaks to you. Maybe it is just a simple "hello." However, there is something real special about that "hello." You begin to realize she is beyond beautiful. At that moment, your world is changed in an instant. You are no longer that boy you were just seconds before. She's no longer that girl you passed by before. Though the population of the earth is six billion, at that moment only she and you exist. As times marches on, you attempt to bring it to a halt. For you, at that moment, time does not exist. When time resumes its spin, you later spend countless other moments attempting to get back to that first special moment.

I don't really care to remember the beginning with my "first love" in 2008. The experience I just described above applies to my experience with my love, the girl I was dating in the fall of 2010. I was at Hampton, and she was back at Banneker Academy in Brooklyn. I cursed the distance, and it was one more matter that made Hampton less appealing than it could have been. In the fall of 2010, I was not sure where my "first love" was attending school. She was at another college somewhere in the big, wide USA.

When I met my "first love" at 15 in 2008, she had me singing with Ne-Yo, "Can't nobody strut like her, can't nobody touch her...." I was beginning my junior year at Banneker when I really began to notice Charlene. During my first two years at Banneker, I had been caught up in my books and basketball. I had been a star on the junior varsity basketball team, and I had developed friendships with many girls at Banneker. Maybe a few had been interested in me, but I hadn't really noticed. Going all the way back to my days in elementary and middle school, I was accustomed to having many female friends with whom I had no romantic interest. So, it was no big deal I had not developed a romantic relationship at Banneker before entering my junior year.

When I met Charlene, windows to a new and different world stood before me. And, like Alice, I descended down into the rabbit hole, according to dad.

Charlene was pretty, shapely, and very intelligent. Those qualities caught my attention, and she had my attention. Whenever there were free moments at school, we would attempt to spend them together. After school, we started attending a community service program, to learn and to be together. Charlene had three younger brothers and a sister to look after so her time after school was restricted. Her parents were also very strict so there weren't many opportunities to get together on weekends. Therefore, the two of us enrolled in the same Saturday SAT prep program at another school.

In the beginning, God created the heavens and the earth and God said, "That's good." Well, in the beginning, my relationship with Charlene was in one of those heavens.

At the beginning of my junior year I assumed everything would flow as smoothly as in my first two years. However, my guidance counselor had made the big mistake of programming me for eight consecutive classes with no lunch period. Banneker was an academically demanding high school, so to stay on top of my grades I was up regularly way past midnight writing papers and doing homework. Thus, by the time November rolled around, I was physically and mentally exhausted and didn't know it. Charlene and I were also becoming increasingly frustrated that I didn't have the freedom of a lunch hour to be with her.

At home I became very cranky and started to get into constant arguments with mom. Mom said I was being disrespectful and my behavior with mom led to constant arguments with dad. Looking back, I can see I was a little rude and disrespectful, but during that period I considered my behavior totally justified. During that period I began to pull away from mom and dad for the first time. The fun times and love we had shared for 15 years so suddenly seemed oh so distant.

At 15, I woke up each day to spend time with Charlene. With her I was the perfect gentleman in Ne-Yo's "Year of the Gentleman." Charlene had my R-E-S-P-E-C-T. She didn't have to demand respect, which mom and dad now had to earn as I demanded more and more independence.

No matter how much we wanted to be together, we just couldn't find enough time. So we started to look forward to the college tours offered by

Banneker just to be together. We went together to Howard, Syracuse, and Binghamton. We met former Banneker students at each campus who told us about their experiences on campus. We were thinking that we might end up at the same university once we graduated.

In October 2008, on the trip to one university, couples paired off in the back of the bus for some heavy kissing. Charlene and I locked lips for extended periods. It's sort of funny that with heavy kissing you relearn how to breathe exclusively through your nose. Anyway, at the back of the bus, the pairs locked in embraces allowed their friends to take pictures to share via Facebook and AIM when we got back to Brooklyn.

Back in Brooklyn, dad and mom saw the pictures one day when I was looking at them on the computer.

"Akhenaton, is that Charlene?" dad asked after glancing at the monitor.

"Yes. What do you think of her, dad?"

"Oh, she looks like a nice girl. Why don't you bring her over so we could meet her?" Dad asked in an innocent tone that I wasn't buying.

I told myself, "There ain't no way I would even entertain the idea of bringing Charlene before mom and dad. My parents have such strong opinions and could say something that would piss me off!"

Then I told dad, "Well, her parents are very strict and do not know that she has a boyfriend. So it's not possible." I had responded with the truth, which was just fine enough with me.

"Well, that's too bad. We would love to meet her." Dad may have been very disappointed, but his tone did not expose him.

A few weeks later, I was a bit more open about discussing Charlene. As dad prepared dinner, he casually asked, "How are things going?"

"Everything's cool. Charlene's parents are very strict, so it is hard to see her," I replied. I wasn't sure he could hear the disappointment in my voice. Unbelievably, a part of me wanted him to probe deeper with questions about my relationship.

"Yeah, I was wondering why you all do not go to the movies on the weekend."

"Well, they wouldn't even let her go to the movies with friends if they thought any guy she knows would be there."

"Wow, that's being a bit too strict. It's got to be very difficult for you to date someone who you cannot even take to the movies. What are they going to do when she goes to college and is not always under their watchful eye?"

"I don't know. Dad, do you know Charlene has other issues?"

"Naw, what do you mean?"

I could see dad's eyes uncontrollably perk up with anticipation. I had to make a quick decision regarding whether I would reward his anticipation and his probing eyes and mind. I could sense he was trying to look right through me to read my mind and emotions.

"She's moody," I stated, in what I thought was the most neutral tone I could command. As soon as the words left me, I felt relieved yet determined to say no more.

"Like what?" Dad asked in what was probably the most neutral tone he could command. This was the dad of the first 15 years of my life, the dad who talked with me more like a big brother and a mentor. This was the pre-eleventh grade dad, the pre-Charlene dad.

"That's all I am going to say. That's all I am going to say," I responded as the 15-year-old man who had determined he knew best about what to do. That 15-year-old man possessed a wisdom that was beyond the reach of his dad who had lived in an ancient world when life for teenagers was not as challenging. He didn't have the experience to understand what I called "the reality of now."

"Oh?" dad managed to stutter with a one syllable word when I announced I would say no more.

It must have taken tremendous self-control for dad not to say anything other than "Oh?" I was glad he was exercising self-control. I had a lot on my mind and was not caring to focus on dad and any thoughts he might have wanted to share with me.

In November 2008 during that same junior year, I made a big decision not to play basketball for Banneker. Coach Wendell Saunders appealed to me and dad. Dad wanted me to play, and he told Coach Saunders he would attempt to convince me. However, his attempts and the coach's attempts were all in vain. I was my own man and capable of making my own decisions. Plus, I had too much going on: a very demanding academic load, Charlene and the desire to maintain our relationship, conflict at home with mom and dad, and seniors on the team who thought it was all about them.

Dad attempted to understand my decision. He couldn't, but he said it was my decision to make. I must admit his decision not to pressure me made it easier for me to live with my decision. However, I would soon get pressure from other adults at the school and students who thought I was letting the school and the team down. Some of that pressure rattled me and added to the anxiety I was experiencing at that stage in my life about who I was and whether I was preparing myself to be the best man I could be.

Thus, from November through February, my high school basketball team played without me. I was putting everything into Charlene, my school work, and figuring out me. I managed to keep in focus my desire to make sure I would meet the challenges of my heavy academic load to have a chance to attend the college of my choice. I knew college admissions staff members look at the eleventh grade report cards very closely.

Dad was happy I was focusing on school. He had taken early retirement in January 2008. Then he started a consulting business which provided an opportunity for him to work from home about half of the days he consulted. Thus he was able to help me deal with my heavy class load and would often stay up late beyond midnight while I did tons of homework. He would bring me Red Zinger tea and hot chocolate. Often I had to wake up at 5:30 a.m. to finish typing my papers, and he was up with hot chocolate and freshly baked corn muffins. If I needed a ride to make it to my first period class, he would drive me to school. I made it through that semester with a B-plus average.

By the time March rolled around, I was beginning to have some serious difficulty in school. I was no longer willing to stay up past midnight doing homework and typing papers. I had a personal conflict with a teacher who was verbally abusive to me and most of the students in her class. She only lectured at the blackboard and did not have good teaching strategies to teach a complex subject. When we could not follow her, she treated us as "special education students," although we had all succeeded in entering a very competitive academic high school.

I started to cut her classes when I felt as if I were going to explode if she were to say anything again to offend me and my classmates. After all, who wants to learn anything from a teacher who is detested by her students? Unfortunately, once I started cutting her classes, somehow it became not too difficult to start cutting other classes, including the classes of great and caring teachers, to spend time with Charlene.

I would cut class when Charlene and I had to talk during periods of our ups and downs caused by her mood swings or simply when I had to comfort her as she dealt with her internal stress. I thought I was doing what was best for me, but somehow I felt a contradiction and didn't know how to make better choices. I was cutting classes to be with her, but she was attending all her classes. Huh? WWIT?! Did I hear someone whisper, "*El estupido*?" Huh? (I told dad I would be pissed if he put the "*El estupido*" line in this memoir.)

From the point dad discovered I was cutting, he would come to the school and confront me as soon as he got a complaint from the school about me not attending class. One time he actually found me in the gym and escorted me to class. My blood boiled. I was pissed! HTH/How the hell did he find me? Then he started to call the school weekly to check up on me like I was back in elementary school.

Whenever dad confronted me about my choices, dad was the real problem, not my choices. I told him he was just a "well-educated dictator" who was trying to impose his will on me. I told him, "You might be the head of the family, but our family is a democracy!"

BTW, teenagers of America, I want to give you a strategy for holding your dad in line. It works. The key is not to use it too often because it would lose its potency. About once every four to six months should be sufficient to keep your dad from overbuggin'. Use it when you know he is upset about something big that you have done wrong.

When your supportive dad first criticizes, try to ignore him but keep a concerned look of remorse on your face. When he starts again, tell him, "Stop already. I know I was wrong. How do you think I feel when I know I have screwed up?" Then, when the criticism goes on and on and is even brought up the next day because he doesn't believe you are remorseful enough, that is when you let him have it. With a demonstration of intense exasperation, you call him the name of an individual or historical figure he detests the most. Then you tell him how his behavior compares with the behavior of that individual.

In response, subconsciously he will know that he overplayed his hand and will back off and attempt for a while to not be overbuggin' again. During the next several weeks, you should be able to get away with more than usual. Choose wisely the things you want to get away with. Free passes don't come every day.

Referencing dad as a dictator would get his blood boiling. For him, someone like Hitler was the "son of Satan," and he didn't appreciate being compared to any dictator. Thus, our conversations were no longer conversations. They were episodes of psychological warfare. Yet, even when I felt I was winning, I often wondered about the price I would pay for winning. At times I would ask myself: "Would a win really be a defeat?" However, the question about the price of winning would fade completely in the midst of the next confrontation because all of my brain power was again devoted just to winning.

Thankfully (or unfortunately according to dad), the 16-year-old brain gives you confidence in the midst of a confrontation that you are always right and your parents are always wrong. Because they are, aren't they? If parents were right, they wouldn't be able to give birth to teenagers who would do wrong.

Even if you are wrong a little bit, it is really because they created the conditions and circumstances to cause your error. They didn't give you the right kind of love. They didn't consider your feelings. They made your errors seem bigger than they were, didn't they? They won't let you make your own mistakes, which never really carry the penalties they expect. They lived in another time and do not know the reality of now. That bull they give about having been teenagers themselves is just bull! Isn't it? Huh?

In mid-March 2009 on a warm Friday afternoon, dad and mom arrived at Banneker for open school day. Dad came around the corner to the basketball courts on Waverly Avenue to get me. I wasn't pleased to see him. Most of the other guys were able to continue playing because their parents didn't show up or did not require their sons to attend open school day.

As usual, most of the parents in attendance were there for their daughters, and most were expecting to hear good things from the teachers. Maybe a tenth of the parents were there for their sons, and many, like mine, were concerned about what they would hear. In three years, mom and dad had never missed open school day. Even during all the semesters when my grades and behavior were tops, they brought me along as well. Why must our parents attend even when our grades are great?

As we went from teacher to teacher that day, they reported on my grades. Most of the reports were good. Math and science were not so good, but we were given clear instructions of what I needed to do to get them better: "Do the homework."

In my Honors English class, I had a perfect 100. I loved Miss Cook-Person, not just for the grade, but really for the quality of her teaching and the quality of her relationship with me and the other students in the class. She was demanding but fair. The topics chosen were interesting. She expected and respected our intelligence. She inspired students to want to learn, to want to do the work, and to want to do their best. I went to every one of her classes. When she demanded 25-page papers that met her standards, everyone was eager to meet her challenge. She was the kind of teacher students wanted for every class and that parents wanted for their children. If all teachers were a Miss Cook-Person, we would solve the problems of the public schools of America within a short period of time.

On the way out of Miss Cook-Person's classroom, we noticed a group of four girls in a corner looking at me and dad. The girls were giggling with big smiles. Angela, Charlene's best friend, whispered my name and stuck out her tongue. I said "hi" and dad and I kept walking.

As soon as we left the classroom, dad had some questions. "Akhenaton, who was that girl who stuck out her tongue? Is she interested in you?"

"Dad, that's Charlene's best friend."

"Wow, and she stuck her tongue out in such a sexually suggestive manner while licking her lips? Does she have a thing for you? What's that tongue about?" Dad's forehead was wrinkled as if he were in deep thought with deep concerns as the questions rolled forth.

"Nothing, dad. She has no interest in me. She's Charlene's best friend. I have no interest in Angela, and I am sure she has none in me. So drop it, dad! You know nothing about how teenagers think today!"

From my tone and body language, dad could determine that continuation of the conversation would lead to a public display of conflict between us.

"Okay, if you say so." With those words dad appeared to drop the topic and we continued walking. As we walked down the hallway, we could see the joy on some parents' faces and the disappointment on others. We entered the stairwell leading downstairs and saw the dark anguish on the faces of some of the students and parents going upstairs.

As we exited the building, we encountered a confrontation between another junior and his parents. His father was putting him on blast about his attendance, poor grades, and the possibility that he would not move on to his senior year. His father gave him a verbal beat down in front of everyone on the sidewalk on Clinton Avenue. He kind of deserved it because everybody in the school knew he was skating on thin ice by cutting classes and leaving school to engage in behavior he probably wanted to keep private from his parents. At that moment, I was happy that I was me and not him.

When we arrived home, dad returned to the subject of Angela's greeting. "Akhenaton, I want to tell you to watch out for Angela. She may be Charlene's best friend, but I can tell just by the way she stuck out her tongue she has a thing for you." Dad's tone was the tone of a guidance counselor issuing an important caution in a way that suggested he has a bit of confidence in my judgment.

"Dad, that's impossible," my judgment responded.

"Trust me. No girl is going to stick her tongue out in such a sexually suggestive manner unless she has an interest in you. You might think that I am too old to know, but living is what gives you the experience to know. And she did it right in front of me in a classroom, not a club, while three of her girl buddies looked on. She has not been taught any self-respect. You need to avoid girls like that."

"No, dad, you're wrong," I responded with a rising tone of irritation with the conversation. I opened the fridge to get some juice and to turn away from him. I was hoping that would be his cue to drop the subject. He was annoying and wrong, and that is a bad combination in parents. He had no experience which would give him the knowledge to fully know what was happening with my friends and my generation.

While not taking my cue and continuing the subject, dad said, "I can see her right now working to break you and Charlene up. Trust me. I was a teenager, and I am a man. I know from experience that many relationships are broken up by the best friends of women who want the men for themselves. In fact, some girls and women become the best friends of other girls and women just to get close to their men. Trust me. I know."

"Uh huh. Yeah, you know, dad," I responded sarcastically. "Yeah, dad, you really don't know."

"Everybody has known this for a long time, and people have even written songs about it. In the 1980s, even the disco group Skyy had a hit song entitled, 'Call Me.' In this song, a woman gives her number and a dime to her best friend's man and tells him to call her anytime. That game is as old as time itself. Maybe I should play that song for you?"

"Dad, it ain't like that. Trust me." I was confident that I was right and attempting to be confident dad was wrong. I wondered what mental madness could make him jump to that conclusion. I had seen girls plot to steal boyfriends on Nickelodeon television shows like *Degrassi*, but I was not prepared to entertain the idea that Angela would act in that manner. Yet, I couldn't understand why dad was on the topic. If he were to continue, I knew I would become very annoyed and say some harsh things to suggest he was clueless and talking madness. Thankfully, he let it go.

About two weeks later I was prepared to return to the conversation. Dad was in the study writing a proposal to secure funding for a national organization when I arrived at about 4:00 p.m.

"Akhenaton, you're home early today," dad called out from the study as I passed by on the way to my room.

After I dropped my bag, I went to the study to talk to dad. I walked over to sit on the black leather couch opposite the computer desk where dad sat.

"Hey, dad, Charlene and I broke up today," I began. "And, you were right about Angela. Yeah, she was in the middle of our breakup," I announced, as I attempted to keep any hint of emotion out of my voice. Yet, I wasn't concerned dad would say "I told you so."

"What happened?" dad asked as he spun in the computer chair to face me.

Despite my best efforts, the emotions had begun to rise so I cleared my throat. I wanted to stare beyond dad's eyes to the Dell flat screen monitor directly behind him. His head blocked my vision and his eyes seemed bigger than usual. After a few awkward seconds, I cleared my throat again, and I was prepared to respond.

"Angela confronted us in the hallway today," I began. "She told Charlene she was spending too much time with me and no time with her and their girl-friends. She said Charlene needed to make up her mind and choose between spending time with me or her and their friends. Uh, uh, uh."

"And what did Charlene say?" dad asked, in a very straight-forward, non-emotional manner that stood in contrast to my own.

"She said she did not want to be forced to choose."

"Huh, she said what?" dad asked, with an air of disbelief. He shook his head "no" and frown lines shaped his face to emphasize his disbelief.

"She said she did not want to be forced to choose. She said that she wouldn't choose."

"Now that's a silly girl listening to a crazy girl! Can you imagine one of your boyz asking you to choose between spending time with him or any girl you are dating? You'll tell him, son, get the f*** outta here!"

"Well, I told Charlene she didn't have to choose, and I stepped," I responded in a voice that suggested I was in control of the situation.

"Good for you! Now you must remember when you turn a corner never to go back down that same street. As a matter of fact, you have to forget you ever walked down that street. Corners are there to be turned!" Dad was once again being the counselor. I was willing to listen up to a point.

"Dad, I stepped, but I didn't tell Charlene that for the last two weeks Angela has been trying to get me interested in her when Charlene wasn't around. Once when I greeted Angela, she turned her head as if to ask for a kiss on the cheek. When I placed my cheek next to hers, she grabbed my head and kissed me on the lips. I was glad I had my mouth closed 'cause she tried to, well, you know what."

"Yeah, she tried to stick out that nasty tongue! Wow! Didn't I tell you that she had a trick up her sleeve? And your girl was dumb enough to fall for it!" Dad smiled and shook his head as if answering "yes" for me. I followed by mildly shaking my head in agreement.

"Dad, until recently Angela seemed so smart and nice. She gets a straight A in every class at school."

"Maybe in Banneker she is a straight A, but I could tell when I first saw her with that tongue out she was acting like a player all the way. Don't think that she has given up on you. She might not show her intentions tomorrow, but give her time and she will. She has not learned any self-respect."

Later that evening as I prepared for bed, I was listening to Ne-Yo's "Mad." I had been listening to that song regularly for the past several weeks since Charlene and I were already going through some highs and lows in our relationship, the highs and lows that need no explaining.

Listening to Ne-Yo, I sought to calm my storm. I didn't want to go to bed mad at her. I breathed in melancholia. I sought to breathe out disappointment. I breathed in disappointment. Melancholia wouldn't allow me to breathe melancholia out. I struggled with physical discomfort. The mattress was suddenly hard and lumpy. The 18-foot ceiling in my bedroom descended and stifled me. I tossed. I turned. I rubbed my eyes. I turned off the lights. I turned on the lights. Finally, I dropped off to sleep listening to "World of Fantasy" by the Five Stairsteps, not Lil' Wayne's.

At school the next couple of days, I was cool on the surface. I had to develop new routines. I started to notice I was spending more time thinking about what I was thinking before I engaged in most activities, especially activities done at times when I would normally be with Charlene. It seemed that everyone was looking at me differently. I wondered if news really travelled so fast while time then seemed to travel so slowly. I wasn't in the mood for questions, so I just looked right past the probing eyes. I also started to notice several girls were speaking to me with unusual sweetness in their voices about topics which required no sweetness.

Toward the end of the week, dad and I found ourselves arguing about a chore that I had failed to do. I wasn't ready for any disagreement at home. Chores should have been suspended while I dealt with my feelings, I thought. Isn't that the way it should be? When a teenager is dealing with his emotions, all chores should be suspended by the decree of America's most respected psychologists.

"Dad, why are you bothering me about that?" I asked. "You don't even care that me and my girl broke up! Can't you see I have a lot on my mind?"

Speaking with the voice of authority and not of the counselor, dad responded, "Man, you need to get over that girl! As you would say, man-up!"

"I am over her, but that does not mean that I feel good about it!" I protested.

Speaking casually with what I considered fake empathy dad explained, "Look, it happens to all boys your age. When it happened to me at 16, I got over it by playing basketball every opportunity that I got. I just kept bouncing the ball and, with each bounce, I bounced out some of the feelings I had for beautiful Cynthia until all the feelings were gone or at least had lost their power over me. That's what you need to do."

Thankfully, mom was standing near the refrigerator and overheard our conversation in the dining area. "Askia, don't tell him to just get over his feelings," mom interjected. "His feelings are important. It takes time. He was in love."

Dad asked mom in a sarcastic tone, "Love? Did you say love? Huh, love! *Dame un breaque!*" (Spanglish for "Give me a break!")

Speaking with authority in defense of her son, mom firmly responded, "Yes, love, Askia. And you cannot make it seem that it should be so easy for him to get over the breakup. He needs time to deal with his feelings about the breakup."

In a tone that had lost some authority, dad responded, "I didn't say his feelings were unimportant. I am just trying to advise him about a way to get over them."

Then, turning to me, he uttered, "Akhenaton, you will meet another girl. There's more than one fish in the sea. You don't have to take sand to the beach. You're handsome and intelligent. Other girls will come along, and you will have your choice of the most beautiful and intelligent."

"Dad, what madness are you talking about? Fish in the sea and sand at the beach? That's why it's so difficult to have a conversation with you about any girl. Huh! Sand at the beach!"

I had quite a bit of rising anger toward dad for advising me about getting over my feelings. What does he know about love and feelings among teenagers? I wondered. Why was he speaking madness about "fish in the sea" and "taking sand to the beach?" It wasn't even summertime. He might have been right about Angela, but he was surely wrong about how to handle the breakup, I thought. Plus, I had no clue about the identity of this Cynthia he mentioned, and I knew nothing about what had happened between the two of them. WTHC/Who the hell cares! What 16-year-old imagines his father at age 16 with a girl? Even if dad had a girl at that age, he learned nothing that is relevant for me in the 21st century, I thought.

A few days later that March I had to turn my attention to playing basketball with the New York City Boys Club in a very competitive league. I was determined to improve and display my skills after missing the season with my high school varsity team. I wanted to be ready to be a star on that team my senior year. I quickly became the star of the Boys Club team, and the most valuable player when we won the Manhattan Borough Championship in the Housing Authority League at the beginning of April.

So with the bouncing of the basketballs, the remaining feelings had unexpectedly begun to bounce away in a matter of a couple of weeks following my argument with dad. When I saw her in the hallway, an imaginary basketball bounced in my mind. Even though Charlene and I attended the same school and would see each other daily, the feelings bounced away just as "mad dad" had said they would.

As B.B. King sings, the thrill was gone. When our paths would cross, I was always polite and would nod and smile. But, in my eyes, Charlene's smile no longer had any special charm. There was no longer any beauty in her eyes. I certainly had no intention of calling her name, and I hoped that she would not call mine. She became no more than a misty shadow of a distant face moving within an anonymous crowd.

While writing this story I had to remember what had attracted me to Charlene. I had to ask myself, "What was I thinking?" Oh, it was that smile. Oh, it was that pretty face. It was that shapely body. It was her intelligence. It was the sweetness of her lips. But within five months after we first started going together, all of that had lost its appeal as if its appeal had never existed. Unlike Anthony Hamilton, I was not moaning, "Oh, oh, oh. Charlene, baby if you're listening, call on me...."

You know you cannot really see a personality at the beginning. Chris Rock says when we first start to date a girl we are dating the girl's "representative," or the person she wants us to see. I was introduced to the sweet and affectionate Charlene. It took me a while to meet the moody and inconsiderate Charlene.

Today I still think Charlene is a very nice girl, but she was never the right one for me. Luther Vandross sang, "I can't love anybody walking on a one-way street (anyway, anyway, anyway). If I can't find somebody, it will be all right with me." It's funny how going in I couldn't see that Charlene was strutting down that one-way street without a map to where it would take her, and our relationship was all about her. Now, like Luther, I don't want to be a fool, ever again.

Thankfully, I have learned there is more than one fish in the sea. I have caught one that makes my heart sing. But I have yet to understand what dad meant about not taking sand to the beach. Post on my Facebook page if you do.

No teenager wants to be assuming incorrectly when his father is seen assuming correctly. How did old dad assume correctly about Angela? How did he know to advise me on bouncing basketballs? It can't be based on his life experience with girls. I guess it's based on what a wise philosopher once said: "Even a broken clock, whose hands don't move, is right twice every 24 hours."

As dad and I spoke just before we began working on this memoir, he revealed a feeling that he had kept to himself during the entire time I dated Charlene. Dad explained he and mom never thought Charlene was right for me. They didn't understand why I would want to date someone whose parents would not allow her, in eleventh grade, to go to a movie with friends on a Saturday afternoon. They didn't understand why I would date someone who was moody and would take me on an emotional rollercoaster. They thought she had played a negative role in encouraging me to cut classes and in turning my attention from the basketball team.

However, rather than express their concerns, they chose to hold their tongues, to remain silent. "We knew if we had questioned you, we would only have pushed you closer to her. So, instead of questioning, we prayed," mom explained, and dad agreed. "And now that you are no longer together, we can shout like Madea, 'Hal-le-lu-jer!'"

You know, mom and dad, I can also say, "Hal-le-lu-jer!" Amen!

And, wherever Charlene is, I wish her love.

Chapter 26
The House Negro

On Saturday evening May 30, 1992, six months before my arrival, dad hosted a reunion party for about 60 friends who knew him as a student at Brooklyn College. Son, I wish I could have been a fly on the wall. Instead, I was a growing babe in mom's belly without the privilege of hearing the discussions.

Years later in the spring of 2006 at age 13, when dad sat me down to give me the details of that party, I was hoping to hear about the crazy mistakes he had made as a teenager that might have come up at the reunion. Dad had decided to tell me the story of the reunion after Juan, one of my classmates but not a close friend, was suspended for bringing a pellet gun to MS 89 and going on a rampage shooting kids. Besides being somewhat of a "wannabe thug," Juan was also a "porn star" who spent time teaching the naïve kids at MS 89 "the tricks of the trade."

I imagine I was like so many other kids in America who were introduced to porn by their classmates. In middle school when a kid hears talk about pornography, he is immediately curious. Porn is a subject that is taboo. Going on a computer and looking at porn is also taboo. Schools place filters on their computers to prevent students from going on porn sites. So when a guy comes into class talking about porn, he immediately gets noticed by all the other guys who know nothing about porn.

One warm spring day in 2006, when Juan came into the gym class talking about porn, he drew a crowd of seven curious listeners: two African Americans, two whites, one Hispanic, one Asian, and me. He described what he had seen on the porn sites. He talked about things that I couldn't even imagine.

Of course at 13 no one wanted to admit being clueless, but I bet I wasn't the only clueless one in that group. He said we couldn't learn anything from listening to our teachers in sex education class because the teachers never had sex. He asked, "Can you imagine Miss Blanks ever having sex?" At the same time we all responded, *"Eww!"*

The more Juan talked, the more the guys nodded their heads as if they knew what he was talking about. Still, there were a few questions that came along with the "Wows!" For example, when Juan described one act, a kid named Jason asked, "Man, do people really do that?"

Juan replied, "Yeah, and more than that! I wish I could show you on the computers in the library."

With answers like that, our seven pairs of eyes saw Juan as a mad cool guy during that three-minute lecture. That day, his lecture was more interesting than the lectures of many other teachers in all of the other subjects.

Toward the end of Juan's lecture, he asked the seven of us if we wanted to know the web address for the porn site that offered the best videos of sex in action. I don't remember anyone saying "Yes." Maybe our minds were too involved in the descriptions he had given to hear his question. However, when he took pieces of paper out of his pocket with the website listed, Jason's hand grabbed one and six other hands quickly followed, including mine.

With the papers hot in our hands, we looked to make sure we could read Juan's handwriting. Juan was known for not being a good student or a good speller. The seven recipients of Juan's lesson were successful students in our classes and throughout the school. When we looked at the paper, to our surprise we discovered Juan had written everything we needed to access the site, including ".com." We placed the papers in our pockets and fist bumped Juan. He didn't know any math, but he knew some porn.

When I got home that evening, I had to figure out how I could get access to the site without dad and mom discovering my actions. I had a few things in my favor: (1) dad and mom had trusted me with computers since I was almost 3; (2) the computer was in the study, and the study had a door I could close pretending to be doing my homework; (3) dad and mom would often go to bed before I completed my homework; and (4) the filter on the computer had not been activated. They trusted me fully at that point in my life.

After mom and dad went into their bedroom around 9:50 p.m., I went in to say good night. I wanted to also make sure they had settled in for the night. They were sitting up in bed watching television. After saying good night,

I asked if they wanted me to close the door to the bedroom. They told me to leave it open so that they could keep the fresh air circulating.

Within seconds, I was in the study with the door shut. I could feel my heartbeat accelerating. I have since learned that is what normally happens when a person does something he shouldn't.

Within a few more seconds, I quickly logged on and I went to www. ushouldnotBwatchingthis.com. What I saw I cannot describe because there are laws against putting it in writing. However, I can tell you that my eyes opened wider and wider and my heart beat faster and faster with each passing second. Within 30 seconds, I became really involved in looking; in fact, I became so involved that I didn't hear mom's footsteps toward the study.

When mom opened the door, I had been in the world of porn for about 45 seconds, but it took less than the fraction of a second for me to leave that world. I quickly closed the page so that a different website appeared on the monitor. Yet, I was very concerned that she might have heard the heavy breathing and sounds of the porn stars and the sexy music as she approached the door.

"*Bambino*, what are you looking at?" she asked as she came over to look at the screen.

"Nothing, mom, I'm doing my homework." The homework helper page on the monitor gave me the appearance of perfect innocence, or so I thought. I turned a few pages in my schoolbook nearby hoping to reassure her.

"That didn't sound like homework to me. Get up and let me see the computer," she commanded.

With my heart racing, I got up and mom sat and opened up the history and discovered the website. My courage left me. Within seconds, she was on the website and looking at more breasts, female and male organs, and butts than she cared to see. Meanwhile, dad was on his way to the study. Dad entered huffing and puffing and ready to blow the house down.

I was so embarrassed, and I felt so "stoopid." Can you imagine being caught by your mom? WWIT?! I am sure I wasn't the first kid in America to be caught, but the fact that I was not the only one did not matter that evening. I was deeply humiliated from the moment mom walked in, and I instinctively knew dad was ready to make sure that humiliation would not disappear with a good night's sleep.

I cannot remember everything dad said, but I do know it wasn't pretty. I believe it went something like the following, and I am paraphrasing here:

> I cannot believe you are in here looking at disgusting porn. Haven't
> we taught you better than that? What you see those people do,

most of it isn't even natural for humans! A lot of those folks are sick in their minds and in their bodies. But they are not going to show you the low self-esteem, the AIDS, and the other diseases that they carry. You do not need to put that garbage in your mind because it can mess up your thinking about what is a healthy relationship with a woman!

Dad said a lot more, but that is as much as I can remember. However, the impact of that evening has stayed with me. God, please understand that is humiliation I do not want to experience again.

When dad paused to give me the opportunity to speak, I told them certain things about Juan and about Juan's lecture about porn. After listening, dad said that Juan was "headed for big trouble." He said life has taught him that kids like Juan needed strong guidance that they often fail to receive. He told me to watch out and stay away from Juan to avoid the trouble headed his way. Dad spoke with the confidence of a man who could see the future, and I listened and accepted his warning.

Dad said I had to make good decisions so that the kinds of actions I would become involved in would have lasting value, "not the garbage acts encouraged by some rappers and misguided teenagers." He said, "Folks on the porn sites do the weirdest things as if they were normal or the way sex should happen between a man and a woman." He said there were certain poisonous images and thoughts we should not allow to enter our minds.

Two weeks after the humiliation I experienced in the study, Juan arrived at school and went on his shooting spree. He ran from class to class with a smile on his face while shooting students with a pellet gun. As he attempted to escape from the building, he ran into me in the staircase. I had avoided talking to him for two weeks, and I guess he didn't like that I had ignored him. He turned and shot at me. He escaped from the school building without being captured.

I believe all the students in the school were against Juan's stupidity. He had hurt innocent people for no reason except for "fun." He had no enemies who were bullying him. He was the bully with a gun. I felt he deserved whatever was coming his way. He was no longer mad cool; he was just a simple fool.

When I arrived home that evening after the shooting incident, I was eager to tell dad the cops were looking for Juan. I was impressed that dad had been able to see the future. I explained what Juan had done. I told him I was glad he had warned me that Juan should be avoided because he was headed for trouble. I wondered how it was possible for dad to predict Juan's troubles. I didn't have a clear answer, but I was glad dad had warned me.

The following day, Juan was arrested at his apartment. I informed dad of his arrest, and we talked about the possible consequences he would face. He explained, "As a 13-year-old, Juan is most likely headed for a juvenile detention center where he may be sentenced to two or more years based on any prior record of criminal activity. He will be away from the people who love him.

"He will sit in classes taught inside of a jail cell by instructors who most likely would prefer to be elsewhere. They will not have the computers, books, and the educational materials found at MS 89. The teachers will not have the background or training necessary to educate so many inmates who are educationally far behind students of similar ages.

"Moreover, there will be little, if any, counseling to deal with the anger, confusion, and low self-esteem that many of the kids bring with them. Some will be angrier and tougher than Juan, and Juan would need to watch his step to avoid becoming a victim of their anger. Juan and most of the inmates would need to worry about becoming a victim of violence and rape. For every year spent in detention, Juan would most likely fall at least one or more years further behind the classmates he left at MS 89.

"Upon release, the public school system will never allow Juan to attend a school of the quality of MS 89. He will only be accepted in a 'low performing' or what most would call a 'bad' high school. Being far behind and unable or unwilling to do the work, work he would probably consider uninteresting, he would most likely drop out. He would most likely face a future of more crime and imprisonment."

"That's horrible, dad. For that one bad mistake it sounds like he might suffer for a long time."

"Unfortunately, many kids fail to see in advance all the long years they are likely to suffer for a dumb and dangerous mistake that only takes a minute to perform."

With that remark we both noticed that we were a bit depressed after discussing the challenges Juan was likely to face. Thus, dad reassured me that it was possible that Juan could rise above the challenges he would likely face and find inner strength to turn his life around. We discussed Malcolm X's rise from dropout, prison, pimp, and drug dealer to scholar, intellectual, and international leader. We agreed that Juan might discover an organization, a teacher, a counselor, a family member, or someone else who might take an interest in his life and give him the second chance, support, and guidance necessary to become a productive adult.

I knew Juan did not have a mean and evil spirit; instead, he had a confused and immature spirit. I think he wanted to be popular and wanted to be in control. Instead, he had become unpopular and had surrendered control of his life to people and a system he didn't even know. Juan was a 13-year-old who had made some bad decisions that should not haunt him for a lifetime. However, the school and criminal justice systems saw him as a statistic and had no sympathy. I am hopeful he will find it elsewhere.

After our discussion of Juan, dad decided to tell me the story of the Brooklyn 19 and the time when the police had arrested dad as a teenager and put him on trial to face more time than he or anyone else could expect to live. Of course, I was all ears and eager to hear the story about the man who appeared as if he could do no wrong. I figured he must have screwed up even worse than Juan and was going to tell me his story so that I would not make the same mistakes and would avoid other teens who might make such mistakes.

So, focusing on the reunion story dad was going to tell me after I told him Juan had gotten suspended, dad began by telling me that on May 30, 1992, he hosted a reunion at our brownstone on Park Place. The reunion was a gathering of black and Puerto Rican student activists who had attended Brooklyn College in the late 1960s and early 1970s. The party marked the 23rd anniversary of the release of dad and the rest of the Brooklyn College 19 from prison. Dad's friends embraced him as they entered. They were greeted by the aroma of barbecue chicken and dad's famous vegetarian chili with brown rice.

David P., one of the Brooklyn College 19, was there with his son, Daoud. Dad had not seen Daoud since 1975 when he would babysit for Daoud and his sister Zawadi in exchange for the times David and Treva (Daoud's mom) would babysit for my sisters Ife and Kakuna. Dad was impressed with Daoud's muscular stature. He said that Daoud looked as if he were ready for kick boxing. In fact, he was so impressed he lost his cool and said something I'm quite sure Daoud was embarrassed to hear: "Brother, look at those muscles. I cannot believe the last time I saw you I was changing your diapers." (Today, Daoud is a successful writer and film producer.)

Knowing what I know now, I could imagine, if it were possible, saying from inside mom's womb, "Daoud, welcome to my world to come." You see, since that party I have had many occasions with my friends present when I did not want to hear the words coming out of my father's mouth when he would display a photograph while saying or revealing uncool things about me.

Can you believe that mom and dad still have hanging in the study a picture of me naked in the bathtub when I was 2? Granted, I am covered in all the right places by suds from my bubble bath along with a lot of toys, but still. I can only imagine what Samori, Lupe, my lady, and my other friends must be thinking when we are playing on the Xbox with that picture positioned directly above the television screen. That is not a good look.

Also, today mom keeps my yellow rubber ducky, seen floating in the tub in that picture, on the stand above her bath tub in her bathroom. I am afraid to ask if she puts it in the water to swim with her.

Njeri, Umakhayir, Kwame, Paulette, Sun, and Dubaka were at the reunion. Cy M., one of dad's closest friends and a member of the Brooklyn College 19, didn't make it. Dubaka, a producer for a major television network and one of the Brooklyn College 19, brought a series of photographs he had taken during the stormy days of the late 1960s and early 1970s. The pictures told stories of the demonstrations on the Brooklyn College and City College campuses and the activist work the Brooklyn College 19 and other students had conducted in communities, especially Brownsville and East New York.

As an activist fighting hunger in the black and Puerto Rican community in the late 1960s, dad was the master chef of the grits, eggs, and beef bacon he prepared for scores of public school students every weekday morning at the breakfast program at Ralph Community Center, 1212 East New York Avenue in Brownsville, one of the poorest areas in urban America. The food for the program was donated by supermarkets in the community. This took place before the federal government fully made breakfast available to poor students in schools across America. For dad, the pictures brought back images of the little black and brown faces in the richest nation on earth that arrived hungry morning after morning at 7:15 a.m. with a look of eager anticipation for a hot meal.

There was also a picture of Susan Taylor, the former editor of *Essence* magazine, as a teenager during one of the protest marches near City College. Instead of the braids she now wears, her head was shaven. Dad said she looked like a younger and prettier version of the model Iman when Iman was in her twenties. Dad and the brothers present remarked about how stunning Susan Taylor was in that photo. Someone remarked, "Uh, she's still fly today."

I think the remark was probably dad's, but he does not want to claim it.

When dad introduced mom at the gathering, David called out, "Yeah, brother Askia is expecting a baby."

"Yeah, we are expecting a baby boy in December," dad replied as he embraced mom.

"Man, you are so chauvinistic. How do you know it's a boy? Have you already had a sonogram?" David asked with a measure of playful sarcasm in his voice. Being called a chauvinist was a label that many revolutionaries who were teens with dad back in the day wanted to avoid. Chauvinists expressed the belief that men were superior to women, and that attitude had sparked the Women's Right Movement of the late 1960s and 1970s.

In response to David's question, dad revealed, "No, we have not had a sonogram. We do not need a sonogram to know. His name is Askia Akhenaton Suleiman Ali Davis," dad announced, brimming with confidence.

"Askia Akhenaton Suleiman Ali," a chorus of voices chanted. "That's a mouthful."

Later that evening as the old school music played, the reunion participants turned to dancing and discussions of their experiences at Brooklyn College as students and members of the Brooklyn College 19. There were a lot of JB, the Temptations, the Jackson Five, the Five Stair Steps, Otis Redding, War, the Watts 103 Street Rhythm Band, BT Express, the Supremes, and the O'Jays.

With many of the songs, they moved with the dances that were popular during those times. Dances in their teens included the Shing Ga Ling, the African Twist, Salsa, the Wah Watusi, the Horse, the Hitch Hike, the Cha Cha Cha, the Boo Ga Loo, the Pony, Mickey's Monkey, the Monkey, Twine Time, the Pearl, Soul Finger, the Tighten Up, the Funky Four Corners, the Dog, Walking the Dog, the Funky Chicken, the Funky Broadway, and the Mashed Potatoes.

BTW, I want to know who would name a dance after a plate of boring food? The Mashed Potatoes? Where's the gravy? The Twine Time? Does that occur in the morning or afternoon? Where's my watch? Walking the Dog? Where's my leash? I need it for dad and his friends. Hitch Hike? We got a car!

I told dad, "I can't believe the names of those dances! I don't want to picture the movements!" BTW, have you seen your old parents do those dances? Have you stopped laughing yet? Well, I am still laughing because I have seen dad attempt those movements as if he thinks he is still 18. He's not.

When my first cousin Symone was visiting from California, she stopped dead in her tracks on her way to the kitchen when she saw dad "dancing" in the living room to Denroy Morgan's "I'll Do Anything for You." Like our first cousin Nicole, she too had this image of dad as super serious and responsible. I hope she has recovered from the shock. Sorry, Uncle Jaime.

Well, dad said I shouldn't laugh. He explained, "Hitch Hike came from Margin Gaye and your generation has yet to produce a Marvin Gaye. The Mashed Potatoes was kept popular by James Brown. It's basically his signature movements where he is on his toes clicking his heels and moving from there, to being on one leg and up on his toes as he shakes his feet, wiggles his hips, melodiously swings his arm, and twists his head all while he sashays across the floor. Those moves are so bad that even Michael Jackson picked up on them, and you can see them in videos of the young Michael. And you know your generation has not yet produced another James or Michael. Or Marvin, Diana and the Supremes, Stevie, Luther, Barry, O'Jays, Temptations, Smokey, Aretha, Delfonics, EWF, Otis, Little Richard, Marley, Jimi, Al, Lionel, Commodores, Curtis and the Impressions, Mick and the Stones, Dells, Chaka, Donny, Jackie, Nina, Prince, Run DMC, Sly, Gil Scott, Whitney, Jacksons, Isleys, Ohio Players, Stylistics, Delfonics, Four Tops, Coltrane, Miles, Ella, etc., etc., etc." (Can you believe I had to listen to all of that? Does he have a point? If yes, don't tell me.)

Today, dad is also fond of telling me that African Americans were more creative in his day as dancers. He says back then new popular dance styles were coming out every couple of months, every time a popular band or singer "hit a new rhythm that the brothers and sisters wanted to roll with." He suggests today's dancing is mostly "the same old gymnastics devoid of imagination. It's about choreography and production, not spontaneity and creativity."

Concerning what he sees as production and not creativity, he asks, "What is Usher doing that Chris Brown isn't doing? Your generation was wasting its time doing the Dougie."

Dad further suggests that black folks should retire most of the "repetitious dance moves" seen in today's hip hop and R&B videos. He says, "The women in those videos (and in cheerleading squads and HBCU's marching bands) have run out of imaginative ways to shake their booties. If you combine all the best moves in all the hip hop and R&B videos and live performances ever produced in the last 18 years, they would not equal the original artistry and creativity in 'Billy Jean' alone. God bless Michael," he concludes.

Dad said African Americans and Puerto Ricans in the 1960s always knew it was time to move on to a new dance when they would look at *American Bandstand* on television and see that the dancers on that show had caught up and learned the steps. African Americans and Puerto Ricans of dad's time did not want to be seen on the dance floor still doing dances that had made it to Dick Clark's *American Bandstand* and the larger American population. He declared that it would usually take about three months for a new dance to make it from the dance halls and basement parties of black America to *American Bandstand* because media back then were not capable of communicating new styles instantly across the country the way media do today.

So, if you were still doing a dance that had made it to *American Bandstand*, you were not going to impress the fly girls in New York in the 1960s. Dad said if you were still doing those dances or "old moves," fly girls would see you as "a lame with no game, a sap with no rap." He said he actually saw girls stopping in the middle of songs to leave guys on the dance floor as soon as the guys started to dance "old moves." Once a fly girl left a guy on the floor, he was instantly an outcast who could not even pay another girl to dance with him. He had the kooties. In the 1960s, no fly girl wanted to dance with guys who were the "Carltons" of the world even before *Fresh Prince of Bel-Air* was televised.

Not wanting to be outcasts, dad and his friends "stayed up on the latest and on the ladies," according to him. He said when he had his apartment starting at age 16, during his high school years his friends would come over and they would work on the latest dances and invent some new ones. He claims he and his friend Elton invented "the Pearl" and "the African Twist." He said that once they had the new dance steps "down" the way they wanted, they would go to midtown Manhattan to the Cheetah or Trik. The Cheetah and Trik were two dance clubs that did not check IDs since checking IDs was not a common practice in the 1960s.

At the clubs, he, Elton, and several male and female friends would strategically situate themselves in different parts of the dance floor. When the DJ played "Get On Up" by the Esquires and "There Was a Time" by James Brown, they would start the new moves and the couples around would slowly stop and stare and begin to try to match the moves. Then he and his boyz would get a corner of the floor and begin to teach the new moves to interested girls and couples. Dad said it made them very popular at the clubs, and he always had some fly girls as dance partners.

Sorry, dad, I can't see it.

Dad further explained *American Bandstand* was the only show in town until Don Cornelius' *Soul Train* came on the air in the fall of 1971 to give full televised expression to African American popular music and dance. He said *Soul Train* made it possible for black dance styles and fashion to quickly move around America and get adopted by the general population.

I told dad, "It is too bad there is no video of you all dancing the night of the Brooklyn College 19 reunion. I would love to have it to show to my friends. I bet teenagers of my generation would have to wear straight jackets in order to be as stiff as you and your friends must have been at that reunion when you all were trying to do the Shing Ga Ling, the Boo Ga Who (or is it the Boo Ga What?) and whatever else you were dancing. Come to think of it, you all should have been the ones wearing straight jackets to prevent harming yourselves as you attempted to dance the whack steps that lately I have seen you do around the house when you are recalling your college years."

Looking beyond the dancing, the Brooklyn College 19 was a group of black and Puerto Rican student leaders who were intensely focused on presenting 18 Demands to the president and administration of the college. The demands called for "open admissions," which would allow more blacks and Puerto Ricans to attend the college, a college that was then totally financed by taxpayers' funds, including taxes paid by African Americans and Puerto Ricans. Other demands included incorporating the study of African, African American, and Puerto Rican histories and literature into the curriculum, as well as the hiring of African American and Puerto Rican professors.

Those matters were considered important because admissions and curriculum standards were designed to keep African Americans and Puerto Ricans out of the college and to deny the contributions of their people to building the nation, its economy, and its educational, literary, and cultural heritages. In those days, the only cultures, history, and literature you could study in most colleges and universities were the cultures, history, and literature of Europeans and European Americans. Even when presenting Egyptian history, there were historians and professors who suggested that the ancient Egyptians were "white," right there in Africa. Professors did not assign Langton Hughes, Julia De Burgos, Maya Angelou, *The Autobiography of Malcolm X, Native Son, Invisible Man*, or Piri Thomas' *Down These Mean Streets*.

Black History Month was not established until 1976 and Hispanic Heritage Month did not begin until 1988, during which time knowledge of the genius and beauty of our people were brought to students in public schools and universities. Those months were established because young people in the universities and black and Latino leaders continued to push to have the contributions and accomplishments of Latinos and African Americans studied and celebrated.

When Brooklyn College's President Peck and the administration rejected the 18 Demands, dad became one of the principal leaders of a student revolt and rallies on the campus. Dad and the students renamed President Peck "Pig Peck," since "pig" was a name reserved by the Black Power and antiwar movements for most negative people in authority who wanted to make sure African Americans and Puerto Ricans remained shut off from fair access to the best public colleges of America. "Pig" also suggested greediness—the desire to maintain much more than a fair share of America's resources and wealth in the hands of a few people in America who represented the power elite or the top "one percent." Dad would lead rallies on the campus where he and hundreds of black, Puerto Rican, Asian, and white students would call out "Pig Peck" for his unfair and poor leadership of the college.

Often, minutes following the same rallies, dad could be found in Peck's office leading negotiations with him about the 18 Demands. He said he didn't feel awkward.

On May 13, 1969, when dad was 18 years old, Peck was fed up with the rallies. Peck agreed with the district attorney to have dad and 18 other students arrested and charged with rioting, conspiracy to riot, arson, conspiring to commit arson, and a list of other crimes too lengthy to include here. Dad said the charges were "trumped up" or greatly exaggerated. He explained he and the other 18 black and Puerto Rican students had led a number of peaceful demonstrations that mostly included loud announcements over bullhorns at times when classes were in session.

Although hundreds of white students from prominent middle- and upper-middle-class families, led by Students for a Democratic Society, had attended the rallies and had expressed support for the 18 Demands, no white students were arrested.

Members of the Brooklyn College 19 came to believe that before the arrests took place the police had planted on campus an older "Negro" man, M. Beatty (dad would not give him the honor of being called black or African American), who reportedly pretended to be a full-time regularly enrolled student. They said the shucking and jiving poser pretended to be a "hip revolutionary student" and infiltrated the inner circle of black and Puerto Rican student leaders.

Beatty, in his twenties, reportedly posed using the "revolutionary look" with his Afro, US Army fatigues, black beret, shades, and lingo. He had been an earlier acquaintance of one of the main black student leaders. That relationship helped Beatty gain credibility which he reportedly used to infiltrate the inner circle.

Looking back, dad said they should have been more aware since even "Satan comes posing as an angel of light." Members of the Brooklyn College 19 came to believe that Beatty participated in meetings to plan the demonstrations and must have become an informant who fed the district attorney and Peck information that led to what, they believed, were false criminal charges. Apparently, after the arrests on May 13, Beatty left the college and was never seen again on campus by dad or the other members of the Brooklyn College 19.

The night of the reunion, members of the Brooklyn College 19 said an informant was the "house Negro" that Malcolm X warned African Americans to guard against. They said Malcolm X explained that the "house Negro" in the era of slavery lived in the master's house and ate the crumbs from the master's table. Therefore, Malcolm X warned, the "house Negro" thought he was better than the masses of "field Negroes" who took unending abuse and were often maimed and murdered by the slave masters. Malcolm X's speech goes something like this paraphrase:

> During slavery, the house Negro loved his white slave master more than the slave master loved himself. If the slave master got sick, the house Negro would ask, "What's the matter boss? We sick?"
>
> If the master's house caught on fire, the house Negro was the first to run for water, even faster than the master. If a slave escaped, the house Negro was willing to snoop and help track down the runaway.
>
> The house Negro was a stooge, an Uncle Tom and a traitor to his race. And there are still house Negroes in America today.
>
> While, on the other hand, the field Negro hated his master. He suffered the sting of the master's whip (and the master's rape of his wife and daughters). So, if the white slave master got sick, the field Negro prayed that the master would die. Yeah, that's right!
>
> If the master's house caught fire, the field Negro prayed for a stiff wind to spread the flames.
>
> The field Negro was the runaway and the freedom fighter. (Nat Turner, Sojourner Truth, Harriet Tubman, and Denmark Vesey were freedom fighters.) I'm a field Negro.[19]

Dad suggests Malcolm X was a revolutionary and a great spoken word master. He further suggests that the Last Poets and Gil Scott-Heron, who are credited for having planted the seeds for hip hop, drew inspiration from Malcolm X and other revolutionaries who were also great spoken word masters of the 1960s and 1970s, including Martin Luther King, Jr., Muhammad Ali, Stokely Carmichael, and H. Rap Brown.

Dad says, "Martin Luther King, Jr., Ali, Malcolm, Stokely, and H. Rap in their leadership and speeches carried not just the rhythm and spoken word artistry of our people, but also the content about our confidence and dignity, our history and culture, and our desire for freedom, equal justice and equal opportunity in education and all meaningful elements of American life. Unfortunately, too many of the rappers and teens of the Hip Hop Generation have little or no clue about the history contained in the lives and struggles of those men and the other great men and women who were trailblazers for the Hip Hop Generation."[18]

Chapter 27

Facing Big Time: Dad on the Rock

So Beatty reportedly infiltrated and then disappeared from campus on the day of the arrest of the Brooklyn College 19. Members of the Brooklyn College 19 assumed he would reappear at their trial as a stooge of the district attorney as is the case with other reputed informants.

The activities of the Brooklyn College 19 were happening during a period when African American and Latino college students across the nation were presenting similar educational demands, as well as demands for civil and human rights and an end to the war in Vietnam. Demonstrations were taking place at schools like City College, San Francisco State, Columbia University, South Carolina State, and even Yale and Harvard. Just as hip hop has spread across the globe today, the struggles of students in America spread to students in other nations who also sought to transform their universities.

President Nixon, the FBI, and state and local governments and police officials became determined in making sure that the rebelling students across the nation would not succeed. In that spirit, 3 black students had been killed and 27 others had been wounded when state policemen opened fire on students from South Carolina State University during a rally on February 8, 1968. African Americans were fighting, dying, and going to jail for things that mattered.

The rallies in the 1960s occupied a great deal of space in daily newspapers and covered television screens during nightly newscasts. Meanwhile, Congress and the FBI launched investigations to determine how to put an end to the activities of the students, Dr. Martin Luther King, Jr., and all the high profile leaders of the Civil Rights Movement, and the national leadership of the Black Panther Party.

Malcolm X was assassinated in 1965. Dad pointed out that Malcolm X's inner circle had been infiltrated by the house Negro Gene Roberts and other government agents seeking to bring about Malcolm X's downfall. Roberts, who worked for the NYPD Bureau of Special Services, was one of Malcolm X bodyguards. Roberts and other infiltrators and informants were in the Audubon Ballroom when Malcolm X was assassinated on February 21, 1965.

Roberts went on to become one of the house Negroes who infiltrated the New York City Black Panther Party. Roberts and Ralph Wyatt, another house Negro, were viewed as star prosecution witnesses in the district attorney's attempt in 1969 to frame Lumumba and Afeni Shakur and the other 19 members of the New York City Panther 21 for crimes they did not commit.

As early as 1957, Dr. King had become a special target of J. Edgar Hoover, the then head of the FBI. In 1963, Hoover declared that Dr. King was "the most dangerous Negro in America." Dad suggested that Hoover's choice of words revealed his lunacy, because although blacks were dying by the thousands in Viet Nam and had died as soldiers in every American war beginning with the Revolutionary War, Hoover words suggested that "Negroes" in general were dangerous, but Dr. King was the most dangerous. Dad said Hoover was suggesting to America that the danger had to be removed, and he attempted to intimidate President Kennedy into giving the FBI a free hand in dealing with Dr. King and other "dangerous Negroes." BTW, while dad was protesting against the war at Brooklyn College and with Dr. King at the United Nations, two of his brothers were in the US Army.

During the Kennedy and Johnson administrations, Hoover spied on Dr. King. He threatened Dr. King with revealing false and damaging evidence about him so that people would lose faith in him. A big part of Hoover's plan was to suggest Dr. King was a communist and womanizer, not a man of God. Dr. King was assassinated on April 4, 1968, with several FBI agents and police officers close by spying. Dad said there are many Americans, including people who were close to Dr. King, who believe the FBI played a role in his assassination.

So Hoover became infamous for his persecution of Dr. King and for cross-dressing as a woman in his spare time. Dad said, "J. Edgar Hoover was a real ugly man so I could only imagine what he looked like dressed as a woman. Maybe Miss Piggy?"

In the late fall of 1968 and early winter of 1969, FBI agents made two visits to dad's apartment to question him about his role at Brooklyn College and in the Black Panthers. Two agents came each time, and both were tall, blond, muscular, and in their late twenties. The agents appeared to want to determine if dad would be willing to provide information about his activities and the activities of others around him.

However, they were unable to get any information or cooperation. Dad told the men that he was not participating in any criminal activity and the right to protest injustice is conferred in the American Constitution. Since he was not involved in criminal activity, they had to leave him alone for the moment. Dad knew they were not satisfied with his response, and he expected the FBI would look for an opportunity to continue to harass him.

A few months later on Friday, May 13, 1969, at 5:30 a.m., dad heard a knock on the door of his Bronx apartment. Initially, he thought (or was hoping) it was his next door neighbor, Sheryl, a woman in her mid-20s he had a crush on and had wanted to "get next to." But it was the "po-po," New York City's "Finest."

When dad opened the door, six officers rushed in with guns drawn. The lead detective quickly placed the cold barrel of the 38 Smith and Wesson on dad's temple as he demanded that dad lie face down on the floor.

Dad told me it still seems strange to him, even to this day, that his heartbeat did not seem to accelerate nor did he feel any sense of fear. Yet, he had many reasons to be fearful of the possibility of the gun so-called "accidentally" discharging in the hands of an overzealous officer. Dad said even though it would be years before he was taught to meditate, it seemed as if he instinctively entered a meditative state. He said it felt like one of the most peaceful moments of his life.

Now that statement alone should give you a sense of how weird dad could be. No, he wasn't high, if that is what you are thinking. He was totally against drugs and had never smoked cigarettes or marijuana or even had a bottle of beer or a glass of wine.

As he remained on the floor, the other officers searched the apartment for guns and bombs. They had built up this paranoia of a gun-toting, bomb-throwing revolutionary. They searched for five minutes and found no weapons or bombs. They reported to the lead detective and, in response, he allowed dad to sit up. Dad sat with his hands cuffed behind his back as the lead detective looked fully at his face for the first time.

"Wow! You're nothing but a kid," the white detective responded as he looked into dad's eyes.

Dad turned his head so as not to look at the detective's thick black nose hairs and white saliva at the corners of his mouth. Dad told me, "The unkempt face and the rumpled cheap suit the detective wore did not match today's image of the fancy detectives on *Law and Order, Law and Order: Criminal Intent,* and *Crime Scene Investigation.* Look around the hood today and see if you see detectives dressing and caring like they do on television. Not in L.A., New York, Chicago, Philly, Miami, or Atlanta. Not in America."

"How old are you?" the detective asked, to draw dad's attention.

"I'm 18 years old," dad sighed.

"Well, you look 14. They sent all of us up here to pick you up? What were they thinking?" he asked as he shrugged his shoulders to suggest annoyance with his superiors.

As the detective prepared to lead dad to the squad car, dad noticed two other officers, who had been stationed outside his window on his fire escape, enter the apartment. He also noticed another officer carrying several Black Panther Party newspapers and some of his books, including *Soul on Ice, The Autobiography of Malcolm X,* Mao's *Little Red Book, Black Skin White Masks,* and *The Wretched of the Earth,* all taken from dad's bedroom. He would later learn the newspapers and books were taken as "evidence" to help build a case of conspiracy against him.

BTW, black and Puerto Rican teens took pride in reading their "revolutionary" books on buses and subways and while eating in restaurants near campuses. Can you believe that reading and discussing certain books was an effective device for getting recognition that you were intelligent and focused? Back then, activists were more popular than wannabe thugs.

Once inside the squad car, the lead detective significantly eased the grip of the cuffs that had begun to leave their mark on dad's wrists. Dad was thankful and he sought to determine the purpose of his arrest.

"Why am I being arrested?" he asked.

"Don't worry about it, kid. You will be out before the end of the day. This cannot be about much of anything," the detective assured him. "You're nothing but a kid," he continued as he shrugged his shoulder again and threw up his hands in a manner that suggested his time had been wasted.

Dad was happy to hear the words and to be well treated by Detective McDonald on the long ride from the Bronx to Brooklyn. He knew of other cases where African Americans had been arrested and savagely beaten before arriving in court. However, he sensed the detective wanted to apologize for the drawn gun placed at his temple. Yet, dad quickly realized, if Detective McDonald wanted to apologize, he could not bring himself to apologize in front of the other officers. The others would have seen an apology as wrong and out of character for any New York City police officer.

"Cops do not apologize even when they know they overreact," he murmured to himself.

In Brooklyn, dad was in for a rude awakening. As dad sat in a hearing room in State Supreme Court, he was astonished to see other cuffed fellow students being brought in one by one, each with an entourage of three officers. Until then, he thought that he was the only one arrested. He quickly developed a sense that something bigger than he imagined was up.

His concerns were affirmed when District Attorney Eugene Gold announced an indictment of 19 felony criminal charges and asked for bail to be set at $15,000 for him and each of his friends. In 1969, $15,000 was equal to almost three years of the starting salary of a New York City school teacher. Dad thought it was an impossible amount to raise, so he prepared himself mentally to spend some time in jail on the notorious Rikers Island, "the Rock."

Judge Dominic Rinaldi, the presiding judge, was notorious for being hard on African Americans and Puerto Ricans. During the bail hearing, he scolded Ray Williams, one of the African American lawyers for the Brooklyn College 19, when the lawyer suggested the district attorney was going after only black and Latino students but not white students who had participated in the demonstrations on campus.

Upon hearing the attorney's comments, Rinaldi leaned over the judge's bench revealing a pronounced hooked nose, pointed his stubby forefinger at Attorney Williams, and told the lawyer, "You better not ever again mention the matter of race in my court!"

The manner in which he scolded the lawyer before the case even began suggested to dad they were in deep "doo doo." Dad suggested the only words that Rinaldi seemed to leave out were "boy" and "nig***."

Dad told me it's impossible to accept the humiliation of being strip-searched where cops check private body parts to ensure you have no drugs. But there he was, with no previous record and having never smoked marijuana, spreading his legs in the most humiliating posture upon reaching Rikers Island.

After the humiliating search, dad was asked by another prisoner to identify the cell block to which he was assigned. The prisoner had called from across the room, "Hey, Davis, what's your cell block?" When dad answered "Cell Block Three," the prisoner made a gesture with his left wrist and body that suggested the cell block had a reputation for rapes of prisoners. After seeing that gesture, dad quickly forgot about the humiliation of the strip search. He now had bigger worries.

My father entered his cell for the first time near midnight after arriving from another holding pen "where they had served a slice of baloney as thick as your hand and tea as thick as syrup." He was hyped and hungry. He walked into his cell in the notorious Cell Block Three while an inmate slept on the top bunk.

In Rikers, a college boy had to quickly learn to become a street tough. Dad had been warned that Cell Block Three was known as the cell block where prisoners were likely to be raped. So dad started to front.

"Man, these f***ing pigs don't f***ing know who the f*** they are f***ing with!" He loudly cursed at an audible level that awakened his cell mate and the prisoners in the cells nearby. He wanted to make the right first impression for everyone so he spat out curses and words of anger nonstop for several minutes toward the unseen police officers, judges and prosecutors. He wanted everyone to know he was ready to "f***" somebody up!

All of the foul language and fronting were coming from an 18-year-old boy who had taught Sunday school for several years starting at the age of 9 and, just a year prior to his arrest, had graduated valedictorian of his high school in Park Slope, Brooklyn.

When his cell mate awakened and sat up on the top bunk to get a close look at dad, dad noticed he was "a lil dude," about 5 feet 8 inches and 135 pounds. Dad figured he could take him on and a few more like him, if necessary, "all at the same time." So after another minute of fronting with the loud f***ing curses, dad flopped on the mattress and slept comfortably that first f***ing dreamless night. After all, dad needed sleep because the cops had awakened him around 5:30 a.m. and by then it was well past midnight.

The next morning, dad was "bopping" (cutting his swagger) as he walked down the hall from the eating hall back to his cell. Dad had skipped on the grits that looked like a bucket of starch and on the bacon that had no lean. He had left toast that was burnt, topped with butter that looked like un-melted lard. So he was light on his feet as he bopped, representing. Suddenly, dad stopped in mid-bop as a Negro corrections officer grabbed him by the back of his neck and pushed him against the wall.

"Who the f*** you think you are and what the f*** do you think you are doing?" the officer began.

Dad instinctively knew the officer did not want him to answer. They were rhetorical questions, and an answer would have encouraged an attack. So he adjusted his breathing to slow his racing heartbeat, and remained silent as he watched the heavy metal object the officer held above his head and felt the heat of the wall on his face.

"You guys come in here when you should be thankful you were in college in the first f***ing place. You think I had a chance to go to f***ing college? Do you think the other Negro officers in here had the f***ing chance you had? I should take your f***ing head off, you f***ing punk!"

The officer appeared to be in his late 20s and had the kind of "chiseled physique," at 6 feet 1 inch and 190 pounds, which inmates strive to get. Dad said this happened at a time when a police recruit had to be in top physical condition to join the force. "Of course, now in New York you have some officers who don't appear to do any pushups and do not appear capable of running one block at a constant pace," he said.

The officer's words and the thought of being assaulted by the metal object caused dad's heartbeat to quicken again, and he struggled to maintain a pattern of slow, deep breathing. Moments later, as he regained the desired pattern of controlled breathing, an African American corrections officer rushed forth and wrestled the shining metal object from his fellow officer's hands.

"Let the kid go, Dawson," the African American officer suggested. "Let him go," the second officer continued as he attempted to separate the first officer's left arm from around dad's neck.

With a shove, scowl, and a warning, the offending Officer Dawson sent dad on his way.

So this Negro corrections officer was a hater, hating on dad for being an educated black man.

Dad was glad to be out of Officer Dawson's clutch, and he decided it was best not to bop the rest of the way to his cell block. So, in prison while going back to his cell, dad walked the way he would walk when entering an office seeking a job interview: head upright, eyes straight ahead, perfect posture and confident strides.

The object that the officer held had been capable of producing major damage. Now, when I think about what dad told me about the possibility of being struck, I have images of the kind of damage Brandon Meriweather inflicted on Todd Heap when the Patriots played the Ravens on October 17, 2010. When I spoke with dad recently, he said even today when he thinks of that encounter he can still feel the fear in his body on that day. He says he could visualize, if he had been hit on the head by Officer Dawson, blood rising like a spout from his head and covering his face as pain surges from his head to his toes.

As dad entered his cell block at Rikers after escaping Officer Dawson's wrath, he saw Wilson, a fellow prisoner he recognized from high school. Wilson had attended dad's high school; at least he did whenever he bothered to show up. Wilson was well known for arriving to school early to wait for certain girls and guys so they could disappear without ever entering the school building. Wilson was the same prisoner who earlier had informed dad about Cell Block Three's reputation for rapes of prisoners. Wilson was sitting on the floor in the middle of a group of 11 other teenage prisoners when dad appeared. Wilson was reading the May 14, 1969, issues of the *New York Daily News*, the *New York Post* and the *New York Times*. The group seemed unusually excited to be reading, so dad imagined that they were reading the sports pages.

As dad drew nearer, Wilson looked up at dad and looked back at the pictures and the article on the front cover of the newspapers. Then he looked up at dad again.

"Man, that is you!" Wilson exclaimed while pointing at the picture and at the list that included dad's name. "Man, you must be one baaaaad mother-f***er!" Wilson proclaimed. "One baaaaad mother-f***er!"

Dad drew even nearer to see the pictures and the articles. It was not a pretty picture.

"Man, it sez here you are facing 228 years in jail! Nig***, that's more time than God has given four nig***s altogether to live on earth!" Wilson continued, "Sez you like to blow sh** up and burn sh** down! Sez you tried to burn the f***ing college down. Sez you are a gun-toting revolutionary. Sez you like to set fires and burn sh** up! Maaannn, guess you don't have to worry 'bout nobody f***ing with you in here! Nig***, I thought you were just some f***ing bookworm! Bookworm, my a**! Maaannn, that show what I know! You are one baaaaad mother-f***er!"

As Wilson continued his monologue, the assembled prisoners' eyes strolled from the top of dad's head to the bottom of his feet and back up again. Dad was 6 feet and 170 pounds and did not even have peach fuzz on his face. He wore his favorite black dashiki, a pair of Wrangler blue jeans, and black Converse sneakers. The prisoners, many of whom had been in prison before, had never seen a man who was facing that kind of time, let alone a teenager. Dad said their look was the look of a kind of fascination that he has yet to find the words to adequately describe.

From that moment on, dad would not have to ever worry about anybody f***ing with him on Rikers. Wilson, who was obviously a serial prisoner with rank among the other inmates, had declared that dad was a revolutionary

N-word and "one baaaaad mother-f***er!" Dad had proper respect because he was facing more time than the total time God had given four N-words altogether to live on earth.

Even though dad now had his props with the inmates, and didn't have to think about attempted rape, he now had an even bigger worry. With that worry surging like a storm threatening to burst his brain cells, dad quickly snatched the paper from Wilson's hands. He figured Wilson was lying and he gave no thought to offending Wilson and his buddies by snatching the paper. Dad could not remember ever hearing that anyone had ever faced 228 years in prison, not even mass murderers and the gangster Al Capone.

However, there in black and white the truth of Wilson's words was exposed. The written words snatched all the courage from dad's heart. Dad was indeed "facing a maximum sentence of 228 years if found guilty of all counts," according to the article. Not even a "baaaaad (18-year-old) mother-f***er" wanted to face that much time.

As dad prepared to slump to the floor with a heavy heart and a dazed mind, he quickly caught himself as he realized he had to focus all of the courage he ever imagined he possessed to begin preparing for a continuous winter in America, an eternity behind bars. So he stood erect and fronted. He swallowed hard. He looked beyond Wilson as if he and his boyz didn't matter. They didn't. He felt as if only he existed. He walked to his cell without ever seeing another face or hearing another voice. He heard only his own heavy heartbeat.

Back in his cell, he felt his innocence did not matter when he thought of the hostile performance of hooked-nosed Judge Rinaldi at the bail hearing. He knew it was not unusual for innocent black and Latino men to be behind bars, especially those who were political prisoners like the Panther 21, fighting for the human and civil rights of black and Latino people. While settling in for the long haul, dad realized later that afternoon that he was the only member of the Brooklyn College 19 in Cell Block Three. However, he quickly discovered that Jamal Joseph, one of the Panther 21, had a cell in the same cell block.

Jamal and dad had been active in the Harlem branch of the Black Panther Party at 2026 Seventh Avenue up until their arrests. Jamal had been arrested with Afeni Shakur, Lumumba Shakur, Zayd Shakur, Dhoruba Bin Wahad, Shaba Om, Michael Cetewayo Tabor, and 16 other brothers and sisters from the Harlem branch. They were falsely accused of planning to plant bombs in locations in New York City, as if they would ever murder innocent people.

On April 2, 1969, the morning of the arrest of the Panther 21, my father had just arrived in San Francisco to participate in a national conference of student leaders at San Francisco State University. He was informed of the arrests by David Hilliard when he arrived at the National Black Panther Party office in Oakland the first morning of the conference. Dad immediately left San Francisco to return to Harlem to help keep the Black Panther Party office open and to continue organizing students at Brooklyn College. He went to the office every day with concern that the cops might "vamp" with blazing guns on the brothers and sisters at the Panther office, as they had at other Panther offices around the nation. Somehow, he found the courage to go anyway.

That morning on April 2, 1969, dad had no clue he would soon join Jamal at Rikers. On May 14, 1969, dad was glad to see Jamal, and he discovered that the second bed in Jamal's cell was empty. So, without asking permission from the corrections officers, dad took his mattress and moved in with Jamal (something a person cannot even do in a college dorm without permission). The corrections officers never confronted him about the move. Dad later figured the corrections officers left him alone hoping he and Jamal would reveal incriminating evidence while they eavesdropped. However, Jamal and dad had nothing incriminating to speak of since they both were innocent of any crimes.

Since they expected dad would be in for a while, because of the high bail, Jamal, who had been at Rikers nearly six weeks, started to teach dad the ropes. One of the most important lessons he wanted to teach was how to keep clothes clean while in prison. As dad looked on the next morning, Jamal told dad he was going to teach him how to keep his clothes clean. Then Jamal lifted the toilet brush and sprinkled a load of Ajax into the toilet bowl. He vigorously scrubbed the bowl while flushing often.

Dad sat wondering what point Jamal was making by cleaning the toilet. When Jamal asked for the undershirt dad was wearing, placed it in the toilet bowl, and proceeded to wash it, squeamish dad got the point. After initially hesitating, the squeamish one dropped to his knees next to Jamal and started to assist. They washed their shirts in a very dirty place hoping to keep sparkling clean. Huh?

Today dad and mom have the nerve to complain about the smell coming from my sneakers, socks, and wet jersey after I have played six hours of basketball. Can you believe that? At least I didn't wash my sneakers, socks, and jersey in a toilet. At least I am not going around like dad and his friend Jamal having to make sure their shirts don't smell like "do do." Were they sure? Huh?

Settling in, dad started to pay attention to the music being piped into the cell blocks. Jamal's favorite seemed to be "Get Back," a No. 1 hit of the Beatles in April 1969. Jamal would stand up on his toes in the cell while swinging his head and upper torso, dancing and singing, "Get back, get back, get back to where you once belonged…. Get back, Jo Jo, go home." Jamal was feeling it. Dad felt he could teach Jamal a few more rhythmic moves; nevertheless, while seeing Jamal's spirited performance dad developed a deeper appreciation for the song.

BTW, today Jamal is a professor and chair of the School of the Arts Film Division at an Ivy League university, and also an acclaimed writer, poet, and film producer.

Dad said there were also three other big hits in May 1969 that had him, Jamal, and the other prisoners singing along in high spirits while spending time enclosed in desolate prison cells. Stevie Wonder's "My Cherie Amour" and Spiral Staircase's "I Love You More Today Than Yesterday" were two top-five hits. He said the third song was the No. 1 pop hit in America which had knocked "Get Back" from the top spot and "had all the prisoners shouting in their cells the way 'holy rollers' shout in Pentecostal churches on Sunday morning." That third song was the Edwin Hawkins Singers' "Oh Happy Day." Dad said he substituted his name in one line of the song and changed "washed" to "walk" as he sang out loud and shouted in his cell:

> "Oh happy day, oh happy day
> Oh happy day, oh happy day
> When Askia walks, when Askia walks (out of prison)
> Oh when he walks, when Askia walks
> Oh when Askia walks, oh when he walks
> Jesus washed my sins away
> Oh happy day, ahh the happy day…."

Chapter 28

The Brooklyn College 19

All of the activities of the Brooklyn College 19 took place during a period when African American and Latino college students and their white and Asian allies across the nation were presenting similar demands. These demands included equal access to America's colleges and universities; access to a good education in quality public schools; recruitment of black and Latino professors; establishment of departments of African American, Latino, and Third World studies; an end to the unjust war in Vietnam; civil and human rights; justice and equal treatment under the law; economic justice and equal access to all the professions; an end to the military draft; and the removal of ROTC programs and military recruiters from college campuses.

Dad said it was impossible to read a newspaper on any given day during the spring of 1969 without seeing several articles related to the activities of students as they sought to press acceptance of their demands. The students were involved in sit-ins, disruption of classes, mass protests, and confrontations with campus security and police agencies, including the National Guard.

While working on this memoir, dad researched the *New York Times* archives for all articles published during May 11 through May 17, 1969, the week of his arrest on May 13, 1969. Dad found more than 100 articles in the *New York Times* that were directly related to the activities of students (and in several cases faculty members) on campuses and/or the activities of students and their supporters who shared the students' desire to see their demands realized. The following list briefly describes some representative articles that had been published that week:

- President Nixon held a special meeting with Vice President Agnew, Attorney General Mitchell, and key administration officials to discuss the problem of campus disorders and actions needed in response.

- The trial of 17 African American students, who brought in rifles to occupy the student center at Cornell, began with the students and their supporters refusing to rise when the judge entered.

- Fifty African American and white seminarians took over Union Theological Seminary and shut it down in support of a group led by James Forman. The group demanded that white churches and synagogues pay African American $500 million in "reparations" for past injustices.

- Students allegedly throwing firebombs, rocks, and bottles drew police tear gas and a few shotgun blasts at Southern University. The police originally said they had been fired upon during the uproar but later said this had not been confirmed.

- The Dartmouth College disciplinary committee decided that 39 students arrested the previous week for seizing the administration building could continue their studies until their individual cases could be heard by the college.

- A committee convened by the Rutgers College dean of students to investigate a racial brawl at the Lamda Chi Alpha fraternity house the previous month ruled that white students involved had exhibited "pervasive overtones of racism."

- Thousands of white students and 50 white professors on the faculty joined black and Latino students and faculty members in boycotting classes at Brooklyn College to protest the arrest of the Brooklyn College 19 and to have a contingent of 75 cops removed from occupying the campus.

- More than 75 cops continued to occupy the City College of New York (CCNY) as negotiations failed between black and Puerto Rican students and the administration.

- A reporter's analysis suggested, "The student protest strategy of massive confrontations with the police that once produced bandaged heads and martyrs in almost equal proportions is being replaced by hit-and-run tactics" at Brooklyn College, CCNY, and other campuses of the City University of New York.

- President Nixon proposed to Congress a major change in policy concerning the armed forces draft. He proposed the induction of the 19-year-old first instead of the then current policy of drafting 26-year-old men first and then moving down the list to the youngest. Nixon also repeated a desire to establish an all volunteer armed services at a future point.

- President Nixon, following years of protests against the Vietnam War, including massive protests led by Dr. King, proposed a mutual withdrawal of American and North Vietnamese forces from South Vietnam within 12 months. Nixon said that America was also willing to participate in negotiations with the governments of North Vietnam, South Vietnam, and the Vietcong or the National Liberation Front.

- A meeting of faculty members from colleges and universities in New York City was being planned for the week of May 11, 1969, by a group of educators opposed to campus disorder.

- Theodore Kheel, America's best known mediator, suggested to the Secretary of Health, Education and Welfare a plan for establishing "a special office for student discussions" at each college and university in the nation. The proposed directors of these offices would have the responsibility of hearing students' demands and bringing into discussions the appropriate officials to "properly address" the demands.

- Students at Harvard criticized its real estate policies and acquisitions which were viewed as driving out blacks and the poor from neighborhoods in Cambridge and Boston.

- The former president of the University of Chicago called for a major reform of colleges and universities and suggested that cops should not be called in to occupy campuses.

- Roy Wilkins, the Executive Director of the National Association for the Advancement of Colored People, at a fund raising dinner attended by hundreds of white and black benefactors declared, "Black study programs in schools about our Negro ancestors is a lot of nonsense. They will only amount to black bull sessions." Wilkins suggested no one was qualified to teach the history of blacks and that students should concentrate on math, making jet engines, and communications. He also blasted blacks who were entering white churches demanding reparations.

- Following demonstrations and confrontations with the police on campus, Stanford University decided to cut ties with the Stanford Research Institute, an enterprise that conducted major research for the Pentagon. Students had protested the university's association with the entity they believed supported America's involvement in the war in Vietnam.

- More than 500 police and National Guardsmen fired on more than 1,500 students while wounding nearly 100 at a park near UC Berkeley. The National Guard was deployed by Governor Ronald Reagan who two months earlier had declared a "state of extreme emergency" on the campus and the nearby community following a confrontation between police and students of the Third World Liberation Front. The Third World Liberation front was comprised of African American, Mexican American, and Asian American students. A 10 p.m. to 6 a.m. curfew was imposed for the city of Berkeley.

- Following more than a year of demonstrations, the City College Faculty Senate endorsed the creation of a separate black and Puerto Rican studies program and called for a new admissions policy that would stimulate the recruitment of students from "poor areas" of the city.

- Following more than a year of demonstrations, the arrest of the Brooklyn College 19, and students and faculty boycotting classes to protest the arrests, the acting president and Faculty Council of Brooklyn College urged the Board of Higher Education to offer a college education to every high school graduate in the city, particularly so-called "needy" African Americans and Puerto Ricans.

At 13 years old when dad first told me the story of the Brooklyn College 19, he asked me to guess the first thought that came to his mind when he discovered he was facing 228 years in prison. Clueless, I responded, "Well, I'm going to die in here?" As I spoke those words I wondered how my middle school classmate Juan was doing in police custody. I wondered how much time he would spend in juvenile detention.

"No, that was not it," dad responded. "I thought I would never walk freely in the sunshine out of doors again. I would never walk in Prospect Park again. I did not think about my family, my girl friend, or my classes. I just thought I would never walk in the sunshine again, and that thought was overwhelming."

But walk in Prospect Park again he did, and it became one of our favorites spots during my early years. He was able to walk in the sun again because Congresswoman Shirley Chisholm, the first black woman elected to the US Congress in 1968 and the first woman to enter a primary of a major political party to run for president, organized the black and Puerto Rican community to raise bail to free dad and his college classmates from prison. Bethany Baptist Church in Bedford Stuyvesant, under the leadership of Reverend William Augustus Jones, and Interfaith Hospital in Jamaica Queens, under the ownership of the noted African American entrepreneur, Dr. Thomas W. Matthews, were used as collateral for their bail.

On Friday, May 16, 1969, they were released after four days of incarceration.

Thousands of white Brooklyn College students and 50 white professors, led by Bart Myers, had join the few African American professors including Dan Meyers and Craig Bell, and the few Puerto Rican professors, including Josephine Nieves, to raise bail money, to boycott classes, and to practically shut down the college to put pressure for the release of the Brooklyn College 19. Hundreds of black, Latino, and Asian students were also instrumental in the efforts.

While they had remained incarcerated, black, white, and Latino pastors had also visited them regularly to make sure they were well treated after hearing about dad's confrontation with Officer Dawkins. Dad was told by a Puerto Rican priest that certain black and Latino corrections officers secretly put the word out to the pastors suggesting they should let the system know the pastors were keeping an eye on the safety and treatment of the Brooklyn College 19.

Within a year, all the charges against dad and the other members of the Brooklyn College 19 were dropped before trial. They had been accused of serious crimes, but it had become very clear that the public and even Judge Rinaldi knew the charges were untrue and the work of an over-zealous college administration and district attorney who wanted to deny students the right to protest injustice and racial discrimination. Even the district attorney's daughter, who was a student at Brooklyn College at the time, was aware the charges were false.

On May 13, 1971, after the longest trial of political prisoners in New York's history, all 21 New York Black Panthers, after remaining in jail for more than a year without bail, were acquitted of all charges in just 45 minutes of jury deliberation. One of the cops and leading witness for the prosecution who infiltrated the Panthers, Ralph Wyatt, admitted in a televised interview that they were innocent all along of the false charges. Yet, as much as two years of their freedom had been taken away.

Dad said there were reasons for celebration, but celebration was not possible because between 1969 and 1971 the FBI and other so-called law enforcement agents had brutally murdered African Americans, including Fred Hampton, a charismatic leader of the Chicago Black Panthers, while he slept in his bed. Also, two black college students had been killed by police officers who fired 140 shots during a peaceful rally at Jackson State College in Jackson, Mississippi.

A year after the confrontation with Officer Dawson at Rikers Island, dad would have a real-life reference for understanding how it feels to have blood spouting from a head wound delivered by an NYPD officer. Following his release from incarceration, dad remained active in the movement including attending rallies of the Young Lords in East Harlem. During one of the rallies, while protesting police brutality outside of the 23rd Precinct on East 102nd Street, dad was smashed in the head by an NYPD officer.

Dad had been hit while reaching to protect Nyisha S. from danger as the crowd scattered to avoid charging officers. She was a friend and fellow Brooklyn College student. As they ran, Nyisha tripped and was about to be hit or trampled. Without breaking his stride, dad reached and caught her. As he moved with her in his embrace to resume running upright, a large Caucasian officer swung his night stick like a baseball bat using both hands to inflict maximum damage. As the pain and blood shot up, dad continued to run, all the while instinctively knowing that stopping would have led to a brutal and prolonged beating. Dad's adrenaline carried him as he carried Nyisha to safety to the corner of Park Avenue and 102nd Street. (Nyisha went on to become a successful public interest attorney, while two members of the Brooklyn College 19 went on to become physicians. Other members became successful professionals in the fields of education, media, government, and construction.)

That was a lot of information for dad to drop on me in one discussion about the reunion and the time he was arrested. I remember after our discussion I tried to imagine what the world would have been like if the charges had not been dropped and he had been sentenced to 228 years or, what Wilson said, more combined life than God had given to four N-words altogether. I quickly realized that I would not have been born, at least not as the son of dad. So I gave up on imagining that world. At that moment, I was happy to be his son.

As a storyteller, dad always has a lesson he wants to get across. Even when the details are fascinating, and I want to linger in the details, he always moves on toward the lesson. Of course, there was a lesson for me in the story of the Brooklyn College 19 that was highlighted in the reunion of May 30, 1992, while I was sprouting in mom's womb.

So dad never saw Beatty again because there was no case needing the testimony of an informant. Beatty no longer appeared for classes at Brooklyn College.

Dad's lesson was that the things you do as a teen or young adult could haunt you for a lifetime in the way he imagined Beatty was now haunted. He imagined undercover house Negroes who infiltrated colleges (and civil rights organizations) in the 1960s would have to live out their days with the harsh remembrances of having reportedly betrayed the best interests of their people who were only seeking to open entrance into the universities to African Americans and Latinos. While some blacks falsely informed against the interests of blacks and Latinos, thousands of white students and their professors at Brooklyn College and hundreds of thousands of white students and their professors across the nation worked to bring about a more just system of public higher education from Brooklyn College to San Francisco State University.

Concerning District Attorney Eugene Gold, the man behind the indictments of the Brooklyn College 19, in 1983 he was convicted for molesting the 10-year-old daughter of another district attorney during a convention of district attorneys in Memphis, Tennessee. He was found in the child's hotel room near midnight one evening and had to pay the price for the worst of sins.

By 1972, Judge Dominick Rinaldi, the presiding judge, was the subject of ridicule in New York City. In an October 1972 article in *New York Magazine*, Jack Newfield had identified Rinaldi as one of the 10 worst judges in New York. Newfield wrote that Rinaldi was especially hard on black defendants but soft on heroin dealers and men involved in organized crime, the Mafia.

Also, in the book *Wise Guy: Life in the Mafia*, Nicholas Pileggi noted that in the 1960s Rinaldi fined Paul Vario $250 instead of sending him to jail for 15 years. Vario was the reputed leader of one of New York's five largest Mafia families. In contrast, in 1921 at age 11, Vario had gone to jail for seven months for truancy.

"Yeah, the Mafia man got more time for truancy as a kid than for reported mayhem, loan-sharking, and organized crime as a Mafia man in front of Judge Rinaldi," dad suggested.

In a second book, *The Abuse of Power*, published in 1977, Jack Newfield presented information which revealed Rinaldi had acted on behalf of another Mafia figure. Rinaldi was reported to have "twice personally gone to police stations to release alleged Mafioso Santo Patti, who had 20 prior gambling arrests, rather than wait for Patti to be arraigned before another judge the next morning. Police records show that Justice Rinaldi did this on April 18, 1969, and again on June 15, 1970." Ultimately, Rinaldi would be pressured to leave the bench with the sword of disgrace above his head.

Shortly after the arrests of the Brooklyn College 19, Acting President Peck was removed by the trustees of City University from the position of Acting President of Brooklyn College. With ongoing demonstrations on campus by black, Puerto Rican, Asian, and white students and faculty demanding justice and equal opportunity to a college education, CUNY leadership did not trust Peck's leadership. He was clearly out of his league when it came to handling the affairs of the university.

Dad says Gold and Rinaldi turned out to be the "real" criminals and were ultimately disgraced. He believes the reported informant Beatty is disgraced and suggests, "No matter how much he fronts, he must confront the deep, dark demons of his heart that made him stand in the way of the progress of African Americans and Latinos."

Due to the efforts of dad and his friends, supported by many white professors and thousands of white students who boycotted classes to demand change, Brooklyn College and City University started Open Admissions in 1970, hired more African Americans and Latinos, and created African American, Puerto Rican and Asian Studies Departments. Dad said the importance of the support of the white students and professors cannot be over emphasized because they were in a unique position to put pressure on CUNY leadership to change because they had more political and economic power and connections than the blacks and Latinos. The white professors were the largest group in the Faculty Council which had a role in establishing and changing university policy. The black and Latino professors were too few in number to have numerical influence in the Faculty Council.

With the doors of admissions opened wider, tens of thousands of African American and Latino students have since gone on to earn college degrees at Brooklyn College and the other four-year campuses of the City University of New York.

Dad said it is a good thing that their efforts also made it possible in 1970 for more Asians, as well as Italians, Irish, and working-class whites from other ethnic groups to enter Brooklyn College in numbers that more closely matched their enrollment in the high schools. The actions of the Brooklyn College 19 made it possible for more of the sons and daughters of Irish and Italian New

York City police officers and firemen to attend Brooklyn College. They too had been shut out when Brooklyn College was considered an enclave mostly for middle- and upper-middle-class whites whose parents and grandparents were college educated. Ironically, the actions of the Brooklyn College 19 also made it more likely that any children of informants would have an opportunity to attend a public university.

So, that's dad. Even when accused of doing something bad, it is because he is doing something good (if only it were like that for me). Dad said that he would not change anything about the history leading up to his arrest and nothing about his incarceration, not even washing his shirts in the toilet. (I would definitely change that part.)

Dad said the experiences and incarceration taught him that, despite feeling fear, you could be fearless and act fearlessly especially when you are incarcerated because you are pursuing higher goals. Dad says, "Lil Kim, T.I., Lil Wayne, DMX, and other rappers should not suggest to young African Americans and Latinos that it's cool to go to jail for dumb things, as if we need more African Americans and Latinos in jail for dumb things."

Juan with the pellet gun went to jail. It was just dumb and "stoopid" to shoot classmates with any kind of gun. He was dismissed from one of the better schools and spent some time behind bars.

Although I am sure Juan got out, I am not sure that he does not continue to pay for that crime. I wonder what jail time was like for him. Dad says, "You can bet it wasn't T.I.'s 'vacation' or a time for drinking, smoking, and sexing in a recording studio."

I think dad is right about some of the messages of some rappers, but I am still singing DMX's "Where the hood, where the hood, where the hood at?" Just can't repeat the N-words in the song in dad's presence.

Every teen learns that parents are very good at reminding you to "do as I say, not as I do." That happens often when they are caught fronting. It must be a great triumph when you catch them fronting. However, when it comes to dad, I have not caught him yet. If getting a gun cocked on your temple and facing 228 years are not "stoopid," then what could be?

Sometimes I imagine that it would be great to sit with my uncles, my aunts, and his former classmates to hear about the mistakes and stupid things he must have done as a teenager. Tell me three "stoopid" things dad did, I imagine requesting. Then I imagine I would get no reply. You know what I mean?

Cy M., Spoiler, Chango, Njeri, and dad's friends from Brooklyn College have spoken to me of him without revealing his faults. His brothers and sisters have shown they would rather talk about how he taught himself to read, how smart he was in elementary school, and how he lived alone in the Bronx at age 16 while putting himself through high school after having only arrived in New York a bit more than a year earlier.

In the 1960s and 1970s, dad and his black and Latino friends, and African Americans and Latino students around the nation, risked their own education and their freedom so other African Americans and Latinos could get a college education.

Dad has told me a small percentage of the African Americans and Latinos, who were then given the opportunity to enter Brooklyn College in September 1970 after the start of open admissions, spent their time "shucking and jiving" while smoking reefers and playing cards in the student center instead of going to class.

So, I ask, was he "stoopid" for fighting for the "shuckers and jivers," or were they "stoopid" for not taking advantage of the new opportunity?

Now, as an 18-year-old teenager, I also ask, "Was dad from some other planet?" Can a teenager really grow up without making major mistakes and doing really, really "stoopid" things? That just isn't possible, not even during ancient times when dad was growing up. I must have inherited some of the "stoopid" things I do from him. One day the curtain will be opened, and a picture of all the teenage stupidity of my father will be revealed. I know it's there.

I plan to take notes and paste them on the bathroom mirror we share with the caption: "From the book of really 'stoopid' things the old man did as a teenager." Swag!

Chapter 29

Jay-Z and the Neighbors Who Don't Know Trey Songz's Name

Sometimes it's less than funny when your boyz like your dad and think he is cool, the very dad you are at war with. But, then again, they don't have to live with him.

In February 2010, dad and I were really at war. I was a senior and cutting classes that I needed to complete in order to graduate. For example, for several weeks at the beginning of the spring semester, I had failed to report to my English class. Dad had discovered my absence by calling my teachers. Of course, his calls would piss me off. Even after I started attending regularly, he would call once or twice a week just to make sure. So, in the middle of my English period, all the students would hear the phone ring and expect dad to be on the other end. Then they would watch as Mr. Miller informed dad I was indeed in class. Oh, my blood boiled.

When I arrived home one afternoon after Mr. Miller's class I declared, "Dad, you need to stop! You don't know how silly you look calling and interrupting Mr. Miller's class. The kids think that you are buggin'."

"Well I don't care what your classmates think. If you don't want me to call, then handle your business."

With that remark, I knew I was not able to make him understand reason. So I gave up and went to play ball. Of course in the next week the calls continued, and I remembered the times he had come to school during my junior year. During one instance, he came to the gym and escorted me to class. He even threatened to come and sit in my class if necessary to keep me focused. Yeah, I was able to imagine him sitting in my class like the mom in the movie "Glory Road" who sat in the college class of her son, one of the basketball players. As a family, we had seen "Glory Road" together. That scene in "Glory Road" was fiction. Remembering that dad had once come to the gym and escorted me to class convinced me that dad was crazy enough to make that scene a reality.

Despite all of dad's faults, he has one quality that is admirable: dad does not let his anger or concern about what I fail to do in one area color the way he deals with me in other areas. He does not dwell on his anger, and he counsels me not to dwell on my mistakes. For example, he might be concerned during the day with my cutting classes, and then he is out enjoying a Knicks or Nets game with me in the evening without ever referring to that concern. If the purpose of purchasing tickets for the Knicks or Nets was to have us enjoy a night out as father and son, then dad was determined that we should enjoy the game. Therefore, the tension that existed would pass like the morning mist when confronted by a rising sun during the game. Although the next morning he would be prepared to call my teachers again if there were any hints that I wasn't prepared to handle my school business.

In February and March, I wasn't handling my school business to the best of my ability. Dad wasn't too happy. Nevertheless, he had already purchased tickets for my best male friend, my girlfriend and me to go with him to see Jay-Z. He was especially pleased I was no longer dating Charlene, and he thought my new lady was special, smart, and beautiful. Dad was no big fan of Jay-Z, but he figured the concert would allow him to get to know my friends better, and he wanted to learn more about the hip hop I loved.

Thus, on March 6, 2010, we were on our way to see Jay-Z and Trey Songz at the Izod Center in New Jersey. Dad was driving, and I was riding shot gun. My boyz Lupe and Samori were in the back. Dad had purchased four tickets and had asked me to choose who I wanted to bring. Since my lady couldn't make it at the last minute, I had chosen two of my closest male friends, Samori and Lupe.

Samori is a big dude at 6 feet 7 inches and 225 pounds. Samori is a Sunni Muslim. He and I have been tight since the first year in high school, and I had missed him a lot when he moved to Atlanta during our junior year. In September 2010, Samori would enroll in Medgar Evers College in Brooklyn.

Lupe's real name is El Hajj and he is about 5 feet 6 inches and weighs 125 pounds soaking wet. He was named for El Hajj Malik Shabazz, otherwise known as Malcolm X. At Banneker, we renamed him Lupe because he bears a striking resemblance to Lupe Fiasco. In addition, he is a great and creative hip hop dancer who fashions and invents moves to capture the imagination. In September 2010, Lupe would enroll in Morgan State University in Baltimore.

"I love the way Jay-Z and Alicia Keys did 'New York, New York,'" dad announced as we cleared the Holland Tunnel on the way to the Izod Center. "So many musicians have written about New York, and that song is among the best."

"Dad, 'Empire State of Mind' is the name of the song," I attempted to educate him.

"That is almost like the title of Billy Joel's great song, 'New York State of Mind,'" dad responded. "Some folks like to get away, take a holiday from the neighborhood," he started to try to sing and, thankfully, stopped. "Wow, Jay-Z did a great job updating that theme and making it a hit that appeals to many generations."

"Dad, my favorite line in that song comes when Jay-Z says: 'Catch me at the X with OG at a Yankee game. Sh*t, I made the Yankee hat more famous than a Yankee can.'"

"Yeah, that's a bad line, more famous that Jeter can," dad twisted the line. "That says a whole lot."

As we took our seats in the Izod arena, the same arena that hosted New Jersey Nets basketball games, dad remarked he had anticipated seeing more African Americans than seemed present in the arena. He said the crowd seemed to be about 80 percent young Caucasians in their early to late twenties. The females seemed to outnumber the males about two to one. Another 10 percent of the crowd seemed to be Latinos, mostly males. Asians and African Americans seemed to represent about five percent each.

Being ever the analyst, dad suggested the crowd for Jay-Z at Madison Square Garden a few days earlier probably had drawn the young African Americans who, he imagined, would have preferred that location. He said he had attempted to get tickets for the Garden "but they were sold out before you could say New York." So he was glad the Izod Center tickets were available when he went online early on the first day the tickets were released to the general public.

"This crowd is very different from the crowd we saw back in November in the Garden for Beyonce," he told me as we waited for the show to begin. "The majority of folks in that crowd were black women in their late 20s and 30s. Man, they had some really fly women that night screaming, 'put a ring on it, I can have another you in a minute, and dangerously in love.'"

"That was a great show, dad." I started to reminisce about that show and the great fun my cousin Nicole and I had that evening.

"She had some unbelievable energy and was incomparably entertaining," dad again pulled my attention. "And that band of all-female musicians. She had some top-flight musicians and some were as fly as she is, if not flyer. I am glad she gave them some time to just play to showcase their talent while she took brief breaks. There was a lot of eye candy that night."

Minutes later after going to get something to eat, Samori, Lupe, and I returned just as the first act was set to begin. I cannot remember the name of the get-the-crowd-in-their-seats act. Later, when Trey Songz came up, Lupe went wild. Lupe stood up for every song. He joined the crowd in singing out every word. "Little Lupe," as dad calls him, was feeling it.

Meanwhile, dad was not impressed with Trey Songz. At that time, he was totally unfamiliar with Trey Songz. He sat nodding out, or pretending to, only sitting up from time to time to watch Lupe sing and to glance at Trey Songz.

Dad had acted the same exact way a few months earlier when he and I were at Chris Brown's concert at Madison Square Garden. When Bow Wow appeared with Chris Brown, dad had yawned out loud, turned in his chair as if turning in bed, and had given the thumbs down signal to everything Bow Wow sang.

But he loved Chris Brown's performance. His favorite Chris Brown song is "Run It." He told me after the concert, "It brings back memories of my disco days when I was single and would steal fly women right from under the noses of their guys using my charm and my fancy dancing.

"Man, I used to fly from New York down to Atlanta for weekends at Mr. Vee's and Cisco's just to dance with some fly Southern black women to Con Funk Shun's 'Got To Be Enough' and Slave's 'Watching You.' Those women would remind me of the world's greatest collection of beautiful girls ever assembled who were in my ninth grade class in Swainsboro, Georgia: Louvincey DeWitt Riggs, Tommie Marie Howell, LaNell Gunn, Eloise Jones, Francis Collier, Jean Marie Miles, Margaret Boston, Geraldine Bentley, Connie Williams, Francis McNair, Dorothy Norwood, Pecola McCloud, Mary Ruth Brown, Delaine Lloyd, and Vernell Lloyd, just to name a few." (He smiled every time he called forth a name as if he were 14 again. I didn't ask for an explanation. Son, I wasn't even trying to hear it.)

Of course, when Chris Brown sang "Run It" that evening, dad sang, danced, and acted like a wild child. He was screaming (not singing), "Is ya man on the flo? If he ain't let me know…." I was glad my friends had not been present to see him "cut the fool." (That's Southern dialect for buggin'.)

Back at the Izod Center, when Trey Songz moved to "Neighbors Know My Name," Samori and I jumped up and joined Lupe in singing along with Trey Songz and the entire audience of 20,000, minus dad. Dad just shook his head and pointed both thumbs down. Once in a while, he would sit up and make a big deal out of covering his mouth as he let out a big yawn before slumping in the seat to close his eyes again.

However, when Jay-Z came up even dad got caught up in the crowd's electricity. Dad jumped from his seat as the entire audience exploded in a frenzy. Jay-Z had his swag on that night. Samori, Lupe, and I sang along on every song. So did everyone around us, including dad, when he knew the words (hardly ever). Dad did not sit for one minute during Jay-Z's part of the concert.

With Jay-Z singing "Hard Knock Life," dad joined in and, thankfully, I generally could not hear him above my own singing because I knew dad was butchering the words and the rhythm. However, when Jay-Z would get to the chorus dad would sing louder. Apparently, he knew the chorus best where the kids are heard singing.

Everyone was into Jay-Z, and he was not looking to disappoint anyone as he moved around that stage spitting every hit we knew. After about an hour, Jay-Z announced he had a "special lady" to bring forth to join him in singing the next song. I roared along with the crowd anticipating Alicia Keys might appear. Moments later, a different woman appeared. Jay-Z welcomed and introduced her.

Seeing that the singer was not the extraordinary Alicia, I didn't catch the name but dad caught her beauty. Dad said, "She's fine, a dime plus, decked out in a flowing white dress that hit every curve from her shoulders to her feet. I don't know if Jay-Z is going home to Beyonce tonight."

Soon Jay-Z was singing "Empire State of Mind." Everyone was alive, moving with Jay-Z as he sang, "I'm out that Brooklyn…." His words were truth. When it was near time for the woman to sing Alicia's part, we all moved with anticipation hoping to stay above in the place where Jay-Z had taken us and where we knew Alicia could keep us. She had a great voice and beautiful harmony with Jay-Z that did not disappoint. So we roared with affirming pleasure.

When Jay-Z finished "Empire," I believe many of us thought the show was over, and we were ready to ask for an encore. However, there was no need to ask for an encore as Jay-Z went right into another hit, and then another.

Afterwards he told the crowd that it was getting late and the band had gone past the scheduled time. We all braced for the disappointment of having the show end. You could almost see joy growing feet and departing.

As joy escaped, Jay-Z spoke to the crowd. "You know, I know where I come from," he began. "I also know who brought me here. You!" The audience roared and the women screamed, "We love you, Jay-Z!"

"So if you want to hear more, you will hear more!" he continued. With those words and the continuation of the concert, joy walked back in.

It was past midnight when we returned to the car for the trip back to Brooklyn. We entered the Camry singing "New York, New York, New York," and we were only about 20 minutes away from seeing the skyline of Manhattan. Inside we talked about the concert and its powerful impact. Dad said it was worth every penny and more. My boyz thanked dad.

As we cleared the traffic coming out of the arena parking lots, dad just couldn't resist contrasting Trey Songz' performance with the performance of Jay-Z. "That Trey Songz is a little dude whose voice was too weak for that big arena. Where did Jay-Z find him?" dad started.

"Mr. Davis, Trey Songz has a great voice," Lupe responded defensively.

"Yeah, dad, he does. You should hear him on his records. Everybody who is anybody loves Trey Songz," I said more forcefully.

"Well, it is probably true his records are okay only because they are cut in a studio where he might not need a big voice. But he needed one tonight. The band drowned him out, and his voice had no strength in that big arena." Then, while shaking his head in a manner to emphasize his point and de-emphasize our points, he continued, "His voice was weaker than the Nets' game, and you know how weak their game is this year. Ha, ha, ha."

"Well, the Knicks aren't doing much better," Samori joined in to defend Trey Songz.

Dad went right past Samori's comment to keep up his monologue about Trey Songz. "Can you believe that little Trey Songz is singing about betting the neighbors know his name? That's a joke. The only way her neighbors would know his name is he wrote it down and slid the paper under their doors! Ha, ha, ha, ha, ha…" Dad was famous for cracking himself up, and his opinion of Trey Songz gave him the opportunity to pour it on.

Continuing to pour it on he suggested, "Ain't no woman screaming his name, unless she's faking, and ain't no neighbors knocking on no wall. They are sound asleep. What woman is screaming, 'Trey, Trey, Trey, oh Trey?' That ain't even a man's name. When a woman screams 'Trey, Trey, Trey!' you would expect she's calling for a 3-year-old with a bad-looking Mohawk to stop running in the streets. Trey Songz may hear 'Trey, Trey, Trey,' but the woman is only screaming 'Money, money, money, oh money!' Ha, ha, ha, ha, ha..."

I declared, "Dad, his name is Tremaine!"

However, dad was too busy hatin' to hear me. Dad's Southern twang was twanging that night, and I must admit it was kind of funny and I wanted to laugh. However, I held my tongue so I wouldn't encourage him. Nevertheless, I had to laugh with dad when he said, "Trey is really a name for a 3-year-old black boy with a bad-looking Mohawk chosen by his mama. There comes a time when a boy has to grow up. There comes a time when a man has to carry a man's name."

During dad's performance, my boyz and I just shook our heads in the manner that suggested we couldn't effectively stop him from hatin' on Trey Songz. I couldn't help Lupe, the biggest Trey Songz fan in the car, if not on the entire planet.

"Neighbors know my name. Hah," dad kept it up. "What bull is that coming from that little dude with that little voice? Trey Songz should keep his shirt on. What's with that anyway, pulling his shirt off to show his puny body? Huh! Do you know what they say about men who speak publicly claiming they do so much with their so-called sexual expertise? The word is: 'Those who do, don't say, and those who say, don't do.'"

"Dad, Trey Songz is over 6 feet 2 inches. He's taller than you, and he's built. And he was a beast playing basketball!"

"Yeah, Mr. Davis, Trey Songz is tall and built," Little Lupe jumped in agreeing with me. However, I quickly realized Trey Songz was no longer relevant for dad. Dad thought he had won that war and was ready to move on.

"You know, that Jay-Z is brilliant," dad remarked as he turned his monologue to the star of the show. "He's on a whole other level than any young person in the game now. He is a remarkable and brilliant businessman. You can see that he is always thinking about what is good for business. Not just writing and rhythmically rapping, but doing business even when he is on stage performing."

"You place him higher than Beyonce?" I asked, as if I didn't know the answer.

"She's incredible, too, but she's no Whitney Houston," he began. "Whitney has a voice that is normally reserved for the angels. Listen to 'All the Man I Need,' and you'll never have to listen to another female pop star sing. That voice and those lyrics: She builds me up, she gives me love, more love than I've ever seen. She's all I've got in this world, and Whitney is all the woman any man needs. That one song alone can take you from here to eternity. God bless her and bring her voice back."

"Hey, dad, Whitney Houston is great, but I was asking about a comparison between Jay-Z and Beyonce."

"Well, Beyonce surprised me," he responded. "Her voice is beautiful and much better than the credit some folks give her. You know when folks were comparing her voice to Jennifer Hudson's in "Dream Girls," it didn't do Beyonce justice. They had different roles and different materials to present. By the way, Hollywood cheated Eddie Murphy out of an Oscar for that movie: 'Jimmy got soul! Jimmy got soul! Jimmy got s-o-u-l soul!' Wow, and Beyonce is a master entertainer. I cannot imagine any woman equaling her as an entertainer. As a master entertainer, she clearly chooses to rely on her talents above gimmicks, substance above hype."

"Yeah, dad, she really performed."

"Yeah, Akhenaton. However, she is not the business person he is. You see how he connected with that audience telling them he knew who brought him there? The sincerity he delivered in that statement was remarkable and more powerful than the words. You'll never hear me complain about you spending my money to download Jay-Z's music on iTunes. Now, Ludacris, and Trey Songz? Well, dem boyz are another story."

Soon we were crossing the Brooklyn Bridge, the bridge that is a popular target for terrorists. It is always guarded by the police in patrol cars just in case. It's such a beautiful bridge leading to the beautiful borough of Brooklyn. After crossing, dad announced, "Lupe, I'll drop you first. What's your address?"

Lupe lived with his dad in Bed Sty, the hood. The "po-po" is always out patrolling big time in Bed Sty. Almost as soon as we crossed the border of Bed Sty and within two blocks of Lupe's crib, we passed a parked police patrol car.

So there we were, four African American men rolling through Bed Sty long past midnight. Since it was a cold night, with the exception of dad, we all had on jackets and hoodies with our heads covered. I was 6 feet 4 inches with a hoodie, Samori was 6 feet 7 inches with a hoodie, and Lupe was only 5 feet 6 inches, but he too was a black man with a hoodie way past midnight rolling in a ride through Bed Sty.

Within two seconds of passing the patrol car, we could see its lights flashing and hear the siren screaming. The cops didn't seem to care that they were waking up the whole neighborhood.

"What do they want?" dad asked rhetorically. "You guys sit up straight, and take the hoodies off your heads. I'll handle this."

My boyz and I were fully awake. We sat erect and our eyes were set on dad.

"Pull over to the curb! Pull over to the curb!" the voice demanded through a speaker system from within the patrol car. Within seconds, as the two officers approached our parked vehicle, their right hands were near their guns which remained holstered. One approached from the left side of the car. The other approached from the right. I wondered what dad would do.

"Officers, my name is Dr. Davis, my name is Dr. Davis," dad announced in a loud, firm, yet polite voice after rolling down the window. As they continued to approach, dad continued to speak. "I am coming from Jay-Z's concert in New Jersey and just dropping off my son's friends to their homes."

As the two African American police officers, who were in their mid-30s, reached where dad and I were sitting in the front, dad dropped his voice and repeated: "Officer, my name is Dr. Davis, and I am returning from a Jay-Z concert in New Jersey. I am dropping off my son's friends to their homes."

"Do you know your left front signal light isn't working?" the officer nearest to dad asked.

"No, I did not know. It must have just gone out." As dad finished saying the words, he asked if he could get out and check.

"No, not now," the officer responded. "Let me see your license and registration!"

No one heard the word "please." Cops are not paid to use the word "please" when requesting information from the taxpaying citizens who pay their salaries. Dad passed the documents and the officers returned to sit in the patrol car and run the documents through their computer.

As we waited, dad spoke to us. "You know they didn't stop me for a signal light that they were not able to see from the position their car was in on this dark night as we approached them. If we were driving in Prospect Heights where I live, those same cops would not have stopped us. But they saw you big guys and Little Lupe with your hoodies riding with me in the hood past midnight. Now they are running information through the computer to determine if they have any information they could use for further action. Of course, they will find none. I do not even get traffic tickets. Don't want to give them free money."

After about five minutes, the officers returned to our car. "Here are your documents," the officer nearest dad spoke. "Why did you feel it necessary to tell us that you were a doctor before we asked you anything?" the officer nearest dad asked in a mildly embarrassed tone.

"I had no clue why you would be stopping us, and I wanted you to know our intent to avoid any possible misunderstanding," dad politely responded.

"Well, you can continue on your way, but make sure you get that light fixed as soon as possible."

"Thank you, officer. I certainly will make sure I get it fixed tomorrow."

As the officers departed, dad said to us, "It only needs a $1 bulb replaced. So they stopped us for that when there are real crimes being committed by real criminals within blocks of here, maybe right down the block. What a waste of taxpayers' money! And those cops are decent but just caught up in a police culture that sees all African American boys and men as potential criminals. I think they walked away being embarrassed they had gotten caught up in thinking we were potential criminals."

"Dad, if they stopped us just for a $1 bulb, why did they have to approach us with their hands near their guns?" I asked.

"It's the policy of NYPD that they must approach us in a manner that maximizes preparation for their safety, not ours. By guidelines of NYPD, it is perfectly acceptable for them to approach the presence of four African American men in a car past midnight with hands on their weapons. They think they have to approach us as if we might respond in a threatening manner," he answered.

"But we would never threaten a cop," I suggested.

"That is true, and that is why it is so insulting to be approached in that manner. Hey, but we handled it well, and we'll just keep on moving knowing from time to time we will need to encounter certain injustices."

Of course, after the drama died down, dad and I teased Lupe about bringing us into the hood after midnight as we rode the two additional blocks to his crib. Dad sang with his Southern twang mimicking DMX, "Where the hood, where the hood at? Bed Sty! Biggie's and Lupe's home." We teased Lupe about Bed Sty knowing dad had secured me an internship that had given me the opportunity to work at the Bedford Stuyvesant Restoration Corporation during the summer of 2009. Also, for more than five years, we had attended Bethany Baptist Church on McDonough Street, just a few blocks from where the cops had stopped us.

When Dad and I got home, I went straight to the bathroom and then straight to bed. I wanted to talk about our experience with mom, but the call of my pillow was just too intense.

The next evening around the dinner table, we had an opportunity to talk about Jay-Z, Trey Songz, and the "po-po." Dad explained there have always been two systems of "so-called justice" in America. He said one system treats

African Americans, Latinos, Native Americans, and often women as inferior, second-class citizens whose human rights should not be fully protected.

He then gave examples of that system: Women may face the cruelty of the system and have to go through extraordinary means to bring a male rapist to justice. Women also face injustice in a system that is often set up to protect the assets of their husbands during divorce, especially if the husbands are wealthy. In that same system, black and Latino men are often seen and treated as guilty before a case has even gone to trial. They could be stopped and searched by the police, with the police using any pretense including a car light whose $1 bulb has blown just a few minutes earlier.

"If stopping us was only about the car light, why didn't they give me a ticket and why was it necessary to run my documents through the police department's computer?" he asked rhetorically. "As Chamillionaire said, they were hoping to catch us 'ridin' dirty.' We weren't even riding in a fancy car, and you know they often think that any black man in a fancy car is a dealer, and I don't mean a car dealer."

"You know we get a great deal of the oil for our industries from the Middle East. But, do you know there are other kinds of oil that are produced right here in New York City and cities throughout America?" Dad asked mom and me as we took a bite of lasagna baked with broccoli and carrots.

"No, dad, I didn't know that oil was produced here in New York City," I responded while waiting for an explanation.

"Oh, yes, Black 'n' Brown Oils are produced here every day. But those oils are not used for the automobile industry. They are used for a different industry that is one of the biggest industries in America. They are produced here and shipped upstate to keep the homes up there warm, and the families in those communities well fed. Meanwhile, the families who produce the oil here are left cold and hungry," dad sighed deeply. Then he paused for 15 seconds to let the meaning of his words sink into my brain cells.

"That's right," he continued. "Black 'n' Brown Oils are our youth and men, and the industry is the upstate prisons. For decades New York City's black and Latino prisoners have been sent to prisons built in upstate Caucasian communities, providing jobs for those communities. Those communities no longer have the factories that once sustained them.

"Now they have the prisons which hire their community members as corrections officers and administrators. The prisons hire their doctors, their teachers, their nurses, their secretaries, and their social workers. When bread is needed at the prison, it often comes from their bakeries. When meat is needed, it comes from their meat markets. When vegetables are needed, they come from their farms. When transportation is needed, it comes from their drivers. When a plumber is needed, he is one of theirs. When an electrician is needed, he is one of theirs. When a carpenter is needed, he is one of theirs. I can go on and on, but you get the point."

Dad paused to take a bite of his lasagna. Mom had made the lasagna, and hers was always a step above dad's although he had taught her how to make it. When mom got up to get the buttered semolina loaf from the oven, I continued to consider the young black and brown faces I had seen led away in cuffs at subway stations after school for missing train passes.

"You know, it costs New York State much more to send a kid to prison than to the State University," mom said as she placed the warm and sumptuous bread on the table before me. "I read prison costs the state more than $25,000 a year for each inmate while tuition, room, and board if you were an incoming freshman at Purchase, or any other state university, would cost about $12,000. Can you imagine how the state and country would benefit if they put that prison money into the kids' public school education?"

"I hope one day I could do something about that. It would be great to help kids stay out of trouble," I suggested.

After dinner, dad and I sat down to watch "March Madness" as the events of the previous night slipped into the subconscious distance. Within moments, we were talking to Evan Turner and our favorite Ohio State players yelling into the television screen, "Take 'em to the hole!"

Chapter 30

Two "Wise Latinas"

In 2010, the stories of two wise Latinas surfaced in the media. The wise Latinas were *dos Puertoriqueñas*/two Puerto Ricans born in the Bronx around the same year.

Sonia Sotomayor received extensive coverage in national and international media. She was President Obama's choice for Supreme Court Justice. Her nomination drew extensive criticism mostly from conservative politicians and conservative activists in the media and organizations set up to influence government and the American way of life. She referred to herself as a "wise Latina" whose life experiences had made her uniquely qualified to sit on the Supreme Court of a very diverse America.

That statement pissed off many haters who do not believe a Latina could be better qualified than a white man to sit on the Supreme Court. But she and President Obama prevailed. In our family, we celebrated.

Gladys Carrion was the other "wise Latina." She did not draw national attention. However, she drew plenty of attention in New York State. My father read articles about her and during a "teachable moment" shared them with me in August 2010 as I prepared to head off to Hampton.

Gladys Carrion is the New York State Commissioner of Children and Family Services. In other words, her job is that of ensuring that children get the services they need to grow securely and productively. She oversees adoption, foster care, and juvenile detention in New York. Dad suggested she is a relentless fighter for social justice. He said she recognizes that elements of the criminal justice system, especially juvenile prisons, are often destructive of efforts to raise children to become productive citizens.

Commissioner Carrion has fought hard and successfully to close juvenile prisons that were notorious for their abuse of kids. In some of the prisons, kids had been brutally beaten by rogue corrections officers, and a few had died as corrections officers restrained them.

Since becoming Commissioner more than four years ago, she has made it a priority to have juvenile offenders remain in facilities in New York City, close to their families. She has also tried to improve their access to education and counseling services in New York City. This has angered many politicians and business owners in the white communities upstate that depend upon a steady flow of black and brown prisoners to keep their citizens employed. They don't want the oil pipe lines shut down or shrunken.

"Northern Disclosure: Shutting Upstate Jails for City Kids Has Made a Fiery Bronx Bureaucrat a Host of Enemies," was an article that appeared in the *Village Voice* about Commissioner Carrion's struggle. In the August 4, 2010, edition Elizabeth Dwoskin wrote an extensive account about Commissioner Carrion's efforts to reform the juvenile detention system. Dwoskin gave an account of the efforts of several white upstate politicians to have Commissioner Carrion terminated by Governor Patterson. Dwoskin made it clear the politicians were upset because they feared their communities would lose the jobs and income the black and Latino prisoners generated. Dwoskin wrote that some white politicians pushing for Commissioner Carrion's termination consider her to be "Satan incarnate" or Satan in a human body.

Despite the pressure, Commissioner Carrion had remained fearless as she pushed to close 18 prisons upstate. Commissioner Carrion was quoted as saying, "I will no longer export black and brown kids to finance the upstate economy."

Dwoskin reported Commissioner Carrion managed to close the notorious Tryon School for Boys in 2009. She transferred all of the remaining inmates. Yet, a clause in the contract of the union representing the upstate prison workers demanded any prison emptied of inmates remain fully staffed for a full 12 months after the departure of the last inmate.

So, after the black and brown prisoners were removed, 129 upstate workers remained fully employed receiving full pay to guard no one at the Tryon School for Boys! Thus, the taxpayers of New York, including the black and brown families whose sons were sent to Tryon, were still paying the salaries of those workers and the other related costs for keeping the facility running for a full year as demanded in the ridiculous union's contract.[20]

Dad says he is big on Commissioner Carrion, though he has not met her. He says she knows the joy of life that jail steals from too many black and brown kids, often for minor offenses that only draw a reprimand for white kids. Dad says he is negative about the few rappers who glorify prison, making a dollar while misleading kids who are not well educated and might not have fathers or someone else to guide and protect them from a prison system that often holds more black and Latino boys than the graduation lines of colleges and universities in America.

He says kids should not be played when T.I. announces in "Winner" he is back from "vacation." He says T.I. may be coming back to fame and fortune, but the kids who buy his hits are coming back to poverty, misery, the prospect of AIDS if they were raped or participated in rapes in prison, and, too often, an early death or early return to prison.

Dad says Black 'n' Brown Oils should no longer fuel the prison industry. He suggests T.I., Lil Wayne, Lil Kim, DMX, and others should reach out to Commissioner Carrion and join her quest to save kids. He said they could reach young people with a different message than that of some rappers glorifying the thug and prison life that claims so many of their fans as victims.

In July 2007, the cops said Lil Wayne was caught "ridin' dirty." On March 8, 2010, he arrived at Rikers Island to begin serving a one-year sentence. When reviewing an article about Lil Wayne's imprisonment, dad remarked he and the rest of the Brooklyn College 19 were arrested and sent to Rikers Island for opening opportunities for African Americans and Latinos to enter Brooklyn College. He asked me if I saw the difference.

I said, "Yes, I do." Then I said, "Dad, I see another big difference. Lil Wayne got rhythm, can rap, and you can't." We both had a big laugh.

Chapter 31

I Believe I Can Fly

At age 18, I was still riding in the back seat of a 1992 forest green Camry that my father purchased nine months before I was born. Whenever mom was in the car, she rode shotgun and I had to ride in the back seat. During the summers of 2009 and 2010, many of my basketball teammates had the pleasure of riding in that Camry as dad chauffeured us from game to game. During those times, I would ride shotgun. My teammates never complained and often competed to get in when there were too many of us to fit comfortably.

However, I had been pushing for a new car for several years, but dad said it runs just fine. He rarely drives it unless he is taking me to an activity.

He asks, "Why buy when all I mostly do is move the car daily from one side of the street to the other to obey New York City's street cleaning rules? Should I pay cash for your college, or buy a new car and let you take out loans? Do you know I can use a Mercedes or Jaguar, which I could buy if I were willing to let you owe $100,000 in college loans?"

"But, dad, everyone says you need another car. Your niece Diane laughs when she sees you drive up in that car. She says you should use some of that money you are saving. Her dad, Uncle Rufus, has two new cars. You are the only one driving a car older than me."

"And I am going to drive it a bit longer. It would be different if the car was shabby, but it's in good shape with a newly painted body and I have never had any problem with the engine. Look, I have often driven past new cars that have broken down on the road. This Camry has less miles than most other cars that are no more than six years old. Anyway, saving for your education is more important and I am also able to help Ife and Kakuna with the high cost of living in New York."

"Okay. I see your point." I reluctantly responded.

I would later learn through another source that a few months earlier dad had given a significant amount of money to a severely ill relative and also to a severely ill former co-worker to ease their financial concerns during their illness. The amount was more than enough to have purchased a new Camry. I began to understand and appreciate dad's priorities.

Dad has also taught me how he is paying for my college through a 529 College Savings Plan he established a few weeks after my birth. He wants me to learn the system of investing so that I could do the same for my kids when they enter the world.

From age one, I would spend a great deal of time in the back seat of that Camry. From that back seat, I absorbed dad's and mom's music. I heard "I'm an ever rolling wheel, without a destination real…." from the Friends of Distinctions singing "Going in Circles." I heard "Last night I dreamed, that you were here with me…." from DeBarge singing "A Dream."

Later, as a teen in 2006, when we would be riding in that Camry I had to listen to dad ridicule many of the singers I was stepping to. One day Michael Baisden and Tom Joyner on KISS FM played Mary J. Blige's version of "A Dream."

"Man, that Mary J. couldn't sing that song if her life depended on it," he began while deliberately emphasizing that Southern twang. It's a sin they would even release her version of that song. The producer is going straight to hell for that sin!"

"Dad, Mary Jane is all right," I mildly protested hoping not to fire him up. But then, there's hope and then there's no hope.

He responded, "Yeah, she's all right when her singing does not require the range of that song! Like when she's singing about getting crunk up in a dancery and not needing any hateration or hollerating." Dad rocked his head in what he called rappers' style as he attempted to sing "Family Affair" but only managed to butcher her song while all the time keeping his eyes on the road.

While listening to dad, I reminded myself that dad actually loved that particular Mary J. song. He had it on his iPod and would often play it as a great workout song when we were kick boxing in the gym. He knew all the words even though you couldn't tell because his singing butchered so many words it sounded as if he were singing in a foreign language.

"Dad! Dad! Dad! Please stop!" I begged, with my hands covering my ears as he continued to butcher her song.

"Okay, but let's listen to the real deal," he suggested, while pointing to the iPod and asking me to locate "A Dream" by DeBarge.

I must admit hearing DeBarge let me know the original version was on a whole other level. The range of Bunny DeBarge's voice just took you to places that were out of reach with Mary's version. Dad said if you weren't in love, hearing DeBarge would make you start searching.

When DeBarge neared the end and started moaning, "Oh, oh oh ooh, ooooooh, come back. Please make my dream come true for me. I need so much for you to see. I need you to love me once again….," dad suggested, "I swear I can hear the angels in heaven singing with them."

Like dad, I must admit that was a baaaaad jam.

"Hey, dad, you know on 'I Ain't Mad At You,' Tupac used the music of that song," I said, with a smile on my face.

"Not one of his best songs. Could have taken the spirit of the music along with the sound and produced some better lyrics," dad responded. "Like when he sampled the Spinners' 'Sadie' for 'Dear Mama' and the Five Stairsteps for 'Oooh Child.' Now those are songs where Tupac really gets your attention."

Oh, yes, I heard many baaaaad jams in the back seat of that Camry even long before I hit first grade. In that back seat is where I first heard:

- Grand Master Melle Mel's "Beat Street"
- "Billy Jean," "Beat It," "Don't Stop 'Til You Get Enough," and "They Don't Really Care About Us"
- "A Song for You"
- "Distant Lover" and "What's Going On"
- "You Can't Hurry Love" and "My World is Empty Without You Baby"
- "Black Butterfly"
- "My Girl" and "Ain't too Proud to Beg"
- Jimi Hendrix's "Along the Watch Tower" and "Foxy Lady"
- "End of the Road"
- "It's Like That (and That's the Way It Is)"
- "When Doves Cry" and "1999"
- Willie Colon with Hector Lavoe on *Calle Luna, Calle Sol* and *Todo Tiene Su Final*
- Hector Lavoe's *Aguanile*
- Ruben Blades' *Tierra Dura*

- Eddie Palmieri's *"Puerto Rico"*
- Ray Barretto's *"Indestructible"*
- Celia Cruz's *"Rie y Llora"*
- "For the Love of Money" and "Love Train"
- "For the Love of You"
- "Tracks of My Tears" and "Ooh, Baby, Baby"
- The Friends of Distinction's "Going in Circles"
- Hugh Masekela's "Grazing in the Grass'
- Manu Dibango's "Soul Makossa"
- Kassav's *"Rete"* and *"Zouk La Sé Sel Médikaman Nou Ni"*
- Youssou N'Dour's "Set' and "Alboury"
- "The Message"
- "I Want You Back," "Dancing Machine," "Got to be There," and "I'll Be There"
- "Brick House"
- "Love and Happiness"
- The Rolling Stones' "Satisfaction" and "Beast of Burden"
- "Word Up"
- Brass Construction's "Movin'"
- Minnie Riperton's "Loving You"
- "I Shot the Sheriff," "Exodus," and "No Woman, No Cry"
- Nina Simone's "Wild is the Wind" and "Four Women"
- "Express Yourself"
- "Hotel California"
- "Try A Little Tenderness"
- "Skin Tight," and "Love Roller Coaster"
- "Please, Please, Please" and "I Feel Good"
- "Keep Your Head to the Sky," "Devotion" and "Reasons"
- "Ain't No Way" and "Respect"
- "Bad Girls" and "Hot Stuff"
- Luther singing "A House is Not a Home" and "Super Star"
- "Fingertips," "Isn't She Lovely," "As" and "Ribbons in the Sky"
- Martha and the Vandellas' "Heatwave"

Those were just enough classics to get me to start rocking in my child seat. While rocking, I also heard the many other classics listed at the end of this book. The list represents hundreds of hours of sounds of classics piped into the back seat and into my being in my early years; classics that have stayed with me a lifetime and have helped to shape my deep appreciation of lyrics.

Dad also played a great deal of jazz and gospel during our trips. I was getting a good dose of Coltrane and Miles in the car during the day and at night in my room when he would leave the radio tuned to WBGO, the jazz station. "All Blues," "So What," "Autumn Leaves," "Equinox," "A Love Supreme," and "My Favorite Things" were often my daily and nightly nutrition. Every year on the anniversary of the birthdays of Miles and Coltrane, we would listen to the 72-plus hours of broadcast of their music on WKCR FM when in the car or at home.

Inspired by Miles and Coltrane, at age 8 I started taking clarinet lessons. Within two years of picking up the clarinet, I would audition for and get accepted into The Juilliard School's Music Advancement Program (MAP).

The gospel songs we listened while driving in that Camry were mostly from tapes of the choir at Bethany Baptist Church, our home church at the time. Dad loved the way the choir would sing "Order My Steps." Even now, after we have moved on to Emmanuel, that song still strikes a note in dad when Total Praise, Emmanuel's choir, sings it. Dad's other favorite was the Commodores' "Jesus is Love." Unfortunately, for me, he would often attempt to sing along. Dad cannot carry a tune even if you put it in a bucket, as he sometimes says of other people's talent.

In October 2010 while at Hampton, I received a text from dad telling me he was remembering the first song he had heard me sing fully with knowledge of all the words. He also sent the text to remind me of my possibilities for greatness.

He texted that I sang the song from the back seat of the Camry in November 1996 when I was almost 4 years old. He wrote that we were on our way to my Montessori preschool. The deejay announced R. Kelly was about to sing. Dad did not like the upcoming song and was prepared to switch stations because he felt the lyrics and melody were too simple. He wasn't feeling it. However, as fate would have it, he did not change the station. So from the back seat, I joined R. Kelly in singing "I Believe I Can Fly:" "I used to think that I could not go on...."

Dad reported he adjusted the mirror to get a better look at me as I continued singing. My little Afro was well formed and shiny from coconut oil. I turned my head so that the morning sun was not in my eye. The blue straps of the car seat were pressed snuggly against the white sweater I wore. Looking on, dad fought to hold back the tears. He was surprised to see and hear how that song was moving me and, in turn, it started to move him. He discovered later that the kids in my preschool and I had been practicing that song for the preschool's upcoming June 1997 graduation.

In 2010 he reported he is still unable to hear that song without getting choked up as the image of me sitting in the back seat and singing with such feeling reappears in his mind.

Within days of that car ride in 1996, we were off to the movies to see "Space Jam." The movie was cool because it had MJ (Michael Jordan), Bugs Bunny, Daffy Duck, and some mean space aliens battling it out in an intergalactic space competition. The aliens played dirty, the way some of the older men now play against young guys at the Dean Street Playground. Of course, MJ ends up doing the impossible with his moves to defeat the aliens in outer space the way he would defeat dad's Knicks on real earth in 1996.

"I Believe I Can Fly" was the theme song for "Space Jam." Dad remembered how we and the other moviegoers left the theatre singing that song. He further stated that in 1997 it was the song most often sung at graduations and at other school functions he would attend that year across New York City as Senior Assistant to Chancellor Rudy Crew. Kids were singing it in schools, on playgrounds, on buses, in the subways, and in the churches.

You know there are many people in New York still crying over the way Jordan denied a championship to Ewing and the Knicks year after year. The only thing they have as consolation is a picture of "The Dunk" where John Starks in 1992 skies over Jordan, Horace Grant, and Bill Cartwright in the Eastern Conference Finals to posterize all three. Today, that poster is displayed in some barbershops in New York City and costs $140 at Amazon. If you are a die-hard Knicks fan and you buy it, remember Jordan got revenge by knocking the Knicks out of the playoffs in 1992, shortly after being posterized.

Starks flew for a brief moment, but Jordan flies for a lifetime.

Chapter 32

Music, Me, and John Legend

Do you remember the first time you heard "Ordinary People?" Do you remember the feeling that engulfed you? Do you remember how you instantly followed every word and every image created in your mind by the song as if you were hearing it for the hundredth time? How old were you? Were you in love?

I remember the first time I heard John's Legend's "Ordinary People." It was February, 2005. I was 12 years and 2 months old. I was riding with my father on the FDR Drive on the way to the 92nd Street Y for basketball camp. We had just left Emmanuel Baptist Church, and I was eager to get on the court. The radio was tuned to KISS FM.

I remember dad and I both became silent with the first sound of the piano keys and John Legend moaning "Oh, oh." He, too, was hearing the song for the first time, and we both knew instantly it would be one that we would love for a lifetime. I knew from the opening bar it would be a song that would just capture me fully with no thoughts of anything else during its duration. So for 4 minutes and 41 seconds, I sat and allowed the sound of John Legend's voice and piano to embrace and renew my spirit.

You might ask, "What does a 12-year-old know about taking it slow? Or what does a 12-year-old know about living, learning, crashing, and burning in a relationship?"

My answer would be, "At that point, I really knew nothing from experience about those matters." However, the amazing thing about the most beautiful music is it can make you feel and live, knowing you know all you need to know as you absorb the sounds into your being.

Dad says, "Our spirits are greater than our experiences and are not limited by those experiences. We know much more than our experiences have taught us. Great music, as it touches our spirit, can often take us to places that are yet out of the reach of our experiences. Great music's true message, the one that reaches our spirit, goes far beyond the pure statements of the written lyrics and the pure sounds of the instruments to inspire the expression of other purer statements and purer sounds in our being. Just ask Coltrane."

Dad further explains, "Although I have had the take it slow and crash and burn experience more than once, the song does not return me to those experiences. When I hear 'Ordinary People,' sometimes I am alone, back in Georgia, 8 years old at the playground, on a swing pumping and pumping to reach higher toward the summer sun. I am back at New York Hospital watching you for the first time in your basinet as I breathe the breath of anticipation of cradling you in my arms for the first time. I am 6, back inside that image of mom taking me into Mrs. Miller's first grade class that would serve as the foundation for my academic learning. I am 15 years old and riding in Mr. Harper's Bonneville crossing the George Washington Bridge going into New York City, my promised land, for the first time. I am 30 and setting my eyes and heart on your mother for the first time.

"I am here and now, in this 21st century, trying to re-visualize and get to that place God showed me so long ago. It is a place that I allowed the requirements for creating a 'successful and morally responsible professional life' to make oh so distant."

Age and even language are not barriers to understanding great music. Dad says that is why Billie Holiday, Ella Fitzgerald, and Michael Jackson were as popular in French-speaking Paris and Japanese-speaking Tokyo as in English-speaking New York.

So there you have it. I, Askia Akhenaton Suleiman Ali Davis, knew all that I needed to know about "Ordinary People" to be as enraptured as any man who has spent a lifetime falling in and out of love.

In August 2008, I had the special privilege of being in the audience when John Legend performed with Stevie Wonder and will.i.am at the Democratic National Convention. I was a member of the Lead America student team at the convention in Denver. It was beyond special to hear John Legend perform "Ordinary People" live in front of tens of thousands there to celebrate the rise of Barack Obama toward being President of the USA.

Do you know who co-wrote "Ordinary People" with John Legend? will.i.am co-wrote "Ordinary People" and the Black Eyed Peas were planning to perform the background vocals on the recording. will.i.am is a master and the Black Eyed Peas are great, but John Legend didn't need them on the background vocals.

Dad adds that in the spring of 2011 when he visited the Blue Note Jazz Club to see Cassandra Wilson, the jazz vocalist, John Legend was there and took the stage to speak of Wilson's influence on his development of his style. Dad used his phone to take a picture with John Legend's permission to send to me at Hampton.

Music is a very important part of my life experience. By the time I was 5 years old, I was already enrolled in piano classes at the Brooklyn Conservatory of Music on Seventh Avenue in Park Slope. I enjoyed the classes so dad soon purchased a Baldwin piano through a sale conducted by the Conservatory. By the time I was 6 I had composed my own little piece of music and performed for mom and dad. My performance encouraged dad to increase the frequency of my lessons at the Conservatory. I also joined mom and dad when they attended performances of jazz greats at the Conservatory.

When I entered third grade at PS 59 in September 2000, I was given a recorder. I performed with the other kids on recorders at special ceremonies at the school. Of course, "Hot Cross Buns" was the first song I remember playing on the recorder.

A few months later, I was given a clarinet by my music teacher at school. I enjoyed playing the clarinet and did well, so my music teacher suggested to mom that I audition for the Music Advancement Program (MAP) at The Juilliard School. MAP, an instrument-instruction program held during the school year on Saturdays, was designed to introduce classical music to black, Latinos, and other students who were underrepresented in the American classical music world. MAP required a highly competitive audition involving hundreds of students from all the public and private schools to fill a total of 20 to 25 positions.

Although I had been taking clarinet lessons for about 6 months and would be competing against kids who had been playing the clarinet much longer, my music teacher at PS 59 thought I should compete. Dad and mom agreed, and I began to prepare for the audition. However, I was not accepted when I first auditioned. I was disappointed, but that was okay. With determination, I began to prepare for the following year's audition.

In November 2001 dad registered me for private clarinet lessons at the 92nd Street Y in Manhattan. So for the first time, I began taking clarinet lessons from a professional clarinetist. Dad soon bought me a Yamaha clarinet.

I seemed to make progress quickly and had the opportunity to participate in recitals at the Y, accompanied by a pianist. Dad also sought and secured a jazz saxophonist, Gerald Hayes, and I began private jazz lessons with him.

At the 92nd Street Y and at the Brooklyn Conservatory, the emphasis was strictly classical music. I cannot count the hours I spent practicing Brahams' "Hungarian Dance Number 5;" Beethoven's "Ode to Joy," "Moonlight Sonata," and "7th Allegretto 3rd Movement;" Bach's "Musette;" Mozart's "Allegro" and "Variation on a Theme;" Tchaikovsky's "Russian Dance/Nutcracker Suite;" and Strauss' "Radetzky Marsch."

Practice takes time and attention. Did I mention it takes devotion? With devotion, I jumped into playing the clarinet at PS 59 and at the Y. At school and at the Y, I received many compliments that increased my motivation.

Preparation for the 2002 MAP audition involved daily practice. I practiced with the piano and the clarinet nightly, often while dad sat nearby in Transcendental Meditation. When practicing on the piano, you don't just sit and start moving your fingers across the keys. Those keys contain sounds. When practicing on the clarinet, you don't just pick up the instrument and start blowing. I had to learn to read music. I had to learn that the notes represented sounds. I had to learn transcription. I had to train my ears to identify pitches, intervals, melody, cords, rhythms, and timbre. I had to learn breathing techniques and how to position my lips. I had to focus on timing using the metronome. I had to play scales over and over again, attempting to produce the correct sound with the correct timing.

Maintenance of instruments was also important. The piano had to be tuned and maintained. The clarinet had to be cleaned and maintained. I had to organize my music sheets. I had to make sure I had the appropriate reeds. I had to make sure I didn't damage a reed when placing it in the mouthpiece. I had to make sure I wet the reed with the right amount of saliva before inserting it into the mouthpiece.

Performances presented other challenges. I had to focus while my teachers listened for errors. I had to focus while my parents and the audience listened for perfection. I had to keep my fingers loose. I had to build and maintain strength in the muscles of my jaws and build stamina in my breathing. I had to coordinate breathing with the movement of my fingers. I had to block out all thoughts and distractions unrelated to the production of the piece of music.

With all of these and other demands, I learned early to appreciate the effort and dedication necessary to produce music. Trust me when I tell you it's much easier to listen than to produce. I was just a novice trying to play sounds using music produced by others, and the effort was challenging. However, I found the dedication within me, and I practiced diligently.

In May 2002, I arrived at The Juilliard School prepared for the audition. I wore a pair of beige khakis, a white button-down Ralph Lauren shirt, and a yellow tie with musical notes in various colors. I do not remember being overly anxious. I had performed recitals at the 92nd Street Y and, before that, at the Brooklyn Conservatory and had grown confident in my ability. I had chosen Mozart's "Variation on a Theme," a complicated piece for a student with less than two years of training on the clarinet. I loved the piece and had played it in practice numerous times on both the piano and the clarinet.

During the audition, I had to play the piece, without accompaniment, in front of two members of the faculty as dad and mom listened outside the door. Before entering the room, I had already prepared the clarinet. After introducing myself, I announced the piece I would play. Then I placed the sheet music on the stand and began to play.

When the piece was completed, the two faculty members thanked me for coming and informed me I would learn about their decision later. However, when I entered the hallway, dad and mom greeted me with big grins and big hugs. "You did it!" dad exclaimed. "You played flawlessly. We are so proud of you. There is no way they can say no."

Juilliard said yes, and I entered MAP for a year. I was at The Juilliard School every Saturday from 8:30 a.m. until 2:30 p.m. I was 9 years old when I began. At first, it was interesting and fun. However, it soon became more like regular school with rigid schedules and activities and students expected to perform at the highest level, even when the activities became repetitive and boring. I attended four classes each Saturday—private clarinet lessons, clarinet ensemble, music theory, and choir. We were taught all of the fundamentals of music. In some classes, we barely picked up our instruments as we focused on learning music theory, music history, and other topics.

We were expected to take what we were learning in class and apply it to our daily practice at home for one hour. We were also expected to be well prepared when we performed a different piece every month before the students and faculty. Every month, each student performed an individual as well as an ensemble piece, and we also sang in the choir. All of these recitals prepared us for the final performance at the end of the year in May. The final performance included individual, ensemble, and full orchestra pieces. We also performed a couple of songs with the choir.

Mom invited *la familia* to this year-end performance, and they sat mesmerized at the high level of talent, skill, and professionalism displayed. My seasonal allergies were bad that day, so I'm glad *la familia* was too mesmerized to laugh at my constant blinking. My eyes were so itchy. Mom captured it all, including the blinking, on the video camera and that video can also be found in the closet of keepsakes.

So as you can see, participating in MAP required a lot of hours of practice and, truthfully, I had never been a big fan of practice. Although I had practiced daily for the audition before entering Juilliard, it was all right because it was only for a few short weeks. When it comes to practicing music, I guess I have a bit of Allen Iverson's attitude in me. Iverson thinks if you are good, it is no big deal to miss practice. Dad said although I practiced only a little, I had to ability to still perform as if I had practiced until I had dropped from exhaustion. That was a blessing and a curse, according to him, because it made me take my gifts for granted. With my interests growing in other directions, later in the year my interest in Juilliard faded even though I completed the year of the program and did well during my recitals. Many other students returned for an optional second year. I didn't.

Looking back now, I can clearly see I must have known then I wasn't destined to be a classical musician. That requires a love for classical music, and extraordinary passion, skills, and dedication just to play the music well, music produced by others often centuries earlier. Also, dad and mom weren't looking to make me a classical musician. They were looking to give me exposure to various experiences to see which would capture my interest and my passion.

While at Juilliard, I also maintained a full schedule which included Scorpion Martial Arts, basketball camp, church, regular cultural performances with my parents, and regular visits *con mis primos y mi abuela*/with my cousins and my grandmother. I was so busy that mom kept a monthly schedule she maintained posted in my bedroom. My *Titi* Miriam teased mom once when she looked at the schedule. "Akhenaton is busier than most adults," she suggested. "Does he get a break?"

Just before entering Juilliard, I had learned to play jazz on the clarinet. I liked classical music but found jazz more interesting. My jazz teacher was Gerald Hayes, a great saxophone man. I loved jazz. Coltrane was most interesting, but too complicated to play. When a 9-year-old hears Coltrane's "My Favorite Things," he knows instantly he shouldn't bother trying.

However, I learned to play "Summertime," which was written by George Gershwin and made famous by Coltrane. I even learned to improvise, trying to mimic Coltrane. I would improvise on jazz tunes I had learned. "Sunny Moon for Two" by Sonny Rollins, "Afternoon in Paris" by John Lewis, "Sugar" by Stanley Turrentine, and "Mercy Mercy Mercy" by Cannonball Adderley became a regular part of my repertoire. The song I would perform most often was "Autumn Leaves" by Cannonball Adderley, recorded with Miles Davis on trumpet and Art Blakely on drums. It was dad's favorite for me to play, and I played it well.

After my year at Juilliard, I stuck with jazz and the clarinet through middle school up until I was about to enter high school. I was still young and willing to accept my parents' belief that I should continue with the instrument. So for several years I continued my lessons and recitals at the Y. I also joined the jazz band in middle school where I quickly became the featured soloist during performances. My use of improvisation generally drew intense applause from fellow students and adults. So clarinet and basketball strengthened my popularity in middle school.

By the summer before entering high school, I knew that my instrument playing days were almost over. I didn't know how to tell mom and dad, especially dad. I was so into basketball, R&B, and hip hop. Nevertheless, when I was introduced to the music teacher at Banneker, I tried to remain open-minded about joining the school's small jazz band to appease dad. However, soon after school began, it became impossible for dad to convince me to practice my clarinet. Suddenly, there were always problems with the clarinet that required repairs.

Mom thought that the problems were due to sabotage by me. It is true that I was not being as careful as usual when handling the instrument, but would I deliberately bend a key on a Yamaha clarinet to the extent that it wouldn't produce the correct sound? Was it really my fault the mouth piece needed replacing after it developed a tiny hairline crack? Was it my fault the only reeds available, when it was time to practice, were all worn down and unusable? I know I greased that cork appropriately. So why was I having a hard time attaching the lower joint to the upper joint? That's it! That's how that key got bent. I was innocently trying to attach the upper and lower joints, and the difficulty I had turning the joints into their proper position caused the damage. (I know, mom. You are going to ask if "the ghost" who left the crumbs on the floor was at it again.)

What American teenager would deliberately commit acts of sabotage as the only way to wear down his parents' will to force him to do something for which he no longer has an interest? American teens don't do that. Where would they get such ideas? Huh?

Sabotage or not, I was old enough and determined enough to make my own decisions. When dad would have wanted me to practice, I was doing my homework. I knew academics always came first for dad. After about a month into my freshman school year in high school, it was clear to him that I was no longer willing to practice. At the same time, he was no longer willing to insist that I practice.

So, instead of insisting, dad tried reasoning with me. He suggested, "You should continue to play because you are good enough to earn a scholarship for a university band. If you earn a scholarship, the money we have set aside for college could be used to buy you a car." I wasn't really feeling it. I was four weeks into high school, and college was four years away.

Like most 13-year-olds and other teens, I was not eager to be burdened with the responsibility of worrying about paying for college. I knew dad had my college fees all figured out with the 529 Plan. So I concentrated on enjoying high school, which included forgetting about playing clarinet and forgetting the suggestion that I might want to play in the Florida A&M Marching Band.

Little did I know that 19 months later I would reluctantly pick up the clarinet again. I had accepted dad's request to perform "Autumn Leaves" at his early retirement party in April 2008. So two weeks before the party, I began practicing again. Dad's party was attended by 250 guests, most of them former colleagues. My sisters, aunts, uncles, and several cousins also attended.

Dad's retirement party was held at Marina Del Rey in the Bronx next to the East River. I spoke in tribute to my father, and then I played "Autumn Leaves," with all the love I felt for dad. I received many compliments for a beautiful performance. Several individuals who had played in high school and college bands said they could never have played that piece without being accompanied by a pianist. I thanked them for the compliments.

That evening was the last time I opened my clarinet case, assembled the clarinet, placed a reed, and blew. Today the piano sits in the living room of our apartment, unplayed. The clarinet sits in its case on top of the piano bench, also unplayed. The metronome rests nearby, silent and still. Maybe I will return to them one day, before passing them on to my sons and daughters. The sheet music, the band method books, and the programs from various recitals rest in folders inside the storage compartment of the piano bench. My transcriptions of various pieces are there, and a review of some would suggest I had learned a great deal about music production.

Music production isn't easy. Dad says most of what we hear musically "is a step above garbage," musically speaking. He says a lot of it is computer production, not music production. Most people cannot hear the sounds of distinct instruments in bad music. In bad music, distinct instruments are often replaced by computerized sounds that do not take much effort and dedication to produce, according to dad.

B.o.B says some African Americans would rather rap than go to school. Even when some are at school, they are spending more time rapping than studying. Do you know someone like that? Is it you? No, it is not me.

Now, don't get me wrong. I don't wanna be hatin' on anybody's dream. However, dad says B.o.B could tell you that for every rapper making a dollar and keeping it through wise living and wise investments, there are many more who are losing that dollar through drinking, gambling, drugs, spending sprees, lawyers to keep them out of jail, and bad investments. He says B.o.B could tell you that too many of the women you see in the music videos, doing what dad calls the "same old hip shaking dance," have a difficult time paying their monthly bills, including their rent.

Like you, dad and I love Waka's "Oh Let's Do It" video, but dad has me wondering how many of the other guys appearing are able to pay their rent in "Riverdale, Georgia." Dad says B.o.B could also tell you that for every Waka, B.o.B, Diddy, Little Wayne, Drake, Lupe, and Jay-Z, there are tens of thousands would be rappers who will never go any further than posting a video on YouTube, if even that far.

My journey has taught me to really appreciate good musicians and the difficult challenge of producing good music. To use an instrument to just play the music that great musicians have produced and to sing the great lyrics they have written takes more than the passion I had for practice.

Yeah, like you, I listen and dance to a lot of the garbage. You cannot avoid ignorant songs at a party. It's impossible.

Yeah, like you, I listened and danced to *"Gasolina"* in 2004. I danced then, but that song *esta muerta hoy*/is dead today.

Yet Alicia Keys' "If I Ain't Got You," also released in 2004, is as fresh as ever. She wrote and produced the song and the album that contains it, *The Dairy of Alicia Keys*. I can still play that song on my iPod for my lady today and find us meditating in our hearts on the power of the lyrics: "Some people think the physical things define what's within…." You can't find that power expressed in the best Hallmark Card.

Don't you hear the opening sounds of her piano keys even as you read this? Don't you hear her sweet and tender opening moan, "*Mmmm, mmmm*"? Aren't you singing the lyrics? Don't you wish your lady or man was next to you right now singing Alicia in your ear as you sink into the love seat in your living room?

Great music is said to be eternal. So Maxwell's "Pretty Wings" of 2009 will still be here 100 years later in 2109 to lift our great, great, great grandsons and great, great, great granddaughters in flight.

"Your face will be the reason I smile, but I will not see what I cannot have forever...."

Chapter 33

A House Divided

Christ said, "A house divided against itself cannot stand." Luther Vandross said "Amen" to that and sang, "A House Is Not A Home."

"Honor thy father and thy mother so that your days may be long in the land that the Lord your God is giving you." That is the Fifth Commandment (including a promise).

Did my father always honor his father and mother? Have I?

My father came from a divided house and ended up fighting his father. I came from a united house and ended up at war and in a physical confrontation with my father. I guess you can say, "Like father, like son."

First, I will give the story of dad's fight with his dad.

African American fathers of my grandfather's generation were noted for the phrase, "Boy, I brought you into this world, and I will take you out of this world!" They were known for demanding consistent honor and respect from their children, and when they thought they weren't getting honor and respect, they would throw out that phrase. I am told the threat usually worked to correct their sons' behavior because their sons knew the phrase was no joke. Corporal punishment was a regular visitor in many families.

Thankfully, corporal punishment has not visited our family, and dad has never used that phrase even during moments of the deepest conflict between us.

During the summer of 2004 at age 11, I attended the Fieldston Enrichment Program (FEP) at the Ethical Culture Fieldston School, a private academy in the Bronx. (I send a shout out to Mr. Thomas, Mrs. Jones, and Mr. Jeremiah for their wonderful teaching and guidance.) Most mornings, dad would drive me to Fieldston. The hour-long trip to the Bronx would provide another opportunity for dad and me to have uninterrupted discussions at the beginning of the day. Songs on the radio were sometimes used by dad to start a conversation about topics presented in the songs.

One bright morning in June as we approached the Brooklyn Bridge on our way to Fieldston, Luther Vandross' new song, "Dance with My Father Again," came up on WBLS FM. As the song came up, dad's voice became heavy with emotion and a tear touched his eye. As he drove, he attempted to sing along with Luther Vandross: "Back when I was a child, before life removed all the innocence...."

Dad sang the entire song, which was rather unusual. My father, with his Southern twang, does not have a voice made for singing, but I managed to respect the emotion. I let him have his moment and his private thoughts. I sat in silence watching the skyline of Manhattan pass as he continued.

When the singing ended, dad turned to me. In a voice colored with deep sadness and disappointment he said, "You know, I don't remember dad ever picking me up as Luther said his father did. Dad was athletic, but I cannot remember him ever throwing a baseball, football, or basketball to me. My father loved to fish, but he never took me fishing. He was a swimmer, but never took me swimming. Dad was known for being very intelligent, the most intelligent man in my hometown, white or black, but he never read a book to me."

"Never, dad?" I asked, in a tone that acknowledged his disappointment. "Never, Akhenaton."

Dad said he remembers when he was 10 years old. He had 11 siblings at the time, all from the same mother and father. There was no baby daddy drama in his house. Nevertheless, my grandfather was a player and a gambler. It was not unusual for him to come home at 4:00 a.m. in a small town where 95 percent of the population was in bed by 10:00 p.m. and all businesses were closed by 5:00 p.m., except the juke joints. Then there were times he wouldn't come home for three or four days. Dad wouldn't know where my grandfather was but had gotten enough information to know that he had women in different neighborhoods in the small town. He learned to assume granddad was sleeping elsewhere.

As a player, my grandfather didn't use much judgment. Dad said he actually "played" right across the street with a certain woman who had about 10 kids of her own; thankfully, not of my grandfather's making. That circumstance created a lot of friction among the children of the Davis clan and the Mullens clan of kids across the street.

One warm afternoon in early May 1961, the friction created a firestorm. One of the little ruffians across the street said something about dad's mom. It included a nasty comment about my grandmother's complexion: "That yallow (yellow) woman…!"

Yeah, dad's mom had "yallow" skin and freckles, and that presented a cause for some kids and adults to make negative statements. On the other hand, my granddad had black skin like the color of black dress shoes. His name was Alonzo, but due to his skin color, almost everyone, including his sister (but not his kids), referred to him by his nickname, Sambo.

Little Black Sambo was a character in one of the most popular children's books for more than 50 years from 1899 through the 1960s. The book also inspired a series of cartoons which were very popular when presented in the movies and on television from 1935 through the 1960s. The book was written by a white Scottish woman who lived in India when India was colonized and controlled by the British.

In her book, Little Black Sambo was a child in a southern India village. He had to use his "simple or limited thinking ability" and good luck to avoid being eaten by tigers that constantly stalked him. His father's name was Black Jumbo, and his mother was Black Mumbo. One day four tigers confronted him. As the tigers began to fight over all the clothes Little Black Sambo had surrendered to them, they ran around chasing each other until the hot Indian sun melted them into a pile of butter. Black Jumbo collected the tiger butter, and Black Mumbo made a pile of pancakes using the butter. Black Mumbo ate 27 pancakes, Black Jumbo ate 57, and Little Black Sambo ate 169 pancakes.

The character of Little Black Sambo was used by racist white supremacists to depict black skinned people of India, Asia, and Africa, as well as blacks in the USA, the Caribbean, Brazil, and South America as simple-minded inferiors to whites or people of European ancestry. (Dad speculates that Little Black Sambo was also the model for Buckwheat in *The Little Rascals*.)

Dad said the basic message of white supremacists using Little Black Sambo and other characters was that people of European ancestry with white skin were destined by God to rule over people with dark skins. Some "Christian" missionaries promoted that philosophy in Africa and Asia, and that philosophy was taught openly in some "Christian" churches through the 1960s in the USA. When dad was a boy, some Southern Baptist and other "Christian" churches openly taught that "God had cursed Ham" and, thereby, had cursed dark-skinned people. Ham, in the Bible, was considered the ancestor of Africans and dark-skinned people of Asia.

Dad says the truth is that Noah, not God, cursed his grandson, Canaan, who was considered the ancestor of the people who populated Canaan before the Israelites arrived. Canaan was Ham's son.

Dad also learned as a child that the Mormons did not accept blacks into the priesthood and believed that black skin color was the curse God supposedly placed on Cain and his descendants for the murder of Abel. In the 1850s, Brigham Young, a founder of the Mormon religion, forbade acceptance of blacks into the priesthood and declared there are "some classes of the human family that are black, uncouth, uncomely, disagreeable and low in their habits, wild, and seemingly deprived of nearly all the blessings of the intelligence that is generally bestowed upon mankind."

However, in 1978 after reportedly "receiving a revelation" from God, "the elders" of the Mormon religion ceased the policy of barring blacks from the priesthood. Dad sarcastically says "the elders" must have told the congregation, "I guess God does change God's mind. God seems to like Negras today!"

The book, *Little Black Sambo,* was widely read in schools and libraries throughout America, a large part of Africa and the Caribbean, and England, then the largest colonial power controlling India and other Asian lands. It was an important part of the curriculum in schools throughout America where it was considered a classic of children's literature. Even in dad's segregated school in Georgia, it was an assigned book that was read aloud in first grade with black teachers in front of the class! Many of his classmates would laugh while reading the book.

With a black-skinned father and a "yallow"/yellow-skinned mother, dad and his brothers and sisters were subjected to teasing from two directions due to the different skin colors of their parents. Dad was the son of "that yallow woman and Black Sambo," according to some of his childhood opponents. Dad and his sisters and brothers suffered taunts because grandma was "yallow" and granddad was black.

In 1961 in the black community, when someone made a derogatory statement about someone else's mom, that someone had to be prepared for war. Among African Americans, there was nothing more important than defending the honor of your mother. African American boys would often ignore an offense to their personal honor and even their dad's honor, but if the offenders would mention their mom, "all hell would break loose." Thus, when the offending ruffian made a derogatory remark about dad's mom, dad and his brothers and sisters were prepared for war.

Dad explained it was impossible for his generation of black males to accept jokes about their mothers since his generation was at least subconsciously aware that black mothers had experienced so much physical and sexual abuse at the hands of men, including white men and white slave masters. They had only to look at all of the varieties of skin color among African Americans to recognize the result of that abuse from white men. Even among brothers and sisters in one family, so many varieties of skin color would be present.

In 1961, dad and his family lived in the housing projects which were about 5 years old. The house that dad lived in had six bedrooms, a living room, a kitchen, and a large pantry. All of the houses in the complex were single-level, red brick, ranch-style homes.

The housing projects carried special status because a significant number of African Americans and Caucasians, including descendants of modern-day Irish travelers, still lived in wooden houses with outhouses in the rear. Often, the outhouses were shared by more than one family. The "toilet man" came around once a week to clean the outhouses. He carried a wheelbarrow and bucket to collect the waste. (Now that's a job that should have motivated even the worst student to study and get a good education.) Also, most of the wooden houses had no running water so the families would draw water from a well shared with their neighbors.

A paved road ran parallel to dad's house. The road was just wide enough to allow two cars going in opposite directions to barely pass one another. Many of the roads in town were unpaved. The road next to dad's home was paved only a distance of about one mile, just enough to take it a few yards past the elementary school for African Americans.

Near the school a stream of water flowed from an open sewer in the woods nearby. The road passed over the stream, and there was a small wooden bridge that allowed the African American kids to get safely to school without stepping into the polluted water. However, on certain days, they had to hold their noses and look out for water moccasins and rattle snakes that would at times appear in their path.

The offending ruffian and his clan, the Mullens family, lived directly opposite dad's house on the other side of the dividing road. The clan lived in a small wooden house that was in poor condition and had an outhouse in the rear. The wood covering the house was a sun-burnt gray. The wood looked as if it had not been treated for water and sun and had never been painted. The house had no running water and no electricity. The house was the "picture of rural poverty" in the 1960s. It was set back about 10 feet from the edge of the road. There was no sidewalk on that side of the road; there was one on dad's side.

BTW, when dad took me to visit Georgia in 2005, he said he was amazed to see that some of the wooden shacks still existed and are still occupied in certain parts of town. They brought to mind the shacks he had seen on a visit to rural parts of the Dominican Republic. "How can this be in rich America?" he wondered aloud.

Within minutes of the ruffian's offensive statement on that warm May afternoon in 1961, all the kids who were at home from both clans assembled on their side of the road. Each side had five kids old enough to fight. The clans had not fought before, but the ruffian, whose nickname was Horse, had crossed the line. Soon taunts were flying in both directions. Then both sides started to pick up pebbles to throw. Since the oldest kids were 13 and many kids were less than 10, no one was accurate with the first barrage. So everyone stopped and began to exchange taunts again, everyone except Gloria, dad's then 13-year-old sister.

As Gloria left her siblings and went into the house, dad paused to watch her movements. Within seconds, she returned with a Coca Cola bottle, the kind made of glass, which was the only kind produced in those days. In those days, the Coke bottles were made of glass that was three times thicker than that of a typical drinking glass.

Gloria had already established a reputation for being a "tough customer," a fierce fighter protecting her younger siblings. She was 5 feet 2 inches, 100 pounds, and "two sticks of dynamite." Once she had threatened to "whup" Sally Ann Sykes, a bigger (140 pounds) and taller (5 feet 10 inches) 15-year-old girl who had furiously swung dad through the air after dad had taunted Sally Ann for having "knock knees." Not even the older brothers in the Davis family dared to offend their sister Gloria because her response would be unpredictable. Her older brother Marcus carried, and still carries, a scar above his left eyelid from a long cooking fork Gloria threw at him for a verbal offense that had occurred a year before the showdown with the clan across the road.

As dad looked on, Gloria swung her arm "like Satchel Paige and Juan Marichal when they warm up." Then she let the Coca Cola bottle fly and, like a guided missile, it hit its target, the head of one of the offending girls.

Dad said, "At that point, the earth stood still for a few moments as everyone in both clans, except for Gloria, stood still in shock. Then the earth started to spin on its axis again as blood gushed from the open wound and the members of Horse's clans, with blood in their eyes, charged like the cavalry toward the Davis clan." Dad and dad's clan quickly entered the safety of their home. They locked the doors and made sure all of the windows were locked. No one was eager to confront a clan that became crazy at the sight of one of their own's blood. There was a general rule among blacks: Don't fight a crazy man because a crazy man feels no pain no matter how hard you hit him.

As Horse's clan retreated to care for the wounded girl, the Davis clan looked in awe at Gloria. Gloria was remorseless because that clan was guilty of dishonoring her mom, and, anyway, Gloria really didn't have an apologetic bone in her body.

About two hours later, dad's father came home 12 hours earlier than usual. Tension filled the air as he entered the house. Granddad was tall and muscular. Dad described him as having the appearance of a tall and pure Yoruba of Nigeria. Rarely would a smile shape his face. He had a thick black leather belt that seemed powerful enough to tame a lion. Dad had always managed to avoid the "whuppings" his dad dished out. Dad was a good kid who had watched the "whuppings" his brothers Marcus and Thomas would receive from time to time for their mischief. Dad said those "whuppings" were enough to convince him that mischief should be avoided.

"What happened this afternoon?" granddad asked after assembling the trembling Davis clan.

"Those bad kids across the street said some bad things about our mother." Gloria answered. "Then they started to pick up rocks, and they threw them and hit the little ones. So I wouldn't let them hit Junior and Danny, who are only 6 and 4 years old. So we fought back."

"Well, do you know that one of the little girls across the street was hit in the head with a Coca Cola bottle?" granddad asked.

"Yes, dad, that's a shame that Horse hit his own little sister while trying to hit one of us. While he was throwing the bottle at us, she accidentally stepped in the way as the bottle left his hand. I wanted to go help her, but you know how bad those kids are. They wouldn't even let me take care of the little girl, and they didn't know how. It's just terrible how he hit his own sister. I wonder how he is going to explain it to his mother."

Gloria had responded speaking rapidly and confidently, saying all that in less than one minute, while dad and the rest of his brothers and sisters stood in terror for what seemed like 10 hours.

"Well, I'll tell you what. I am going across the street to hear their version of what happened. And let me tell you, if I find out if any one of you all had something to do with it, I will beat the black off you when I get back!"

Granddad had spoken with supreme authority. No one doubted his words. He was gonna beat the "black" off them even though all of them were brown, except two who were "yallow."

After granddad's threat, dad began to imagine the expected pain. He began to recall the screams his older brothers, Marcus and Thomas, made from their beds when granddad would arrive home at 2:00 a.m. and, without warning, shake the two of them awake with a stunning leather belt in response to earlier mischief. Then dad started to recall the times that his father would wait until Marcus or Thomas was in the bathtub to bring out the belt to stun wet skin. With those memories running through his head, dad tried to suppress any thoughts of his father's return.

Within minutes of granddad's departure, Grandma Mattie, the "yallow" woman with freckles, arrived home. Grandma was a bit tired after a day of doing work that was common to many black women in those days: cleaning, ironing, and cooking while reading to and taking care of the kids of one of the local Caucasian women. Grandma had returned from working at Mrs. Willis' house. When she entered and "plopped down" on the couch, she let out a deep sigh that was an expression of her exhaustion and frustration that she had to leave her children and home to take care of the children and home of another woman. Even though Mrs. Willis was generous and kind to grandma (and dad who often worked cutting her grass and raking leaves), grandma was usually tired but nevertheless ready to begin almost immediately taking care of the responsibilities at home late into the evening.

The Davis clan could not afford to give her a minute to catch her breath. All ran over to tell her about the confrontation and granddad's threat. Gloria took the lead as usual. She repeated the story she had told granddad.

Grandma responded, "Well, I don't care what he said. He is not going to put a hand on any of you!"

About a half hour later, granddad returned with a menacing look in his eyes. As he prepared to "whup" the Davis clan, grandma told him, "You are not going to beat any of my kids based on anything that woman told you!"

Then grandma stood up to position herself between the kids and granddad. Granddad threatened her and lightly pushed her in an attempt to get to the kids. However, she stood her ground. Then he raised his hands as if to hit her for her defiance. Big mistake! Big mistake!

By that time one of dad's older brothers had returned home, and just in time. No one had to say anything. Gloria, age 13 and ever the warrior, led the charge. Within seconds, six members of the clan including dad, age 10,

Aunt Lillie, age 8 and Uncle Junior, age 6, were all over granddad. They hit and kicked him. They beat him in the living room. He made a break for the back porch. They followed him into the kitchen and jumped on him as he stepped on the porch. They knocked him off the porch. It was only two and a half feet above the ground, so there was no major damage, except to his ego, as the neighbors looked on. They jumped from the porch and continued to kick him for daring to make the mistake of raising his hands against their mom.

After a thorough beat down, granddad stood and walked away. That was the last dad saw of his dad. Granddad was 37 and grandma was 34 and six months pregnant with Aunt Sheila, their 13th child. In 1961, granddad walked out of dad's life on a bright sunny May afternoon with no clouds in the sky and no cloud in dad's heart because granddad had committed an unpardonable sin. He had acted as if he were prepared to hit dad's mother. Big mistake!

In the Bible, fathers may come first, but in the heart of African Americans, moms are always first. Dad says that is the way it should be, even in our own home. "You should never put anyone, including me, in front of your mother," he tells me. Thankfully, I have never had to consider making that choice.

Christ said a house divided against itself cannot stand. Dad's house fell. When granddad was there, some of his money went into drinking, gambling, and loose women. Thus, there were times the family went without enough food and without enough clothing. At times, before dad started school at age 6, he was without shoes. He walked around the neighborhood with bare feet like little kids in rural Africa. Then there were many times when the electricity was turned off. Many winters they had to struggle, at times not having enough money for kerosene to keep the furnace hot.

However, after granddad's departure, the quality of their family's life improved. The brothers and sisters pulled together to work at various jobs to make money to pay the bills. They had worked previously, but some of their earnings had been mishandled by granddad. The lights were never cut off again. There was always enough money for kerosene to keep the furnace warm in the winter. They always had enough shoes, clothes, and food. They became a family and a house united.

In contrast to dad's experience, I've grown up in a middle-class family. My father has often picked me up. He has danced with mom and me. He has carried me up the stairs to bed after I have fallen asleep on the couch. He has thrown footballs, basketballs, baseballs, volley balls, soccer balls, and tennis balls to me. He has taken me to the ocean in Cape Cod almost every summer since birth to swim and share the ocean, sunsets, and family. I learned to read, and I read *Hop on Pop, The Snowy Day,* and *The Cat in the Hat* sitting on his lap as a 3-year-old. I have never had to miss a meal. The idea of being without electricity has never crossed my mind.

Furthermore, I have not had to go barefoot outdoors, or even indoors, because I have always had slippers. I've bought two pairs of sneakers at one time; one for basketball and one for styling. Sometimes within one or two months I would stop wearing them. Dad has given away many of my sneakers that looked nearly new when I no longer wanted to wear them. But, you know, any teen could tell you that gear that might look physically new could look very old from the point of view of current fashion.

Before I entered eleventh grade at age 15, I had travelled to Mexico, Canada, Puerto Rico, and most of the interesting cities in North America (Philadelphia, Atlanta, Boston, San Francisco, Seattle, DC, Orlando, Montreal, Quebec City, Vancouver, etc.). I had even attended the Democratic National Convention in Denver and observed Senator Obama as he accepted the nomination for president.

At age 15 in 2008, I walked the streets of North Philadelphia with dad campaigning for President Obama while seeing huge confederate flags hanging in some living rooms (right in North Philadelphia). A month after turning 16, I was in beautiful Maui. All of those trips were enjoyed with dad and mom, except mom didn't come to North Philadelphia to see the confederate flags in the homes of some of the people we wanted to ask to vote for President Obama. Some of those conversations were very short and yet very interesting.

However, before dad left Georgia at age 15, dad had not travelled more than 60 miles from his hometown and had never visited a city with a population greater than 10,000. By twelfth grade, the only city he had entered was New York.

Despite the advantages dad has provided, by the middle of the first semester of my junior year in high school a war was brewing between dad and me. I started to pull strongly away from dad's presence. Mom was often caught in the middle. Our house was becoming divided, and that division would ultimately lead to a physical fight between dad and me.

You know what they say: "Like father, like son." He fought his father, and I would fight mine.

Chapter 34

My House Divided and Falling Down

By eleventh grade, dad and I were on a collision course. We were headed for a train wreck. I was speeding in one direction, and he was speeding in the opposite on the same track. There were probably warning signs, but I don't think either of us saw them. Then there was an explosion, and our relationship would be altered for two lifetimes.

When I began eleventh grade, I expected a great year. I loved Banneker. I had a B+ average. Dad and mom thought I had not given my best efforts and, during my sophomore year, several of the teachers had informed them that I should be an A student and would be an A student if I applied myself fully to my studies.

As a result, dad and I had argued and dad had threatened to take me out of Banneker and move me to Xaverian High School. There was no way I wanted to go to Xaverian, an all-male Catholic high school in the Bay Ridge section of Brooklyn. I loved my friends and most of my teachers at Banneker. Plus, Xaverian had only a few black and Latino students. A lot of the boys at Xaverian seemed to be the sons of Irish and Italian police officers and firemen. Even the guidance counselor was a retired police officer. Its sister school was full of the daughters of policemen and firemen. Xaverian was a nice school; nice for somebody else.

When I graduated from middle school two years earlier, dad and mom had considered Xaverian, Bishop Ford, Bishop Loughlin, and Banneker, all in Brooklyn, and Xavier in Manhattan. Xavier was a highly regarded Jesuit academy that emphasized leadership and military discipline and the teaching of Christianity.

In the early years of my father's professional experience, he had been trained in leadership and organization development by Brother Joseph O'Connell, an Irish American Jesuit. Dad considered Brother O'Connell a master in the field of leadership and organization development, and it was clear to dad that his expertise flowed from Jesuit philosophy and training. Dad said Brother Joe and his fellow Jesuits helped him to build a wonderful and uncommon foundation for professional success and confidence.

Thus, dad was very open to the possibility of my attending Xavier. I believe he went there having it as the preference in his mind. When we visited, I discovered the school was nice, but I wasn't quite feeling it. The location was great. The library and other facilities were great. The students and teachers were nice and seemed focused. The school was somewhat diverse and it had black and Latino students who were not athletes and seemed to exhibit a leadership role in the student body. However, with military discipline and no girls, well, I wasn't feeling it. But I thought dad would make the final decision so I didn't say much about my concerns. I believe I was willing to accept attending Xavier.

Next we visited Xaverian. It too was located in a great neighborhood and had great facilities. Xaverian had a very strong focus on using technology in the classroom, which impressed dad. However, the school was not very diverse, and the African Americans and Latinos who stood out seemed to stand out for athletics. Xaverian was all boys, and I wasn't feeling that.

Bishop Ford's student population was nearly entirely African American and Latino boys and girls. The teachers and kids seemed cool and focused. The facilities and library were considerably less desirable than those at Xavier and Xaverian. The school was a financially poorer cousin of Xavier and Xaverian.

Bishop Loughlin was located near our condo, and the facilities were nice. The student population was almost entirely African American boys and girls. Academically, Loughlin seemed sound. Financially, it seemed somewhat endowed above Bishop Ford but somewhat below Xaverian and Xavier. Dad left the visit leaning toward Xavier and Loughlin. I preferred Loughlin and I thought he preferred Xavier.

Finally, when we toured Banneker, I knew that I had found my future home. The facilities weren't great, but the teachers and the school spirit were. We met Tyler from my middle school, Big Time from my former martial arts dojo, and other students who were neighbors or ex-classmates from my other schools, and they were thriving. Dad was impressed with the writing center, with several teachers who had attended Morehouse and other Historically Black Colleges and Universities, and with Mr. Askia Egashira, a teacher he had earlier attempted to recruit in the Bronx. He was impressed with a spirit of commitment among the African American and Caucasian teachers who seemed to share devotion for ensuring academic progress of black and Latino students.

Following the Banneker's visit, dad asked which school I preferred. I told him Banneker.

He asked if I preferred to attend a school with girls or one where girls would not be present to distract me. I said I preferred to attend a school with girls. Girls had not distracted me in the past, so I was not really sure about his need to ask that question.

"So you think Banneker is best?" Dad asked.

"Loughlin is nice, but Banneker is best," I responded.

"Then Banneker it is,' he responded.

I was excited and relieved. I had made the decision. It was the first decision I made regarding attending a particular school. At that very moment, it seemed as if I were already walking the halls and sitting in the classrooms and shooting hoops with the team. I was glad there were a lot of pretty girls, but I had no images in my mind of what their presence would mean.

My first year in Banneker did not have much drama. I remember taking a media class that I loved, and it reinforced my desire to study sports broadcasting. I joined the junior varsity basketball team. I was a starter and quickly became the leading scorer and rebounder. Also during my freshman year, dad decided to let me step away from playing clarinet. He wanted me to join a small jazz band in school, but I wasn't interested. I had great ability according to all the music teachers who had taught me, but I wasn't willing to put in the work and practice to improve. With things going my way, everything was cool at home that freshman year.

My sophomore year went very much like my freshman year, except I had one teacher who pissed me off. He really pissed me off. He was old school. He thought he knew everything and everything had to go exactly the way he wanted in class. He had been a friend of my father's when they were in their twenties. Like my father, he also had a doctoral degree, so that made him smart. He was a black man with a doctoral degree who demanded respect and who knew precisely what the black and Latino kids at Banneker needed for future success, according to him.

There was something about Dr. X that struck a chord of defiance in me. Well, for one thing, he was known for not giving any grade higher than an 85, and Banneker had a lot of students with the potential to get an "A" in any class. So I would come to his class with a bagel from Connecticut Muffin on the corner of Myrtle and Clinton Avenues. But there was no eating allowed, so I didn't listen. I thought he should have been thankful that I had arrived on time rather than having stayed outside to eat my toasted cinnamon raison bagel with cream cheese.

When Dr. X spoke, everyone had to listen, except for me since I too was a talker. Of course, friction rose between us. And, guess what, just guess what? My old man didn't like my attitude. Dad showed up for a parent-teacher conference and heard about my behavior. During the conference, dad suggested, "You need to change your behavior or I might have to show up in the middle of your class to correct your behavior." He said he would take a seat and watch me conduct myself properly. He said all that while other parents and kids stood listening nearby.

Even Dr. X must have thought dad was crazy. He responded, "Dr. Davis, I think Askia will settle down, so it isn't necessary for you to come and sit in class."

Whew, I was glad to hear Dr. X say that. Those were some of the most beautiful words that I had ever heard come out of his mouth. Even Dr. X didn't want to be embarrassed by dad's presence in the class.

When we returned to the car, dad repeated the threat.

"But, dad, Dr. X is too strict, and I don't like it. All of the kids say the same thing, but we have to take him because the course is required," I responded.

"Akhenaton, when I was at Columbia University, I had Professor Anderson who had grown up in the South. When he asked all members of the class to give him the names by which they preferred to be acknowledged, I told him 'Askia' when he got around to me.

"With his Southern drawl, he asked in front of the entire class, 'What kind of name is that, and are ya shur you want to be called by that name?' I said, 'Yes.' I remained in that class. I could have transferred, but I wouldn't give him the satisfaction of thinking that I couldn't handle anything that he might send my way.

"Being one of three African Americans in the class, I worked harder than every white, black, and Asian student so that I wouldn't give him an opportunity to mess up my A average. I could have substituted a different class, but his attitude made me want to stay and defeat him. And I did. I proved that no one in that class was smarter than me, including Professor Anderson.

"Professor Anderson had a problem. Some said he drank too much. He would come and start the class and often disappear for more than an hour during that two-hour class. Sometimes he would return a few minutes before the end of class, but many times he failed to return at all. We had to dismiss ourselves. Even though he was not being responsible, I studied and came to class every day on time. There were days he didn't bother to show up. We would give him the standard 15 minutes from the time the class was supposed to start and then leave."

"But, dad, I am not you, and Dr. X pisses everyone off." (Of course, when I look back now, I realize I was exaggerating. But at age 15, an exaggeration seemed truer than the truth.)

"Yeah, you are not me, and Dr. X is not the Columbia professor. Instead, Dr. X is trying to prepare you as a black man for the challenges that lie ahead. He knows you have to be two times better than the best just to get noticed."

With dad's threat of sitting in class recorded in my memory, I toned down my behavior and made it through Dr. X's class. I studied two years of history in one year, taking Dr. X's class and another. I also received an 87, which was a high mark, on the Regents exam. The Regents exam was the indicator for how well a student learned the material in the classes. However, Dr. X gave me a 75 on the report card, 12 points below my Regents grade, when most teachers would have given me a 90 based on the Regents grade. In fact, there was a policy that allowed students to appeal and have their grades raised based on the Regents score. We didn't appeal.

When I brought my report card home, dad took a look and commented. "I see you passed Dr. X's class and scored nicely on the Regents. I also see what you mean about him giving low grades. It's common for teachers to give grades closer to the score on the Regents."

"Dad, Dr. X may be too strict, but I always believed he was a good and smart teacher," I responded.

"Well, you never told me that."

"Yes, I did. I told you he knows his subject and he knows how to teach. That's why all the kids always pass and do well on the Regents. He just needs to chill a bit, but he's cool."

A few months following that conversation, I was starting eleventh grade. I would have a teacher who would make Dr. X seem like a saint. Son, it was time for me to go from the frying pan into the fire.

At the beginning of eleventh grade, I was programmed for Miss Protégé's class and seven others. My guidance counselor had programmed too many classes and no lunch period. At Banneker there was emphasis on getting students to finish almost all the credits required for graduation by the end of their junior year. In late September, dad suggested I drop a class to relieve the pressure of excessive homework. However, I insisted I could handle the load, and he accepted my decision. Of course, I was only familiar with the present and could not accurately predict the future.

The future arrived in October. The future brought with it hours of homework each night and writing papers almost as often. Every night in October 2008 I was up way past midnight with school work. Often, I had to wake up before 6:00 a.m. to complete my assignments. As I mentioned, dad had taken early retirement in January 2008. So on most school days in October, dad was home when I departed for school, and he was home when I arrived from school. His presence was initially a blessing, but would soon at times seem like a curse.

By mid-October, the long hours of schoolwork began to take a toll on my body and my attitude. I became cranky at home. I began having many arguments with mom, the topics of the arguments I really don't remember. They were probably about responsibilities for chores like taking out the garbage, cleaning the bathroom, making my bed, and cleaning my room. I am sure there were arguments about the half-empty bottles of Smart Water and Tropicana OJ, and the bags of half-eaten and spoiled sandwiches that I had left in my room.

I am also sure there were arguments about me not lifting the toilet seat when I would use her bathroom instead of the bathroom dad and I shared. Her bathroom was right outside my bedroom and, therefore, more convenient than the other bathroom which required a walk through the dining area and the master bedroom. When you got to go, you got to go, and every 15- and 16-year-old thinks his preferences are more important than his parents' rules.

Mom had too many rules. She wanted no crumbs left on the counter near the toaster. When she would claim that I left the crumbs, I would tell her that I had not even toasted a bagel. When she would claim I missed the garbage and left food on the floor, I would tell her that I didn't even eat any food. Her response was usually, "Well, I guess 'the ghost' did it." Well, we must have had a ghost in the apartment because I didn't do a lot of messes I was accused of creating.

When I would argue with mom, dad would often intervene. Dad would chastise me for disrespecting mom. I usually "disrespected" her by arguing with her in a sarcastic tone. Dad would insist that I drop the sarcasm. I would insist I wasn't being sarcastic. I would defend my need to argue with her by insisting she was making my life difficult by always bringing up small matters about what I was doing and what I should be doing.

Dad's intervention would generally and temporarily bring a halt to the arguments between mom and me. Sometimes mom would tell dad, "You are not doing enough to make him responsible and to make him respect me."

Dad would ask, "What do you mean? I am the one who is constantly disciplining him and calling upon him to take care of his major responsibilities. I try to pick and choose what I bring to his attention. I can't bring up every concern, because there would never be any peace. Unfortunately, you bring up some things that you should let go of for the moment because there are bigger things to consider. Meanwhile, he's happy because he has succeeded in distracting you from addressing the bigger issues such as making sure he is on top of all that school work he has."

As they would continue their arguments I would sometimes take the opportunity to leave the scene and return to whatever I was doing before mom had interrupted. Sometimes, but not always, I would also stop to clean the crumbs from the countertop, clean the food from the floor near the garbage can, and even throw out the stale food in my room. Of course, that wasn't enough to satisfy her because she would soon find something else to complain about, like the clothes left on the floor of my bedroom.

By mid-October, I was also very involved with my first girl, Charlene. I wanted to have more time with Charlene. I started to attend an after-school community service program and a weekend SAT prep class with her. My time with her meant I had less time for other things, like school work and chores.

When November arrived, an early winter was about to settle into my life at home. November was especially long and rough. Again, as in October, I was up every night long past midnight. Dad was also usually up offering snacks, hot chocolate, and juice, as needed, and guidance regarding any research I was working on. Then, around 5:45 a.m. on most mornings, he was shaking me awake to complete my assignments.

When I would get out of bed at 6:00 a.m., he often had a cup of hot chocolate waiting for me. At times mom would also get up early to help me finish typing a paper before she left for the office while I worked on another assignment. Many times dad had to drive me to school because I could not afford to wait on the bus if I wanted to get to class on time.

At school, Miss Protégé's class started to take its toll. Miss Protégé's had a way of speaking to and dissing the class in a mad condescending manner, something Dr. X had never done. She was mad cocky with a tapped brain and the only teacher in Banneker I knew with that problem. She would refer to us as if we were a bunch of "special education students" when we displayed difficulty in understanding what she was trying to teach.

That pissed off a lot of students, and by November several students had transferred out of her class. Some of her other comments began to feel like direct personal attacks on me and the other students, and she became increasingly unpopular. She said something to my girl about me not being good enough for her. I was pissed and I told dad. He was pissed that she would dare to comment about a student's relationship with another student.

The problem was not me and the other students. Instead, it was the way she taught a lot of complex content in a lecture format. Her lecture was difficult to follow, no matter how hard many students and I tried.

November was also the time the school began to put together the varsity basketball team. Coach Saunders reached out and asked me to join the team. I was undecided. I didn't like the attitude of many of the seniors who would be on the team because they were not into building a productive team spirit. I knew Coach Saunders had a reputation for being demanding. I thought I was prepared to adjust to his demands, but unsure if I wanted to struggle with selfish teammates. I also had the pressure of my academic schedule. It was important to me to keep my average up so that I would have an opportunity to choose the colleges on my top-ten list.

Of course, there was my girl Charlene who had her opinions about what I should do with my time. Playing ball would take time away from her. With her parents' restrictions, we had little time together, and basketball would reduce the little time that we had.

At home, the arguments with mom and dad were also on the rise. Of course, for me they were the cause of all the arguments because they could not understand where I was at that point in my life. They wanted me to do well academically and be responsible with my chores around the house. All I wanted was to be fed, given money, and LTFA/left the f*** alone! Now, is that too much for a teenager to ask? Teenagers cannot all be illogical if we are all asking for the same thing. Why can't our parents see that the request must be necessary and reasonable?

By late November, I had made up my mind. I decided I would concentrate on my studies instead of playing basketball. Coach Saunders was disappointed. Dad was confused. He thought I could do both. Coach Saunders spoke to dad, and dad spoke to me. I explained my decision, and dad was all right with it.

During our discussion, dad said, "Well, you know we have always emphasized academics over basketball. So if you are making this decision because you want to focus on your academics, we are really pleased," dad explained. "Just give your coach the respect he deserves and explain your decision to him face to face. We are with you all the way."

December arrived. Miss Protégé was still out of control and buggin'. I was struggling in her class and in my math class, but I was still putting in the time. There were more late nights and hot chocolate at 6:00 a.m. I was cranky at home because mom and dad just didn't get it, and I wasn't getting enough sleep. The basketball team was playing, and I wasn't even trying to go and see their games. Charlene and I were doing just fine, most of the time.

Up until my junior year, it was common for mom, dad, and me to go together to the movies. Before my junior year, I would even go and see a movie a second time with my parents after seeing it the first time with my friends. I enjoyed our time together and the discussions the movies would stimulate.

However, in the first semester of my junior year, I lost any interest in going to the movies with my parents. I pulled away from my parents. It became increasingly difficult to get me to go to church. I preferred to sleep late on Sundays and get up in the early afternoon. Around the house, I changed from being usually cheerful to being very discontented. I believed my discontent was justified, and I believed that it made me stronger. My discontent meant I was gaining control of my life and defining my present, without being unduly focused on the future dad wanted me to see.

When Christmas rolled around, dad, mom, and I were off to Maui for 10 days. Dad scraped up the money for us to go because he thought it was very important for us to get out of our environment to relax and strengthen our bond as a family after a stressful few months. With careful and thoughtful spending and saving the three previous years, we were able to go on this fantastic vacation. Dad joked that it should last us another three years.

Some people say that Maui is paradise on earth. Maui is Cape Cod plus palm trees that are extra tall, waters that are sparkling blue, and beaches with white sand that stretch on for miles. When you enter the water in Maui, you can clearly see 10 or more feet to the bottom of the ocean, but in Cape Cod you can see to the bottom only in a pool. In Maui, you can even watch fish swim next to and through your outstretched legs, even as mountains in the distance are kissed by clouds.

Every day was sunny and perfectly comfortable in the low to mid-80s. Dad had chosen Maui over the Caribbean because he was confident from the research he had done that the temperature would always be in the 80s. We swam, ate, took a nap under the palms, and swam some more. We toured the huge island by car taking the scenic road to Hana. We drove up to the top of Haleakala ("house of the sun"), a 10,000-foot volcanic mountain, to watch the sunrise. We had to wear heavy sweatshirts and long pants to fight the cold morning air. Then we descended down a winding road passing tourists on bicycles. We left the frosty air at the top and met the tropical air at the base. We left the treeless top only to marvel at the beauty of the tropical trees and other foliage at the base.

Every evening before dusk, we were at beachside to observe the glorious setting of the sun. The sun would seem to bathe us in its orange glow, and we would seem to sink with it below the surface of the distant water. After watching sunsets, we were off to Lahaina, the capital town, with the beautiful catamarans and yachts in its seaport.

In Lahaina, we ate at some great restaurants, and dad and mom usually selected the ones that had menus that included the kinds of foods a teenager would enjoy. Yeah, I was able to get my burgers and fries, steak and fries, and fish and chips. There were times I would eat grilled salmon or tuna. Vegetables for me were tomatoes, carrots, and broccoli, when dad insisted. After dinner, we would casually walk through the scenic town eating the tastiest ice cream cones.

After our walks, we would return to our hotel. I slept in the living room where my PlayStation was hooked up. Some nights while my parents watched movies in their bedroom, I was on Grand Theft Auto: San Andreas and Call of Duty: Black Ops in the living room.

Our room faced the ocean. At night, dad would leave the terrace door open. After I was done with my games, I would fall asleep to the sound of the waves kissing the beach below our windows. That sound carried a special and peaceful melody that made it seem as if anxiety could not exist, as if anxiety were a far distant illusion.

Every morning, dad was up before 6:00 a.m. He would dress and go to the beach. By 2008, dad had become a Bikram Yoga fanatic. So on the beach every morning he would start his yoga routine and move from there into his Northern Shaolin Kung Fu and Tai Chi routines.

Mom and I would rise around 7:00 a.m. most mornings, and I would stand on the terrace and watch part of his routines. He would always have on a West African straw and leather hat, a T-shirt, and light-weight sweat pants. I always thought the hat made him look mad ridiculous, but he thought it made him look like a true warrior. He would always finish his routine kneeling Japanese-style in the ocean doing deep breathing above the water's surface as the morning waves slapped his chest. Mom and I would join him at the beach where we would spend a leisurely day before going up to our room to shower and get ready for the sunset. Mom would work with me to take the sand out of my braids. That was a 20-minute job that involved removing a lot of white sand from among the tens of thousands of strands of kinky hair.

In Maui, we restored the harmony with which we had been accustomed. There were no arguments and no drama. There were no discussions about the challenges we had experienced. As dad would say, "We lived in the moment." And that was refreshing for each of us.

On the last morning of our vacation, an "omen" appeared while dad looked west to face the water just after completing his morning routine. Seeing the "omen," dad hurriedly called mom on her cell and asked her to rush outside and to bring me and the camera. As mom and I hurried through the door of the hotel and approached the beach, we witnessed a scene unlike any we had seen before. As we looked on in awe, we saw a huge rainbow that stretched across the entire horizon and touched the ocean with its northern and southern tips. Mom immediately started snapping pictures, finding it difficult to get both ends of the rainbow in one frame—that's how huge it was. Mom kept saying, "Wow, I have been waiting for one of Hawaii's incomparable rainbows since we've arrived, and here it is. What a magnificent and truly blessed departing gift!"

Several hours later, we were on a United Airlines 15-hour direct flight to New York. When our flight took us over Manhattan, I smiled at the skyscrapers below and looked eastward toward our home in Brooklyn. When we reached the gate of our condo, I announced I was glad to be home after 10 beautiful days in Maui. When I got upstairs, I announced I was glad to be able to sleep in my own bed again. That evening, I slept peacefully even without the melody of the waves sweeping the beach.

The next day I was back at school. I was glad to be back to see my friends and Charlene. When the time arrived for me to attend Miss Protégé's class, I noticed a bit of anxiety creeping up within me starting in my gut. Yet, I went to her class with the glow of Maui still within. It didn't take her long to start casting a shadow on my glow with her condescending statements to the class.

Since it was early January, I had to start preparing for final examinations. At home I found myself back in the past-midnight and early-morning routines. Dad was there again with the hot chocolate and encouragement.

When February 2009 crept in, my schedule was changed, and I was given a lunch period with seven classes. Dad and I thought the homework load would lessen. It didn't. Miss Protégé didn't get any better. Plus I was getting drama from Charlene and the basketball team. Charlene's moody personality presented a challenge.

I was still eligible to play varsity and Coach Saunders reached out again hoping that I would add to the team's potential for success in the playoffs. Certain players wanted me to play and others expressed their concerns to me that I would take away their opportunity to enter the court if I played. The drama became too much.

I spoke with dad and told him I didn't think it would be fair for me to play if it would cause others who had been with the team all year to sit on the bench. I told dad I wouldn't play. He agreed with my decision. However, my decision created more drama as some students, adults, and some team members accused me of being selfish for not using my eligibility to join the team before the playoffs.

In February, going to school became less appealing. I was tired of the drama and the homework. I would complete homework and not bother to turn it in to my teachers, especially Miss Protégé. I started to cut classes and hangout in certain spots in the school. My guidance counselor, Miss Davidson, spoke to dad. Dad would call my teachers and visit the school. Of course, those acts created great friction between us again.

One day in February, dad visited and stood outside Miss Protégé's class. No one in class, including me, was aware that he was outside listening to Miss Protégé's lecture. Later, when I arrived home, dad told me of his presence. He said he was surprised to hear her present the complex material solely in a traditional lecture format. He said he could see the faces of many of the students, and many looked confused. He commented, "When I took that subject in high school, I took it in an honors class. I got an A in class and 97 on the Regents. However, the materials that she presented were more complex than what I studied. With her teaching style, I don't think I could follow her."

"I told you dad. She just keeps talking when it's clear no one understands her. And the school lets her get away with it because most of the kids who stay in her class pass the Regents, and many of those who don't are the ones who leave because they can't tolerate or understand her," I responded.

"Maybe many kids do well because they get tutoring and other support. I am going to look for a good tutor for you," dad replied. "You are going to pass that class since you cannot leave!"

I already had an SAT tutor and a math tutor, and now dad was preparing to find a third tutor. I wasn't pleased with all the time additional tutoring would demand. To meet the demands, I had to arrive home some days immediately after we were let out of school. The demands cut into my time with Charlene, my friends, and basketball across the street at the Dean Street Playground.

The various tutors assisted me in catching up and doing my homework. There were sessions with the math tutor where I would complete three or four overdue assignments. Then I would go to school and not turn them in to my teacher immediately. Mr. Bradhurst was a cool and effective math teacher who had also built a championship debate team at Banneker in his first year there. He was cool, but I wasn't focused enough to turn in my completed homework. WWIT!

By the beginning of March, dad had developed the habit of checking in with Mr. Bradhurst via telephone at the end of every week. Of course, when he heard that I had not turned in my completed assignments, he became very upset. He said he couldn't understand why I wasn't turning in assignments I had completed. However, I vaguely knew why: my thoughts were elsewhere.

With my thoughts being elsewhere, dad and I became locked in even more intense mental battles. To get him off my back, I started to lie, and lying gained serious momentum in my life.

Once, dad caught me in a lie having to do with school. As we sat in the study at home, I told dad, "I am sorry dad. I don't want to lie to you, but I can't help myself. Dad, could you please teach me how to stop lying?"

Dad was very upset about the lie. However, he paused to consider my request. Then, in a calmer voice, he responded. "Lying is a choice that a person makes. If you really want to stop lying, choose to stop."

"But, dad, I really don't know how to stop," I responded, in what I thought was a genuine appeal for assistance. I really wanted to change course but didn't quite know how.

"Yes, you do. Tell yourself, 'The truth is more important.' Then tell the truth," dad responded, in a tone to suggest it should be easy to always tell the truth. At that point it was not despite my best efforts.

In the fall of 2010 while working on this memoir, dad said a better answer touched his spirit. He then realized that the emotions of 2008 had clouded his ability to see a better answer. "I should have said that no one can teach another person how not to lie. However, I can teach you by example how to tell the truth. I can also demonstrate my pleasure when you choose truth over a lie, and I can demonstrate my patience and willingness to help you overcome the results of the wrong choices that a lie would bring."

Nevertheless, with our emotional burdens bearing down on us on that day in February 2008, I was left without a formula that would enable me to stop lying. Dad had given the best answer he could at that moment, but it was not a remedy for what was bothering me.

So the lying and the bad choices continued, and the emotional conflict with dad rose even higher. I wanted dad to just stop, to stop interfering in my life. I had the answers, since I was sure he didn't. I was then a 16-year-old man. I was prepared to live with the consequences of my decisions. I was defiantly confident of my success. I placed a sign on my bedroom door that read, "My success is guaranteed. I am more than you bargained for, and nothing less than real." That sign hangs on my door even now.

Before the end of March, I had broken off the relationship with Charlene. Her mood swings had become a burden I was no longer willing to bear. Our relationship had been a roller coaster ride. It was the kind of ride with a great emotional thrill at the beginning that then left you ready to mentally puke as it continued. Thus, I had to set her free so that I could breathe.

In March 2009, I started travelling with dad to various basketball leagues around town where I competed. According to dad, I had to stay on top of my school work in order to compete. So I did my best to meet with my tutors on time, complete my assignments, and turn in the completed assignments. Even as I did my best, I was still stressed. Miss Protégé was still fronting as a teacher. By mid-April, dad had added another tutor. This one was for Spanish Regents preparation, so tutoring was also a pain. Don't get me wrong, I liked and appreciated the tutors who worked according to my schedule and tutored from the comfort of my home. However, I must have resented all of the academic demands.

I also resented dad. I resented the hot chocolate and the rides to school. I resented his encouragement. I sought desperately to break free. I told him I had teachers and administrators at the school comparing me with him. "Oh, are you Dr. Davis' son? Dr. Davis is so intelligent and has done so much for schools in New York," I reported them saying, with the acidic pitch of sarcasm in my voice.

I told dad I did not want to be compared to him. I also told him I do not want him to compare me to Kakuna, my older sister, who had attended Stuyvesant High School, New York's top high school, and had later attended Rutgers University on an academic scholarship.

"Well, I have never compared you to me or Kakuna. It's hard to believe teachers would compare us when the only way they could know me is by reputation. Anyway, I know you are destined to do greater things than me, so I do not compare you to what I have accomplished," dad responded.

"Trust me dad, they do!" I protested.

After that conversation and by the end of April, dad and I were nearing our train wreck. He would be the little passenger car and I would be the brolic diesel. Toward the end of April, dad was still checking up on my progress with certain teachers. I resented the intrusions, although I must confess I wasn't always doing what was expected of me. I had a required art class that I would cut. I wasn't turning in my assignments that I had completed. When field trips to the Brooklyn Museum were scheduled, I was hooping in the gym with my boys. Dad discovered my actions. He leaned on me, demanding that I get focused.

Then one morning in late April as we neared my school, dad asked me a question about my responsibilities and behavior at school. Neither of us remembers the exact question and neither of us remembers my answer. However, we do remember that my answer was arrogant and defiant. My answer enraged dad and he lost it. He reflexively smacked me hard on my shoulder just as our car reached the perimeter of the school.

WTF! I quickly looked to my right to see if any kids had seen the insult. No one appeared to notice. I then turned to my left, stared at dad, and unleashed my anger.

"I can no longer respect you! I don't care about anything you say to me in the future! I can no longer respect you. Now I want to see what all those teachers who respect you say when they learn you have hit me." After completing my protest, I quickly exited the car. The old man was trying to say something, but I wasn't listening. I wanted to remain in a state of defiance.

When I returned home that evening, dad apologized for his action. He explained it as an unacceptable emotional response without clear thinking. I told him I could not accept his apology.

Looking back now, I see that I was angrier about the intrusions in my life and the demands. The response I wanted was an end to the intrusions and demands. I wanted to make my own decisions about school and responsibilities.

Later that evening, dad and I were off to one of my basketball competitions. Mom was in the audience with the video camera. She caught images of me skying and dunking and dad jumping up shouting, "Be a beast!" On the way home, I got an opportunity to glance at the images on the screen of the video camera. The smack was forgotten. We were laughing and celebrating another win for the Boys Club team.

Oh, yeah, we were also celebrating me being a brolic beast.

Chapter 35

The Beat Down

Of course, all celebrations have to come to an end. So the morning following the Boys Club win, I was back to school, back to responsibilities and demands.

After two more weeks passed, I was ready to explode. With the pressure building, one afternoon in early May 2009 I found myself in the study working on an assignment for Miss Protégé. As I worked on the assignment, scenes from her classroom rolled across my brain. It seemed as if every word I would write would initiate a new unpleasant scene in that classroom. I was drowning in the images! I saw her smirk, and I heard her diss me and the other students. I watched her cheeks puff up with arrogance as she fronted as if she could teach. She was eyeballing me! I saw her evil eyes that claimed they could see into our brains. I felt my heartbeat increase as if I were back in class, back in her miserable presence. I wanted to spit at her disgusting image in my mind.

Soon I began to deeply question the need to complete her assignments. I asked myself, "WTF!? Why should I complete the assignments of a woman who does not know how to teach and respect kids?" I answered with the answer I was sure my father would give: "You need to pass her class because the course is required for graduation." Upon hearing dad's mad annoying answer in my head, my resentment for dad rose. He and she were the same problem, I thought. The two of them were obstacles who stood in my way, demanding attention to academic work that I would never use in real life.

With that thought I stood up. I left the study and walked toward the living room where dad was sitting working with his MacBook. I was prepared to do what every 16-year-old has wanted to do: end the tyranny of his teachers and parents. Ask any teenager; they will tell you it is what we all wish for.

Looking up from the computer dad asked, "Where are you going? You know you have to finish your assignments before we leave for your game tonight."

"I am not doing any assignments, and I am going to my game tonight!"

"Not if you do not do your assignments."

"Oh, yes, I am! I am sick of the assignments, and I am sick of you telling me what I must do!"

"Well, as long as you live in this house, you have to take care of your responsibilities."

I paused for a moment as I felt my rushing heartbeat and heard my quickening breath as I looked down at him. I could feel the blood rush up to my head.

"You don't tell me what my responsibilities are!" I exclaimed as I moved closer to him. "I am sick of Miss Protégé and you, dad. You make me sick to my stomach! I could just, I could just…"

"You could just what?" dad asked as he rose from the couch.

"I could just knock you out of this world!"

"Boy, you need to go back in there and do your work."

"And if I don't? The days of you telling me what to do are over! I said over!"

Within seconds we were chest to chest, breath to breath, and racing heartbeat to racing heartbeat. Dad was 6 feet and 175 pounds and well conditioned. I should have been concerned because when I was 8 I had seen the power of dad's punches. We had been on Park Place during the West Indian Carnival. Dad was talking to this senior citizen, Miss Kee. These four guys in their twenties approached. One decided he could not hold it any longer, and he took it out and peed in her yard right in front of us.

Miss Kee started to protest, but dad told her to forget it. She didn't listen, and dad asked her again to forget it. She kept protesting. Her protest angered the guy. He said, "I'll smack you, old lady," as he raised his right hand. Dad stepped between them. The guy threw a punch, which dad blocked. Then dad stepped into a bow and arrow stance and delivered a solar punch that lifted the guy off his feet as if he were a rag doll. I had only seen that done in Kung Fu movies when they are using stunts and ropes to pull the guy into the air.

Within a split second, dad was surrounded by the other three guys. Seeing the fight in dad, one guy tried to calm things down as mom called 911. They started to talk, and while they were talking, the guy dad had punched picked up a broom stick nearby. He sneaked up as they talked and hit dad near his right eye with the stick. Dad grabbed the stick and chased all four guys. As he chased them, the cops arrived. They were already patrolling on the block due to the millions who attend the parade. They grabbed dad and the four guys. They put dad in handcuffs because they thought he was the aggressor since he was chasing the guys. Mom and Miss Kee protested and explained the situation. They took off his handcuffs.

At the station, the cops appealed to dad to press charges. Dad thought the whole situation was unfortunate and said no. Before running the guys' names through the computer, two African American cops explained that the same four guys had committed other felonies in the past and suggested dad should not leave without pressing charges. Dad did not believe them and was unwilling to press charges. Dad was more focused on his own embarrassment to have been fighting in the streets and his disappointment that Miss Kee had not listened to his advice.

As dad continued to sit without accepting their request, they tried to hold the four guys. They ran their names through the computer. Nothing came up. Dad was happy with that because he knew the cops would have to set the four young brothers free. He felt that the guy who hit him had made a bad judgment to impress his friends by showing he would not tolerate anyone dissing him. Dad did not want to see four more African American males caught up in the system for the stupidity of one. Dad left the precinct relieved and went to St. Mary's hospital for sutures to close the wound under his eye.

As dad and I continued to square off for our battle, I was thinking that no matter how well conditioned he was, in my eyes he was an old man. Sure, he knew Kung Fu, but I was prepared to show him the better man. I was 6 feet 4 inches and 195 pounds.

Today, neither of us can remember who sent the first blow. I remember blocking a right palm hand to my chest. He remembers a solid right above his heart. The battle was on.

I had several advantages in the battle. I was bigger, younger, and stronger. He was the old man Sonny Liston, and I was the young Muhammad Ali. I had rehearsed kicking a** in Tekken and so many video games while playing on my Xbox and PlayStation. I knew the kicks and punches that would crush his puny body and crush his useless pride. I took out a front tooth with a punch. I sent a Mixed Martial Arts right side kick to his left leg and followed with a left straight kick to his groin. As he crouched from the blow to his groin, I jumped and sent a knee to his left eye. He was on the floor screaming to express the pain, and I put him into a choke hold until he was close to losing consciousness. I rose, spat in his face, and walked out the door for an early arrival at the site of my game. I was free! Free at last!

When Muhammad Ali was in the prime of his career and unbeatable, he told Ernie Terrell, another No. 1 contender for his title, "If you ever dare to dream you beat me, you better wake up, call me, and apologize."

Well, the next day I wanted to apologize to dad for the dream I had, but I couldn't. You see, most of the description of the fight above is actually from a real dream I had the evening following our confrontation. That dream was prompted by the real confrontation dad and I had that May afternoon. When I told dad, "The days of you telling me what to do are over," I pushed him with a strong force. The force rocked him. I remember waiting for his response so that I could knock him out. I remember the look of disbelief in his eyes. I remember him returning at some point and sitting on the couch. That is as much as I remember today in terms of the actual physical altercation.

It is strange that dad says he remembers no more than that. He doesn't remember responding physically. He doesn't remember pushing me or striking me. He only remembers a fierce look of determination in my eyes. We both know more than what we remember actually happened, but somehow we have chosen to stay in memory's fog rather than expose memory to sunlight.

Even as this memoir was being written nearly two years later, we have never gotten around to fully discussing the incident and its impact on our relationship. I think for both of us it's hard to think about, so we have decided to let it be.

Everyone says they want answers. Really? Everyone says they want to know the full truth. Huh.

Yet, everyone finds in their lives there are times when they just can't handle looking at the full truth.

TITT/That is the truth!

Chapter 36

Hoop There It Is!

To dunk or not to dunk? That is never the question for a man who is able. From the first time a boy picks up a basketball, and even before he has the muscles to shoot it to the rim, he has a desire to dunk the ball. Today, when a 3-year-old sees JaVale, Dwight, DWade, Blake, and DRose going up for a spectacular dunk, he immediately dreams of being able to one day do the same.

When I was 3, everybody wanted to be like Mike. Dad had purchased a toy Fisher-Price basketball hoop for me. It had a plastic yellow stand, a yellow pole, and a white backboard. The height was adjustable. I would have dad raise it high at about 6 feet when I would stand in our backyard at a distance and shoot. When I wanted to be like Mike and dunk, I would have dad lower it.

In 1998, at age 5, dad took me to the Garden where we had the special thrill of seeing Mike dunk on Ewing and the Knicks. Of course, we were Knick fans but, like thousands of other Knick fans, we had come to the garden that evening to see Jordan at his best.

Michael Jordan was such a graceful and fantastic leaper Chicago ultimately built a statue in his honor. Before then, Nike had already created the Jumpman Logo representing Jordan in flight. That logo became one of the most recognizable logos in the world and is still making money for Jordan and Nike today.

In 2002, Bow Wow starred in the movie "Like Mike," and dad, mom, and I were in seats at the UA Court Street Stadium 12 enjoying the performance. Bow Wow plays Calvin, the main character. Calvin lives in an orphanage managed by some shady people who force the orphanage kids to sell cheap chocolates at expensive prices outside the LA professional basketball arena.

One day, Calvin meets the owner of the LA Knights while trying to sell him some expensive candy. The owner is impressed with Calvin's knowledge of basketball plays, statistics, and the players. He invites Calvin to a game where, during half time, Calvin is invited to go one on one with Tracy Reynolds (played by Morris Chestnut), one of the players on the LA Knights.

Calvin is surprised when the sneakers he had purchased from the Salvation Army Thrift Shop give him super jumping abilities. The sneakers have the initials MJ written on them to suggest the possibility that they had belonged to the young Jordan. With the sneakers, he does some fantastic dunks and defeats Tracy.

Thus, at the age of 14, Calvin is allowed into the NBA. With superior jumping abilities, produced by the sneakers, he dunks on David Robinson in a game against the Spurs. He later leads the team to defeat Gary Payton and the Seattle Supersonics. He even wins the Slam Dunk Contest and becomes the main topic of sports broadcasters. However, when he goes up against the Toronto Raptors, his sneakers are ruined in a pile-on and his magic fades, but his team manages to win anyway.

As we prepared this memoir, dad said that movie was a real fairy tale. "That movie was a 100-minute commercial for Nike," he suggested. He reported that soon after that movie I asked for my first pair of Air Jordans. He was reluctant to buy the sneakers. He did not want to "contribute to the practice of buying overpriced sneakers produced by workers in Vietnam who put in 12-hour days and are not paid enough to buy a decent dinner or have pure drinking water for their families."

Dad further said, "The Vietnamese worker gets paid a few hundred dollars a year so Nike can earn billions and pay athletes and coaches many millions, earned from sneakers bought by many American families who are just getting by making a few thousand."

I actually got my first pair of expensive sneakers a month after first seeing the movie from Uncle Nick when my mom and I were visiting family in Florida. Without asking my mom first thinking it was no big deal, Uncle Nick bought me a pair of Jordans while we were at the mall. After all, what are uncles for?

At 10 years old, like all American kids who wore Nikes, I wasn't concerned about the workers in Vietnam. I am glad dad did not tell me his thinking at that time. I probably would have said, "I ain't trying to hear that."

My first pair of Jordans cost $139, but I wasn't the only one of my peers trying to be like Mike. Even NBA stars wanted so much to be like Mike they appeared in the movie. Other NBA stars who appeared included Allen Iverson,

Jason Kidd, Chris Webber, Tracy McGrady, Dirk Nowitski, Steve Nash, Alonzo Mourning, and Jason Richardson. They were willing to allow themselves to be posterized by a 14-year-old boy wearing sneakers that Jordan may have worn as a boy.

With my new sneakers, I wasn't ready to dunk, but I was ready to try. Around the age of 12, I joined my first out of school competitive team under Coach Cynthia Hall. She's a lawyer who played college basketball. She taught me discipline and helped me develop the drive to improve my skills. By the time I reached age 13, after having purchased other Nike sneakers, I could smell the rim when I went up and came just a little short. Finally, after many attempts, a few months after turning 13, I went up wearing my Melos and put the ball through the hoop at the Dean Street playground. (Dad had finally relented, yet he insisted on buying them on discount on Eastbay.) I had arrived at my destination. I attempted the dunk again, and I succeeded again. Then I was ready to take on the world.

That evening when I saw dad, I told him of my success. The next day, he came to see me in action. I succeeded again with a basic two-hand dunk. Immediately, my mind began to imagine various other kinds of dunks my body could learn to do.

In the spring of 2006, the Dean Street Playground was not in the best of shape. It looked like one of the many playgrounds forgotten by the Parks Department in many neighborhoods around the city. The nets were tattered. There were 10 baskets. One of the baskets was lowered at eight and a half feet. Many of the kids first learned to dunk there. At age 10, I was dunking there also. Two of the baskets were crooked. The floors on the five courts were all concrete. In some places the concrete was cracked and grass grew between the cracks.

After school, the two main courts were usually full of black and Puerto Rican kids playing ball. Some days, older guys would come to play, and the young teens would play on teams mixed with young adults including some of the young adult whites who had recently moved into the community.

Almost every day after school I would spend an hour or two playing. I had a lot of fun and was able to run with the guys who were serious about their game. Although I would talk smack at home into the television, I preferred to allow my game to talk smack on the court. However, when I would dunk in games, the older kids would talk smack to the older players who I had posterized. "Man, you let that kid posterize you. Ha, ha," was one of the common remarks they would make. In response, the older guys would use their weight to try to keep me from going up, but I would often find my way up anyway. I became a favorite player chosen when teams were being selected.

Dad and mom were cool with me playing at Dean Street. The guys were serious and not into a lot of negative conflicts on the court. There wasn't a lot of cursing, and any threat of a physical confrontation between players was extremely rare. The guys loved the game and were into playing the game.

When dad would come and watch, he was pleased to only rarely hear the N-word and to never witness a fight. Dad would pass through many days on his way to or from Bikram Yoga Park Slope. Dad said the older men who played on Sunday mornings could learn a lot from the kids who played after school. He said the guys on Sunday morning would curse, fuss, and talk louder than their play. Dad only had two complaints regarding my play. He would become upset that I would often leave my ball and sometimes not have it returned. He would also become upset when he would see me shirtless or not clothed warmly enough for the weather.

In 2006, Prospect Heights was going through an intense period of gentrification. By 2008, the Dean Street Playground was in the process of renovation. The largest area containing six basketball courts was renovated and covered with artificial turf for baseball, soccer, and touch football. Nike renovated the two remaining basketball courts with new baskets, boards and courts made of materials less damaging than concrete.

Following the renovations, middle-class and upper-middle-class families and crowds from Park Slope and the surrounding communities began coming to make use of the turf. The Parks Department began to pay greater attention to cleanup and maintenance. Dean Street Playground quickly became one of the city's most attractive public parks.

In September 2006, I entered Benjamin Banneker Academy. I tried out for junior varsity. I made junior varsity and became the star power forward. I continued playing junior varsity in my sophomore year even though I was invited to play varsity. I loved the spirit of my junior varsity coach and my teammates. I finished the year averaging 18 points and 15 rebounds. My team made the playoffs and was defeated in the third round.

In my junior year, I received a great deal of pressure from Coach Saunders to join the varsity team. However, I was feeling the pressure of keeping my academic average above a B while taking eight classes with no lunch break. I was also interested in spending more time with Charlene, my first girl friend. Dad encouraged me to play. However, I did not join the team.

As the playoffs approached in the spring, Coach Saunders continued to ask that I join before the time limit for eligibility would pass. Some of the players asked me not to join because they were concerned I would take their spot, while others encouraged me because they believed the Banneker Warriors would be much more competitive in the Public Schools Athletic League playoffs if I were playing. I chose not to join. At the end of the season, the Warriors were defeated by Westinghouse for the third consecutive year and eliminated from the playoffs.

Beginning in March 2009, following the playoffs, I joined three teams belonging to different city leagues. The first team was the Police Athletic League team of Lower Manhattan. The team coach was Louie, a short *Borinqueño/* Puerto Rican who had love for the game. Coach Louie worked hard and managed to assemble a very strong team that included me as the 6-foot-3-inch center/power forward.

With Andrew as point guard and Xavier as shooting guard, we were ready to face all challengers. Andrew was unusual as a high school point guard because he really preferred to drive and dish for assists versus hogging the ball and shooting. Xavier had great shooting and handling skills and could play point as well. They got me the ball down low often, and I was a "beast."

Yeah, "Be a beast!" are the words dad often shouted from the stands when I would posterize someone with a dunk or vicious block. When I would make an incredible block, his shouted words to the opposing players were often, "Take that whack back to your neighborhood!"

We went undefeated in the league, and I averaged a double-double, with 25-plus points and 20 rebounds. My efforts eased my anxiety regarding not having played for my high school varsity team my junior year.

In April, Louie informed Coach Will Curry of the Boys Club that I could be available to join his team for the New York City Housing Authority League. Coach Curry called dad, and dad gave his consent. Thus, twice a week, dad drove me to Manhattan for practice at the Boys Club in the East Village. Coach Curry and Coach Amar had more experience than Coach Louie, and our practices were intense and focused on game strategy and plays. The competition was much stiffer than what we had encountered in the league with Coach Louie.

With the Boys Club, I began to really discover my potential. I started as center/power forward and averaged a double-double. I won the MVP trophy for the Manhattan Championship after averaging more than 20 points and 20 rebounds. I was also the defensive star. As usual, dad got me to every game.

That was important because there were times when other key players would be absent.

Given my success with the Boys Club, dad placed me with the National Collegiate Scouting Association (NCSA) so that I would begin to get exposure with college coaches. NCSA created, posted, and made available to coaches a three-minute video which highlighted my abilities. Soon I began receiving comments and questions from college coaches. Several expressed interest in learning more about me and some suggested I consider applying for their teams.

When the summer of 2009 arrived, I continued to play for the Boys Club. We played in several leagues. I was also being asked to play for other clubs, but I stuck with the Boys Club because dad and I trusted Coach Curry.

However, the Boys Club had a problem because we would arrive at some games with one or more of our key players missing. I was always present, and dad was always there as well. With key players missing, we lost playoff games. Some probably had legitimate reasons, such as jobs and family matters, and others were probably just being negligent.

In a game near Lincoln Center, more than half the players were missing including three of the starters. Worse yet, an assistant coach wasn't there as planned to replace Coach Curry who was out of town.

With the time for a forfeit approaching, dad decided to step in to coach because we needed the win to advance to the championship game. Dad had no coaching experience, but he had good relationships with the guys on the team. He was the parent who would buy dinner before dropping some of them home. He was the parent who would buy water and bananas for me and other members. He was the parent who would talk to and encourage all the players, not just me.

With the game about to begin, there were just 4 of us versus 10 on the other team. We had defeated that team in an earlier game up in Harlem when one of its star players and one of ours were absent. I could see in their coach's eyes the look of anticipated joy that we would have to forfeit the game. However, five minutes before the time we would have had to forfeit, a fifth player arrived. We quickly huddled around dad, and he gave us his game plan.

Dad could have used a plan to set plays and defense. His plan was to have us play hard and avoid fouls because no one could afford to foul out. He told us we knew each other's strengths and weaknesses and that we should go with our strengths.

In the first half of the game, they "whupped" us good. The score was 31-18. At the beginning of the second half, they continued to pour it on. Dad called time out with them leading by 18 and asked us to play better defense. I began to block more shots, and little Julio, "*el Puertoriqueño*," began to steal, drive, and dish to me. Our guys began to hit outside shots. At the end of regulation, the score was tied at 58.

With the five-minute overtime about to begin, we gathered around dad for more instructions. We felt we were on the course to victory. We knew they doubted they could defeat us. At the end of overtime, the score was 72-70, 72 for them and 70 for us. Dad took some of us to Checkers and then home. That was my last game with the Boys Club. It was not a Hollywood ending, but dad says life rarely ends the way Hollywood paints the picture. He says we have to find the beauty and meaning in the picture that Hollywood doesn't paint. I am still trying to fully appreciate what he means by that.

There are some important lessons I learned with the Boys Club. I learned the importance of discipline and being reliable. I learned you cannot win if you don't show up, and showing up presents the possibility of winning. (Dad says he is still trying to teach me the importance of showing up in other aspects of life including consistent, on time class attendance.) I learned you can grow in confidence even in defeat. I learned the importance of practice and teamwork. I learned encouragement could be a two-edged sword, both good and bad.

When I began playing for the Boys Club, dad always had comments about what I should and should not do. He wanted to encourage me. However, I succeeded in convincing him it was most often best to hold his comments and just let me play. I told him I had a coach and that some of the things he suggested were opposite of what the coach wanted.

For example, Coach Curry might ask me to begin offense near the top of the key when dad wanted me to begin below the foul line. What dad wouldn't realize is our guards could not be as effective in some games getting the ball to me in the post because of the defense used by other teams. Coach Curry would expect for me to get the ball, turn, and move toward the basket on men that I could maneuver around and jump over for the shot. At other times Coach Curry would want me to toss the ball back out, set a pick, and roll toward the basket.

Dad also learned to hold his tongue from watching the behavior of other parents who would counsel their sons, often in direct defiance of the coach's desires. For example, we had a parent who would tell his son not to pass to an open man but to go to the basket to "get your points." The same father would scream loudly whenever his son missed an open outside shot. His son would become so nervous and embarrassed that he would often miss. Then the father would scream out that his son needs to be benched. When the coach would sit his son down, the father would make loud comments about other kids, at times asking, "Why did he sit my son down instead of that kid?"

Meanwhile, all of the players on the bench and court could hear the parent. To tone things down, dad would shout encouragement to that father's son. My father would suggest we needed his son and persuaded his son to keep his head in the game.

Dad said my teammate's father loved and was devoted to his son. He suggested the father wanted what was best for his son but was at times missing the concept of teamwork and making his son too nervous by the constant focus on his individual play.

I agreed with dad's analysis. The only time his son played well was during games when his father was absent. Then you could see the beauty of his outside shot and his rising confidence.

After the defeat up near Lincoln Center, dad received another request for me to join the NY Knights, an Amateur Athletic Union (AAU) team, under Coach Terrence Felder. There was just one problem—I would have only one opportunity to practice with the team before leaving for the AAU tournament in Orlando, Florida.

Once again, dad dutifully drove me one Thursday night in July 2009 to Haverstraw, NY, a round-trip distance of 90 miles. That night I met most of the guys who would travel to Orlando. Xavier was a member, and he had been the person who had recommended me to Coach Felder. Dad was immediately impressed with Coach Felder. Coach Felder was a retired African American police detective who had experience playing and coaching. Coach Felder was also financing the team primarily through his own resources and a small fee collected from parents to help with the cost of travel and lodging.

Since I was supposedly attending summer school classes for math, I wasn't able to travel to Orlando by van with most of the team members. Instead, dad got me airline tickets for a JetBlue round-trip flight.

Orlando was a wonderful experience. We played at Disney's Wide World of Sports. The Wide World of Sports Campus is 220 acres big. The Milk House, where the games were held, was incredibly large and beautiful. There were at least eight basketball games going on at once.

My new team, the Knights, had a lot of talent, but we would go up against some teams whose members had been playing together for three or more years while most of our members had been together less than three months. So our players did not have a strong knowledge of each other's strengths and preferences, and we had a limited number of offensive and defensive sets we could run. To add to our challenges, our two starting guards failed to appear. I was switched from starting power forward to shooting guard. Our center was 6 feet 6 inches. He had a lot of potential but not an equivalent amount of discipline, especially the discipline and desire necessary to play defense.

Nevertheless, we suited up and played hard. We won a few and lost a few. Although I played out of position, Coach Felder told dad I played well. He suggested that he wanted me to return the following year. Dad agreed to have me play with the Knights the following season believing we would have an opportunity to assemble a team whose members would have more experience playing together.

During the following season in April 2010, Coach Felder called the team together. Dad drove me the 90 miles round trip every Thursday night to Haverstraw. Nate, our center, had grown to 6 feet 7 inches, but he weighed maybe 185 pounds. He could jump, but I told him, "Son, you need to lift in order to build upper strength to hold onto rebounds." Nate was a great guy who preferred kidding around instead of practicing hard. He had a nice outside shot which he preferred rather than going to the basket unless he was on a fast break.

However, we had Big Will as a new prospect who would become our starting center with Nate coming off the bench. Big Will was 6 feet 7 inches and 230 pounds with legs like a tree trunk. He was strong and disciplined, but needed a bit more polishing to stay on the floor out of foul trouble.

Our guards AJ, Malcolm, and Sheldon seemed ready to contribute. AJ was 5 feet 7 inches and quick. Malcolm and Sheldon were both about 6 feet with good handles and outside shots. Michael, the coach's son, was a substitute guard. He had a great outside shot.

Mike, our small forward, was ready to be a fearless spark off the bench. He was 6 feet 1 inch with a good handle and a great bounce. He was a good passer as well. Maurice was the other forward. He resembled Evan Turner. His strength was his outside shot. (Maurice joined the squad at Providence College in 2011.) Xavier, my friend from the Police Athletic League, was expected to be the starting small forward, but he went off to play for another team, and that represented an important loss for our team.

At the beginning of the season everyone seemed serious, and we anticipated we would be able to do some real damage in the run-up to the AAU Championship at Wide World of Sports. I was selected team captain. Our first major test came at the Hooperstown Classic in Mount Vernon, New York, where we competed against regional AAU teams mostly from the suburbs of New York City. All of our players attended the weekend tournament. The competition was stiff, but we won all of our games and the championship. I played great defense and averaged more than 20 points and 15 rebounds. I was the leading scorer and rebounder of the tournament.

After Hooperstown, certain members of our team became unreliable. Most would skip practice although all of them lived within a few miles of the practice facility. However, dad made sure we made every practice by driving the 90 miles round trip every scheduled Thursday night. When guys began to miss games, the coach and everyone became concerned.

One Sunday, we played a game in Manhattan with just five of our 12 team members present. I was one of only two starters there. I was accustomed to playing the entire game, but none of the other four players had that experience. We played a great game and should have won. However, three open layups in the final two minutes were missed by a fatigued player. We lost by one point and walked away very disappointed.

To dad's credit, he continued to take me to practice and the games even though there were times when several key members would not show up at all and others would show up for the later games, after we had struggled without them in the morning games. Dad always kept a positive attitude, and I was enjoying his support. For every game, he would bring bananas, water, and donuts to keep everyone energized. My teammates appreciated his presence and listened to his encouragement.

During one tournament, Malcolm, our best point guard, cursed the coach and seemed prepared to fight because he didn't like the coach's instructions. His actions were out of character and unanticipated because he had a long-standing and positive relationship with Coach Felder who had done so much to help him with life's challenges the past few years. Malcolm had refused to run a play as instructed and had resisted when the coach called him to the bench. The coach dismissed him from the team because, as a role model, Coach Felder never cursed any of us. He preferred to teach and encourage. Later, dad stepped in as a mediator and was able to get the coach and Malcolm back together so that we would not lose his floor leadership.

At the regional AAU tournament at SUNY Westbury in June, we again started with absent members during the Saturday games. One of our best outside shooters showed up late without his jersey with seven minutes left in an important game. Despite the challenges, we played well and won enough games to qualify for the AAU Division I Tournament in Orlando. I played well and had many highlights which mom recorded and then put into a promotional video. An assistant coach from a Division II university came to observe me. The head coach had spoken with dad and had indicated I should attend, but he didn't have scholarships available for 2010. Dad said it made no sense for him to pay $40,000 to send me to the university where I would not receive a scholarship the first year and would not be guaranteed one later.

At the AAU Championships in Orlando, we were again without all of our starters. We went up against teams that had been polished over the years. In our bracket, we won two and lost two and did not make it to the next level. However, it was a great experience for dad and me. I had developed strong friendships with great teammates. From observing and listening to Coach Felder, I had learned a great deal about my abilities and the things a team required to be a winner on the court. I plan to use his teachings one day as a coach for a high school team.

Concerning the formula for winning, we had the necessary talented and devoted coach. Coach Felder had good plays for offense and defense. He would spend a great deal of his time, money, and blood pressure providing guidance to some teammates who were what some people would call "knuckleheads." He would call to wake members up. He would buy them lunch when they had no money. He would pick them up and bring them to games. He would drop them home. He would call their parents to get them out of jams so that they would have an opportunity to play. He was honest and fair with everyone. He showed no favoritism toward his own son who would often be left out of very competitive games. He would stick with the members despite the grief they would cause. He was a wonderful role model and an exceptional and compassionate teacher.

Dad said Coach Felder did all of it for a higher purpose. Dad declared Coach Felder knew that guys like Nate and Malcolm were worthy of having adults who would continue to support their development as responsible young men even when they weren't acting responsibly. Dad suggested Coach Felder's attitude and coaching skills made it easier for dad to drive me the 90 miles round trip to avoid letting the coach down.

We also possessed another ingredient for a winning formula—many individually talented members. However, we were just a group of talented individuals who never had enough time together to truly become a complete team. We were from many different schools and cities in the New York City metropolitan area. We had to face teams from smaller cities whose members were talented and had known each other and played together since elementary school. Like the USA Olympic Basketball Team of 2004, we learned that talented teams will beat a group of individual players who might be more talented but had not developed as a team.

Of course, there were many parts of a winning formula we did not possess. We had members who were at times undisciplined and unreliable. We had members who ignored the instructions of the coach. We had members who did not give much thought to doing the hard work necessary to take their skills to the next level. Yet every single teammate was a great individual and a wonderful friend.

Although the Knights failed to come together as a team, I was confident in my senior year that the Banneker Warriors would emerge as a team. In November 2009, tryouts for the Warriors' upcoming season began. I had skipped the previous season but was ready to play. My best friend Samori Wright had returned from attending a prep school in Atlanta. Samori and I made the team. I was selected as the starting power forward at 6 feet 4 inches, and Samori would be the backup center at 6 feet 7 inches. Omari Bennett, also at 6 feet 7 inches, was our designated starting center. Mathew Walker, 5 feet 10 inches, was selected as the starting point guard, and Andrew Batts at 6 feet 2 inches was the shooting guard. Maurice Colson at 6 feet 2 inches was selected small forward.

Just before the season began, the New York City newspapers began to take notice of our team and its prospects for the upcoming season. In a November 2009 article in the *New York Post*, a sports writer suggested Banneker would have a good season with Samori, Maurice, Omari, and me supplying the size Banneker had been without in previous seasons. The writer wrote that I was "at the top of the list" of Banneker's talented big men and that I was "blessed with guard skills."

I believed what the author wrote, and I was determined to live up to the expectations my coach and team members had of me. I began spending most of my free time at school in the gym. As a senior, I had only four classes so I had considerable time for the gym. Soon I was forgetting to leave the gym to attend certain classes. After all, I was a senior, and I felt I knew what was and was not important.

Of course, dad was lurking ready to make sure I was handling my business. When he found out I was missing certain classes, he came and spoke to Mr. Fernandez, the gym teacher, who agreed to monitor my schedule and put me out of the gym. Though I would leave the gym, the senioritis fever that was developing was not leaving me. But that is a story for the next chapter.

After several early season wins, we were on a roll. Our first big test came ın exhibition tournament and nonleague game against Bedford Academy ᴅuring a Christmas break tournament at St. Francis College. Bedford Academy and Westinghouse High School were rated at the top of the league. The scouts and writers expected Bedford Academy would easily defeat us. I was dealing with the flu when the game began. During the game, I could barely hold my arms up. The music that usually flowed through my head was missing.

Despite the flu, I played the whole game and performed well with defense and rebounds. I scored 10 points, well below my average of 18 points. Matt and Samori were the stars of that game. Matt killed them with penetration and shooting more than 20 points. Samori killed them coming off the bench with rebounds and defense. We defeated Bedford Academy and that game gave us added confidence that we were well prepared for the rest of the season.

During the Bedford Academy game, Coach Saunders was out of town. He had not been there to see us at one of our finest hours. He had not been there to see the fire Samori brought off the bench that made a big contribution in our win. That was unfortunate because Coach Saunders and Samori soon found themselves in conflict.

Within three weeks of the victory over Bedford Academy, Samori quit the team. Dad was shocked and disappointed when he arrived at one of our home games in mid-January to discover Samori in street clothes. He tried to talk Samori into attempting to return, but Samori wasn't trying to hear that. Dad had watched Samori at the game against Bedford Academy and felt we would be more powerful with him. Dad said Coach Saunders was the demanding type, and Samori was the sensitive type who allowed the coach's demands and comments to get under his skin. Despite Samori's absence, we won that game and continued to win others that kept us at the top of our division.

In New York, sometimes winning can create a problem for a team. There were at least two games when winning brought intimidation and threats from the losing teams and their fans. When we defeated Erasmus Hall at Erasmus Hall, we had to stay together afterwards and be escorted out of the neighborhood to avoid confrontations with enraged fans. At Grand Street High School we had to run down the streets to the subway for our safety from fans, including adults who were angry at losing. During those games, I played well with the music flowing through my head. However, the music had quickly left when I found myself running from a mob.

Dad had attended the Erasmus game, and he told me the experience reminded him of his time at John Jay High School. He said many John Jay fans would not attend football games against Boys High School because they feared being beaten if John Jay would win. He said he and others would leave the games at the beginning of the fourth quarter when John Jay was fortunate enough to be winning. Even then, he said at times they would need to run from guys waiting outside for any John Jay students who might try to sneak out.

As the playoffs approached, we were at the top of our division at 11-3 and were seeded No. 9 among 36 teams for the playoffs citywide. Our nemesis, Westinghouse, was seeded No. 1 and picked by all to emerge as champion. Westinghouse had defeated us twice that season.

By the beginning of the playoffs, we had become a real team, a real band of brothers. Surely we weren't perfect, but we had learned to be more focused on teamwork and less on our individual preferences. Coach Saunders was relying on Matt to provide point guard leadership, distributing the ball at the right time. Matt had come a long way from an earlier encounter when he had confronted Coach Saunders with some nasty words and left the team in the middle of a game because he was unwilling to accept the coach's criticism of his playing. Thankfully, during the encounter Coach Saunders had kept his cool even though it had happened inside the gym at Banneker in front of students and adults. We needed Matt if we were going to have any chance of advancing in the playoffs.

During the first three rounds, we smacked our opponents. Our toughest game of the three rounds came against Brooklyn Collegiate at their home court. Brooklyn Collegiate was seeded higher and picked by some critics to make the final four. A large crowd of Brooklyn Collegiate fans turned out to make some noise. Even the band was present as if it were a college game. The school's principal walked the sidelines revving up the crowd. She questioned the referees when some calls didn't go their way.

When the game started, Collegiate was off and running. The crowd's noise was intense. Dad was in the midst of the small Banneker crowd trying to get it to make some noise. Mom, as usual, was at courtside recording the game since Dad tended to record the ceiling lights, the gym floor, or someone's shoes in his excitement watching the game. Toward the end of the first half, dad was leading the cheers of the Banneker contingent as we began to close the gap. At the beginning of the second half, we caught up with intense defense. We started to press and disrupt the passing lanes. When there were turnovers, I was often breaking for a pass from Matt to end up with a dunk at the other end. Collegiate's center was 6 feet 7 inches, and my dunks were designed to take his heart out. I had played against him and defeated him the previous spring in the NYC Housing Authority Manhattan Championship, and I was determined to defeat him again.

We prevailed against Collegiate. Matt scored 23 points and had a ton of assists and steals. I scored 23 points, 15 rebounds, and 10 blocks. Lareik Taylor and Jose Jensen had come off the bench and combined for 10 steals that made it possible for us to rally. Lareik had hit the go-ahead bucket that put us ahead for good in the fourth.

With the win against Collegiate in the third round, we were ready to meet Westinghouse in the quarterfinals. Westinghouse was the favorite to win it all as they had done in the previous year after "whupping" Banneker 79-44 in the quarterfinals. Since Coach Saunders' arrival at Banneker, Westinghouse had been the one opponent who would stand in Banneker's way of advancing in the playoffs most years. The critics said Westinghouse had Banneker's number. Westinghouse had already beaten us in two close regular 2010 season games. We wanted to prove them wrong, for ourselves and Coach Saunders. To prove them wrong, we knew we would have to play our best team game yet.

The quarterfinals were held at City College's Nat Holman Gymnasium on March 7, 2010. Westinghouse had defeated us during the regular season, so the team came with many fans and an air of confidence that they would send us home again to do what Charles, Kenny, and EJ sent NBA teams off to do: "go fishing." On the other hand, we were seeking revenge and felt confident we would win.

During warm up, I went through my usual routine. I was hooked to my iPod with the songs that I wanted to flow through me during the game. Usher's "More" stuck and would become the song I would often come back to in my mind during the course of the game. As the warm up ended, I looked toward the bleachers to see mom, dad, uncles, aunts, sisters, cousins, and my lady. I checked and was thankful to see mom had the video camera instead of dad.

During our first possession, we scored. Then we pressed the inbounds pass, catch, and dribble. Coach Saunders had prepared us to focus on our defense because defense wins playoff games. Within the first two minutes, I had two blocks and Omari had one. As the period continued, Andrew was cooking on offense, but we had several turnovers from our guards. I had the task of guarding the paint in our zone defense. This put me directly against their big man who was two inches taller and 30 pounds heavier. However, I held him in check and had several additional blocks and two points before the period ended. At the end of the first period, we were down 13-8.

In the second period, we picked up our defense. Omari and I continued to block shots. Our offense picked up, and we cut down on turnovers. The period ended with us down 27-24.

During the third and fourth periods, Omari and I started to stifle their offense. During the first few minutes of the third period, I had four additional blocks and Omari had three additional blocks. Omari was in foul trouble, and he fouled out leaving me alone to disrupt their defense with blocks. Soon the damage was complete and Westinghouse had become hesitant when testing the paint. When I wasn't blocking shots, I was often altering shots.

Meanwhile, Andrew, Terrell, and Matt were leading the offense in a very close contest. By the end of the third period, we led 36-30 after holding Westinghouse to three points. We looked in their eyes and saw the fear, and that fear fed our confidence.

In the fourth quarter, Westinghouse increased its defensive intensity. They forced some turnovers and made a mad rush to catch us before the end. Coach Saunders called time to settle us down. We finished our scoring, with me hitting a foul shot. We won 53-48. We gathered and danced our routine at mid-court around Andrew, our leading scorer with 16 critical points. Terrell danced as we celebrated his timely 10 points. We saluted our guards for the turnovers they forced and Matt for his floor leadership and 7 points. We bumped chests with Omari in recognition of his strong defense and 6 blocks. We were delirious as if we had won the championship.

I finished the game with 12 rebounds and 13 blocks. Later, when I reviewed the tape, I saw that in 4 instances I had come up with the deflected ball after making the blocks. In 3 other instances I had blocked the ball into the hands of a teammate. In addition, there were at least 4 instances where I had altered the shots of my opponents, without blocking, to make them miss. Although I had been the team's leading scorer during the regular season and playoffs, there were no passes to me in the paint because of Westinghouse's man-to-man defense against the guards. Nevertheless, I scored 10 points, mostly on put backs and breakaways.

After the game, we were interviewed by the *New York Post* and the *New York Daily News*. Zach Braziller wrote in the *Post* that we had arrived with high, pent-up emotion to face Westinghouse. He wrote, "Banneker didn't shy away from its Westinghouse ghosts. The Warriors (Banneker) embraced them." He went on to quote our great Coach Saunders, who said, "I told them there is this bad taste in our mouths from last year. Let's spit it out!"

Braziller described our dance as our emotions overflowed on the floor after the win. He wrote, "Once it was over, those emotions came flowing out in a wild celebration that included a mosh pit and Soul Train-like dance circle at half-court." He went on to quote me. I said, "It was like winning a championship without actually being in the championship game. We got in their heads with all the defensive plays. Me blocking shots, everybody else getting loose balls, getting rebounds, boxing out. When we saw their facial expressions that told us everything."

As everyone knows, a semifinal follows a quarter final. We had proven we were one of the four best teams in PSAL-A and one of the top seven teams in all of New York City. Afterwards, we wanted a championship, and we would face Bedford Academy for the second time. We had beaten Bedford in the holiday tournament and believed we were prepared to beat them again.

We didn't! Their full court press rattled our guards and led to costly turnovers at the very beginning of the game. The guards handled the ball and tried dribbling too often through three defenders who would surround them as soon as the ball was thrown in. After so many turnovers, our body language spelled defeat. That was truly a game where we had been defeated in the first quarter. Maybe we had been emotionally exhausted after defeating Westinghouse. Analysts often say teams who get very high emotionally after a big win often do not have enough emotional intensity to win the next game in a playoff series. We all came out flat, and we stayed flat.

Like every other basketball player in America, I wanted a Hollywood ending. I wanted the championship. I wanted to see my name in the headlines. I wanted to be the talk of the town.

But dad reminded me that Hollywood endings are for Hollywood. He says we can find deeper meaning while living in reality.

With the season over, I had an opportunity to look back on what had been a great year. Most of all, I appreciated my growth as a person and as a player. I appreciated my mental toughness. I appreciated my "band of brothers," my teammates who went to war with me. Most of all, I appreciated Coach Williams and Coach Saunders who had worked so hard to develop me.

Also, I appreciated dad and his crazy shouts from the stands when I had skyed for those dunks: "King Kong ain't got nothing on me!"

Chapter 37

Senioritis and Its Cure

Senior year. Senior year. Senioritis.

Senioritis is a disease our parents and teachers say we all get in our senior year. For them, they would prefer we had the flu because they say the flu comes with less drama.

Senior year is a time when we all feel we no longer need to listen to the bull from those teachers who are teaching subjects that are just plain boring or that we will never use in life. We think we are on our way out the door and into a new world of freedom.

Yet, the teachers and our parents tell us graduation is not guaranteed unless we continue to do our homework and pass our classes. However, we are not easily convinced because each of us knows someone in a class before us who graduated without doing the work. Maybe he graduated because he was a star athlete. Maybe he graduated because the teachers liked him. Maybe he graduated because they wanted to hurry and get him, the problem, out of the school. Maybe he graduated because the school wanted to say it is successful at getting kids to graduate. I bet the reader can give the names of students who got over for various reasons.

Even the colleges conspire with our parents and teachers to keep the senioritis sunflower from blooming. They send notices suggesting they will look at our final grades even after they have accepted us for admission. They tell us they might take back admission if our grades drop in our senior year. Now that is just mad "stoopid."

Senioritis is a rite of passage which all American teens should experience. We have earned the right to throw off the oppressive demands of our parents and our teachers once we get that far. Isn't that correct? Hey, even dad had senioritis! Can you believe it? He was the valedictorian-in-waiting and not attending his classes regularly.

Yeah, in his senior year dad found it difficult to attend class. He would roam the hallways after his classes had started. If his classes were 45 minutes long, he would often come in 20 minutes late after stopping to get a late pass from Miss Fitzgerald, a teacher and college advisor. Yeah, he admired Miss Fitzgerald and she covered for dad. Miss Fitzgerald was a great social studies teacher who had encouraged dad to keep developing his interest in Africa and African American history.

When she wasn't covering for him, Miss Martorano, his most favorite teacher for all time, was covering. Today, he still speaks fondly of Miss Martorano, and he describes her with this smile on his face as if he were looking right at her.

"She was 5 feet 6 inches and 130 pounds, in her late 20s with a pretty smile, beautiful face, wonderful spirit, and blond hair rolled up into a tall mound like television character Peg Bondy on *Married with Children*. I loved her because starting in tenth grade she opened up another world for a little country boy from Georgia. She was Italian American and didn't see me as just one of the few African Americans in honors classes. She saw me simply as a young man with a lot of promise and treated me accordingly. She was a blessing and a guardian angel who protected and nurtured me even when I didn't know I needed and was receiving protection and nurturing. All the students loved her. Wherever she is, God bless the wonderful spirit that she is."

Senioritis had dad for several months. But, of course, being the "perfect one," dad came up with a solution for senioritis. Now ain't that some sh**? He came up with a solution for senioritis!

Now, I want all the kids in America, Canada, England, Nigeria, the Caribbean, Puerto Rico, and Mexico to take out you notebooks and pens and write down the prescription for curing your senioritis, a prescription that most medical doctors don't even know. Parents, put your pens away! Kids are you ready? Are you sure you want to be cured?

Ta da! In late November of his senior year, while being totally bored at school, dad, on his own, with no prompting from anyone, decided to use his credits to graduate at the end of the semester in January to start college in February. Yeah, the "perfect one" went from senioritis in November to Brooklyn College in February 1968. Now ain't that some sh**?

Dad could have stayed at John Jay. He was popular and had many friends from all backgrounds. He was cool with the honors kids or the "bookworms." He was cool with the near dropouts. He was cool with the athletes. He was cool with the super cool, many of whom would cut to go hang out in groups with the girls at nearby houses. He was cool with and had friendships among the Irish, the Italians, the Jews, the Puerto Ricans, the Asians, the African Americans, the Caribbean blacks, and the Latinos from South America. He was never involved in the mini riots which sometimes occurred after school among the various racial groups in the school. Because he was in honors classes that lasted beyond the regular school day, there were times he would leave school after a mini riot had taken place outside on 7th Avenue with kids reportedly having raided the nearby hardware store for tools to use as weapons. Although he would have to walk alone through the overwhelmingly white neighborhood around the school, he was never harassed by his white school mates or the other white boys who lived in the vicinity.

In those days, even fights between only two individuals usually occurred outside the school building. When things got hot, it was common for someone to suggest, "Y'all better take that outside." At John Jay, if two kids chose to fight inside they usually had to deal with Dean Riccio. Dean Riccio had a reputation for taking fighters to the gym and giving each a pair of boxing gloves. Each was then expected to box with Dean Riccio who reportedly had a punch like Rocky Marciano but looked more like Jake Lamotta. Dean Riccio had a reputation for knocking out quite a few "knuckleheads," and he had the respect of the guys in the school.

As valedictorian-to-be, dad dressed the "super cool" part fitting in with the African American and Puerto Rican boys. Puerto Ricans and blacks generally socialized together, including Puerto Ricans with "white" skin like dad's friend and party buddy, Joey Morales, and those with brown skin like dad's honors class buddy, Angelo Echevarria. Dad wore a black leather cap backwards, with a black leather coat, gray "sharkskin" pants, and black lizard skin shoes while "bopping" down the hallway of school carrying *The Autobiography of Malcolm X* in his hand.

The principal, Mr. Maloff, didn't like the image, but Miss Martorano and Miss Fitzgerald were cool with it, and they were the only adults in John Jay High School who mattered to dad. Today he cannot remember the name of any other teacher he had during his three years at John Jay. Today dad sends a shout out to the two ladies and regrets that he didn't thank them appropriately when he was in their care.

Yeah, dad gave the speech as the valedictorian at the graduation ceremony in January 1968 in John Jay High School in Park Slope, Brooklyn. On February 1st, he made his fateful entry to Brooklyn College. He travelled from the Bronx to Brooklyn five days a week. He was always present and always in his classes at least five minutes before starting time. Senioritis was dead with a stake driven through its heart.

Well, at Banneker, I was not dad. I was not trying to follow in the footsteps of the "perfect one." I must have had senioritis early in the second semester of my junior year. Yeah, I had junioritis. (Was I the first to have it?) I had Miss Protégé, and her class was full of misery. Her class was the main cause of my junioritis. As a result, I fought with dad who insisted that I meet my responsibilities.

Through all of the challenges in my junior year, I passed Miss Protégé's class, and I performed well on the Regents. I am sure the school gave her credit, but the real credit goes to Paul Hoftyzer, a department head at Brooklyn Technical High School. Upon the recommendation of Jennifer Chu, a math teacher at Brooklyn Tech and a neighbor in Prospect Heights, dad selected Mr. Hoftyzer as a tutor and in the three weeks prior to the Regent's he came to our apartment and taught me all I needed to know and could not learn in two semesters in Miss Protégé's hell hole of a class.

I also scored high on the Spanish Regents, thanks to my Spanish teacher and my Spanish tutor, Juan Arevalo, a middle school teacher in the Bronx.

However, that spring of my junior year I struggled with the Math B Regents, which was given on the same day as the Spanish Regents. Can you imagine sitting nearly three hours for a Spanish Regents and nearly three hours for a Math B Regents all on the same day? In six hours I had to demonstrate all that I had learned in three years of advanced mathematics and three years of Spanish. Who were TIIC/the idiots in charge who came up with that schedule? They must have been adults buggin'. Yeah, they were adult idiots with fancy titles.

Anyway, I had more than enough credits to move on to my senior year, but I was expected to go to summer school and take the Math B Regents class again. Math B is a complex course that maybe 20 percent of the kids in New York go through. There were less demanding courses that could be substituted by kids not interested in being scientists, mathematicians, or engineers. Of course, I was really looking forward to applying all my complex Math B knowledge in sports broadcasting. Not really.

I wasn't feeling summer school. If any teenager says he is, he's lying. So I got up every day and pretended to go to school. Summer school was the playground. On top of having to go to summer school, I had to be home around noon for math tutoring twice a week. Most days I made it on time except when I had to posterize some posers on the court. I would come in a few minutes late to be greeted by drama from dad who was paying the tutor by the hour.

When August rolled around I took the Math B Regents again and this time I passed. I did much better with the help of my math tutor, Michael St. Cyr. But I had just one problem—I needed to have attended the summer class in order to get the credit. Class had been hoops. So, although I had passed the Regents, I did not get credit for the math class. Had I gotten the class credit, I would not have had to take any more math classes during my senior year.

September 2009 rolled around. I was then a real senior with serious senioritis and no desire to use dad's cure. Senioritis was junioritis to the tenth power. I had a light class load since most of my credits required for graduation had been completed. I was enrolled in math (yes, math), art, English, and a psychology elective. I wasn't enrolled in gym, but I wanted to spend a lot of time there. I believe my plan would have worked if dad had not discovered my plan. With the discovery, dad came up to school early in the first semester of my senior year and made a deal with Mr. Fernandez, my real cool gym teacher. He informed Mr. Fernandez of my plans, and my mad cool gym teacher agreed to monitor my schedule and make sure I was not in the gym when I should be in class. My mad cool teacher conspired with dad. Now ain't that some sh**?

Of course, dad didn't stop there. Why should he? He's dad. He was interested in making sure I would stay in my art class and complete my assignments. He was concerned because during the previous semester I had dropped my art class. So he reached an agreement with Ms. Iverson, who would keep him informed of my progress. Unfortunately, that agreement led to a call one day in October when I was missing from class.

Within minutes of the call, dad was at the school. I am not sure that he even took the time to shower before arriving. As he stood outside the class Miss Iverson informed him I was in class and that she had mistakenly called to report my absence. You see, dad had her so hyped she forgot that she had given me a pass to go to the senior lounge to take care of a graduating class matter.

As they spoke in the hallway, I sat pissed off in the class with all eyes on me.

I whispered to myself, "Why me? There are guys right in this school who smoke blunts. There are guys who drink. There are guys who cut to go have sex. There are guys who don't show up in class for weeks. There are guys in trouble with the law. There are guys who flunk everything. Yet, their fathers never show up at school. They don't have to deal with the drama that I have with my father, and I do not do any of the things they do. They are free, and I have a dictator on my back. Maybe if I were like them he would feel powerless and leave me alone!"

When December rolled around, I was on the varsity team. I was on my way to being the leading scorer and rebounder. I was getting good press, and our team had a lot of potential. Dad began attending the games. He was often the only parent at the games. Right away, he was in the middle of everything. Can you imagine, he became a favorite of the students from my school who attended the games? From the court, I could hear him shouting, "That's my son! Whew, did you see that dunk? Don't tell me Superman can't fly! That team ain't bring no kryptonite wit 'em!"

At times, I would glance toward him and see my lady and friends giving him high fives while laughing at his performance. (Please remember they could enjoy him because they didn't have to live with him.) At other times, I would listen as he revved the crowd up and led the entire gym in chants. At one home game after a dunk, he stood, pounded his chest like a drum, and shouted for everyone to hear, "King Kong ain't got nothing on me!" Each word had been accompanied by its own beating fist on his chest. My school mates roared with laughter and gave fist bumps to dad and each other. Dad was contending for the Oscar that Denzel Washington didn't get for "Training Day."

I should have been embarrassed, but I was already used to that side of his crazy personality. Plus, how could I be angry when my friends were laughing and talking about how "mad cool" dad was? He wasn't "mad cool," but I always welcomed his presence at the games. He encouraged me and rarely criticized the team for not passing the ball. I had told him earlier I did not want to hear criticism of my teammates from someone not on the team. I had told him we were a team, and I preferred to focus on the progress we were making as a team. So he backed away from criticism and accepted my preference.

I got through the fall semester and entered the spring semester. Senioritis was still in full bloom in February 2010, and I felt as if I were living in a field of sunflowers and thornless roses. I had taken the SAT and had been accepted academically to some great schools including Hampton, Old Dominion, Seton Hall, Montclair State, SUNY Purchase, Delaware State, Florida A&M, and St. John Fisher. With the academic acceptances in hand, dad and I turned to discovering possible opportunities to play basketball. I had emails from more than 30 Division III coaches asking me to consider joining their teams and exploratory responses from several Division I coaches.

Even as we turned our eyes toward college, dad kept some time for his eyes to be focused on me finishing up at Banneker. He read out loud in my presence the notices from the colleges which stated they were prepared to withdraw entry if grades fell in the senior year. I wasn't trying to hear that. That was so much "blah, blah, blah, uh huh, uh huh."

I had registered for the 8:10 a.m. English class. Eight semesters of English were required to graduate in New York City. I was 17, and you should know how a 17-year-old body regards time and the need to be on time. Even though I had taken the English Regents for graduation in my sophomore year and passed, I still needed to attend English classes.

Now I want all of the men in America who are seniors and willing to get to school every morning for an 8:10 a.m. English class to stand. For those few who stood, can you really say you are real men? Well, I was a man and I wasn't having any part of it. I wasn't having any part of it, that is, until dad found out. When he found out I wasn't getting to class he picked me up at school one afternoon when we had to drive to the photographer's studio to take yearbook pictures. As soon as I got in the car that beautiful March afternoon he put me on full blast.

"I heard you are not going to English," he began. Then he paused while I put on my seat belt. Once my seat belt was on, I expected him to start up the engine. He didn't.

"Let me tell you something," he started up again. "You may be planning on not finishing in June so you could be with your girlfriend and friends in New York this summer, instead of away at pre-college. Last year you lied about attending summer school. If you have to go to summer school this year, let me tell you what will happen. I will drive your f***ing a** to f***ing school every f***ing day. I will walk your a** to your f***ing desk. I will f***ing wait outside your f***ing class. I will make sure you have a f***ing job at f***ing Burger King or the f***ing Regal Movie Theater. I will take you to your f***ing job and pick your a** up after the f***ing job. I will take your f***ing a** home, and you will not see a f***ing friend all f***ing summer! I will shut you off that f***ing Facebook, and you will not send out another f***ing tweet. That's right, you will not see or communicate with you girlfriend or any friends the whole f***ing summer! F***ing try me! F***ing try me if you think I am f***ing kidding!"

OMG/Oh, my God! Dad said all of that without breathing more than once. I was shocked because dad is not a person who uses profanity. I heard "f***ing" and "a**" more in that one minute than I had heard from him in 17 years, and he said it all without spitting foam on me.

I couldn't come up with a reply. As a matter of fact, I was too shocked to even try. That quick thinking and wise me, who usually had a swift reply that would explain my actions to lessen the impact of dad's words, did not exist in that car. I remained silent as I pondered his words and emotions. I was deeply convinced he meant every word, so I realized that there was but one thing for me to do.

Son, I did what all wise young American teenagers would have done. That afternoon I quickly made arrangements to get to class every day. I also worked out an agreement with my English teacher who allowed me to come to a later class if on rare occasions I would run late for the first period class because I was completing an assignment.

Thus, dad had found another cure for my senioritis. I became more cooperative in other areas as well. I even brought my girl Regina home to introduce her and include them in that part of my life. Regina was smart and beautiful, dad and I agreed. She was 5 feet 1 inch, but a killer on the volley-ball team. She was not loud like some of the females you see on the bus and subways of New York. She had a lot of self-respect and self-confidence. When you have that, there is no need to shout and be outrageous to be noticed, and you don't really want to be noticed except by a special someone. She was 16, but carried herself like she was more mature than any 16-year-old you could find. She was intelligent, sweet, and fun to be around. (She would enter NYU in the fall of 2011.)

Dad and mom liked her a lot and were so happy that she seemed nothing like Charlene. They invited her, and she came to Easter service with us at Emmanuel and then dinner at the Lemongrass Grill after the service.

Dad even ate the little beef franks rolled into biscuits that Regina would make when she visited our home. He must have really liked her in order for the health fanatic to eat Hebrew National franks and Pillsbury biscuits. Of course, dad always had to be there the few times she would visit. Dad even met her mom when her mom picked her up from our home.

In March, dad, mom, my best friend, Samori, and I visited Hampton and were greeted by the welcoming crew. The girls in the welcoming crew all seemed nice, smart, and beautiful. I noticed, but my mind was on my lady, because I prefer to give all my romantic attention to one girl. Dad and mom sensed it, so on the way back they teased me for having my thoughts on her.

Dad started with, "Hey, Nydia, what is that song by B.o.B?"

"Isn't it the one where he says they got nothing on you?" mom responded. "Yeah, that one. Find it on the iPod."

So with B.o.B and dad singing, we rolled across the long bridges connected to the Chesapeake Bay Tunnel toward New York. Samori laughed because he had been free to really notice all the beautiful girls at Hampton in the welcoming crew and the student center.

In June my lady was my date at the senior prom. She was a junior. Dad got me a tuxedo and gave me the money for the shared limo. As dad would say, I was "sharp and decked out." (ELF/Every lady's fantasy!)

That was an evening full of joy because we all knew we had reached an important turning point in our lives. We danced, we talked, and we laughed. We posed for pictures. We were all handsome and beautiful. We greeted each other as if we were bound to one another forever, although we knew that we would all soon be scattered to the four corners of America and eventually the four corners of the world.

In mid-June, I graduated with a B average and a Regents Diploma, the highest diploma New York grants. It's ironic that Banneker's graduation ceremony was held in the Walt Whitman Auditorium on the campus of Brooklyn College, my father's alma mater. My father had graduated from Brooklyn College in 1972. However, he had chosen not to attend his own graduation at Walt Whitman Auditorium because in 1969 the college's administration had cooperated with the district attorney in seeking his arrest for campus demonstrations. When dad graduated, Brooklyn College sought to recruit him as a counselor, but dad refused to consider their offer though he had no other job waiting. He did not want his credibility and influence to be used to pacify students. Dad just wanted out with no ceremony. So I became the first Davis to participate in a graduation ceremony inside the Whitman Auditorium.

The ceremony was perfect; it was just the right length with just the right speeches. I must have received a million and one kisses. I welcomed each with a smile. We marched in looking to see our parents' smiles of joy. We smiled with joy to match their smiles. Our school band, led by Omari on piano, was a big hit leading us in the school's song. We sang with passion. We clapped with every sentence of the speeches of the valedictorian and the salutatorian. We blew kisses and shouted out to our teachers, our counselors, and our principal. We tossed our caps into the air. We turned and embraced a special embrace saluting each other for our great accomplishments.

Graduation from high school was a big thing for all the students and their families. We had reached a mountaintop, the first of many to be reached. We could look off in the distance and see all that the earth has to offer displayed before us. We could see so many roads and so many pathways before us. We could see the roads and pathways taken by our parents and generations of our family members. We could see their footsteps. We could see the sign posts and the oases they had established to sustain us on our way to places they had only partially seen in dreams and visions. We could hear the wind whisper that we had an opportunity to reach higher than they had reached because they had established those sign posts and oases. We could hear the wind whisper that we have to carve new and different pathways to those dreams and visions and beyond. We could hear the wind whisper that we are "the promise." Indeed we are "the promise!"

Okay, the last paragraph above reflected what my father wanted me to see and hear. He wrote those lines. Don't forget, he was the one who said Hollywood endings are for Hollywood. Below is what actually happened.

Graduation from high school was a big thing for all the students and their families. We had reached a mountaintop. I was thrilled and thankful. I felt smart and, like Flyleaf, "Fully Alive." I loved my family and was very proud that my family members seemed so happy with my accomplishments. In a state of rapture, I posed for pictures with my parents, my sisters, my family, my classmates, my teachers, and my basketball teammates.

However, as I headed toward the Camry after the last hug and the last goodbye, I had to consider that it was time to move on. But on that sunny June afternoon, I could not see clearly toward what and where I was moving.

The graduation ceremony ended close to 1:30 p.m., which left me no more than 30 minutes to say goodbye to friends. I had another appointment—a 4:00 p.m JetBlue flight back to Hampton University. I had arrived two days earlier from the pre-college session at Hampton, my first choice on the list of universities I wanted to attend. Yet, I had very ambivalent feelings about returning. I really wanted to spend the summer in New York, but I knew there was no chance that I could convince dad, even with mom's help. I wanted to be with mom and dad, and I wanted to complete and enjoy the relationships with friends developed at Banneker. I had Brooklyn in my heart, not Virginia.

Concerning the wind, unlike dad, I didn't hear the wind whisper anything. Therefore, on the plane back to Hampton, I could see the faces of my parents and my friends and our relationships, that had been so familiar and so meaningful, fade into the background. I wasn't sure that the tradeoff was worth it. I was on a plane back to Hampton, but the destination in my heart wasn't Hampton. While looking out of the plane's window, I didn't feel connected to anything. No birds flew. No flowers bloomed. No life was visible in the bodies of water below. The countryside seemed desolate and alien. Everything and everyone around me seemed so anonymous like images in a bad movie. When the plane landed I didn't know where I was.

I started a frantic search for the absent me. He remained unformed and hidden!

Postscript

"Warrior of the Void," is dad's nickname for me. The Void is that empty, challenging, and treacherous space that must be conquered by a special awareness, a special existence, and a special warrior. The Void is the space that exists between who we are and who we are called to become. It is the space where we encounter so many flamboyant demons while searching for a few discreet guardian angels.

Who are the demons? Dad answers, "Our demons are our self-righteousness and exaltation of self, our self-assurance denying blessed assurance, our love of instant gratification, our pursuit and worship of deceitful successes, our fixation on faithless fears, and our embrace of enchanting illusions. Our willingness to opening our minds to a flood of embraceable media, technological, and cultural delusions are among the most challenging ones. With those at work in our minds, Satan can take a long vacation."

Sensei Soke tried to teach me as an 8-year-old long ago that my principal enemy would be "the man in the mirror," the mind that I express, and the "me" whom I prefer to choose to represent to the world. Now, at 8 years old, or at 18, or even 80, who could really understand that?

Dad has told me Moses was 80 when he was told by God to go back to Egypt to confront Pharaoh. Moses looked within at his own weakness and suggested to God to send someone else. So even with God being with him, Moses didn't have confidence in "the man in the mirror." He wasn't eager to confront the demon of self-doubt.

As a teen, I often look in the mirror and like who I see. I leave the mirror and look into life and see dad. I am fighting him. Am I fighting myself?

Even with all of my flaws, I am still dad's Warrior. His faith assures him that I will reach the promise because he has faith that "God is faithful to complete a work God has begun in us."

Even with all of dad's flaws, I love him.

Concerning me, I too am faithful. Even when I have questioned myself, I have never doubted that I will find the answers and the success. I am my own Warrior. I am fighting the fight to be my own Warrior. I try to understand when dad says my flaws must become my stepping stones.

You see, dad says, "In order to get to a greater place, you must first be in a lesser place." Immaturity precedes maturity, no matter how much dad wishes to have me mature instantly. Dad knows that doubt always precedes Faith. So, even as I live with doubts, my Faith is always being strengthened. Dad says, "Folly always precedes wisdom." So, even in the midst of my foolish actions, wisdom embraces and expands within me. Dad further suggests, "Folly calls for punishment, but love sends you Grace."

Dad says, "Love, Faith, Wisdom, and Grace are the four cornerstones of my foundation for reaching that greater place, for conquering that Void." There's an inner part of me which understands that.

Therefore, I, Askia Akhenaton Suleiman Ali Davis, whisper, "I am the promise. I am the Warrior of the Void. Swag!"

Conclusion

Warrior of the Void
Plan of Action

Our goal in writing this memoir was to bring light and inspiration to young people coming of age in the early 21st century and to those adults helping to guide them. We recognize that there are many other compelling stories in their experiences, and we want to encourage them to share their stories. Thus dad and I plan to take this message to the public, using a format that will encourage participants to tell and write insightful chapters about their lives.

We understand that sons, dads, human beings are not perfect. It is only our struggles with our imperfections, the enchanting demons, which make life interesting and meaningful.

For Your Listening Pleasure

(Recommended for the Hip Hop Generation and Everyone Else)

The songs on this list might generally escape the attention of many in the Hip Hop Generation, but they should not be missed in a lifetime. Dad selected the list. The songs are not listed in order of popularity and not necessarily the biggest hits of the artists or necessarily the biggest artists. However, my dad considers all of the 300 songs great songs. Dad assumes you may have heard other hits of many of these and other old school artists, so he attempted to exclude some of those hits and artists you might have already heard. For example, don't look for the Temptations. Also, you will not find "For the Love of Money" by the O'Jays, but you will find their "Ship Ahoy" because it's a great tune and dad believes it carries a special message for the Hip Hop Generation.

Enjoy! The songs are available on music sharing sites including iTunes and YouTube.

300 Old School Hits

Title	Artist
If You Think You're Lonely Now	Bobby Womack
Exodus	Bob Marley
These Arms Of Mine	Otis Redding
Beat Street	Grandmaster Flash & The Furious Five
People Everyday	Arrested Development
My Philosophy	KRS One
My Mind Playing Tricks On Me	Geto-Boys
Triumph	Wu-Tang Clan
Rockit	Herbie Hancock
Atomic Dog	George Clinton
Hoochie Coochie Man	Muddy Waters
Emotions	Mariah Carey
The Greatest Love Of All	Whitney Houston
Loving You	Minnie Riperton
Unforgettable	Nat King Cole and Natalie Cole
Dindi	John Lucien
Let Me Be Your Angel	Stacy Lattisaw
Anacaona	Fania All Stars
Puerto Rico	Eddie Palmieri
Bemba Colora	Celia Cruz
A Dream	DeBarge
What Kind Of Man Would I Be	Mint Edition
Something In Your Eyes	Biv Bel DeVoe
For You	Kenny Lattimore
We Are the World	Quincy Jones, Michael Jackson, et al.
What's Love Got To Do With It	Tina Turner
Outa-Space	Billy Preston
Disco Inferno	The Trammps
One Nation Under A Groove	Funkadelic
Planet Rock	Afrika Bambaataa
Marcus Garvey	Burning Spear
Rumours	Gregory Isaacs
Rastafari Is	Peter Tosh
Alboury	Youssou N'Dour (Senegal)

Title	Artist
La Asesina	Bonny Cepeda
C.R.E.A.M.	Wu Tang Clan
Basketball	Kurtis Blow
Tune Up	The Dramatics
Can't Stay Away	LeRoy Hutson
In A Sentimental Mood	Duke Ellington & John Coltrane
Mr. Magic	Grover Washington
Wild Is the Wind	Nina Simone
Sunday & Sister Jones	Roberta Flack
Is It A Crime	Sade
Body Music	The Strikers
Might Mighty	Earth Wind & Fire
The World Is A Ghetto	War
Here Comes The Judge + The Trial	Pig Meat Markum
Human Beat Box	The Fat Boys
La Di Da Di	Slick Rick and Doug E Fresh
The Freaks Come Out At Night	Whodini
Dance To The Drummer's Beat	Herman Kelly & Life
U Can't Touch This	M.C. Hammer
The Message	Grandmaster Flash & The Furious Five ft. Grandmaster Melle Mel
Express Yourself	Watts 103rd Street Rhythm Band
Funky Broadway Parts I & II	Dyke and the Blazers
I Was Checking Out While She Was Checking In	Don Covay
Who's Making Love To Your Old Lady	Johnnie Taylor
Land Of A Thousand Dances	Wilson Pickett
Lonely Teardrops	Jackie Wilson
Got To Be Enough	Con Funk Shun
Keep In Touch (Body To Body)	Shades of Love
Dying To Be Dancing	Empress
Show Me Love	Robin S.
Sinner Man	Sarah Dash
Turn The Beat Around	Vicki Sue Robinson
Stomp	Brothers Johnson
You Are My Friend	Sylvester & Two Tons O' Fun (Live)

Title	Artist
Obeah Man	Exuma (Bahamas)
Ragamuffin	Daddy Yod (France & Guadeloupe)
Zoul Le Se Sel Medikaman Nou Ni	Kassav (Martinique & Guadeloupe)
A Kou Tchou Kou Tchou	Tabou Combo (Haiti)
Sa Sa Yea	Mighty Sparrow
O' La Soca	Arrow
Blue Skies	Ella Fitzgerald
Watching You	Slave
Searching to Find the One	Unlimited Touch
Don't Stop the Music	Yarbrough & Peoples
I Like What You're Doing To Me	Young & Company
Hot Shot	Karen Young
Love Sensation	Loleatta Holloway
I'll Be Good	Rene & Angela
Over Like A Fat Rat	Fonda Rae
We've Got the Funk	Positive Force
Victim	Candi Staton
I Will Survive	Gloria Gaynor
Ain't Nothing Going On But The Rent	Gwen Guthrie
A Love Supreme	John Coltrane
So What	Miles Davis
The Creator Has A Master Plan	Pharaoh Sanders & Leon Thomas
All Blues	Miles Davis & John Coltrane (Live in Stockholm 1960)
500 Miles High	Return To Forever
Autumn Leaves	Cannonball Adderley ft. Miles Davis
I Didn't Know What Time It Was	Billie Holiday
End Of The Road	Boyz II Men
All the Man I Need	Whitney Houston
Hurry Up This Way Again	The Stylistics
Ready Or Not	After 7
Anniversary	Tony Toni Tone
Can We Talk	Tevin Campbell
Fight The Power	Public Enemy
Sound of Da Police	KRS One
Ain't No Half Steppin	Big Daddy Kane

Title	Artist
Wild Wild West	Kool Moe Dee
Cool Like That	Digable Planets
No Woman No Cry	The Fugees
Hip Hop Hooray	Naughty By Nature
Walk This Way	Run DMC & Aerosmith
The People	Common
Anytime	Brian McKnight
Love Don't Live Here Anymore	Rose Royce
It's Been A Long Time	New Birth
Brick House	Commodores
I Want Your Love	Chic
Boogie Wonderland	The Emotions & EWF
The Best Of My Love	Emotions
Soul Finger	The Bar-Kays
Let's Straighten It Out	Lattimore
Don't Look Any Further	Dennis Edwards
I'm Not Going To Let You	Colonel Abrams
I Do Love You	Billy Stewart
Make It Happen	Mariah Carey
Something On Your Mind	D Train
Love Shoulda Brought You Home	Toni Braxton
A Song for You	Donny Hathaway
Going in Circles	Friends of Distinction
One Hundred Ways	James Ingram
One In A Million You	Larry Graham
Please Mr. Postman	The Marvelettes
Spill the Wine	Eric Burdon and War
Heatwave	Martha and the Vandellas
Boogie Oogie Oogie	Taste of Honey
Creep	TLC
Boogie Nights	Heatwave
Bertha Butt Boogie	The Jimmy Castor Bunch
I Want Someone	The Mad Lads
World Of Fantasy	Five Stairsteps
Living All Alone	Phyllis Hyman
All Along the Watchtower	Jimi Hendrix

Title	Artist
Searching	Change ft. Luther Vandross
Silver Shadow	Atlantic Star
Here's To You	Skyy
Fencewalk	Mandrill
Movin'	Brass Construction
Don't Let Go	En Vogue
The Boss	Diana Ross
Rie y Llora	Celia Cruz
Mas Que Nada	Sergio Mendes and Brazil 66
Karukera Madinina (French Boogie)	J. A. S. & Guilou (Martinique)
Esquinas	Djavan (Brazil)
The Harder They Come	Jimmy Cliff
Try Jah Love	Third World
Forever My Lady	Jodeci
If I Ever Fall In Love Again	Shai
Ain't No Way	Aretha Franklin
Stay In My Corner	The Dells
I Feel Good All Over	Stephanie Mills
One More Try	George Michael
I'll Give Good Love	Babyface
My Funny Valentine	Miles Davis
Night In Tunisia	Dizzy Gillespie & Lillian Terry
Compared To What	Les McCann and Eddie Harris
Who's That Lady	The Isley Brothers
Put It in Your Peace Pipe	BT Express
Running Away	Roy Ayers
Dance Dance Dance	Chic
Caribbean Queen	Billy Ocean
Get It Up	The Time
Quimbara	Tito Puente & Celia Cruz (Live)
Todo Tiene Su Final	Hector Lavoe & Willie Colon
Bang Bang	Joe Cuba
Boogaloo Blues	Johnny Colon
Indestructible	Eddie Palmieri
Secret Garden	Quincy Jones ft. Barry White
Last Dance	Donna Summer

Title	Artist
Bad For Me	Dee Dee Bridgewater
She's Got Papers on Me	Richard Dimples Fields
The Rain	Oran 'Juice' Jones
On the Wings of Love	Jeffrey Osborne
Everything Must Change	Quincy Jones
If I Were Your Woman	Gladys Knight and the Pips
Love TKO	Teddy Pendergrass
So Fine	Howard Johnson
I Miss You	Klymaxx
All Cried Out	Lisa Lisa & Cult Jam
Wishing Well	Terrence D'Arby
The Message	Dr. Dre
Gangster's Paradise	Coolio
I'll Take You There	The Staple Singers
Who Is He and What Is He to You	Bill Withers
This Masquerade	George Benson
My Favorite Things	John Coltrane
St. Thomas	Sonny Rollins
You Belong to the City	Glenn Frey
Sledgehammer	Peter Gabriel
Somebody Else's Guy	Jocelyn Browne
Give Me The Night	Shannon
Last Night A DJ Saved My Life	Indeep
Jungle Boogie	Kool & The Gang
Slow Jam	Midnight Star
Fantastic Voyage	Lakeside
Time Has Come Today	The Chambers Brothers
Give Me Some Loving	Spencer Davis Group
Calle Luna Calle Sol	Willie Colon and Hector Lavoe
Tierra Dura	Ruben Blades
Beast of Burden	The Rolling Stones
Hotel California	Eagles
Black Magic Woman	Santana
The Thrill is Gone	B. B. King
Soul Makossa	Manu Dibango
Separate Lives	Phil Collins

Title	Artist
A Drop of Water	Keiko Matsui
Hold On to What You Got	Joe Tex
Take Time to Know Her	Percy Sledge
How Do You Mend A Broken Heart	Al Green
Still	Commodores
Four Women	Nina Simone
Coal Train (Stimela)	Hugh Masekela
Peace Be Still	James Cleveland and the Southern California Gospel Choir
Oh Happy Day	Edwin Hawkins Singers
All Night Thing	Invisible Man's Band
Victim	Candi Staton
Ring My Bell	Anita Ward
Rivers of My Fathers	Gil Scott Heron
I've Known Rivers	Gary Baartz
Skin Tight	The Ohio Players
Say It Loud, I'm Black and I'm Proud	James Brown
Pillow Talk	Sylvia
Jungle Fever	The Chakachas
House of the Rising Sun	The Animals
For the Love of You	Isley Brothers
Love Is A Hurting Thing	Lou Rawls
Shake It Up, Do the Boogaloo	Rod
Bad Girls	Donna Summer
This Time Baby	Jackie Moore
Ship Ahoy	The O'Jays
Baby I'm for Real	The Originals
Close Your Eyes	Peaches and Herb
White Lines	Grand Master Melle Mel
Expansions	Lonnie Liston Smith
Harlem River Drive	Bobbi Humphrey
Mama Used to Say	Junior
Love Makes the World Go Round	Deon Jackson
You're All I Need to Get By	Marvin Gaye & Tammi Terrell
Oops Upside Your Head	Gap Band
Baby, You Need to Change Your Mind	Eddie Kendricks

Title	Artist
Grooveline	Heatwave
Heartbeat	Taana Gardner
Foxy Lady	Jimi Hendrix
Moondance	Van Morrison
Another Brick in the Wall	Pink Floyd
Dazz	Brick
Aquarius/Let The Sunshine In	Fifth Dimension
Smoking Gun	Robert Cray
You're the Only Woman	Ambrosia
Dynamite	Jermaine Jackson
For the Lover in You	Shalimar
Let's Start the Dance	Hamilton Bohannan
Fragile	Sting
Dance to the Music	Sly and the Family Stone
Confusion	Aleem
Shame	Evelyn Champagne King
It Seems to Hang On	Ashford & Simpson
And the Beat Goes On	The Whispers
You and I	Rick James
Sweet Thing	Rufus ft. Chaka Khan
Like A Rolling Stone	Bob Dylan
Coco Sec	Midnight Groovers (of Dominica)
Back to My Roots	Fania All Stars with Gato Barbieri
Black Butterfly	Deniece Williams
Woman To Woman	Shirley Brown
Silly	Deniece Williams
Love Ballad	L.T.D. ft. Jeffrey Osborne
Get On Up	The Esquires
Lady Marmalade	LaBelle
Tell Me Something Good	Rufus ft. Chaka Khan
Stand By Me	Ben E. King
Do You Love Me	The Contours
Shop Around	Smokey Robinson & the Miracles
Hello Stranger	Barbara Lewis
What'd I Say	Ray Charles
Johnny B. Goode	Chuck Berry

Title	Artist
Long Tall Sally	Little Richard
Stagger Lee	Lloyd Price
Going Out Of My Head	Little Anthony & the Imperials
Chain Gang	Sam Cooke
Jesus Is Love	The Commodores
The Lord's Prayer	Mahalia Jackson
Healing	Richard Smallwood
Your Grace and Mercy	Mississippi Mass Choir
Safe In His Arms	Rev. Milton Brunson & The Thompson Community Singers
I've Been In The Storm Too Long	Mighty Clouds of Joy
Magnify Him	Total Praise
That's Why I Praise You	Kelly Price
Worthy Is The Lamb	Brooklyn Tabernacle Choir
Stand	Donnie McClurkin
Crazy Baldheads/Running Away (Live)	Bob Marley
Our Love	Natalie Cole
Ad Anah/How Long O Lord?	Hebrew Psalms Radio (http://www.hebrewpsalms.org/)
Dieuzbu	Musa Dieng Kala

Here are a few music titles from my dad that reflect various messages of Hip Hop. The list does not reflect any order of popularity.

75 Hip Hop Hits

	Title	Artist
	Work Out	J. Cole
	In Da Club	Fifty Cent
	99 Problems	Jay-Z
	I'll Be in the Sky	B.o.B.
	Oh Let's Do It	Waka Flocka Flame
	Not Afraid	Eminem
	Daydreaming	Lupe Fiasco
	Mama Told Me	Wale
	The Light	Common
	Dear Mama (Remix)	Tupac ft. Anthony Hamilton
	Sole Survivor	Akon and Young Jeezy
	L.A.	Murs
	Put My Swag On	Soulja Boy
	My Chic	Ludacris
	Mr. Carter	Lil Wayne
	Beautiful	Akon
	PJ & Rooster	OutKast
	Otis	Jay-Z & Kanye West
	Deceiving	Drake
	History	Mos Def
	Like A Star	J. Cole
	Rude Boy	Rihanna
	Touch the Sky	Kanye West ft. Lupe Fiasco

Title	Artist
Izzo (H.O.V.A.)	Jay-Z
Lookin' Fly	Murs
Where da Hood At	DMX
Congratulations	Drake
Ridin'	Chamillionaire
Cash Moves Everything Around Me	Wu Tang Clan
R.O.O.T.S.	Flo Rida
Ain't I	Yung L.A.
Dead and Gone	T.I.
Monster (video)	Kanye West
The Show Goes On	Lupe Fiasco
Gangsta's Paradise	Coolio ft. L. V.
Gold Digger	Kanye West ft. Jamie Foxx
Dame Dame	Que No ft. Dicky Ranking & Abusivo
Jigga What, Jigga Who	Jay-Z ft. Big Jaz & Amil
Hey Ya!	OutKast
Boom Boom Pow	Black Eye Peas
Green Light	John Legend ft. Andre 3000
I Love College	Asher Roth
All the Way Turnt Up	Roscoe Dash & Soulja Boy
4 My Town	Birdman, Drake & Lil Wayne
Hope	Faith Evans & Twista
N.Y. State of Mind	Nas
No Diggity	Dr. Dre & Blackstreet
Teach Me How to Dougie	Cali Swag District
Rider pt. 2	G Unit & Young Buck
I Know You Want Me (*Calle Ocho*)	Pitbull
Hypnotize	Notorious B.I.G.
Mosh	Eminem
My Time	Fabulous & Jeremiah
Remember the Name	Fort Minor ft. Styles of Beyond
Stoopid	Gucci Mane
All I Do Is Win	DJ Khaled
Heart of A Champion	Nelly Ft. Lincoln U Vocal Ensemble
The Second Coming	Juelz Santana
Dirty Money —Coming Home	Diddy

Title	Artist
Gin and Juice	Snoop Dogg
It Was A Good Day	Ice Cube
The War	Wale
Hip Hop Is Dead	Nas ft. will.i.am
The Winner	Drake ft. Jhene Aiko
God's Gift	J. Cole
Keep Ya Head Up	Tupac
Fat Booty	Mos Def
Fire Burning	Sean Kingston
Hey Ma	Cam'Ron ft. Juelz Santana
Ambitious Girl (Pts. 1 & 2)	Wale
Till I Collapse	Eminem ft. Nate Dogg
Let the Beat Build	Lil Wayne
Universal Mind Control	Common
Whatever You Like	T.I.
Big Poppa	Notorious B.I.G.

Notes

1. Billy Joel, the piano man, used to have hair! You can see that hair as he sings "New York State of Mind" at http://www.youtube.com/watch?v=UZh8YjbDiVk.

2. You can also watch the "Beat Street" video on YouTube countless times at http://www.youtube.com/watch?v=rhkOPNRV8Pk.

3. For an article about the yearbook controversy between Crew and Giuliani, see http://articles.nydailynews.com/1997-04-02/news/18028546_1_yearbooks-schools-chancellor-rudy-crew-mayor-giuliani.

4. For the Human Rights Watch report about the criminal justice system treatment of the poor during the pre-trial period, see http://www.hrw.org/news/2010/12/03/new-york-city-bail-penalizes-poor.

5. For a *New York Times* article regarding the madness that is leading to the prisons being full of first-time, non-violent offenders incarcerated for marijuana possession, often for as little as one joint, see http://www.nytimes.com/2011/06/15/nyregion/in-new-york-a-call-to-shift-policy-on-marijuana.html?ref=nyregion.

6. For more information on the legislation to destroy the NYPD database, see http://www.silive.com/news/index.ssf/2010/07/governor_forces_nypd_to_delete.html.

7. To read the article about Chancellor Walcott's encounter with New York's Finest, see http://www.nytimes.com/2011/05/01/nyregion/police-look-into-complaint-by-new-york-chancellor-after-traffic-stop.html?scp=1&sq=NYPD percent20stops percent20Chancellor percent20Walcott&st=cse.

8. For a report on the Ziegler confrontation, see http://www.usatoday.com/news/nation/2008-05-10-1736174211_x.htm.

9. For your Pong hookup and an opportunity to see an ancient game, see http://www.youtube.com/watch?v=LPkUvfL8T1I.

10. To hear FSU's war cry, go to http://www.youtube.com/watch?v=mMLd6WzevT4.

11. For an article on the origin of language, see http://www.nytimes.com/2011/04/15/science/15language.html?scp=1&sq=Origin percent20of percent20human percent20language&st=cse. For information regarding our common ancestry as revealed in *The Journey of Man: A Genetic Odyssey*, see http://news.nationalgeographic.com/news/2002/12/1212_021213_journeyofman.html.

12. For an artist's rendering of Bin Laden's "fortress," see http://www.edward-jayepstein.com/nether_fictoid3.htm.

13. You can hear the Mask Man and the Agents sing the song "One Eye Open" at http://www.youtube.com/watch?v=OKJpjCLHkys.

14. For more information on Vincente Guerrero and the history and presence of blacks in Mexico, see PBS documentary series "Black in Latin America," produced by Harvard scholar Henry Louis Gates, Jr., specifically the episode entitled, "Mexico & Peru: The Black Grandma in the Closet" at http://www.pbs.org/wnet/black-in-latin-america/featured/full-episode-mexico-peru/227/.

15. For photos of Ali with El Hajj Malik Shabazz, see http://images.search.yahoo.com/search/images?_adv_prop=image&fr=chr-yie9&va=Muhammad+Ali+and+Malcolm+X+photo.

16. For photos and an article on the young Cassius Clay, see http://www.courier-journal.com/article/99999999/ALI/90617014/The-legend-became-Muhammad-Ali.

17. For an article on Jay-Z's efforts, see http://abcnews.go.com/Nightline/story?id=2681905&page=1

18. To hear Malcolm in his own words that he wrote after four little black girls were killed in the bombing of the 16th Street Baptist Church in Birmingham, Alabama, by white supremacists on September 15, 1963, see http://www.youtube.com/watch?v=znQe9nUKzvQ&feature=related

19. For the Hip Hop Generation, Mos Def has attempted to introduce the speeches and philosophy of Malcolm X. To hear Mos Def reading the Malcolm X speech, see http://www.youtube.com/watch?v=RzC3ZKzkTOM.

20. For an article on Commissioner Carrion and the notorious Tryon School for Boys, see http://www.villagevoice.com/2010-08-04/news/gladys-carrion-upstate-jails-for-city-kids-bronx.

Glossary —Texting Terms

BTW: by the way
ELF: every lady's fantasy
EOR: end of rant
HTH: how the hell
LMAO: laughing my a** off
LTFA: left the f*** alone
OMG: Oh, my God
OMW: on my way
POTS: parents watching over the shoulders
ROTFL: rolling on the floor laughing
TBBH: to be brutally honest
TBT: truth be told
TIIC: the idiots in charge
TITT: that is the truth
WTF: what the f***
WTHC: who the hell cares
WWIT: what was I thinking
YGTR: you got that right

About the Authors

Askia Akhenaton Suleiman Ali Davis

NYC PSAL Quarter Finals, March 2010

Askia Akhenaton Suleiman Ali Davis is known to family as Akhenaton and to friends as Askia. He is the son of Dr. Askia Davis and Mrs. Nydia Lassalle Davis, with whom he lives in the Prospect Heights section of Brooklyn.

Askia Akhenaton is a lover of spoken word, slam poetry, lyrics and various genres of music. He reads music, plays the piano and clarinet, and is an aficionado of Garage Band.

Askia Akhenaton is a 2010 graduate of Benjamin Banneker Academy in Brooklyn. At Banneker he was a successful student in honors English classes and the starting power forward and most valuable player leading Banneker's basketball team to the semifinals of the Public Schools Athletic League in 2010.

Askia Akhenaton is currently a student in City University of New York. He is active in several local basketball leagues. He is majoring in communications and mass media. His professional goals include sports broadcasting, teaching, and coaching.

Dr. Askia Davis

Dr. Askia Davis was born in rural Georgia and at the age of 15 joined "the Great Migration" of African Americans to cities in the North. At age 16 Askia lived independently in the borough of the Bronx in New York City while travelling to the borough of Brooklyn to attend John Jay High School. Also at age 16 he "stumbled upon" *The Autobiography of Malcolm X* and his view of the world was transformed.

Soon after, in 1968 he joined the Black Panther Party in Harlem (not to be confused with the so-called "New Black Panther Party"and its positions on race and violence) and became its Lieutenant of Education, leading classes in studying revolutionary books and literature that provided a context for community service. In 1968 he also became a leader of the successful struggle to open enrollment of Brooklyn College and City University of New York to blacks and Latinos. At Brooklyn College in 1969 he was arrested, along with 18 other African American and Puerto Rican students, and held on Rikers Island facing the threat of being sentenced to 228 years in prison.

Askia later completed a doctoral degree at Teachers College at Columbia University in 1983. Professionally, Askia has been a teacher, a counselor, an administrator, the senior assistant to three successive chancellors of the New York City Public Schools, superintendent of schools in Harlem, and deputy regional superintendent for 140 schools serving 99,000 students in the Bronx.

Askia is currently a writer and an educational consultant, specializing in strategic planning, team building, curriculum change, Models of Teaching, proposal development, and leadership.